First Steps in Acting

Lake Matoaka Amphitheatre,
Williamsburg, Virginia

The Reapers and Sowers

From The Common Glory
by Paul Green

Samuel Selden

*University of California,
Los Angeles*

FIRST STEPS
IN ACTING

SECOND EDITION

NEW YORK

APPLETON-CENTURY-CROFTS

Division of Meredith Publishing Company

PREFACE TO THE FIRST EDITION

IT WAS MY PRIVILEGE a good many years ago to work in several of the early Eugene O'Neill productions, one of which was the Eastern Road Company of *Desire Under the Elms*. I was associated with it as stage manager. Most of the actors in the troupe were veterans of long experience and very fine players. In all the cities we visited on our tour, the response was enthusiastic; the audiences enjoyed the play; and they liked the performance of every member of the company—every member, that is, except one. That unfortunate individual was the young man who played the role of Ephraim Cabot's son, Eben. He was one of the replacements in the troupe, having joined us only a short time before the close of the New York run. He was by nature a very fine person, intelligent, sensitive, modest, and friendly; and both visually and aurally he fitted the part of the youthful farmer for which he was cast. He had a good voice; he was handsome, vigorous, and thoroughly masculine. His back and shoulders looked as if they could wrestle with an ox, yet he moved about the stage with a remarkably easy grace. The morning he came from the casting agency to read the part of Eben, the director thought he had made a find.

Audiences, however, had no liking for him. Filled with curiosity, I tried to analyze the failure. The portrayer of young Eben, I found, had become indoctrinated with the all-too-common notion that an actor must identify himself with the part he plays. He had done this so long, in spite of some considerable rough and tumble experience in stock companies, that the idea had become an obsession with him. Gripped by the desire to bore into the innermost

v

soul of Eben, to breathe *his breath* and pulse with *his blood,* the actor was one of the most sincere and earnest individuals I have ever encountered. Early every morning of the four long months we were "on the road," alone in his hotel room or in a far corner of a Pullman car, he would pore over his part, studying it anew, trying to wrest from the author's lines and stage directions some bit of fresh meaning for that evening's performance. And yet, somehow, the portrayal missed. The interpretation was not accepted. The characterization was said to be "aloof," "cold."

There was very little criticism of the role in the first two acts. The actor managed the difficult passages which show the enmity of Eben toward his father and his growing love for the woman, Abbie, really quite well. The role went to pieces in the tragic crisis near the end of the play. In that short scene, Eben, learning from the lips of Abbie that she has killed the child who, she believed, stood between them, gives vent to his horror.

Quite ironically, this was the spot on the preparation of which the actor daily expended his greatest effort. Every time the moment of terrible realization arrived in the performance, the actor would gather together and throw into the response every ounce of feeling he had concentrated on it. He would contract his hands, twist the muscles of his face and shoulders, make a gasping cry, and fall shuddering to the floor. The following speeches with Abbie were almost unintelligible, because the words which Eben uttered broke from his throat like guttural sobs. There he remained in a tortured knot, shivering, with the blood almost bursting from the veins of his neck, until the curtain fell.

This was an example of living one's part if there ever was one! The actor, although endowed by nature with a powerful physique, was nightly so exhausted by his exertions that he was forced to sprawl on the stage floor. Because he was too heavy to move, and because he was unable to crawl under his own strength into the wings, we were forced to delay for several minutes the curtain for the following scene. After these many years I can still recall vividly the figure of my friend the player lying prostrate in the middle of the Cabot kitchen fighting to regain his breath, while property men, electricians, and other actors waited in a patient, sympathetic circle around him.

The complete inability of all this very genuine pain to affect the audience at all made a deep impression on me. I kept asking myself where the fault lay. Certainly not in a lack of sensitivity! Positively not in a want of sincerity. The actor I was observing had these in abundance—a considerably greater amount of both, as a matter of fact, than any of his more successful colleagues. Finally, I arrived at the answer: the actor had the feelings for the part, but he did not project them; they remained in a little self-contained bundle in the middle of the stage, separated from the spectators by the footlights and the orchestra pit. That was why the actor in his most emotional scene was judged to be aloof, apart from his audience. And the reason there was no projection was that the actor's premise was wrong. He assumed that concentration on his part, living it with all his might and main, would automatically make a living performance. Precisely here, of course, lay his error. Living is the *source* of acting; but living itself *is not acting*.

In a stage presentation of a child, the two ends of behavior may be very close, for a child's thoughts and feelings are manifested openly for all to see; but in the grown individual, the most powerful elements of a man's experience, the part which perhaps wracks him from his head to his feet, tends to be inward, and therefore hidden. The portrayer of Eben in *Desire Under the Elms* was behaving indeed as his prototype in an everyday world would behave; in this he had succeeded beyond any shadow of doubt. But he had not yet begun to act. His suffering was visible to one or two companions on the stage, but that was all; the audience was left out of it. That is why the audience felt that the actor was negative, "cold."

In the many years I have spent teaching young actors since then, I have thought often of that role of Eben. The longer I work, the more I am convinced that the first problem of the player is not psychological characterization, but dramatic projection. Characterization will come later—and when it does come, it will occupy most of the player's thoughts. However, at the beginning, he must devote himself to the recognition of his medium. He must sense the forces that operate in a world of natural living, and then feel how these forces are opened out, enlarged, strengthened, and ordered for a theatric presentation. He must be affected by space and distance; he must sense the pull and push, the lift and depression of the human and inanimate presences around him, and then be able to respond to them, not in little flickers of movement, but in clean sweeps of action easily recognizable many feet away. And he must use words that are more than intellectual murmurs drawn out of a dictionary; rather, words that, like the pantomime, possess the magic of motion expanded, made understandable, made compelling.

The present manual was written to record this point of view. It is thus unavoidably somewhat technical. Considerable space is devoted to discussion of and to exercises for the four "fundamental movements" that are designed to work in both the pantomimic and vocal phases of the actor's performance so they fulfill a dual purpose. They are planned (a) to help the actor sense the dynamic factors in his role, and (b) to help him find methods for the projection of his part. But none of these "fundamentals"—or any of the many other "principles"—set down is intended to imply any fixed system of playing. They are meant simply to serve as starting points for the actor's own exploration, to be disregarded and forgotten as soon as he discovers better ways of his own. While the book stresses technique, it attempts also throughout to give reasons for the methods outlined so that the apprentice may be able to see, and *feel,* clearly what he is trying to do. He is encouraged to observe always the central principles from which his various devices spring—and to see these rooted, not in the wooden floor of the stage, but in the deep, warm, rich soil of everyday human life. The student player is, however, emphatically *not* encouraged to do one thing; that is, to sit down for a purely sedentary appraisal of his work. From beginning to end, the assumption is made that he is *in action*—not just thinking and talking. Hence the title of this book.

S.S.

PREFACE TO THE SECOND EDITION

IT IS SEVENTEEN YEARS since I wrote the first edition of this book. In that period of time I have added considerably to my experience of coaching and directing young players. Though I think I have learned a lot from this supplemental experience I have found no reason to change my original conviction that the first great lesson the actor must learn is not how to construct an elaborate inner attack upon his work, but *how to communicate.* When he prepares himself to appear on the stage he must give thought to the substance of his role, of course, but he cannot stop there. The actor may work out in his mind what seems to him to be a wonderfully interesting characterization. Yet, if he cannot get the thought and the feeling of this across to a spectator seated fifty or seventy feet away from him, he has actually created nothing of value at all.

In the early years of his appearance in front of an audience the performer must depend mostly for the interpretation of his parts upon the guidance of his older and more worldly-wise director. In time, his own wisdom with regard to *why* people in certain circumstances do what they do will grow. As that wisdom matures he himself will assume the primary task of working out the inner motivations for his outward actions. He will then be a complete performer. For the initial period, however, when he is readying himself for the greater tasks of interpretation still to come, he will turn his principal effort to the perfection of his projective techniques.

This new edition emphasizes two lines of training: first, the recognition, planning, and communication of evocative stage imagery, and second, the development of the pantomimic and vocal instruments for the communication of this image to the audience. Considerable space here is given to the building of a dramatic role. The actor is asked to see this, however, not as a vague abstraction of inner deliberation but as something in motion which from the start *a spectator can see and hear.*

In other words, this is a book for the beginning performer—it is a guide to the *first steps* in acting.

Once again I wish to acknowledge the help of my students in the preparation of this book. Many of their thoughts and some of their actual words are quoted in the text.

S.S.

CONTENTS

Part Two
TWENTY-FIVE DRAMATIC SCENES

part one

✕

The Forms and Techniques
of Acting

I

★

THE ACTOR'S OBJECTIVES

The Two Doors into the Theatre

THERE ARE TWO WAYS to an understanding of the theatre. One is through the Stage Entrance. Inside this door the student of dramatic techniques comes upon a bustling world of writers, designers, players, and other artists, each busily performing a task in accordance with a very personal conviction about the best method for it. If the visitor to backstage can keep himself from becoming bewildered, if he observes long and keenly enough, and if he asks enough questions of those who have time to reply to him, he will learn many enlightening things about showmanship.

"If you wish your stage setting to produce an exciting effect," the scenic man may advise him, "include in it at least one strong diagonal line."

"Speak first in a low voice, then in a high voice," an actor will say, "and you will roll them in the aisles with laughter." Or, "Move vigorously across the room, then stop as if there is something you want to utter, but cannot quite put in words and you will draw tears from your spectators' eyes—like rain!— Anyone can do it! But you must do it right!—See?"

If the young investigator of theatre ways wishes to become a writer, or designer, or player himself, he may choose the Stage Entrance and limit his field of study to the small world inside. Learning carefully from the actions of those who inhabit that re-

3

gion of artificiality, he may acquire a marvelous number of good tricks for his work. But if he confines his learning to the Stage only, no matter how hard he may try thereafter to avoid the taint, he will always affect his products with the odor of grease paint, with a manner a little unreal. The life he will attempt henceforth to depict will be secondhand—the love, laughter, and sorrow of people seen through the technical eyes of other craftsmen.

But there is another door. Through this entrance every serious observer should pass, not once but many times, if he wishes to arrive at the true secret of the theatre. This is the Front Door. It is the one used by the audience—the people for whom the dramatic artist creates. If the writer, designer, or player really wishes to win their approval for the things he makes for them, he must learn to know them. He must recognize them, not as a mass of men and women seated in orchestra or balcony chairs at so much admission per person but as individuals. He must associate with them intimately in their daily lives, in their homes, in their places of business. He must speak to them, walk with them, find their inmost thoughts. Then he will go to the playhouse—not *his* playhouse, but *theirs*—and sit down humbly beside them. He will feel their breath stop expectantly as the lights in the auditorium dim slowly, and he will watch their eyes open hungrily as the dark curtains part on that little place of wonder called the Stage. Constantly he will ask himself: "Why have these people come here?" Only when he has found the true answer to that question can he begin to shape his creative efforts into real eloquence.

Why the Audience Comes to See the Play

If the artist were to inquire of a number of lay persons why they attend the theatre, he would doubtless receive some very different replies. Each man has his own reason.

Mr. Jones is the senior accountant at the Mark Johnson Department Store. Unmarried and without many friends, he spends long days over order sheets, bill forms, and ledgers. At night he tries to forget these things. He likes the theatre. Sometimes he attends one of the touring attractions at the City Auditorium, and sometimes he goes to a play presented by the university actors up on the campus. But often he prefers the movies. Punctually at eight o'clock he enters the mystical darkness of the Mercury Theatre and is straightway transported to the tropical shores of Tahiti where he romps in the sun, the wind, and the waves with long-lashed, brown-skinned girls; or to the chamber of the British Prime Minister where he plots with soft-spoken diplomats for the control of the Suez Canal; or to the hills of Montana where he battles with a sheriff and his posse for the capture of the baby-faced desperado barricaded in a lonely ranch house for his last stand. Through a magical two hours, Mr. Jones' existence is immeasurably freshened. His eyes, accustomed to figures and store print, varnished furniture, and the gray outlines of his office, eagerly trace new images. His mind, full of the click-clack of typewriters and adding machines, is purged with the sound of pleasant voices. Mr. Jones has for a while stepped out of himself into another world. . . .

Mrs. Williams, married to the proprietor of a small hardware store, lives comfortably but uneventfully. She is not quite rich enough to afford that maid she has long desired, nor so poor as to ever be worried about the monthly bills. Mrs. Williams is really very fond of her husband and her two children; but she has to admit to herself occasionally that she gets rather tired of tending to them day after day—getting their breakfasts, making their beds, cleaning the apartment, and then preparing lunch in the same old kitchen, with never a change. Her one form of stimulation is the theatre. Her eyes shine when she thinks of it. Every Tuesday evening after the supper dishes, she hangs her apron on the hook inside the pantry door, puts on her hat, calls "Good night" to the children at their lessons and Mr. Williams seated with his paper, and walks downtown to one of the playhouses. She selects her entertainment with care. Especially she likes stories about the family, dramas of growing children, the heartaches and laughter of young married people, and the bravery and wisdom of their elders. As she watches their problems unfold and follows their gallant efforts to solve them, her emotions, leveled by the monotony of her own changeless existence, are stirred once more into active life. She feels fearful, hopeful, sad, full of tender longing, happily satisfied; and she enjoys every bit of that experience.

When she goes out into the street at the close of a particularly good performance, she feels strangely lifted. She walks home on light feet. Back in the apartment, she glances affectionately at her sleeping children, and sometimes, in a gay mood, she even kisses her husband. Mrs. Williams is still feeling the glow of her evening's adventure when she slips into bed. . . .

Dr. Jordan and his wife are very busy people. He is the county health officer and she is active in welfare work. They go to the theatre whenever they have an opportunity. It is their one form of outside recreation. They enjoy almost all the plays they see, but they prefer those that are thoughtful. They like to watch the kinds of characters and stories which offer a critique of life— dramas which discuss current social problems, and those which deal illuminatingly with the more timeless conflicts between man and his environment. Dr. and Mrs. Jordan have an insatiable interest in human behavior. The plays they see often give them fresh perspectives. Weeks after they have attended a performance, sometimes at lunch or at supper, the doctor will suddenly drop his paper, or his wife will set down her cup, and remark: "You know, I have just thought of something in connection with that play." And then he, or she, will talk about a new point of human psychology or philosophy which has occurred to him. The life which they see around them holds so much confusion that the moments in the theatre which bring clarity seem very precious to them. . . .

Mr. Jones, Mrs. Williams, and Dr. Jordan and his wife are by nature different individuals, so their reasons for attending plays vary. If the young artist should inquire of any ten persons just why they like to frequent the theatre, he would doubtless receive ten answers which viewed superficially would seem to be wholly unlike. But if he probed long enough into the minds of the persons he interviewed, he would find certain similarities. Every man wishes to feel himself alive to the fullest extent of his being! In the theatre, he may realize this desire more completely than in any other place on earth.

The Way the Spectator Responds

This book discusses the particular problems of the actor. Dedicated but professionally inexperienced persons have often disagreed with the idea that the actor should be concerned with the spectator's attitudes. "In order to keep oneself completely honest in what one does in the theatre," the young player is apt to declare bravely, "one should give thought to no one's opinion but *one's own*." This concept of artistic integrity is admirable—except in its failure to recognize one fundamental fact of the playhouse: this is a place which was erected for the purpose of having a group of people present some words and actions *for the enjoyment of other people*. An audience comes only because it wants to. If it receives no pleasure, it leaves. The young person who likes to recite lines on a platform in a bare room *for his own satisfaction only* has every right in the world to do that; but he cannot logically call himself an *actor* until he attracts other persons to hear him. If he wishes to draw them to his performance, he must respect their desires. We must start, therefore, with the assumption of two premises: that the playhouse exists for an audience, and that it is not only the privilege but also the obligation of the actor to please that audience.

When the young man who wishes to understand the stage has found the reasons for a spectator's appearance in the playhouse, then he will certainly wish to continue his investigation by studying that spectator's behavior after he has arrived. A spectator's response to a dramatic performance, he will discover, involves at least three things: perception, participation, and mental comment. Little need be said about the first, for that factor of the perceptive response is obvious. The spectator sees a player's body and hears his voice. The only thing he asks with respect to perception is that the player appear in enough light for his physical presence to be seen, and that he speak distinctly enough for his words to be heard. The second point in the response, however, offers a problem considerably more complex. Upon the player's ability to get the spectator to *act with him,* depends the success or failure of his whole venture.

In what way may a member of the audience participate? Clearly, he cannot walk down the aisle, climb onto the stage, and engage himself in the movement and speech of the players—actually. However, he may do what is practically the same thing: he may *feel* himself up there. In imagination, he enters the body of the actor and becomes united with him in everything he does. Part of that participation is purely mental make-believe; but there is also another aspect. It is a sensuous response which involves the whole organism of the beholder, physical as well as mental. It is a kind of participation similar to that experienced by the spectator at a sports event.

Anyone who has attended a football game will remember how the people in the seats play along with the men on the field. If a favored member of the team seizes the ball and starts down the field with it, his friends on the sidelines lean a little in the direction in which he is going, contributing their own muscular and nervous energy to help him reach the distant goal line. They "feel into" his action. Similar behavior may be seen at a horse race, or a dog race, or at a track meet where contestants jump or run. Sometimes the spectator "jumps" or "runs" so hard with the man whom he hopes will win that his body aches and there is no breath left in him. Physiological investigations have shown that the secretion from the adrenal glands of the onlookers is often equal to that of the athlete.

The impulse to feel out sensuously the shape and quality of objects that interest us is manifested in our daily lives. There is a name for it: *empathy.* The objects which so excite our participatory responses need not be in motion or even animate. We see a polished granite ball, and we sense at a distance its smoothness, roundness, and weight. While we contemplate its heaviness, we feel no urge to dance, or to walk lightly on our toes. We "feel" solid, established, just as if we were holding the great bulk of the stone in our arms. Through the glass of a store window we gaze at a piece of fur, and we can imagine our hands caressing it, our fingers twisting through its softness. We look at a marble column and speak of being "lifted," because inceptively we reach our arms along its tall sides. We come suddenly upon a view of the sea, and our chests rise and our palms reach out to feel the spaciousness of it. Our senses go out to the wide expanse of water and sky, and we respond with every part of us.

But it is the active objects which appeal most strongly to this strange urge for "feeling into." The swaying of tall trees in the wind, the graceful motion of a white sailboat, the sleek running of a hound, the rhythmical walking of a handsome woman—such things have a compelling effect upon our empathic natures. We enter into them. We feel their movement. Perceptively, to those who watch our outward bodies, we may not sway, or glide, or walk, but we do have a tingling of the senses, a little tightening of our muscles. What these stirrings lack in breadth they make up for in intensity. So we do in truth experience in ourselves the motion we contemplate.

The kind of participation described is clearly evident in the theatre. The spectator arrives with a desire for action. As he sits waiting expectantly for the curtain to rise he has his whole person set for an active response. Then, when the moving bodies on the stage are revealed, the spectator's sensory-motor organism, already attuned, begins to stir. He responds dynamically with every part of himself. His whole being "moves" with the moving stimuli. He walks with the players, sits and rises with them, enters into every slightest motion of their hands and faces. He also speaks with them; and as the muscles of his throat search out the tonal changes of their voices, he achieves an emotional understanding of the characters whom they portray which he could never attain if he listened objectively to words alone.

But too much participation may destroy itself. Stories are told of the old mining days in which playgoers, transported with anxiety for the lovely heroine hard pressed by evil, stood up in their seats and shot the villain. That kind of all-out participation is obviously not to be desired. The man with the pistol identified himself completely with the fortunes of the fair lady, but when he did that he stopped playing the game. For him, the theatre was no longer a place of make-believe; it was the real thing. And so he missed a lot of fun. He ceased to play.

What the performer seeks from the audience, then, is not a blind, hundred percent identification, but a pleasurable *sharing* of action. Between complete identification and effective sharing lies a margin of difference which leaves the playgoer space for the movement of his own personality. Thus he can retain some freedom of choice as to how he will handle his game of make-believe. If the play is well written, and the acting of all the parts is good, he will doubtless enjoy the art of the performance as much as he does the characters themselves.

And, with regard to those characters, he is at liberty, if he wishes, to extend his participatory adventure beyond the ingratiating heroine and her handsome lover and to associate himself with other figures—including the villain. Though naturally he may fear this man's actions, he may, at the same time, develop a sympathy for him—he may even have an affection for him. The spectator can take an empathic satisfaction in feeling out the boldness and smoothness of a character whom, from the viewpoint of the story, he is bound to shun intellectually. In a similar way, he can enjoy the sheer skill with which a certain comic role is presented—a figure with whom the spectator might never wish to identify himself at all.

In the marginal territory of participation just described operates that important third phase of the playgoer's response, his running mental comment. If the acting has quality beyond the basic portrayal of character, if it has grace, vitality, and style, the spectator will note this, and by the measure of that observation will the intensity of his pleasure be increased. Every member of the audience, if he be experienced at all, likes to imagine himself as playing a triple role: the character portrayed, the actor portrayer, and the critic; and not the least of his satisfaction comes from the third part. When he is in the presence of a good thing he enjoys the process of analyzing it. He likes to recognize the features of skillful designing. He likes to examine them, to trace them, and to caress them with his thoughts.

So far in this discussion, all references to the audience have been made as if that audience had a single and unchanging personality. Nothing could be further from the truth. An assembly composed chiefly of Mr. Joneses is bound to be very different from one comprised of persons like the Jordans and the Mrs. Williamses. The members of all three groups, it is true, would doubtless be drawn to the theatre by the same three desires for diversion, stimulation, and illumination, but the ways in which the groups respond to the play would vary considerably. The Mr. Joneses would seek a participation close to the point of full identification; so they would resent everything in the way of style which would affect the "naturalness" of the interpretation. For this audience, the actor would have to design a realistic performance, dressed in "straight" costumes in a lifelike setting.

Mrs. Williams would not care so much about the manner in which the play was acted as about its ability to stir her emotions. Dr. and Mrs. Jordan, on the other hand, would probably enjoy a considerable amount of formal design. Without style, the performance would seem to them flat, pedestrian. For them the performer would work especially hard to attain grace of speech and movement. For them, he would sharpen delicately the phrases of double meaning, the oblique references, the sly rejoinders. For them, he would refine the means for creating mood; and he might spice his whole performance—if this seemed fitting—with subtle bits of humor which would increase the sense of playfulness. He would enlist the assistance of the costumer, the scenic artist, and the lighting expert, and they would help the actor to bring out all these nuances by reflecting their spirit in the visual environment. Music and sound effects, also, might lend their aid. If the efforts of the actor, helped by his companions, were successful, the enjoyment of the spectators who comprise this third audience would be twofold. Like the Mr. Joneses and the Williamses, they would participate sensuously and emotionally in the dramatic figures of the story; but, differing from the others, they would also have a real share in the performance itself. And they would take pleasure in their recognition of its fine points. They would have the satisfaction of playing at the same time the parts of character, actor, and critic.

Sooner or later the successful player has to deal with all kinds of audiences. He learns early to recognize them and to adapt his technique accordingly. Frequently he finds all of the kinds of people gathered together in one assembly. Then he has to know how to appeal to all of them at the same time. In the presentation of the same play through six days of a week, he will inevitably have to alter his performance to fit the changing proportions of human temperament between Monday and Saturday. The remarkable thing is that, if he is a sincere artist who respects his obligation to the playwright's script, and is at the same time a man of imagination and flexibility, he will be able to adapt his interpretation without once being false to the basic dramatic idea.

The Actor's Means of Communication

The actor's medium is himself. What he wants to affect is the imagination of the spectator. This he cannot do if he simply repeats parrot-like the words set down in the script and if he executes mechanically the "entrances," "exits," and "crosses" indicated there. He must do all this in a *certain way*. In the first place, the player must stir up and call forth the spectator's interest in his presence, and then, by additional stimuli, he must induce the spectator to follow his actions throughout the play. The means for that kind of stirring-up lie in a special language of acting which is related to, but goes beyond, the lettered symbols in the playwright's score.

The actor's mediums of communication are three:

(1) Words—without their tone-coloring	Mental and acquired (deliberative, definitive, unemotional)
(2) External bodily movement—posturing and gesturing (3) Voice-tones—the sounds of the active body	Physical and natural (impulsive, intuitive, emotional)

The actor as the playwright's translator lifts the symbols from the dramatic script, turns them over in his mind, and then projects them in a new form across the footlights. But the measure of his talent does not lie in the quality of his memory or the purity of his diction. It lies rather in the kind of feeling with which he surrounds those words, a feeling which he makes audible through the music of his voice, and visible through a sensuous dance of his body.

The spectator responds to the player's performance only if the player makes that response inviting. In order to evoke this desirable reaction, the player must see to it that the movements of his body and the tones of his voice are the kind that the spectator would enjoy feeling himself into. His pantomime must be right for the character and situation he is attempting to depict. His steps must be of the correct length, neither too long nor too short, neither too fast nor too slow. He must use his hands just enough and in the right places. And when he does use them, they must have—unless the character is supposed to be dull—an impression of sensuous life, as if they really feel the objects they touch and are ready to do something about them. The actor must keep his face mobile and, at the same time, avoid grimaces. His pantomime must be clear and precise; there must be no awkwardness of movement—for that would destroy participation immediately. It must be rhythmical and richly varied.

In the same way, the actor must give thought to his voice. The spectator will refuse to play along with him if the tones he utters are too high or too low, or if they lack the right timbre, or if they do not have the correct intonation for the character they are trying to impersonate. There must be rhythm, tempo, contrast, and an exciting music in that voice if the actor hopes to catch the spectator up in it and make him a part of it.

The player's success in vividly projecting the author's images depends upon his technical skill in employing the three mediums of communication. But finally something more than mere technique is involved. The other factor is the player's own personality. During the process of translation the actor must add something of himself, or the images will die. The images must be touched by his imagination, stirred by his pulse beats, thought and felt by him anew; thus the vision becomes enriched as it passes through him to the spectator. In this way, the actor is not only the interpreter of the playwright, he is also his creative collaborator.

The Twofold Objective of the Actor

The performer then is a dual personality. The first self is the part of him which reads a script, conceives a character, and, from the materials so acquired, creates a human image of sound and action.

The second self is concerned with the presentation of this image so that an audience will grasp it not only with senses but also with mind. The actor as instrumentalist is both an expert projector of the image, and a keen critic of the effectiveness of that projection. In this way the actor in motion complements all of the spectator's desires for participation, stimulation, and mental comment.

Here are indicated very simply the two basic responsibilities of the actor, and, in their light, what he should set up as his two principal objectives. The first is to conceive the character with which he is entrusted as clearly, as vividly, and as completely as he can; and the second is to present him as a composition in movement and sound in such form as will make the spectator accept him in all his parts. Practically, the actor will devise a personality, and by means of art induce the spectator in his imagination to play him. If the actor does this efficiently, both he and the spectator will be pleased with the collaborative experience.

The Actor's Program of Training

Generally speaking, there are four steps in the training of an actor. First is his broad education. To do justice to the wide range of parts which will come his way when he has matured his art, he must have many references from which to draw. Therefore, as a young person he should take a great many courses in science and literature, both prose and poetry, and supplement these with history, music, an appreciation of painting, and philosophy. He should also study language. There is little he can study in high school and college which will fail to contribute valuable grist for his mill.

The second step is an enlargement of the scope of his living. An actor deals with human nature. He cannot deal with it effectively until he knows it thoroughly, and this in turn he cannot do until he himself has lived life intensively, inwardly and outwardly. He must know many people in many walks of existence, talk with them freely, share with them their hopes and dreams, their loves, their pains, their terrifying frustrations, and their joys of freedom. He himself need never become the governor of a state or a bum on Skid Row, but he should at some time in his experience come close enough to them to feel the warmth of their personalities and to respond to the shapes of their thoughts.

The third and fourth steps are training for the fulfillment of what we have just described as the actor's two principal responsibilities. This third step is the preparation of the mind for dramatic image-making; and the fourth the disciplining of the body as instrument for the transmission of that image to an audience. It is to these two last phases of the actor's development that most of the following chapters of this book will be devoted.

II

THE ACTOR AS IMAGE-MAKER

Human Images in Motion

THE FIRST BUSINESS of acting is the making of an image. Out of the literary figures of an author's script, out of his word-symbols, the player must draw forth a mental vision; he must see it and hear it in his mind. Then, standing on a stage and with the aid of devices of tone and gesture, he must translate that inward vision into an outward image compellingly sensible to a group of spectators.

What the player creates is a tangible form of voice and action. Yet it is not practically speaking a reality. It is a semblance only. In preparing his role the actor makes up his face. He puts on a costume. He assumes a posture, a manner of walking, a style of speaking—none of which is actually his own. Then he steps into a setting which *appears* to be a real place—the sitting room of the Mayo farmhouse, perhaps, or the side of a New Hampshire roadway at sunrise—but which in truth is a group of wooden and canvas screens lighted by electric lamps. The aim of the actor in this makeup, this costume, and this setting is not to *be*, but to *seem to be*. Throughout his appearance on the stage he strives to stimulate the spectator's imagination in such a way as to make him see and hear much more than the actual stage depicts. Therefore what the actor produces is beyond reality; it is an implication, a picturization of shapes in motion designed to stir imagination.

The image made by the player has its physical presence on

16

the stage; it walks and talks in the body of the actor. But its features and movements, in so far as they *seem* to be the living expression of dramatic personalities, depend for their meaningful existence on the mind of the audience. Stage imagery is ever the result of collaboration; the actor creates, and the spectator sees— what the actor wants him to see.

The Dramatic Personality and His Stage Environment

To build the dramatic image requires technical and psychological understanding. There are, as the preceding chapter suggests, two approaches to the problem, and both must be explored. One is to observe how fellow performers handle imagery. The other is to do some exploring in the human backgrounds of everyday life. The actor is wise if he follows the second path first. He will look at someone of his acquaintance—any ordinary individual—and ask himself, "What are the simplest human facts about this person?" The man, he will see, is a personality with an inner (hidden) self and an outer (visible) self. He lives in a universe of restless forces, some of which imply a better existence for him, and some of which mean harm. He continuously makes adjustments so that he may live as securely, as comfortably, as completely as possible. A young man may take his girl for an early morning ride in a bright new car. He drives it fast because he wants to impress her with his skill. But he takes great care not to strike anything that will dent a pretty fender and frighten the girl, for to do this would make the next ride in the car less desirable for her. At home, his mother is involved in far less adventurous pursuits, perhaps, but she too will be responding pro and con to the objects around her. She wants to get the sleep out of her eyes, so she prepares some coffee. She places the percolator on the gas flame to heat it. She takes care, however, not to poke a finger in the flame because that would cause a pain. If she does get it in the flame she jerks it away. When the coffee is ready she pours it into a cup. But she drinks the hot liquid cautiously. She wants to enjoy its wonderfully stimulating effect, yet she wishes also to avoid burning her tongue. Perhaps the sun shines in her eyes. She draws the shade. The air from outside smells fresh, so she opens a door to let some of it into the kitchen.

Then the phone rings. Now she must make a decision. Who is on the other end of the line? She would like to talk to the pleasant Mr. Ainslie. But the person on the phone may be that whining Mrs. Harwood! Shall she lift the receiver? She decides to take a chance. So the day goes on, with some involuntary and some deliberate responses.

The most important reactions which the previously mentioned young man will direct to his surroundings during the coming hours will be those he makes, not to inanimate objects, but to people: his girl friend, his boss, his fellow workers at the shop, his parents at home. His mother will have to deal in turn with the mailman, the paper boy, the grocery clerk, her neighbor across the road. The young man's father at the office will probably have to act and react to fifty or a hundred different people before the end of the day.

Since everyone wishes to extend his existence in as positive a way as possible, he must recognize quickly the difference between the beneficial and the harmful forces represented in the shape and quality of objects, but mostly in the speech and movement of people—and react accordingly. No sooner will he achieve one adjustment before he will be driven to work for another. The forces are never still. His life is a continuing series of crises, from the little one involved in correctly interpreting the sensation on the soles of his feet that will enable him to descend a flight of stairs safely, to the big one involved in approaching a bank president for a substantial loan.

The awareness which precedes response depends upon the outward self; the nerve ends which serve the senses are external. But a sensation is not completed until it passes inward and records itself on the mind. That interaction is automatic; the individual has no control over it. Outward conditions cause inward changes. The reverse process, however, does not always take place. Although inner changes (feelings, thoughts, emotions) *tend* to reveal themselves outwardly, they do not *always* do so. Outward reactions are natural to children and uninhibited primitives, but they are commonly repressed in socially-trained adults. It is the rule rather than the exception that the more deeply a civilized man feels, the less he will show it.

At this point, therefore, the actor will have to stop studying his acquaintances from the everyday world and begin to consider the requirements of the stage. The dramatic figure which it is the business of the player to project in imagery must be self-revealing. Since the spectator cannot by any effort read the mind of the actor without the outward symbols, the actor must devise ways for making his character *demonstrative*. Even when the playwright calls for an interpretation executed with the "utmost restraint," the performer realizes that a "restraint" on the stage is only a comparative one; *inner feelings must be made sensible to the audience*.

The writer of a novel can take a figure in repose—a man drowsing away a whole afternoon beside a sunlit canal—and, by the manner is which he portrays him, make him absorbingly interesting. The dramatic artist, however, cannot do this. On the stage, a quiescent figure is meaningless. He must be stirred into action; thus only can he reveal his essential personality. He must be shown to be affected by stimuli, and then be seen doing something about them. The whole substance of the dramatic image exists, therefore, in visible and audible action and reaction.

Inward and Outward Attention

Most of what the actor has to depict is what the man whom he is personating does about the dramatic people and objects around him. From time to time, however, the man depicted will turn from the forces outside himself to certain other forces inside. These may be voices of experience, or temptation, or fear, or conscience. In effect, he will enter into conversation with inward spiritual or mental entities—they may be conceived as "councillors," or "devils," or "angels"—whom the audience cannot see but whose presence the audience wants to recognize. How can he do this so that the audience may be aware of what is going on?

The first step in an acting technique is to show where one's center of attention is located. The actor must always create his image with outward symbols. These must be clearly visible and clearly audible to every spectator in the playhouse—including the person way back in the last seat in the balcony. But the actor can use these symbols in such a way as to *suggest* whether at a given moment the core of his thought is related to something in his environment, or something within him.

If the center of the actor's dramatic attention moves from outside to inside there will tend to be some change in his posture. The best symbol of the fully enclosed individual is that of the fetus in the womb. When the individual is in the beginning stage of his development he is completely unaware that any kind of environment exists. He is folded inward with his head bowed and his arms and his legs drawn up to his chest. His principal vital organs —heart, lungs, stomach, intestines, reproductive apparatus—as well as his sensory organs, are all turned inward. When he emerges into a world of environmental forces his body will open up, but the sensitive, most actively responsive part of him will still be in his frontal area. When the character on the stage moves back into himself, therefore, it will be natural for him to drop his eyes— away from contact with the environment—and to lower his head. He will probably move out of the region of other action on the stage and he may sit down. If he speaks, he will drop the pitch of his voice a little. If the character depicted is so sophisticated— that is, so trained by his social breeding that he must resist the impulses to resume the form of the fetus—he will simply turn his head or his body away from other action; and he may walk off into a quiet or shadowy part of the scene. Perhaps that is all he will do. If his dramatic impulse to retire into himself is overpowering, however—too strong for his breeding in self-control to master—he may crawl into a bed, curl up, and turn his face to the wall.

When the dramatic center of attention is outward—which will be most of the time—the actor's image-making actions will work in reverse. He will show his responsive awareness of an object or person in the environment by opening out his body, straightening his back, lifting his head, and looking directly at the source of the stimulation. When he speaks to it he may raise the pitch of his voice a little and strengthen the intensity of his tone. He is now receiving impressions from outside and projecting his responses back to the source of the stimulation at some distance from himself.

The Shifting of Attention Illustrated

The actor's purpose in changing imagery by moving his center of attention from inside to outside can be illustrated in a sequence of actions for one of Hamlet's soliloquies and in what immediately follows it. The soliloquy opens:

> To be, or not to be: that is the question.
> Whether 'tis nobler in the mind to suffer
> The slings and arrows of outrageous fortune,
> Or to take arms against a sea of troubles,
> And by opposing end them. To die; to sleep;
> No more; and by a sleep to say we end
> The heart-ache and the thousand natural shocks
> That flesh is heir to. 'Tis a consummation
> Devoutly to be wish'd. To die; to sleep;—
> To sleep? Perchance to dream! Ay, there's the rub; . . .
> For in that sleep of death what dreams may come,
> When we have shuffl'd off this mortal coil,
> Must give us pause. . . .

The stage is presumably empty. If Ophelia is present, she must be standing so far upstage in a dark corner that the Prince cannot catch a glimpse of her. He enters slowly and quietly with his head and eyes lowered, paying not the slightest bit of attention to his surroundings. We in the audience hear what he says to himself, but his voice is lowered—obviously his words are not intended (from his point of view) for any one but himself. Hamlet is here turning over in his mind the dark question of possible suicide. So, surely he will not seek for the development of his thoughts the center of the hall, nor will he climb the steps to any eminence as if he were trying to enlarge his effective presence. Rather, he will probably move off-center and lower himself onto a bottom step or a stool—the smaller and less prominent the better.

At the close of Hamlet's inward communion with himself Ophelia enters, or emerges from the concealing shadows, toward him. He notices her:

> —Soft you now!
>   The fair Ophelia!

His manner changes. He lifts his head. His back and shoulders begin to straighten. When she gets part way to him he rises and extends his voice a little, still talking to himself rather than to the young woman, but clearly directing his attention to her.

>   Nymph in thy orisons
>   Be all my sins rememb'red.

When Ophelia reaches the Prince she speaks to him with the full voice of outward interaction:

>   Good my lord,
>   How does your honour for this many a day?

The Prince answers with a kind of grim good humor on the same level of full interaction:

>   I humbly thank you, well, well, well.

And so the scene continues to the end, when Ophelia slips back a little into herself on Hamlet's exit.

A stage character's center of attention moves in various ways in different circumstances. Depending on the nature of what attracts it, the center may move reluctantly or gladly, slowly or rapidly. For the young girl waiting for her lover, the sound of a light knock will draw her attention to the front door immediately. When Laertes in *Hamlet*, hearing about the ruin of his sister, Ophelia, angrily seeks the King, his center of attention leaps from the outside of the castle clear into the heart of it, and the crash of his voice shows the violence of its movement. When Lear gazes at the still warm body of the dead Cordelia in his arms his center of attention moves achingly just a few inches to her lips. By the force of his attention he tries to make the lips quiver again in life. When he finds that he cannot will action into them he sorrowfully draws his eyes from them and turns his gaze to his friend, Kent.

The Motivation of the Actor's Response
to Another Presence

In every case, what brings about an active response in an attendant individual is not so much the bare physical being of an observed object or person as its *effective presence,* a power which it has to titillate the sense and at the same time to stir the mind of the particular person who is looking at, or hearing, or touching this source of stimulation. Because no two responsive individuals have identical ways of feeling and thinking, and because even the same man's sensory and mental trends vary from moment to moment, the object's effective presence changes continually. What makes one person laugh may make another cry. What incites to action today may put to rest tomorrow. The effectiveness of an object's presence (at a certain place and a certain time) depends therefore on two factors: (1) the sensuous power of the object, and (2) the relationship of the object to the past experience of the responsive individual, and to his present needs and desires.

When Mr. Smith turns to speak to Mr. Brown on the stage, he projects a force of stimulation. His bodily appearance fills Brown's eyes, the sound of his voice strikes Brown's ears. The visual and auditive presence of Smith makes a sensory impact on Brown. Now, if Smith not only walks up to Brown and speaks to him, but also grasps his hands, or aims a blow at his face, the sensuous fact of Smith is intensified. In either case, Brown becomes physically aware that Smith is there. Consequently, he begins to respond. What he does in return is conditioned by the power of the physical contact—the size of Smith's body, the pitch and volume of his voice, and the strength of his hands. But equally important in the calling-forth of action from Brown—frequently far more important—is Brown's own condition of receptivity. This is influenced by many things: the kind of life he has lived, his past dealings with Smith, his present bodily and mental poise, and what at this moment he would like to gain or avoid in his association with Smith. If Smith is his friend, he will take one attitude toward him; if he is a stranger, or an enemy, there will be another attitude. In any event, the presence of Smith challenges him. It makes him gather up his energies in resistance to Smith, or let those energies flow in compliance with Smith; it makes him move toward Smith, or try to escape from him. Finally, the effective presence of Smith causes Brown to do something specific with regard to their relationship. Brown may simply laugh at Smith. That all depends on the character of Brown's preceding experiences, and on his current needs and desires, in so far as these may be associated with Smith.

Without having to go very deeply into the complex psychology of stimulation-and-reaction, the player readily discovers that every object of attention (animate or inanimate) on the stage exerts certain dynamic forces, or *spurs;* and that these cause in the individual who sees, or hears, or feels, a response which has three parts, three steps in action:

> (a) Sensation
> (b) Preparation
> (c) Attack

When the responsive individual becomes aware of an object his whole nervous system is stirred. Then he is prepared to do something. He lifts his energy to meet the force of the object's presence, or drops his energy because he does not wish to resist its influence. If he is affected by it positively, he moves toward it; if negatively, away from it. Finally, in a third step (if he has gone toward it) he handles the object. He picks it up, fondles it, changes its shape; or he destroys it. If the object is a person, he embraces it, caresses it; or he strikes it, or pushes it from him. This, at any rate, is what the responsive individual *tends* to do. That is what he has an *impulse* to do. The actor on the stage must deal constantly with these tendencies, impulses, for out of them he builds the skeleton of his performance.

The Form of the Response: Fundamental Action

Stage action, and this means those movements and vocal utterances by which all dramatic characters respond to one another, can be divided into two kinds, fundamental and accessory. The first is gross, broad, and generally impulsive. Its character is primitive; it may be seen in young children as well as in grown-ups.

The second kind of action, the accessory, is typically marked by complexities of thought. It is therefore the more sophisticated action. A thirsty man reaches for water; that is fundamental. He puts what he is about to drink in a cup; that is accessory. A susceptible young man moves toward a woman—fundamental. He pays her a compliment—accessory. Fundamental action is by nature automatic, involuntary, while the accessory is learned, deliberative.

Because of their fundamental association with primitive behavior, the fundamental movements can reveal to the audience much more directly than the accessory the forces of stimulation and reaction. Consequently, they form the basic part of every piece of acting. There are four of them, and they may be lined up this way under the three steps of the dramatic response outlined in the preceding section:

Sensation

Opening out the senses to the presence of the stimulating object	Closing in

Preparation

Rising	Sinking
Approaching	Withdrawing

Attack

Building up the forces of the stimulating object	Destroying it

Movement No. 1 is an unfolding of one or more parts of the body in such a way as to reveal to the spectator how the actor is aware of the object confronting him. He lifts his head, he turns his head, he opens his eyes, he raises and bares the palms of his hands, or he extends his arm or his foot to touch, to make sensuous contact. The movement of Sensation may be large or small, involving a single part or all of the body. It may be swift or deliberate; that depends on the situation. Expertly performed, however, it should tell the spectator three things: (a) the place of the stimulating object (right, left, high, low, here, there, or over yonder); (b) the form of the object's presence (whether it is visual, auditory, olfactory, gustatory, or tactile; and what is its size, shape, or quality); and (c) the force of that presence. There are many ways in which the sensory impact of the object can be shown; the actor has to be prepared to experiment freely. The negative phase of Movement No. 1 is the reverse of the positive, that is, a closing in of the senses to put an end to sensation. (In this respect it is related to the outward and inward movement of the center of attention previously described. In effect it is the same movement viewed from a different angle.)

The two movements of the Preparatory step serve to place and condition the actor in anticipation of the third step, the Attack. There are two preparatory movements. The first is rising-sinking. If in the initial act of sensing, the actor perceives the object to have beneficent or malignant qualities, he will have an impulse to gather up his resources of energy—to meet the challenge of the confronting presence—or to let the resources of energy flow away in fear or resignation. Rising energy is reflected in a lift of the body, ebbing energy in a drooping or sinking. Upward movement is associated with life—a growing plant, a young child, a man of vigor seeks to push from the surface of the earth, to reach skyward in conquest of gravity—and downward movement is related to death—the sick man, the weary and discouraged sink toward the grave. The fundamental rising-sinking action is executed on the stage as a lift or fall of the body as a whole, or of single members only. The individual may jump up or sit down suddenly; or he may lift or lower himself very slowly; or he may raise or drop just his hand in one of a variety of gestures. In those scenes which demand subtle suggestion rather than full statement, the individual shows his energetic response to another presence by a small tilt and sag of the head or chest, or by a slight elevation or depression of the shoulders.

Sometimes the rising or sinking constitutes all of the second step. Usually, however, the individual's perception of the good or the bad qualities in the object impels him also to change his position in relationship to that object. He finds the dish of food or the handsome woman he contemplates attractive, so he advances toward the object; or he notes that the food gives forth an evil odor, or that the woman holds a gun, so he withdraws. Or he is angry with the thing before him and steps up to it in order to force down its presence; or he is disgusted and moves in retreat. If the qualities the individual senses in the object are immediately compelling, he jumps forward or backward. If they are of a less critical nature, he may take a single slow step toward or away, or perhaps, turn himself only. In a situation of restraint, the individual may simply shift his feet slightly, rock his weight forward or back on his heels, swing his hand, or just quietly incline or avert his head.

The Attack Movement takes many forms. Reflecting as it does the urge to increase or diminish the effective activity in another body, it may be a movement of lifting up (something fallen), a fond pat on the back, or a comforting embrace. Or, on the other hand, it may be a tearing down, a striking apart, a throwing aside. It may be a fondling or a strangling. As a fundamental action, it is always very simple in form, the kind of movement which would be natural to a child, a savage, or even an animal. As part of a sequence, it may serve as a basis for more complicated action which will start as soon as the intellect of the individual begins to work, but in its first raw state it is crude and direct. For this reason, when the Attack Movement is performed by persons of self-control, it is often partially masked. But vestiges of it are certain to be revealed in tensions of the body as a whole, and particularly in convulsive gestures of the head, the hands, or the feet.

Corresponding to each of the fundamental movements described is a characteristic fundamental vocal response. Motivated similarly by sensory stimulation, by forces which draw forth, rouse, and urge the individual to increase or diminish activity in the object which confronts him, the human voice purrs and cries with excitement; it rises and sinks, and reaches toward or away; and it caresses or lashes at the other presence—just as the body does. Commonly, the vocal response accompanies the pantomimic. Not infrequently, particularly in those dramatic moments when the body must for some reason be kept immobile, vocal action serves as a substitute for the pantomimic. In situations of this kind, the tones of words, and those incidental but expressive sounds like whistling, groaning, and sighing suggest vividly what the visible person would do if he were free to move.*

As an expressive agent on the stage, tonal speech ranks with bodily movement. The full concept of fundamental responses must therefore include both elements, the auditory along with the visual. From scene to scene the proportions may vary; here the stress will be on pantomime, there on voice. Occasionally one will have to serve for both. But where either of the two elements is submerged, its action has to be clearly implied. When the actor pantomimes, the audience demands to *feel speech;* when he speaks, it wants to *sense movement*—for both are parts of the self-same expression.

Although every basic stage response includes, either by statement or by unmistakable suggestion, something fundamental, it will not necessarily involve all four of the actions outlined in this section. Frequently the response goes no farther than the action of the first step (Sensation). More often it includes also the first, or both, of the second step (Preparation). If the general nature of the response is negative, the actions may stop at that point; but if it is positive—that is, if the individual presses forward with rising energy—the third step (Attack) will be apt to follow. The best of theatric behavior is always economical; it shows openly just enough to stimulate the thoughts of the audience, and leaves the rest to imagination. *This means that when the whole series of fundamental actions is not specifically needed for fulfilling some reference in the dialogue, good stage practice tends to let the sensorial or preparatory actions alone stand for the completed response.* In a scene of restraint in which the various forces of opposition have already been adequately described, and the audience is therefore quite clear about them, a swift glance of recognition, and a slow widening of the eyes, or a slight stiffening and rising of the body with a small inclination forward, may be sufficient to intimate the full power of an individual's urge to step up and destroy the object which troubles him. But it should be obvious to the actor that if the series of four actions stops at any point, he must see to it that the *remaining actions are all clearly*

* Problems of fundamental kinesthetic speech are discussed in Chapter IV.

implied. Amateur players usually indicate too little in this regard rather than too much. Nine times out of ten the so-called "ham" acting of inexperienced performers is really underacting; that is, it is acting which shows too few of the inner impulses.

Each of the fundamental movements and tonal activities of Preparation has both an aggressive and a recessive phase. Opening out, rising, and approaching are aggressive; while closing in, sinking, and withdrawing are recessive.* A response usually stays in one category or another. An individual is not very apt at the same time to come forward and fold inward, or to run away and expand. Both phases of Attack belong on the aggressive side; but building up may be designated as positive and destroying, as negative.

Several fundamental actions run in sequence; but frequently they move together, blended practically as a single action. All the elements of a full stage response are linked with one another like the notes in a phrase of music. When the audience listens, it gives attention to the harmonic design as a whole, rather than to any of the separate parts. However, to achieve that effect of unity the musician must prepare all the separate elements. Likewise, in his field, the actor has to give careful thought to each of the several components in a unity of expression.

The Form of the Response: Accessory Action

Fundamental actions make up the skeleton of a dramatic performance. All the other actions, both pantomimic and vocal, are accessory. They connect, develop, and elaborate on the effects of the fundamental. A man who is hungry approaches food. That movement is fundamental. He eats the food. That also is fundamental. If he is a savage, he may limit his movements to these. If, however, he is a civilized man he will increase for himself the pleasurable effectiveness of the food by further actions. He will spread a napkin on his lap, take up a knife and a fork, and proceed to carve his food before he eats it. This is accessory. Most of

---

* The order of sequence for the recessive actions is often the reverse of that for the aggressive. Aggressive: opening out, rising, approaching. Recessive: withdrawing, sinking, closing in.

the many little actions involved in the preparation of that food—cooking it, seasoning it, and serving it—are also accessory actions.

The accessory actions, as already stated, are the learned voluntary actions. They are typical of the adult individual who has trained himself by long experience to manipulate things efficiently in order to make them yield their greatest values. The actions include the movements and speech patterns associated with formal communion and persuasion, with many of the details involved in putting things together and in taking them apart, and in the building up or lessening of the stimuli which cause sensation. Saying good morning, asking for the time of day, writing a letter, mixing a cake, repairing a clock, playing the piano—all these are accessory actions. Through the aid of precise speech and movement, they handle certain points in the relationship of the individual to his environment which cannot be managed by the cruder, more impetuous fundamental actions.

It is true that the accessory sounds and gestures form the bulk of what the actor does on the stage. Since, however, the requirements for these are in every situation rather obvious, they do not need to be classified and examined separately. Instead of worrying very much about the accessory actions—except for the secondary purposes of clarity, grace, or characterization—the player wisely turns his attention to the fundamental actions. He strives to understand and master them, for they are the key to a vigorous, basically dramatic performance. Without the help of fundamental actions, every other effort of the player lacks conviction.

Fundamental actions, bodily and oral, do not occur in a clear-cut form at every moment of a performance. They serve chiefly as focal points, points of greater emphasis. Between them are transitional passages of accessory movement and speech. But it would be a mistake to think of the transitional parts as being in any way devoid of dynamic feeling. Actually, the particular movements and voice-tones which have here been termed "fundamental" are just the more easily sensed manifestations of dramatic forces working continuously under the surface. Practically speaking, every moment of a scene is affected by urges to sense more clearly—in order to understand more keenly and so become better prepared to adjust;—to align oneself more closely with persons one favors, or to escape those one fears; to extend good activity, or to stop bad activity. A person affected by a certain presence in a certain way may be impelled to cultivate it or destroy it, and then devote three whole acts of a play to doing this.

What this means is that no action is a detached unit. All movement and all speech parts are related to others. Drama depends on interaction. One stimulus sets off a response; that response serves as a second stimulus; and so the play progresses. Interaction proceeds without a break from the beginning to the end, and way beyond—for there was action before the play began, and there will be action after this segment of the story of life is over.

Action and Interaction Illustrated

How the player may recognize the different types of action in a dramatic scene which he observes and, conversely, how he may exploit such actions in his own performing, can be illustrated simply. The following passage comes from the beginning of Act III of *Romeo and Juliet*. The young lovers from the opposing houses of Montague and Capulet have just been joined in Friar Laurence's chapel, and Romeo, because of his attachment to his wife, has decided to become friendly to the rival family. Two of his companions are strolling along a street, talking.

BENVOLIO. An I were so apt to quarrel as thou art, any man should
      buy the fee-simple of my life for an hour and a quarter.
MERCUTIO. The fee-simple! O simple!

> (*The men are walking slowly and relaxed. Their conversation is amiable. They sense each other's presence, and, in a quiet way, they are turned out to each other. But, since neither of them recognizes in the present situation any kind of challenge except a mildly intellectual one, they*

*reveal to the audience no note-
worthy gathering of preparatory
forces. Now suddenly, however,
they change.*)

BENVOLIO. By my head, here come the Capulets.

(*Both men tense a little as they
view their hated rivals. They
show clearly by their eyes and
the posture of their heads the direction of their attention, the
form of their sight, and the force
exerted on them by that sight—
although the audience cannot yet
see the newcomers.* BENVOLIO
and MERCUTIO *prepare for a possible shock encounter by standing a little straighter and lifting
their chests out.* MERCUTIO *decides almost at once to pretend
to ignore the intruders. He deliberately starts to walk away.*)

MERCUTIO. By my heel, I care not.

(*Enter* TYBALT *with others.*)

TYBALT. Follow me close, for I will speak to them.

(TYBALT *keeps his voice down,
somewhat inward, when he
speaks to his men; then he
throws it out toward the two figures he wants to stop.*)

Gentlemen, good den: a word with one of you.

(MERCUTIO *stops instantly and
turns with an insolent air. Both
his body and his speech have ex-
pansion. He looks his braggart
enemy straight in the eye. He is
prepared to deal with him.*)

MERCUTIO. And but one word with one of us? Couple it with something; make it a word and a blow.

(TYBALT *gathers up his energy
for the reply. He stands straight
and filled out. The two men begin to lash at each other with
their voices.*)

TYBALT. You shall find me apt enough to that, sir, an you give me
occasion.

MERCUTIO. Could you not take some occasion without giving?

TYBALT. Mercutio, thou consort'st with Romeo,—

MERCUTIO. Consort!

(*Choosing to interpret* TYBALT's
*accusation in the worst possible
light, he reacts visibly as if
struck.*)

What, dost thou make us minstrels? An thou make minstrels of us, look to hear nothing but discords. Here's my
fiddlestick; here's that shall make you dance. 'Zounds,
consort!

(*On the reference to the "fiddlestick," he points to his sword and
takes a threatening step forward
—as if he is prepared to annihi-
late* TYBALT. BENVOLIO, *who has
been standing by nervously during this noisy interchange, tries
to check the activity of the other
two men by stepping between
them and speaking quietly.*)

BENVOLIO. We talk here in the public haunt of men:
Either withdraw unto some private place,
And reason coldly of your grievances,
Or else depart; here all eyes gaze on us.

(MERCUTIO *brushes* BENVOLIO's
arm aside.)

MERCUTIO. Men's eyes were made to look, and let them gaze;
I will not budge for no man's pleasure, I.

(*Enter* ROMEO.)

TYBALT. Well, peace be with you sir; here comes my man.

(MERCUTIO *and* BENVOLIO *turn to see their fellow Montague.*)

MERCUTIO. But I'll be hang'd, sir, if he wear your livery.

(MERCUTIO'S *tone is still insolent and taunting. He speaks as if he deliberately wished to provoke* TYBALT. MERCUTIO *is prepared to fight, but he has not yet touched his enemy.*)

Marry, go before to field, he'll be your follower;
Your worship in that sense may call him "man."

(TYBALT *turns from him disdainfully, and addresses* ROMEO, *who stands somewhat preoccupied—turned inward.*)

TYBALT. Romeo, the hate I bear thee can afford
No better term than this,—thou art a villain.

(*The last word spoken by the lips of a Capulet stings* ROMEO. *He turns out of his own inward thoughts with a snap, and looks steadily at* TYBALT. *For an instant his body tenses, and his two companions tense with him, expectantly. Then* ROMEO *smiles, and he relaxes the muscles of his back, his neck, and his shoulders. The eyes of the two* MONTAGUES *nearly pop from their sockets.*)

ROMEO. Tybalt, the reason that I have to love thee
Doth much excuse the appertaining rage
To such a greeting: villain am I none;
Therefore farewell; I see thou knowst me not.

(*He tries quietly to pass* TYBALT, *but the Capulet fiercely follows him.*)

TYBALT. Boy, this shall not excuse the injuries
That thou hast done me; therefore turn and draw.

*(ROMEO turns back to TYBALT.
He starts to tense his arms, raise
his head, and lift his chest as if
he has a strong impulse to strike
the other man. But he speaks in
a low, controlled voice.)*

ROMEO. I do protest, I never injured thee,
But love thee better than thou canst devise,
Till thou shalt know the reason of my love:
And so, good Capulet—which name I tender
As dearly as my own,—be satisfied.

*(He regains his good humor, re-
laxes, and utters the last words of
his speech almost quietly. The
outraged MERCUTIO leaps forward.)*

MERCUTIO. O calm, dishonorable, vile submission!
Alla staccato carries it away. (*Draws.*)
Tybalt, you rat-catcher, will you walk?

*(TYBALT turns to MERCUTIO with
a snarl.)*

TYBALT. What wouldst thou have with me?

MERCUTIO. Good king of cats, nothing but one of your nine lives;
that I mean to make bold withal, and as you shall use
me hereafter, drybeat the rest of the eight. Will you
pluck your sword out of its pilcher by the ears? Make
haste, lest mine be about your ears ere it be out.

TYBALT. I am for you. (*Draws.*)

*(After the considerable period of
preparation to fight, the two men
are ready now to put their impulses into action. Each means to
destroy the other. ROMEO tries to
check them.)*

ROMEO. Gentle Mercutio, put thy rapier up.

(But they brush him aside.)

MERCUTIO. Come, sir, your passado.

(They fight.)

ROMEO. Draw, Benvolio; beat down their weapons.

> (*Then he addresses the others again.*)

Gentlemen, for shame, forbear this outrage!

> (*He steps in and tries physically to restrain them. For a moment they succeed in pushing him away.*)

Tybalt, Mercutio, the prince expressly hath
Forbidden bandying in Verona streets.

> (*He seizes* MERCUTIO, *pinning down his arms.*)

Hold, Tybalt, Good Mercutio!

> (TYBALT *under* ROMEO's *arm stabs* MERCUTIO.)

MERCUTIO. I am hurt.

> (*For a moment he is more surprised than anything else. He contracts himself a little on the side of the wound to make certain sensorially that it is there. Maybe he twists his face around to see the blood. Then, still in* ROMEO's *arms, he cries out in sudden pain.*)

A plague o' both your houses! I am sped.

> (*The last three words are said more to himself than the others. He slips downward and shrinks into himself for a moment. Then he turns outward again, looking wildly about.*)

Is he gone, and hath nothing?

> (*The whole fight and its aftermath have taken place so swiftly that* BENVOLIO *has not yet quite grasped what has happened. Maybe he has taken an angry step after the fleeing* TYBALT.

But now he comes over solici-
tously to MERCUTIO.)

BENVOLIO. What, art thou hurt?

MERCUTIO. Ay, ay, a scratch, a scratch, marry, 'tis enough.
Where is my page? Go villain, fetch a surgeon.

(*The page boy runs out in search
of help, and* ROMEO *and* BEN-
VOLIO *tend* MERCUTIO *anxiously.
But he sinks rapidly. Affected
sympathetically by his pain, their
bodies slump visibly with his.* RO-
MEO *especially shrinks downward
and also inward when his beloved
friend accuses him of causing his
death. He is still in this mental
and physical attitude of depression when* BENVOLIO *lifts* MER-
CUTIO *out of view and* ROMEO *is
left alone to commune with himself.*)

ROMEO. This gentleman, this prince's near ally,
My very friend, hath got his mortal hurt
In my behalf; my reputation stain'd
With Tybalt's slander—Tybalt, that an hour
Hath been my kinsman! O sweet Juliet,

(*His voice loses its bitterness as
he speaks her name, and his body
opens out a little as if he wishes
to touch her image.*)

Thy beauty has made me effeminate

(*He stiffens a little.*)

And in my temper soften'd valour's steel!

(*Soon, when* TYBALT *returns,* RO-
MEO's *remorse turns to furious anger and he lunges into the skillful
but cowardly* CAPULET *so vigorously that he destroys him almost
with his first blow.*)

This selection from *Romeo and Juliet* shows distinctly how experienced players depict a dramatic situation—the changing thoughts and feelings of the characters they are personating and their relationships to the objects and people around them—by means of responsive movements supplemented by responsive words. Certain of the actions are accessory. But the effective core of every presentation is constructed out of the fundamental elements. All four of the basic movements described in preceding sections of this chapter were employed in the imaginary performance outlined above. Each of the four characters involved demonstrated his visible awareness of the other persons on the stage in terms of direction and form of attention. They were keenly appreciative not only of each other, but also of their swords. The force or intensity of their sensorial responses was in nearly every instance strong. Possibly only in one place was there a sensation which might be called mild; that was Romeo's when he made his first entrance. Then his thoughts were so preoccupied with Juliet that he saw the men he met in the street rather vaguely. His eyes were half closed. He opened them wide, however, as soon as Tybalt addressed him.

The two fundamental movements of the Preparatory Step were also in evidence. All raised their energies in visible pantomime to meet the challenge of opposing presences; and nearly everyone in the group took turns at approaching and withdrawing (or avoiding). Romeo and Mercutio had their periods of sinking. In the third fundamental step of Attack at least three men participated in efforts to destroy each other, and Romeo and Benvolio tried to "build up," nurture the stricken Mercutio.

In the performance of a play of heroic proportions, such as *Romeo and Juliet,* the fundamental action is bound to be broad, readily sensible to the audience. In most comedies of every type the basic movement must be obvious. The feelings of the personalities are revealed in the open; they show their sensuous awareness of each other, their fondness or dislike for each other, and their impulses to extend or to limit each other's activity, in clear-cut terms. The players presenting the little episode from *Mr. Roberts* reproduced in this book, for example, should reveal the lively feelings of the Captain and the Lieutenant without much restraint. Those interpreting the passage from *Suppressed Desires*, on the other hand, might employ just a little more reserve. They should manifest the fundamental impulses of their roles with greater emphasis on suggestion. Nevertheless, the kind of performance they give should still be fairly open, one which invites the audience to see every part of the skeletal framework without too much dependence on the imagination.

Subtlety must be employed in such seriously realistic scenes as the following from Paul Green's *The House of Connelly*. In playing this type of drama all the inner impulses should be intimated rather than stated frankly. Evelyn and Geraldine have completed their preparation for Christmas supper in the great, ghost-filled dining room of Connelly Hall, and viewing the gleaming table with tremulous anticipation, they decide to call the family.

EVELYN (*picking up the leather-headed gong stick*). Shall I ring now?

GERALDINE (*standing back and appraising the table*). Our Christmas supper is ready at last. Yes, ring. (EVELYN *turns to the sideboard and strikes the gong with slow measured strokes. The two women grow still in their tracks listening as the soft musical tones go echoing through the house.*)

> (*In order to convey the fact that they hear those echoes in distant hallways and faraway rooms, the two women will doubtless lift their heads a little and focus their eyes on points beyond the surrounding walls. At least EVELYN, the younger and more impetuous of the sisters, will do this. Perhaps GERALDINE will deliberately look out quietly in front of her; while EVELYN raises her face, and then turns it as if to follow the course of the musical tones. She listens a long moment before she speaks.*)

EVELYN. I never get tired of listening to it.

GERALDINE (*softly*). Yes, it's beautiful.

> (*Under the spell of the sound, the bodies of both women lose their tiredness. Perceptibly, they lift a little. EVELYN's body also opens outward slightly, as if she were hungry to sense the images of the past recalled by the music.*)

EVELYN. Something so lonely beautiful in it. (*Half musing.*) For a hundred years it has called people into this dining room. (*Softly also.*) A hundred years.

> (*The sharp pang of memory makes GERALDINE almost lose her self control. She tries to shake off the spell of the gong.*)

GERALDINE (*turning with quick nervousness towards the door at the left*). I was forgetting the coffee.

> (*She goes into the kitchen, and EVELYN moves over to the hearth and leans her head against the mantel. After a moment GERALDINE returns with the coffee pot, which she places on the table.*)

EVELYN (*staring at the fire*). Through all the rooms it goes calling. (*Echoing the gong with sentimental and heart-aching mournfulness.*) Nobody. Nobody.

> (*Here the actor playing EVELYN might deviate from the action suggested in the stage directions by raising her head just a little on the first line—as if with a forlorn hope she still expected possibly to hear an answer from a distant corner of the house—and then dropping her head on "Nobody! Nobody!"—to indicate the death of that hope. Her sister,*)

GERALDINE, *sensing the slump,*
attempts vocally to lift EVELYN.)

GERALDINE. Of course there's somebody.

EVELYN (*with sudden and tearful melancholy*). How warm this
fire is. It burned like this Christmas years ago. I was standing
here and Father came in from town. He brought me a new
fur coat—you remember that coat, Deenie?

(*The beautiful form and warmth*
of that coat are now so real to
EVELYN *that she lifts a hand to*
touch its lovely softness on her.
She has forgotten the shapes of
the present that surround her in
the room.)

GERALDINE. Let's think of tonight, not some other night.

(*In order to keep her own atten-*
tion from slipping into the past,
GERALDINE *shifts some object on*
the table.)

Now that's it.

EVELYN. Oh, there was so much fun then. We had so many friends.

GERALDINE (*with a touch of sharpness*). We have friends now,
Evelyn.

(EVELYN's *pictures of long ago*
fade a little under GERALDINE's
rebuke, and she sinks and closes
in once more.)

EVELYN. Yes, Mother, and Will, and Uncle Bob, and you and me.

(*Immediately she smiles again;*
her head and shoulders lift, and
her arms open out.)

There were so many more then. Father—Grandfather—

(*She sees each of them vividly—*
feels so powerfully the force of
their living warmth that she
trembles in their presence.)

Aunt Charlotte and Uncle Henry.

(*They are all different; but each*

*in his or her way is a glorious
person! Then suddenly,* EVELYN'S
*vision returns to the existing
scene. She begins to sag again,
gradually, until, in the last line,
her voice is small and shrunk-in,
as if she saw her own grave before her, and was trying in terror
to draw back from it.*)

Soon there'll be Uncle Bob and Will and you and me; then
you and me and Will; then—*

Here Geraldine once more puts a check to Evelyn's downward and inward movement by turning attention sharply to the
ivy leaves. Evelyn attempts to hang onto her memories; but presently she gives up, and, at the bidding of her older sister, she
leaves the ghost-filled room to summon her uncle to the meal.

Players performing a scene like this should express their
changing thoughts and feelings by exploiting exactly the same
kind of fundamental movements and voice-actions as those required for *Romeo and Juliet.* The only difference between them
with respect to form should lie in their magnitude and mobility.
While those in the Shakespearean performance are large and free,
those in *The House of Connelly* should be small and constrained.
They should reveal themselves to the eyes and the ears of the
spectator in the audience more by suggestion than anything else.
However, the limitation of scale for *The House of Connelly* does
not imply any mildness of passion. Evelyn and Geraldine feel just
as intensely about their problems as Romeo and his companions
do about theirs. All use visible and audible symbols to manifest
those feelings. The variation between the freely heroic and the
tightly realistic actions reveals itself only in the freedom or the
restraint with which the symbols are employed.

Surface and Under Imagery

The intellectual and emotional drives which stand behind dramatic oppositions are sometimes very simple, but more often they are complex. Among the most potent of the drives are those which develop out of man's primitive, biological urges and through his civilized, socially conditioned desire to conform. Since the primitive forces are constantly trying to assert themselves in dynamic action, and the civilized impulses are just as determinedly trying to hold the primitive forces in check, these two sides of the individual are ready at all times to breed lively dramatic conflicts.

The business of the actor is to create imagery. Some of the figures he makes are fairly concrete. Some can be intimated only, and these are often dramatically the most important. For this reason, the player has to distinguish carefully between one image and another. On the surface is one kind of image which the spectator can see and hear. This is the part of the general stage imagery which may be photographed and recorded. In this phase of the dramatic action, the characters reveal all the restraints imposed by natural obstacles such as costumes, furniture, walls, doors, chains, and bars, but particularly by the learned controls which spring from social breeding. Beneath the surface image is a second one which, though never revealed openly, is implied. This is the picturization of what the characters are actually feeling or desiring to do. In the under image all constraint is removed, and the characters behave broadly and completely. They sense deeply, without embarrassment, stride freely toward or away from the presences that confront them, leap or lie down, and fondle or destroy, in accordance with their inmost urges.

Since every man who wears a shirt, sleeps in a bed, and says "good morning" politely to his neighbors is, at the same time, both a savage and a civilized being, the two images of his dynamic personality take form together. The man is hungry. If he were simply a savage, and he saw meat on the table, he would grasp it in his hands, place it in his mouth and eat it straightway. His action would be direct, uninhibited. However, because he has been trained to regard the feelings of other people, he controls his violent impulses. Instead of grasping the meat and gulping it down, he sits quietly beside it, spreads a napkin on his knees, and proceeds to pick at his food with silver tools. While he eats, he talks to his companions at the table, graciously, unhurriedly. But his appetite is still primitive. No amount of white linen, gleaming cutlery, or conversation about the coming elections can alter that feeling. Therefore, a dramatization of the fact of hunger in a scene like this would have to give some hint of the inner urge. It could be presented in a number of different ways: the way the man approaches the table, perhaps, or the way he sets his lips, or the way he cuts the meat, or the way he tastes it, or the tone of his voice when he comments on it. Bare words alone would not tell the truth of his present satisfaction, for he might only be complimenting his hostess. Tone also would have to speak. Tone would give the conviction—tone which echoed, even though distantly, the sound of the wild man growling over his food.

Perhaps the man has cause to be angry at another man. If he were altogether a savage he would seize the nearest rock and beat out his enemy's brains with it. Since his social upbringing, however, has taught him that direct action in rage tends to defeat itself in the end, he will curb his primitive impulses. Instead of striking his foe, he may smile at him—a bit tight-lipped, probably, —and offer him a cigarette. He may even talk about the weather. Beneath that suave exterior, however, still crouches the tense-muscled form of the savage; and if the situation is to be visualized on the stage, the audience will have to see glimpses of that hidden form. Little involuntary movements—apparently impulsive but actually rehearsed, of course,—might be what will reveal him: a sharp intake of breath, an interrupted gesture, a quick flexing and slow unflexing of the fingers, a stiff posturing of the neck and shoulders.

Often the clearest indication of the wild man under the skin of the gentleman is an exaggerated display of control. If the person exercising restraint moves and speaks with an unusual calm, his behavior becomes immediately suspect. The spectator senses the strain of control; consequently he watches with considerable excitement to see if the savage will tear loose from his bonds.

Perhaps the man loves a woman. As a savage, his action would be swift and simple. He would take hold of her, carry her to his lair, and make her his. As a person of more civilized tastes, however, he tempers his biological hungers with thoughtfulness. He does this so that in the end he may enjoy more fully all sides of the woman's personality. So he courts her. He takes her riding. He dances with her. He plays tennis with her. He compliments her clothes, he reads to her, writes to her, takes her gifts. If the man really loves the woman, he may spend ten years trying to win her. But none of this devious behavior ever for a moment destroys the basic fact of sex. It is the most primitive urge of life which gives power and richness to all the rest. Without that, the whole relationship between the man and the woman would be a graceful but meaningless display of social customs.

From a study of such actions as those described, it will be seen immediately that under and surface imagery are closely allied with the fundamental and accessory action described in preceding sections. Under images tend to be formed largely of fundamental movements, and surface images, in great part of the accessory ones. This division is only approximate, however, for the under, hidden images often include some accessory movements while the surface, manifested images include all parts of the fundamental movement which can actually be observed. These outward manifestations of fundamental action are related to the inward phases of the same fundamental actions. But they are not exactly the same thing. The little actions which the spectator actually sees are the *clues* to the hidden images; they are not the images themselves. *The under images exist only through the eye of the spectator's mind. But to be able to picture those under images, the spectator must have the clues.*

In every dramatic scene the under images are apprehended most keenly in moments of stress. Then it is that the lines of the hidden forms project themselves with the greatest power. But effective playing does not limit the ground on which these images operate. Since the under images provide the elemental, emotional driving force for all the surface imagery, their existence can never pale entirely into oblivion without danger to the scene as a whole. At all times, even during the most intellectual, and therefore abstract, passages, there should be sensible vaguely, at least, the struggling of persons to search out other persons, to approach or to avoid them, to sink or to rise higher because of them, and to extend or curtail those other persons' actions.

Surface imagery is like a saucepan, and under imagery, the stew which boils inside it. That stew is in a state of turmoil, but the onlooker will never be able to sense its action unless the saucepan emits from beneath its cover occasional puffs of white steam and a sputter or two.

Imitation and Invention

Obviously, all of the material for stage imagery cannot be derived from the playwright's script. Neither can it be taken wholly from the actor's imagination. A very great deal of it will have to come from life study. The actor must observe long and patiently how people behave, not on the stage, but in the common world, and learn to imitate their methods. But when the player brings the fruits of his research to the stage he should be ready to adapt. He must choose and combine various elements; then he must point up their most important features, discard the irrelevant ones, relate them and proportion them, in order to secure from all the most eloquent action possible. From first to last he will remember that he has a function as an artist to exercise his imagination, to invent when necessary. But his invention will be held within reasonable bounds, for forms drawn only out of thin air are apt to be sterile. Somehow, directly or indirectly, every image built out of the mind of the artist has eventually to be connected with his own vital experience as a human being.

Conclusion

Usually, in the progress of an actual performance, a player will construct his images not deliberately but intuitively. For the student of acting who has had to read through nearly thirty pages of instructions on "outward and inward centers of attention," "three steps in response to a stimulus," "fundamental and accessory movement," and "under and surface imagery," this statement may sound like a grim jest. How, he will ask, can one keep in mind all the directions set forth in this chapter and at the same time be *intuitive?*

The answer has two parts. First, the "directions" set down here are not intended to be—can never be—fixed instructions. *They are meant to serve only as guideposts to exploratory experiments in the feeling out of action patterns.* Each piece of responsive action described is based on a readily observable behavior pattern in human life outside the theatre; it has just been simplified and exaggerated for use in the theatre. But implicit in the description is certainly no rule to be memorized.

Second, the actor will appreciate the fact that a few exercises in the conscious construction of active imagery—extended out into the full range of its *possible* dimensions—will help him to rediscover sensuously the free forms of expressiveness which were naturally his during childhood. As soon as the actor as an adult finds these forms and makes them once more a part of his intuitive apparatus, he can—and should—forget all the mechanical aids he used to achieve the rediscovery.

An analogy on this point might be drawn between the actor and the pianist. The pianist looks at a score and from it constructs a mental image of the sound of music. Now he puts his hands to a keyboard and translates that inward image into something that will impinge on, and please, another person's ear. If every time he sat down to the piano he had to recount the white and black keys, remind himself of the different tonal qualities associated with the upper, middle, and lower sections of the keyboard, and think about the psychological effects of major and minor keys, sharps and flats, accents and contrasting rhythms, he would quickly paralyze himself. At some stage in his training he will have had to investigate *consciously* the full potentialities —the expressive dimensions—of his instrument. Then and only then can he take them for granted and direct his principal attention to the overall musical impression he wishes to produce on the listener. He cannot arrive at this final good product if in the past he merely sat down at the piano, thought a little about what he would like to do, then just impulsively tinkled a few of the keys under his fingers.

The actor like the pianist then must devise a way to create richly and eloquently. He must feel out all the aspects of the image he wants to project, then work on the instrumentation of its projection. The following two chapters will deal with the second aspect of his art. Chapter V will return to the problem of image making.

III

★

THE ACTOR AS INSTRUMENTALIST – PANTOMIME*

The Purpose and Form of Stage Pantomime

PANTOMIME is the bodily movement of the actor. It is often called the "stage action" and sometimes the "stage business." A part of it is described in the play script, but much of it has to be invented by the actor and his director. The purpose of this pantomime is to create imagery; to suggest visibly the personality of a dramatic character, his inner thoughts and feelings, and his relationship to other characters, in such a way as to stimulate the imagination of the spectator.

The form of pantomime is large and free. Even for the most "naturalistic" of plays, plays that are supposed to be "just like" real life, the movement must have a boldness which is essentially theatrical. In the first place, the gestures of all the stage figures have to be made clear for the spectators, some of whom may be seated seventy or a hundred feet away. This action must be exaggerated for dramatic reasons. Even those stage personalities who are designed to resemble closely their counterparts in the everyday world have to be broadened somewhat so that they will

* This chapter and the following chapter are, of necessity, rather technical. The student using this book may find it to his advantage to do some reading in Chapter V and some practical work in exercises pertaining to that chapter before going deeply into Chapters III and IV.

49

be dynamically interesting. Their performance will demand a manner of walking which is more definite, more purposeful than that of the average person outside the theatre. The head will normally be held higher; and the swing of the arms will show, in contrast to elbows and wrists, more play of muscles in the shoulders. This is the behavior of the "life-like" figures. Those who are designed on more heroic lines, figures from the pages of the Greek classics and from Shakespeare's dramas, for instance, demand basic patterns of stage movement stretched even larger. Oedipus, Hamlet, and Falstaff cannot be adequately portrayed except by large action.

While stage pantomime is free, it is also precise. It is detailed. Every part of it is carefully planned so that nothing is crude, inexact, or confused. Every phase of it is filled out completely. The pantomimic elements are selected thoughtfully and they are so well ordered that every one of them points to the right thing at the right time.

Vitality is another fundamental attribute of this movement. Every aspect of the player's effort to make a stage personality breathe and walk is backed with energy. An actor with lazy muscles is no real actor, even though he may have the most beautiful voice in the world.

The Means

The means of pantomime is the actor's body. It is made up of four agents.

The Torso. The most important member of the pantomimic group is the central one. In the trunk, or torso, first, are the vital organs—the stomach, the heart, the lungs, the bowels, the various glands—which are intimately associated with emotion, and so with the impulses of the body to move. In the torso, second, are the primary muscles for action, those of the waist, back, neck, shoulders, and hips.

The most expressive movements of the human body are the four pertaining to the second step of Fundamental Action outlined in the preceding chapter. All of these in their broadest form involve the use of the torso. Closing in and opening out are forcefully indicated by a bending or unbending of the trunk, sinking and rising by a similar flexing, and approaching and avoiding by a forward or backward leaning or turning. In the primitive body, the child's, for instance, this movement of the torso may be seen clearly. In the civilized adult body, however, the central part is likely to be inhibited and the impulses representing positive and negative responses to objects are then made manifest in the action of the secondary agents—the legs, the arms, and the head. In the aged body the torso remains inexpressive, except in a passive way, because the joints of the backbone have become stiffened. One of the things which characterize the elderly person is his general inability to show effectively his fundamental impulses with the central part of his body. In moments of violent attraction and re-pulsion, however, the primary movements take place even in the aged body.

The characteristics of the forward, backward, bending, and turning urges of the torso are, of course, influenced not only by instinctive, but also by acquired, "states of mind"—grief, despair, humility, indecision, joy, wonder. If the primitive emotions are manifested through action, the acquired emotions are often mani-fested through posture. Posture expresses also simple physical states—strength, weakness, exhaustion.

The actor gives much attention to the pantomimic value of the back and waist. The human body is formed of two elements, (1) a bony supporting frame which is not rigid but is·hinged in numerous places; and (2) muscles which are hung on this frame and which move it by a complicated system of tugs and releases. The most interesting, and in many ways the most useful, unit of the body frame is the backbone. Made up of a series of smaller, cartilage-connected bones called vertebrae, and held erect by a group of powerful muscles, the backbone functions as a kind of mainspring for all the larger and more vitally expressive move-ments of the body. David Belasco used to remark that an actor acts with his backbone.

The most flexible, and therefore the most active, part of the spine is the lower part which lies between the ribs and the pelvic bones. The waist is the great, central, master-joint of a man's body. Those larger movements and postures of the torso expressive of primitive urges and emotional attitudes are controlled at this point. If one thinks of the actor's torso as being the most important member of this physical family of pantomimic agents, one should recognize his commonly much despised waist as the most important part of his torso. Within the region of an actor's body between the lower edge of the ribs and the pelvic basin are located all the numerous viscera (with the exception of the lungs and heart) and also the great diaphragmatic muscles which control breath and tone in speech.

The Legs. The legs are expressive chiefly as the carrying agents for the body. By bending or unbending, and by moving backward and forward in action patterns we call "steps," they extend and accentuate the manifestations, given by the torso, of a man's impulse to sink or rise, or to make or break contact with objects. Through the manner of their movement, they show also the state of mind which accompanies the impulse. The actions of the feet indicate more clearly, perhaps, than those of any other part of the body (with the possible exception of the face) a man's feeling of happiness, sorrow, indecision, embarrassment, determination, pride, or joy of living. The actions of the feet show unmistakably likewise the physical condition of the man. Think of the contrast between the manner of his walk when he goes to his shop or his office in the morning, and the manner when he returns in the evening.

The effective use of the legs in acting depends upon a close coordination between those members and other members of the body, especially the torso. The roots of the hip muscles which motivate the legs are implanted in the base of the trunk, and through them the legs draw, from the vital centers above, those rhythmic impulses which develop unified expressiveness. A kick swung from the knee is purely humorous; a full-membered movement initiated by a muscular tension in the waist is no laughing matter.

Independent, that is, unrelated, action always appears to be false, and for that reason awkward. One is often treated on the amateur stage to the sight of a pair of gay, young feet bouncing thoughtlessly back and forth in front of the scenery, without the slightest nuance of time or character, while the members above are doing their best to communicate a whole range of emotions, from shock and indecision to joy and determination. The effect is grotesque in the extreme. The legs are two of the most highly expressive instruments of the human body. It is to be regretted that they are so frequently used on the stage only for ornamental purposes.

The Arms. Like the torso, the arms are expressive of an individual's impulse to turn into or out of himself. When inhibitory influences are absent, the hands tend to reach in the direction of the point of attention—in toward the personality, or out toward the other object. The arms alone, or working with the head, and often the torso and the feet, are expressive of the force of sensation, and of the impulse to increase the sensation. They reach forth to touch, they react from touching.

The arms, in common with the torso and the legs, are expressive also of impulses to sink and to rise, and impulses to make or to break contact with other objects. When the torso slumps and the legs bend, the hands tend to fall at the side. When the torso unfolds, and the legs straighten in an upward push, the arms also tend to lift. When the torso leans forward toward a desirable object, and the legs carry forward, the arms also reach forward to touch, to grasp. When the torso leans or turns away from a repulsive object, and the legs carry away, the arms also drop away from contact, or they rise to ward off, or to push off the object which the body wishes to avoid.

The hands are two of the body's chief instruments of sense. Much of their expressive value lies in their tactility. The palms and the tips of the fingers are the sensitive points; they lead in gestures of contact. The hands may suggest a great deal directly by the way in which they respond to the touch of soft or hard, warm or cold, light or heavy objects; but they may suggest even more of human drama indirectly through their responses to emotive symbols. The manner in which a person fingers a silver coin or a piece of jade, or the manner in which a woman places her hand on the head of a man, may say more concerning character and situation than many pages of dialogue.

The arms are particularly eloquent with respect to the last of the fundamental movements, the furthering and checking of other action. The hands are man's primary agents for building up, raising up, healing, nurturing, and caressing. They are also first in tearing down, striking down, and destroying. Hands are creative, hands are tender, hands are cruel.

Finally, the hands share with the head the ability to communicate purely intellectual ideas. They signal, they point, they write, they mark out this and that. Citizens from different lands, knowing not a word of each other's language, are able nevertheless to exchange many thoughts through the gestures of their arms and head. Deaf mutes can carry on elaborate conversations with the hands alone.

The arms, especially the hands, become by training the most flexible of the human agents involved in making, altering the shape of, and otherwise controlling the things around an individual. They tend, therefore, to be most active in the accessory type of movement which complements the fundamental.

The manner with which the arms make or break contact with objects indicates the same general states of mind—happiness, sorrow, indecision, pride, sense of youth or age—as those manifested by the other members of the body. The way in which the arms are held and the way in which they are moved show clearly also the man's physical state; his strength or weakness, his calmness, restlessness, or exhaustion.

In common with the legs, the movements of the arms seem to gain in effectiveness, in depth of emotive significance, when they have some "body" placed behind them. A gesture from the elbow commonly looks weak, while one from the shoulder or from the waist seems strong.

The Head. The head is expressive in two aspects: (1) in its entirety, (2) in the face alone.

The backbone, with its attached muscles, extends, as we have already observed, all the way up the back and functions both as a pivotal support and as a mainspring for the actions of the torso. The spine does not terminate at the upper edge of the torso but continues up through the neck. The head is fastened to the top of the spine as a large knob. As such, the head is expressive chiefly through its relationship to the torso as a kind of second, emphatic joint to the main trunk below—like the point of a finger. In response to a general impulse to approach or to avoid an object the head tends to turn and reach toward or away from the object, in the same direction as the torso, but farther.

Physical and mental states are reflected clearly in the posture of the head; a bowed head does not mean much unless the torso is also bowed. The reverse is likewise true. When spirit comes into a man bent with the thought of his own worthlessness, breath enters his lungs, his waist muscles tighten, his chest expands, his backbone stiffens,—and then his head rises. His head does not rise first, unless it is to observe the source of promised inspiration, that is, to offer a channel through eyes and ears for the inflowing. When spirit comes, it affects the central sections of the body first. A realization of the importance of the posture of the head in indicating a man's estimation of himself should emphasize the value of an erect carriage for all dominating characters on the stage. A hero or heroine with slumped head and shoulders loses spirit. One cannot in this posture give the impression of being filled with the zest of life.

But the chief expressive values of the head lie in the face. The face is the focal and emphatic center of physical and mental expression. After observing the more general posture and action of the body as a whole, one looks to the face for a sharpening of the impression. The face is man's most important reception center. There are senses here for sight, hearing, smell, taste, and, to a certain extent, touch. The expressiveness of the face is largely concerned with indications of these sense activities.

The eyes and the mouth are the only two features capable of independent posturing, though the nose can move to some slight extent, in sniffing, for example. Hearing, and nearly all forms of smelling, must be indicated by a movement of the head as a whole. The eyes, however, are capable of considerable independent action which may involve the eyeballs or the eyebrows. The movement of the eyebrows is particularly effective in giving shape to facial expression. Eyes as perceptive agents are not used nearly enough by young actors. When a new and unexpected presence is introduced to the stage there is a tendency not to notice it at all or, as in the case of a sudden entrance of a new character, to swing the whole body around at the first impulse instead of letting the eyes go first.

A similar remark could be made regarding the use of the ears (indicated by a posturing of the head). The actor learns that re-action comes *after* perceiving—even if not more than an infinitesimal fraction of a second later. Reaction never *before* perception!

The Body as a Whole. The four pantomimic agents, the torso, the legs, the arms, and the head, employed by the actor to communicate his message to the spectator have been considered separately in these pages, not in order to emphasize any independently expressive qualities in each, but to show how much each member has to contribute to the expressive whole. The larger organism of the body, made up of all the physical members, plus the voice, should sit, should talk, play, work, seem happy, discouraged, weary or strong, sense the presence of objects, be attracted or repulsed, as a single instrument. The movements of the torso, the legs, the arms, the head, and the features of the face should be synchronized absolutely, and the sum-action of the pantomimic body fitted carefully to the time and tone of the voice, for the purpose of producing *one* dramatic effect.

The Control

In order to use well his pantomimic means the actor must develop control. Like the athlete and concert dancer, he must train himself through exercise to be strong, flexible, and prepared, capable of performing every kind of movement, large or small, and ready to do it instantly on command. And he must train himself also to make all movements neatly, without any apparent waste of energy. As we have already observed, efficiency is one of the primary marks of good pantomime. The moment by moment supply of that effort which an audience is willing to expend in its attention to a performer's action is limited. When the action observed is awkward, when it fails to accomplish its objective without fumbling, the attention of the spectator is distracted. Through the sensations derived from "feeling-into" (discussed in Chapter I), every observer has a tendency to suffer the same kind of bodily discomfort as that experienced on the stage by the ineffective actor himself. Fine movement, on the other hand, tends to lift, to exhilarate both the player and the spectator. Herbert Spencer describes grace as "motion that is effected with economy of force." That definition suggests succinctly the purpose of control.

The price of a set of strong, live, *dependable* muscles is exercise. Sports provide admirable training, but they are not enough. Swimming, baseball, and tennis should be supplemented by setting-up exercises specially designed to strengthen and quicken those particular parts in the player's body which have a tendency to become flabby: the shoulders, perhaps, or the neck, or the hips. The kind of physical drill which modern dancers employ to build up their bodies is excellent for this purpose. Some of these exercises in modified form are included at the end of this volume. Above all things, the actor should plan to do plenty of walking. This is very important if the routine of his daily living requires him to spend much of his time in a seated posture. A brisk walk, with the head erect and the arms swinging naturally, keeps the vital waist muscles toned up and tends to awaken all the other parts of the body as well.

The development of pantomimic control is fostered by daily practice under the direction of concentrated thought. A vague, half-hearted running-through of two or three of the exercises— with the mind way off somewhere else—will accomplish little. At each practice period, consideration should be given first to good posture, then to muscular preparedness, and then to quick response to mental command. At every step, the results aimed at in the exercises should be related to actual dramatic problems so that the practice work may never be pursued for itself alone.

Among the several aspects of control which each actor strives through his practice to achieve are these: (a) relaxation, (b) flexibility, and (c) continuity. Preparation for any performance begins with relaxation. An actor who is physically tense is never effective in his movement. He cannot play at all if he walks out before the spectator with his muscles frozen. It is the aim of the actor, therefore, to foster through progressive physical and mental exercises a fine sense of ease throughout all his members in order that he may be able to approach each new problem of bodily expression with a completely free instrument.

But relaxation, though it means lack of undue tension, does not mean collapse. The relaxed actor is not a weak actor. He has a feeling of ease, it is true; yet, at the same time he is thoroughly alive, every fibre of him tingling with eagerness for action. His muscular organization is strong, alert, eminently ready like that of a wild animal for the call of new movement at an instant's notice. This state of preparedness is the basis of flexibility. The actor who is relaxed, and at the same time alert and strong, is able when stirred to point his energies in any direction. But flexibility means more than choice of action. It means also control of the force which shall be applied to that action and the time and space that shall be consumed by it. In working for flexibility, therefore, the player will strive to build on the foundation of relaxation a vibrant readiness for every kind of movement—large or small, general or detailed, violent or quiet, quick or slow. And he will prepare himself to change neatly from one form to another.

The development of a sense of continuity gives assurance that every part of the pantomimic action will flow forward, grow, and come to a point without jerks and stutterings and without confusing gaps in the motion. All units of more emphatic action are then connected by transitional movements or postures which keep the feeling of life—sensation, thought, emotion—going on. Each phase of the pantomime is worked out to a logical end in keeping with the character and situation. The movement "follows through." When every new action group is started it begins with authority, it finishes its initial course, or else it modulates definitely through transition into another action. There is no petering out. In this respect, good pantomime is like music. It grows, it ebbs, it pauses, it changes constantly its time, pitch, and intensity; but, from the moment the first note is struck right through to the finish, it carries forward without interruption.

Therefore, the actor will include in his training plenty of work in continuity to supplement his efforts in relaxation and flexibility. Some practical suggestions are contained in the exercises at the end of this book.

Normal Posture and Movement

There are two types of posture and movement with which the actor must make himself familiar. They operate in both the fundamental and the accessory action discussed in Chapter II.

Normal posture and movement—unparticularized conduct
Characterized posture and movement—particularized conduct, suggestive of some distinct personality

Characterization is a principal goal of the player's effort, for
only through intelligent characterization can the dramatic personality be made to behave as a distinct individual. The training
of an actor for characterized conduct begins, however, with his
training for normal conduct. Normal conduct is the standard. Departures from it must be made with care. In the playing of a
"character" role, even a decidedly eccentric one, the performer
who adapts his pantomime thoughtfully out of the materials of
normal posture and movement is bound to get nearer to reality
than the man who attempts to fashion his actions out of hetero-
geneous bits unrelated to normal patterns. Characters not based
upon normal patterns invariably lack subtlety and proportion.
Amateurs characterizing old men and old women often round
their backs into crippled arches, vibrate their knees and arms, and
duck their bodies up and down when they converse (always in
strange nasal squeaks). They are horrible examples of inhuman
characterization.

The performer with his body tuned for normal action is the
prepared performer. He has put his muscular equipment in shape
and is ready for an expressive effort in any direction. A normal
posture is an alive posture, one which gives the maximum impression of strength and alertness. Normal movement is easy, youthful
movement. It is springy, rhythmical movement with all the muscular contractions shaped and timed to conform most efficiently
with the laws of physics. Within each of us lies, at least in a potential state, a high sense of physical design in action. The player
cultivates this sense until it operates for him naturally and habitu-
ally—without his having to think about it.

Standing. Good posture depends on good alignment, the correct vertical superposition of the masses of the body in space. This
begins with the arches of the feet and builds upwards through the
ankles, the calves, the thighs, the hips and pelvis, the back and
upper torso, the shoulders, the neck and head. The actor who
wishes to assume good posture places his feet fairly close together
and keeps his body poised—directly over neither the toes nor the

heel, but the arch of each foot. When the head faces to the front, the ear, the shoulder, the hip-bone, and the arch of the foot on each side should be on a line.

In order to make the contours of the body as straight as possible, special attention must be given to three parts: the back of the neck, the spine, and the abdomen. The back should be straight, curved neither forward nor backward, but held in a position in which the separate vertebrae, which together form the "backbone," are fairly well aligned. The hollow which has a tendency to form in the small-of-the-back should be pushed out by tightening the stomach muscles and tucking the tip of the spine under, "out of sight." The old-fashioned military pose in which the chest was thrust violently forward and the buttocks away out behind was as wrong from both an esthetic and physiological point of view as the slouch it attempted to correct. The buttocks should be made as inconspicuous as possible. This can be done very easily by rolling the thighs (not the feet) out slightly; that is, by pivoting them away from center without destroying the straight line of the leg.

The body should be erect. In order to find out what parts of the body need retirement, the actor can place together two chairs with vertical, unslanted backs, and try to squeeze between them sideways. Next, he can stand with his back against a wall, heels up tight, and try to level out his back in such a way as to bring as many points of his anatomy as possible—calves, thighs, the full length of the backbone (including the center), the shoulders, and the head—all into contact with the wall. Now he pulls his feet out just far enough from the wall, perhaps half an inch, to bring the weight of the body over the spring of the foot, and notes carefully the distance from the heels to the wall. He uses this as a test position. Whenever the actor is in doubt as to whether or not he is standing correctly, he can put his heels at the correct distance from the wall and see how the back feels. It is impossible to assume the right pose in this position without tucking in well the lower tip of the spine.

The body should have good contour as it is viewed, not only from the side, but also from the front or rear. In moments when the actor is at ease, he may rest the weight of his body a little more on one foot than the other; but there should be no impression of weakness. The muscles of the supporting side must remain firm. A slouched hip is more destructive of poise than a slouched shoulder.

Except when one is playing a part specifically calling for a bent frame, one should carry the head and body erect. Let the actor remember what Belasco pointed out regarding the importance of the backbone. Even with the rest of the body relaxed, the backbone should have a strong upright position, as though a steel spring had been run through the length of it. The upper body hung on such a backbone may be bent freely, forward, to the right, or to the left; but it prefers in repose to be straight up and down. Above all things, the actor must learn to keep his feet under him. One sees all too frequently on the nonprofessional stage the strange spectacle of a person with his feet nailed to the floor in one direction, while his head and shoulders are twisted around in another.

There should be a sense of strength, but not strain, in a good standing posture. The shoulders should hang naturally. In order to eliminate flabbiness and to establish and maintain a fine, strong line in the body, the actor must exercise four sets of muscles constantly: those of the abdomen, the buttocks, the back of the shoulders, and the neck. When the stomach and gluteal muscles are tensed and the neck is held well back, the rest of the body is likely to take pretty good care of itself. Simply raising the chest a little will do a great deal to establish good posture.

Walking. When one is walking, the weight of the body should be borne by the arch of the foot. The actor is instructed not to throw the weight on the heel or the toe, but on the spring of the foot. The heel on each step will strike the ground a little before any other part of the foot, but the burden should not rest there. The actor keeps his heels together, toes spread a little, but not too much. Arthur Murray, the well-known teacher of ballroom dancing, remarks: "Nothing makes a woman so ungainly as to spread her heels." The remark applies as well to men.

Swing the leg from the hip, not below. Raise the knee freely and keep it moving in the direction of the foot on each step. A good-looking leg has a straight inner line. The knee should be relaxed but firm. A surprising number of people suffer from weak knees—the result no doubt of sedentary habits. They have a tendency to stiffen their thighs and to walk by flipping out their lower legs loose-jointedly from the knee. This member of the leg generally keeps its correct position when the abductor and adductor muscles at the front and rear, just above the knee joint, maintain a normal tension. These muscles need constant exercise for good behavior.

The legs should move rhythmically, without jerkiness. Lift the thigh strongly (letting the rest of the leg follow); place the foot on the ground with purpose, but quietly; draw the body forward, shifting the weight smoothly, without throwing it; lift the other leg, and continue. Give attention also to the upper joints of the body. Keep the body moving straight forward, not letting it shift from side to side nor bounce up and down as though it were being carried over a corduroy road. Have the head erect, eyes up, shoulders and lower torso fairly still, and the backbone, strong but springy, in direct control. It is often helpful to imagine oneself a puppet suspended by a stout cord from a smoothly rolling truck overhead. The weight of the body is borne by the truck and the legs move simply to push the body forward.

Posturing of the Arms and Hands. Two of the most typical signs of self-consciousness are elbows glued to the sides of the body and restless hands. Unless movement is specified, the arms should hang straight down, easily and naturally. When the actor walks, the arms may swing a little, but when he stands they should remain quietly in repose. The elbows should be free, suggesting that when the call for action comes again the arm will be ready to move all the way up to the shoulder; the hands should be relaxed and still. There must be no unnecessary fumbling for pockets. The actor who tries to counteract a sense of awkwardness by hiding his hands succeeds only in calling attention to them.

Turning. The actor learns to turn freely and naturally, taking a few steps in a semicircle if necessary to avoid awkward, cramped angles. He is careful not to spread or tangle his feet.

The secret of good turning lies in being prepared. If an actor makes himself ready to shift the weight of the body quickly and easily from one foot to the other, he cannot very well be caught off guard (the cause of awkwardness). The actor makes himself ready for all demands for movement by training himself never to slump on the weight-bearing side. He keeps the two sides of the body strong even in rest.

One must remember to make the feet follow the direction of the body. Never let them be left behind in a turn. At the same time, in trying to acquire efficiency take care not to fall into military habits of strong "faces" to the right and left.

Sitting. One should sit relaxed but upright. Do not slump, unless the part calls for slumping. Remember that a strong backbone, springy, not stiff, makes for smartness on the stage. Do not sprawl the feet. Keep your knees (especially if you are a woman) close together. If you throw one knee over the other, you must avoid a "proppy" look—that is, one with considerable open space between the higher and the lower knee—as though the legs were too stiff to lie comfortably beside each other. (What *looks* comfortable is what counts, not what *is.*)

Pay attention to the arms. If you are sitting near a table you may place an arm comfortably on it. But do not slump. If you rest your arm on the arm of a large easy chair or the back of a sofa, let it *rest*—do not hang your body from it.

To get into a seated position, the actor should bring at least one leg right up against the chair or sofa, and let himself down straight and smoothly—that is, without poking out or waving his buttocks, and without seeming to fall into place. Above all things, he should avoid doing what many young players do, starting to sit down before arriving at the spot for sitting. Each action should be in its place. When he rises, he should bring his feet in under him in order to establish a good balance, then rise straight up smoothly, easily. In normal movement he should never throw himself onto his feet.

Going Up and Down Stairs. Ascending and descending stairs should look like graceful, easy walking. It should be smooth and rhythmical—never seem to be hard work. What must be avoided is unnecessary jerkiness, the jumps going up and the drops coming down. The secret of a good staircase technique lies in continuity of muscular tension. When a trained person goes up, instead of thrusting himself forward from one step to the next, he rises quietly, making all the muscles of his feet, legs, and torso contribute in the movement. When he descends he does not allow himself to fall from one step to the next. He uses some intermediate tension so that, instead of dropping, he seems to be letting himself down.

Falling. If the player falls stiffly he will likely hurt himself. Instead of throwing his body straight onto the floor he should crumple, starting the collapse in his ankles, and then breaking his fall with, in turn, a knee, a hip, a hand, an arm, and perhaps a shoulder. If he performs the action quickly and neatly, the devices for the fall may be concealed.

Lifting. To lift an inert body lying on the floor, the player should kneel close to the body (upstage of it, if possible). He should grasp the near elbow of the body with his own far hand, and pull up sharply, slipping his other arm under the shoulders. Then he should free his first hand. Now he should get his knee, on the same side as the hand first used, well under the knees of the body and using his free arm lift the body toward himself and up, letting the strain bear more on his legs than his back.

If the person to be transported is a man, and fairly heavy, the actor may have to employ the "fireman's carry." He turns the man on his face and, facing toward the head, steps astride his body; he then places his hands under the armpits and raises the body to its knees. He next clasps it around the waist and raises it to its feet. While he supports the body erect (with a little undercover help from the "unconscious" man), the actor passes around to where he can face it. He grasps the right wrist of the body with his own left hand and pulls upward; then stoops quickly and passes his right arm between the legs of the body, at the same time drawing the body across behind onto his left shoulder. Finally, he passes the body's right wrist to his own right hand, and, if he so desires, reaches back with his left hand to grasp and pull forward the body's left wrist in order to steady the burden.

Embracing. Embraces always need to be carefully rehearsed. The bodies of the two persons involved should be close to each other; attempted in any other posture, the embrace is always awkward. The position of the feet should be plotted in advance so that each player will know just whose foot goes outside and whose foot between. The actual embrace is then worked out in such a way as to make it seem easy and natural, and also so that the two faces will stay in view of the audience (if that is desired). In some situations the girl—especially if she is considerably shorter than the man—lets her downstage arm slip under his. Sometimes she puts it above his and allows her hand to slide upward to encircle his neck. Occasionally she lets the arm remain folded inside the embrace, with her hand resting on his chest or holding his coat lapel.

If the kiss that accompanies the embrace is supposed to represent more than a sisterly peck or a train-side farewell, it should be unhurried. It should be preceded by a moment of anticipation—the eyes looking, the hands touching the other person—and it should be concluded with a memory of the kiss—the hands still touching the other body, before the embrace is broken.

Entrances and Exits. Entrances and exits to and from the stage must be made by the player in character with his part and the dramatic situation, neatly, on time, and in such a way as not to delay the action of the scene. Doors on exits may be handled in this way: If the player is making an exit through a door on stage left, he grasps the knob with his left hand instead of his right, in order to avoid an awkward and unnecessary turn. Then he pulls the door open, passes, and draws the door shut with his right hand. When he enters through this door, he opens it with his right hand, passes in, and closes it with his left. An exit or entrance on the other side of the stage would be executed, of course, in reverse.

Gesturing. The actor's gestures should be clean-cut, free, natural, and spontaneous. Gestures with a bit of curve to them are commonly more effective than straight ones. Usually to be avoided in any form of movement on the stage are sharp, sudden angles, which are rarely expressive.

Tradition says: "Do not use gestures which cross your body." The wisdom of the following rule depends, of course, on circumstances. There are moments on the stage when it is necessary to reach across the body. The principle involved is simply that the body should be kept expressive in as big a way as possible, and it fails to be so when parts of it are hidden unnecessarily behind limbs. Gestures in front of one's face, for instance, tend to cover up the features and are for that reason distracting. It is very simple to avoid cross gestures. Imagine yourself seated in a chair between a friend standing on your right and a table, on which is a letter, on your left. You wish to pass the letter to the friend. You could twist clear around in your seat to seize the letter with the right hand; but it would be much more reasonable to lift it with the left hand, pass it to the right and present it with this hand. The easiest way is usually the right way.

Characterized Posture and Movement

Characterized posture and movement, as already defined, are particularized conduct, conduct suggestive of some distinct personality. Basically, it is related to normal conduct. Characterized posture and movement do not spring from some different, remote pattern of living; they are simply normal ways of doing things, changed by force of circumstances. The limp of a lame man is the behavior of a person who once walked like everyone else, but has suffered an injury and now cannot use one leg as efficiently as he did. The stagger of a drunken man is the behavior of a usually able person whose natural powers of perception, and whose regular sense of balance are temporarily affected. In every case, the normal patterns serve as the starting point for the comparison.

The problems of characterized movement are complex. Since they involve highly individualistic traits of temperament, they cannot be dealt with very successfully in the general terms of a book. One man's lameness, or drunkenness, or physical mannerisms will be quite different from another's. However, a few broad observations about those typical changes of conduct which are caused by age may prove helpful.

If we disregard the effects of possible illness, we may say that the man or woman of forty is just about as strong physically as the youth of twenty. Frequently he is stronger. But one thing he has lost; that is agility. The middle-aged person no longer bounces. More "settled," with a heavier body, he usually moves more slowly. His feet stay firmly on the ground; there is not much twisting and turning. The tempo of his movements is steady—he seems to be much less affected by conflicting impulses than when he was younger. One reason is that his senses are somewhat duller. So he is much less apt to be driven this way and that by cross currents of sensation.

But there is another reason for the steady tempo of the middle-aged man. Years of experience have given him the power to select certain of the many stimuli in his environment to which it is best for him to respond. The period of experiment is past. So he walks (and talks) with directness, with assurance. He makes fewer gestures, but he makes each count. Much less ready than the youth to adapt himself to sudden emergencies, he is nevertheless able to plod along the established ways of daily life with far less waste of energy.

Very young actors tend to have more difficulty playing middle-aged parts than elderly types. This is probably because there are few real eccentricities to exploit. In general, the factors to be remembered are those which can be associated with (a) heaviness, (b) economy, and (c) assurance. The middle-aged person stands typically with his legs slightly separated and his weight distributed more or less evenly on both of them. He moves deliberately and with a kind of certainty, making each step and each operation of the hand accomplish something definite. When he turns, he does not twist much at the waist; he prefers to shift his whole body around. His neck is comparatively inactive. The middle-aged person is quite capable of turning his head, but he tends to do this much less than the younger individual; and when he does shift it, he usually does it more slowly. Entirely absent from his behavior are the many twists and jerks of the neck typical of youth. Girls attempting to play matrons need especially to watch this part of their pantomimic anatomy.

A man of eighty may still be fairly vigorous; but he is much more apt to show the effects of disease and a general breakdown in the whole physical body. Age brings a certain collapse in all the parts. An old man may show this collapse in a stoop of the shoulders or of the back, but he need not be bent (in spite of the hoary traditions of the amateur stage). Some very aged men stand quite erect. But in every one of them there is to be noticed a perceptible sag, a sinking down into oneself. A person at eighty, standing as straight as he can, is usually an inch or more shorter than when he was forty. The sag is shown in the slope of the shoulders, the droop of the abdomen, and often also in other parts of the body as well.

If the middle-aged person has less bounce than the youth of twenty, the aged individual has no bounce at all. He tends to walk in a very flat-footed manner. He brings heel and toe down together, and lifts his foot again without much spring from the toe. Since his sense of balance is usually impaired, he stands and walks with his feet well separated—like the child first learning to toddle. Unable to trust himself on one foot any longer than neces- sary when he steps, he lifts and then drops each member quickly, so that during most of the course of his progress both of his feet are touching the floor at the same time.

One of the characteristics of an old body is stiffness. The muscles are inflexible, and the joints are apt to be swollen by arthritis. Consequently, the aged person husbands his move- ments, and when he does execute them they appear tight and angular. Another characteristic is the lack of cushioning tissue, especially between the bone ends. An old man or woman con- stantly complains of how his "old bones rattle together." Because of the pain caused by jolting of any kind, the octogenarian usually sits down and gets up in a gingerly way. Kind attendants place sofa cushions behind his back, and everyone takes care not to push him needlessly.

It is true that some aged persons are very spry. They dart around from place to place in a nervous, angular sort of way. More typical, however, is the very slow movement. Because the person is without much strength, because his body is stiff and his bones rattle, and because his sense of balance is rather untrust- worthy, he tends to move carefully. Often he employs a cane to steady himself. Perhaps the best way for the young actor to arrive at the feeling of an aged action is to remember how he behaved when he was very tired—how he dragged on his feet, and put his hand out to the table or the back of a chair to support himself as he passed.

Very frequently, the general breakdown in an old man's body is not equal in every part. Some member has given way more than another. Consequently his sag on one side is slightly greater than on the other; or one knee or elbow is stiffer; or the person, because of neuritis, is able to turn his head in one direction but not in another. Deafness in one ear also may affect his posture. Such differences give the actor an almost limitless number of opportunities to vary his characterizations of old people.

Movement with Other Bodies

The steps in the preparation of dramatic pantomime commonly run somewhat like this:

(1) The actor works out his general behavior, giving thought to awareness, response, and the general requirements of stage imagery.

(2) He sharpens up the points of characterization which he has selected to particularize in the figure he is portraying.

(3) He puts his movements into good spatial relationship with those of the other actors.

Because it is difficult for a player at the same time to concentrate effectively on his own part and to view the stage as a whole, the modern theatre has developed a supervisory artist called the "director." It is his function to work out a master plan of performance and to guide the actors in such a way that each will fill out logically his particular segment of it. However, no good director wishes to be an autocrat. He prefers to draft, in only the broadest kind of lines, a tentative design, and then to depend on the players to collaborate with him in the perfecting of it. Instead of resenting initiative he usually welcomes it; the director does not like to have to deal with puppets. Below are listed a few general principles of design which commonly serve as a point of departure for both director and actor. They cover certain spatial relationships between the figures on the stage, and all players are expected to know them.

Space around a stage personality tends to individualize him; the removal of space unites him with another person or object. Even characters who are supposed to be dramatically distinctive have to make many movements toward or near others; the working out of natural responsive contacts demands this. But they

should avoid all unnecessary hugging of furniture and long,
jamb-up positions besides other people. Inexperienced actors have
an unfortunate inclination to walk into a huddle, like frightened
sheep, and then to stay there. Attention should be given to keeping the group loosened up. The players, with the help of the director, must look for opportunities to introduce out-movements
from time to time. Sometimes the crosses are provided for by the
script, and sometimes they must be inserted independently. Every
cross, however, whatever its purpose, must be properly motivated.
If the reason for the movement is not stated specifically in the
script, a reason must be invented so that it, in common with all
the other action of the stage, may seem thoroughly logical.

Clear lines of sight are important. The characters on the stage
should keep each other's faces in easy view, and the audience
should be able at all times to see everything that is going on. This
means that although every part of the acting area is used by the
performers, comparatively there will be more action moving back
and forth across the stage, where it can be spread out for the
audience to see, than up and down stage, where one actor is likely
to stand in front of another actor. In ordinary duologue conversation, when the faces of the two figures involved are about equally
important, the actors normally stand "on a line with each other"
(equidistant from the footlights), commonly faced halfway toward each other and halfway toward the audience. In moments of
tension they will probably turn and face each other directly—in
order to bring to bear on each other the full force of their personalities.

For the sake of variety, or in order to throw one face a little
more into the view of the audience, the actors may move onto a
diagonal. But they must be careful not to let themselves get into
such an upstage-downstage relationship as to hide their mutual
reactions from the view of the audience. Although it is a sound
general rule to keep all active faces pretty much in sight of the
audience, no player should be afraid to turn his face occasionally
upstage. Sometimes a very eloquent effect can be secured when a
figure twists his face away from a companion (to hide his pain,
for instance) and shows only his back to the spectator.

The reverse behavior, however, is usually to be avoided. A

full-face to the audience is seldom convincing. A player showing this aspect seems to be speaking directly to the spectator, and to have broken all dramatic connection with the other figures in the stage scene. Even when a character is delivering oratory, or is indulging in reverie, he should refrain from looking the spectator straight in the eye. If he angles his face only a few inches to the right or left, and up in the air slightly, or down, he will place himself back in the picture plane with his fellow character.

Contrary to what some books say, there are no set rules for "crosses" (moving from one place on the stage to another). Modern practice is usually to take the nearest path to one's objective; but, when two alternate paths are about equal, one takes the path in front of other people. This is just another application of the general principle that as much of the stage action as possible should be open to the view of the audience. During the progress of the cross, all important contacts between persons should remain unbroken. If one character must pass behind a second character in order to reach another spot efficiently, and the second character is supposed to watch him cross or speak to him as he crosses, the second man (the one behind whom the first crosses) should pivot around so that he may keep his face in continuous contact with the other, even though this means that he must momentarily turn his back on the audience. Quite objectionable is the practice common on amateur stages of having actors look stiffly over their shoulders in order to search out other figures behind them.

If a person is to be crossed in front of, instead of behind, and he finds himself in the line of walk of the moving person, he may have to give way a little and then return to his normal position after the cross. If this action is done quietly, it will not be noticed by the audience.

The working "center" of the stage is the area around the midpoint on the line across the opening just behind the proscenium, or as near to this spot as efficient overhead lighting will permit actors to stand. This area possesses a magnetic attraction for the action of the play; all movements tend to converge toward it or to radiate from it. The normal position for two or three standing persons, not otherwise attached, is in or around stage center.

When two characters are standing near center and a third

character, entering from down-right or down-left, must cross to speak to the farther person, the three characters commonly do this: The entering character walks over to the farther character and stands near him but slightly upstage of him. The third person, the person in front of whom the newcomer crossed, "gives back" to make room and, taking a couple of easy steps around in an arc, comes to a position a little to the side of his former position. The newcomer is now at the apex of a small triangle, an arrangement which puts him into easy contact with the figures right and left of him.

The influence of the magnetic center is felt particularly by standing or walking players. When they are seated they must, of course, be located wherever furniture is. At the same time, the attractive force of the middle point of the picture can never be completely neutralized. Too much or too obvious use of stage center tends, however, to grow tedious. The wise plan is to keep the dramatic center of interest in the picture moving around a little.

One very important factor of spatial design is what is called "dressing the stage." This means distributing the various characters around the acting area so that they will make a pleasing, well-balanced composition. Although the chief responsibility for this arrangement must rest with the director, the actor should use his own common sense to help work out the picture. If he finds, for instance, that one side of the stage is getting crowded while the other side is bare, and he can discover a good dramatic reason to move over into that unoccupied section, he should do it—without waiting for the director to give him the order. When he enters from the rear he may have to hold an upstage position for the delivery of certain important lines. If, however, that position is not necessary for him, and if he notices that a number of people are already standing or sitting around center while a spot down-right or down-left is unfilled, he can move quietly toward it. The director depends on his players' feeling of design to work out most of the obvious points. This leaves him free to watch the less obvious details.

Compulsive Movement

The examination of stage pantomime in this and the preceding chapters has led so far, roughly, through expressive and then tactical movements. What remains to be investigated is compulsive movement. Compulsive movement has already been defined as persuasive movement, movement possessing certain qualities which compel the spectator to participate in it. It is movement which is logical and which fits admirably the dramatic situation for which it is designed. But it is more than that: it is movement which is *sensuously appealing*. It induces the spectator to "feel into" it, and to move along with it.

A primary factor in compulsive movement is efficiency. This is another way of saying that compulsive action is graceful. It is performed—at least apparently—with a minimum of effort appropriate to the situation. No movement is wasted in unnecessary fumbling: an actor walks straight to his goal, he turns the nearest way, he sits down lightly, he lifts an object with one neat gesture. Every action looks easy. It is efficient. It is "graceful." Often the actor has to work strenuously in order to get the *appearance* of effortlessness. But whatever the cost of it is, he strives for it because he knows its value. He is aware that for the spectator one of the chief charms of the theatre lies in the fact that it provides an escape from the aches and the sweaty odors of daily toil. Consequently, if the stage action which the spectator comes to the theatre to see is expertly done, he feels into it hungrily, joyously; thus he is caught up in it. Through sensuous participation, he becomes a part of important movement unhindered by human frailty. He strides across vast areas of experience on winged feet.

A second factor in compulsive movement is rhythm. When it is present, pantomime has a smoothness of flow, an ease of transition, and a power of growth. It develops, changes, and goes on without stuttering. Rhythmical movement is movement affected freely by pulse beats. The beats are not set in as rigid patterns as those typical of musical forms; nevertheless, they throb continuously deep within the action, and their influence is manifested clearly in the way the player walks, sits down, rises, moves a chair to the table, and passes an object to another person. Rhythmical movement is marked by periodic alternations between greater and lesser activity (frequently punctuated by rests), and by periodic stress and ebb. Everything the player does, whether the action be quiet or violent, is done as if to music heard by the ears of his mind. The spectator, watching the outward action of the player and sensing through it the hidden pulse beats, hears by imagination the same inner music and is caught up in the spell of it.*

The third great factor of compulsive movement is variety. The able actor never lets the visual (and auditive) elements of his performance become monotonous. Since he knows that any long repetition of the same pattern of action, or the same tempo, or the same stress, or the same intensity of force, will put the audience to sleep, he strives vigorously for change. He tries to stir the senses of the spectator from as many different angles consistent with the material with which he is dealing as possible. A wise use of contrasts serves a double purpose: it helps to develop the dramatic factors in a situation by directing the attention of the observer to different sides of it and it helps to keep the observer sensuously alert and interested.

* The whole problem of rhythmical acting, compared with the technique of the dancer, is discussed at length in the author's *The Stage in Action*.

IV

★

THE ACTOR AS INSTRUMENTALIST – SPEECH

The Nature and Form of Stage Speech

THERE IS A GAME played by children in which letters of the alphabet take the place of words. Employing these letter sounds with the aid of tonal action supported by appropriate gestures, they are able to carry on a fairly effective dramatic dialogue quite understandable to each other. The conversation in a typically playful mood will run somewhat like this:

A B C D?

(The thought conveyed: *Do you love me?*)

PLO–O–O!

(*Yes, with all my heart!*)

Q X R Z–M Y

(*In that case, kindly step over here and let me present you with a flower.*)

O F–J K S–M–N!

(*Thank you. You are kind, sir. This is a most fragrant blossom!*)

H–G E V T W.

(*You are welcome. Now let us run down to the lower end of the garden to see what the others are doing.*)

I

(*All right.*)

U!

(Come!)

Printed starkly on a page, or uttered aloud in a flat, neutral voice, these letter symbols are, of course, absolutely without meaning. Yet, when they are touched by tone, they immediately assume a marvelously expressive power.

One often hears an inexperienced stage actor remark that he has "learned his part" in a play, when in actuality perhaps he has only memorized the verbal framework of it. What he does not yet realize is that the words to which he has so earnestly devoted his attention are just one of the elements of his role. There is another important factor he has still to grasp; that is tone. Tone is the melodic color of speech. It is inflection, and quality, and volume, and rhythm. Words without tone are barren of expression. Let anyone who questions this take the one word "No," and ask himself what, in plain terms, it suggests. Then let one intone the word. Affected by changes in quality and inflection, it may mean several quite different things. It may signify simple negation, or indicate a doubt. It may ask a question, or express irritation, or a great weariness. On the contrary, it may speak a joyous hopefulness. There is a mischievous *No,* an inviting *No,* an angry *No,* a *No* which implies a command, a *No* (frequently!) which means *Yes.* A short sentence containing this word may acquire a dozen meanings simply through alterations of tone:

No, I shall never think of you again.

Innumerable stories are told of actors who have been able to affect their hearers practically without words. Madame Modejeska once brought tears to the eyes of an English-speaking audience by reciting with feeling the multiplication table in Polish. An actor from Italy swept the emotions of a tableful of companions by vocally interpreting a menu. A famous comedian convulsed a party of friends by reading a list of names and numbers from a telephone directory. Caruso made certain commonplace remarks to his fellow performers on the stage an effective part of the duets he sang with them. When the popular entertainer Carmen Miranda toured the United States she was a sensation, though she sang and spoke Portuguese only.

No one acquainted with such experiences could suggest for a minute that words are fundamentally unimportant in the theatre. The normal development of nearly every dramatic scene definitely requires them. Sustained effects depend on the clear understanding of situation; and an audience cannot follow the progress of the stage story with very much assurance unless it has a certain knowledge of how the principal characters are verbalizing themselves, each other, and their surroundings. At the same time, such experiences as those mentioned suggest powerfully that the magic of speech consists of something more than just the vowel-and-consonant symbols lifted from the dictionary. It transcends these. The conclusion at which every student of vocal communication is bound to arrive inevitably is that bare words in a line of talk are like bones of a skeleton. They may have form, but no animation. The bones must be covered with warm flesh; there must be breath and pulse around them if they are to have life. The verbal flesh is tone.

Like stage pantomime, stage speech has a general technical form which is founded on everyday behavior patterns. But those patterns have to be adapted; they must be made to meet certain requirements imposed by the size and purpose of the theatre in which they are employed. That means that speech for the stage has to be enlarged. It has to be clear and loud enough for everyone in the auditorium to hear it easily. It must have a swing that will give it dramatic force and provide good support for the pantomimic action with which it is united. At the same time, it cannot rely for its effect on just projective power. It must have subtlety. It must have detail. It must be able to reflect with the utmost sensitivity every kind of change in thought and feeling. Also, like the pantomime, it must be affected by inner vitality. The very sound of it, quite aside from the words involved, should suggest to the listener that things of importance are taking place.

The Means

The means of speech is a marvelous complex instrument consisting of reedlike membranes in a bony box, three resonating chambers, a tongue-and-lip-controlled outlet, and bellows, all subject to sensitive adjustment by more than thirty muscles. With training, the instrument can make a series of notes extending over two octaves with many changes of quality. Tonal changes include timbre and other factors affected to an infinite extent by variations in pitch, time, and force. The human speech apparatus is the most flexible musical instrument in the world and every tonal resource connected with it is used in speaking.

Two basic problems confront an actor preparing to talk effectively from the stage:

(1) Good word formation

(2) Expressive tone

The problem of word formation is a technical one. It involves the correct manipulation of the voice mechanism in order to get the maximum of clarity and power with the minimum of effort. Its aim is easily and pleasingly intelligible speech sounds. By studying enunciation, articulation, and projection, an actor prepares himself to form words well. The problem of expressive tone, on the other hand, is a dramatic one—and therefore, from the point of view of the effect on the audience, a much more extended one than the other. It involves finally nearly every factor connected with the life of man.

Since the problem of diction has been dealt with more than adequately in books which specialize in the technical aspects of speech, it will not be discussed here. Attention will be directed rather to a few of the most important aspects of tonal design.

Kinesthetic Tone

The tonal design of dramatic speech is founded solidly on a concept of action. If one utters the word-symbol "woman," or "house," and then examines the effect of it, one notes some interesting facts. Devoid of tone, the word has a certain intellectual meaning. That meaning is carefully defined in the dictionary: a woman is "an adult female person," a house is "a structure for human habitation." However, the real significance of "woman" or "house" does not begin to emerge until the utterance gives some intimation of the speaker's personal feeling regarding that particular object, his inclination *to do something about it*—to approach or to avoid it, to extend its activity or to destroy it, to sense it more fully or to cast it forth from the realm of his experience. The kind of movement implicit in the speaker's mind at the moment of utterance is reflected in a vocal coloring which affects the sound of the word. Therefore we say, in general, that human voice-tones are connected with the sense of muscular tensions. They are *kinesthetic*.

The kinesthetic influence is most likely to reveal itself, of course, when the speaker is actually doing something. If one utters the term "cake" while one is tasting a particularly delectable morsel of it, one is apt to make an image of the tongue rolling sensuously over its goodness. That is natural. If one says "scoundrel" while one is throwing something at an unpleasant person, the sound of the word is bound to reflect the accompanying action. Any listener in an adjoining room out of sight of the movement and not hearing (in the presence of other noise, perhaps) the crash of the missile, would still be able to surmise what is happening just by hearing the tone of "scoundrel." But one does not actually have to move one's muscles in order to produce the sound of action. All one has to do is to *feel* movement. The words "cake" and "scoundrel," or "woman" and "house" can be made to seem the center of action through the kinesthetic imagination of the speaker. His feeling is reflected in tone, and the listener senses a physical stir.

Thus tone in speech may be significant of action in many different situations. It implies activity naturally when it accompanies present movement—when the person speaking is actually doing something at that time. It tends to reflect the same movement if the speaker himself is not the active agent but is an interested, sympathetic observer affected by *empathy*, the impulse to "feel-into," described earlier in this book. But the speaker does not have to be actively moving or even watching movement. He can simply be thinking about it—projecting his senses into the future, or remembering the past.

An example may serve to illustrate. Robert Browning's miniature story in verse, *Meeting at Night*, is a recounting of a human experience.

The gray sea and the long black land;
And the yellow half-moon large and low;
And the startled little waves that leap
In fiery ringlets from their sleep,
As I gain the cove with pushing prow,
And quench its speed i' the slushy sand.

Then a mile of warm sea-scented beach;
Three fields to cross till a farm appears;
A tap at the pane, the quick sharp scratch
And blue spurt of a lighted match,
And a voice less loud, through its joys and fears,
Than the two hearts beating each to each.

One can imagine the poet speaking these lines in our hearing
—forgetting for a moment the lilt of his verse and simply telling
the adventure as he remembers it. To us as listeners, the "gray
sea" sounds, as he speaks, wide but colorless; the "land" long-
extended but "black." The dark aspect stretches our sense of
touch, perhaps, but closes in our sense of sight because in the
murkiness we can see no details. Feeling the speaker's tones as he
describes the moon, however, we become aware of its vibrant
brightness, its bigness and its low-hanging position in the sky. The
"startled little waves" move quickly and nervously, but the prow
of the boat is slower and steadier. The sand brings all motion to
a momentary stop. All this we see and touch because the speaker,
reliving past experience, enters actively once more into a sensuous
feeling-out of the several objects and motions; and this dynamic
condition is reflected in his tone. That in turn affects us.

But the occupant of the boat in the story does not remain in
his seat. Now he is striding down the mile of warm sea-scented
beach, and the kinesthetic tone of the speaker travels with him.
It helps him to cross the three wide fields—freshly plowed, perhaps, or grown with tall grass which impedes the impatient walk-
er's progress—to find at last the dark form of the farmhouse. The
tone holds its breath for the tap on the pane, and the quick
scratch and spurt of the match. Then finally, in a joyous release,
it embraces the fond object of the speaker's journey.

To repeat, the active quality of kinesthetic tone may spring from a present participation in real action, or from the memory or the anticipation of it. On the other hand, it may grow simply out of a transient, inner sense of action unconnected, except indirectly, with any actual movement. When Swinburne wrote *A Song of Time of Order*, he was only *imagining*.

> Push hard across the sand
>   For the salt wind gathers breath;
> Shoulder and wrist and hand,
>   Push hard as the push of death. . . .

Nevertheless, a speaking of these lines could imply as much of movement as if they were based on an actual experience. In effect, the speaker does have an experience as he talks; he senses physically the action created by his imagination, and the dynamic tone of his voice communicates this feeling to the listener.

All active values, like these illustrated, are to some extent natural in everyday speech; but they are especially cultivated for the dramatic language of the theatre. The values are selected, intensified, and pointed up in order to produce the greatest possible motivity.

The Four Fundamental Tonal Actions in Stage Imagery

Kinesthetic tone is a vital factor in building the kind of fundamental action described in Chapter II. Through changes in quality and pattern, tonal actions express the same responsiveness to stimuli as that pictured in the fundamental pantomimic movements. They indicate clearly the excitement of sensation, and they show also the impulse to gather up one's forces and to do something because of that excitement. They reveal in a general way an individual's self-extension, his energetical change, and his attack upon the object; and they point specifically to the way in which each of these broad urges moves in a given situation. There are four fundamental tonal actions, which correspond to the four fundamental bodily movements already outlined. They are:

Sensation
        Opening out the senses to   Closing in

the presence of the stimulating object
Preparation

| Rising | Sinking |
| Approaching | Withdrawing |

Attack

| Building up the force of | Destroying it |
| the stimulating object | |

Since the forms of dramatic expression depend so much on personal factors in the individual performer, and since they are conditioned to such an extent by shifting elements of circumstance, no one can lay down any fixed rules for tonal design. It is safe to make one generalization, however: *tonal forms tend to follow the shape of the physical movements with which they are associated.* A vocal expression brightens in sound and changes in volume and tempo to show that the human organism is being stirred by sensation; it changes in pitch and in quality of projection to indicate the direction of that sensation; and the whole tone pattern rises and strengthens, or falls and softens to reveal the growing or ebbing of excitement. When the speaker utters these sounds successfully, the listening audience senses the opening of eyelids, the quick, alert turning of a head, and the general tension or release of muscles all over the body, even when—as in the case of radio—it cannot actually see the speaker.

When the responsive individual sees vividly (actually, or in imagination) some object like a star "high, high beyond the clouds," he is apt to feel himself reaching upward toward it. Consequently, the tones with which he describes his sense of it tend to rise with the implicit reach. When he speaks of digging for gems or precious minerals "deep, deep within the earth," he feels his hands toiling down there, and the pitch of his voice goes down with them. Things sensed by the speaker as near and far, "here," "there," and "yonder," likewise reveal their positions by the tones of his voice. Those tones, like movements, suggest the place of attention.

But it is the descriptive aspects of sensory speech which most specifically suggest the pantomimic counterparts. Sounds of "bigness," "smallness," "heaviness," "lightness," "hardness," "softness," "roughness," "smoothness" bring up instantly the images of hands measuring, hands weighing, hands feeling. These images arise, as already stated, because the sensuously-affected speaker thinks not in terms of abstractions, but of concrete physical experience. When he refers to a stone, the weight of which is impressing him, he says "stone" in such a way as to make the listener feel the weight of it in his arms. If the speaker talks of a "mansion" experienced by him as big, the listener in the audience senses the speaker walking through long halls, or lifting his face to lofty ceilings, or stretching his arms wide to feel the spaciousness of the rooms. In a similar way, vocal sounds may create images of hearing, smelling, and tasting.

Similarly, the intensity of a tonal action intimates the force of a sensory response—just as the movement does. A speaker's voice touches "lightly" or "heavily," relaxed or with the snap of shock. It may be smooth and mild, or vibrate deeply. It may cry out in pain. But always in it there is the image of physical action.

Affected by sensation, tonal design suggests the speaker's impulse to turn in on himself or to turn out to another object when that design follows implicitly the closing in or opening out of the body. When a man's thoughts in revery or in deliberation are turned upon himself, the voice tends to grow quieter and to slip back a little in his mouth. It "retires." When the man's attention reaches away from himself, his voice tends to reach also. It strengthens in force and pushes out at the front edge of his mouth; it "goes forth" to make contact with the other body.

Tone movement drops wearily, dejectedly, when the body feels like sinking; and it lifts, gathers speed, and dances brightly when the body feels an upward surge of life. It goes forward aggressively like the body to meet the objects of desire. It retreats in fear, or shame, or grief when the push of the opposing influence is too great to be withstood. In this way the voice can show as clearly as physical action all the shades of feeling connected with the fundamental step of Preparation.

The kinesthetic tonal changes often show most strongly when they spring from impulses to build up or destroy the activity of another body. They sound like striking fists, or soothing hands, or stamping feet even in the absence of visible action, if the physical-emotive impulse is there. "I shall shut your lying mouth!" may well sound in its savageness like a real strangling, while the lingering utterance of "darling!" may suggest most vividly a loving caress. Expressions of "lifting," "patting," "fondling," "hugging," or of "biting," "tearing," "whipping," and "breaking into pieces" can be very eloquent in their suggestiveness.

How several of the fundamental tonal actions here described may work together in a single brief passage of speech can be illustrated in a little verse picture by Paul Eldridge. Here is the poem:

> Night—
> An old woman sitting at the window—
> Dreaming . . .
> Suddenly,
> Softly,
> Her name is called—
> "Florence—Florence—Florence!"
> She shivers—
> Rises—
> Bends out—
> A neighbor's window opens,
> A gentle voice whispers—
> "All right, dearest—come up—I am alone" . . .
> An old woman standing at the window,
> Dreaming . . .[1]

And here is the kind of mental diagram the speaker might work out for his vocal interpretation of that poem:

> Night—
>
> > (*A time of stillness, a period when human contacts draw away from distant horizons and become centered on small, close circles of activity. Therefore, a kinesthetic sense of closing in.*)

[1] Paul Eldridge, *Vanitas* (Boston: The Alpine Press, 1920).

An old woman sitting at the window—

> (*She is frail and tired, and she is seated. Closing in and sinking.*)

Dreaming . . .

> (*Quiet, detached, unhurried. Showing vague form and mild force of stimulation, in a person turned-in on herself.*)

Suddenly,

> (*Now a change. The body of the old woman—and therefore the voice of the speaker—becomes tense, alert; and it turns out expectantly.*)

Softly,
Her name is called—
"Florence—Florence—Florence!"

> (*The sound which now strikes the ear of the figure by the window comes "softly." It is almost a whisper. The speaker's voice which describes it should be low and intense.*)

She shivers—
Rises—
Bends out—

> (*The sound of the word "shivering" is guided by a bodily sensation. Then "rising" and "bending out."*)

A neighbor's window opens,
A gentle voice whispers—

> (*The old woman is still leaning out, listening intently. Tonal action: Sensation.*)

"All right, dearest—come up—I am alone." . . .

> (*What she hears touches an inner chord of youth in her. For a*

moment she feels exhilarated—
lifted. A slight pause. Then—)

An old woman standing at the window,

> *(She retires into herself once*
> *more—a little less lifted. Tonal*
> *actions: Closing in, sinking.)*

Dreaming . . .

> *(A misty, sensorial quietness.)*

This is, of course, just a very rough drawing of what might pass through the mind of the speaker. As he tries to put the little word portrait into sound, he could never allow himself to think thoughts actually as laborious as those diagramed—and certainly he would not dare permit himself to count off the various tonal changes as numbers. To do that would make the whole inner experience which he aims to create in order to give life to his speech, intellectually static rather than dynamic. However, the notes suggest the kinesthetic drift of his thinking.

The Tonal Actions Illustrated

Probably not every reader would translate Eldridge's verse picture exactly as it is outlined here, but doubtless he would use all of the first three tonal actions somewhere in the course of his rendition. The only action which would find no place in the rendering would be the last one, the Attack. The old lady, although she experiences something rather exciting, has no opportunity tonight to carry her feelings over into action affecting another object. The movements of her body and of her thoughts impinge now on no one except herself.

While the tone of aggressive action cannot be illustrated in the particular poem just quoted, it is, nevertheless, a very common one. Examples abound. Typical would be the rendition of any quarrel scene, like the one between Kent and Cornwall in *King Lear*. Here Kent manifests in the clearest possible terms vocally how much he would like to put his fists on the "knave" he abhors.

CORNWALL. Why art thou angry?
KENT. That such a slave as this should wear a sword, . . .
    A plague upon your epileptic visage!
    Smile you my speeches, as I were a fool?
    Goose, if I had you upon Sarum plain,
    I'd drive you cackling home to Camelot.

Such scenes of destructive import appear, of course, all through the dramas of Shakespeare, and all through the works of other playwrights old and new. Equally common are the scenes which reflect inner impulses to fondle and build up the other person. One will recall immediately any number of such lines in a play such as *Romeo and Juliet*.

    See, how she leans her cheek upon her hand!
    O, that I were a glove upon that hand,
    That I might touch that cheek! . . .

    Sleep dwell upon thine eyes, peace in thy breast!
    Would I were sleep and peace, so sweet to rest! . . .

    Gallop apace, you fiery-footed steeds . . .

All of the examples so far, poems and dramatic excerpts, are strongly descriptive; they are passages in which the moving imagery is plainly indicated. Their vocal rendition calls rather obviously, therefore, for the aid of kinesthetic tones. The speaker on the stage would make a mistake, however, if he believed that the use of the four fundamental actions described in this book can be limited to picture scenes only; they must ever serve as an inner framework for dramatic language whatever its form. The need for them in the building of every kind of scene becomes apparent as one goes on with the problem of interpretation. Under the broad as well as the restricted areas of dialogue the listener should feel the movement of approach and withdrawal, of rise and fall, and of destruction and creation, for this gives him certain vital clues to the emotional flux of the speaker's thinking which he would be unable to obtain in any other way. Even a Shakespearean soliloquy, uttered when no one except the speaker is present, needs abundant use of fundamental kinesthetic action. Here is how an actor might tackle the speech addressed by Hamlet to himself in Act II, after he has dismissed the players.

O, what a rogue and peasant slave am I!

> (*He depreciates himself with a falling tone. Viewing his own sickly presence with disgust, he sounds also as if he wishes to turn away from it.*)

Is it not monstrous that this player here,

> (*Averting his face, as it were, from the craven figure of the man called "Hamlet," he sets up the contrasting image of the actor whom he has just seen. This he views with a kind of bitter fascination. Starting low, the speaker's voice rises a little as the image takes shape.*)

But in a fiction, in a dream of passion,
Could force his soul so to his own conceit
That from her working all his visage wann'd,
Tears in his eyes, distraction in's aspect,
A broken voice, and his whole function suiting
With forms to his conceit? And all for nothing!
For Hecuba!

> (*His rising voice falls a little for a contemptuous "Hecuba," as if he realizes the inherent sham in the image he is creating and wishes to destroy it. Instead of tearing it down, however, he turns on it and challenges it. His words increase their force.*)

What's Hecuba to him, or he to Hecuba,
That he should weep for her?

> (*The image of the actor holds*

firm. Approving its resolute vigor, he dresses it in his own clothes and contemplates it intently. HAMLET's *voice drops a little on the question, and acquires new stress as the vision clarifies. The picture finally becomes so vivid that he feels himself moving and speaking with the actor.*)

What would he do
Had he the motive and the cue for passion
That I have? He would drown the stage with tears
And cleave the general ear with horrid speech,
Make mad the guilty and appall the free,
Confound the ignorant, and amaze indeed
The very faculties of eyes and ears.

(*He has spoken the last few lines almost with enthusiasm. But now the vision vanishes, and his mind turns once more to the anemic figure of the man called "Hamlet." The sight of him makes his voice drop and turn in on itself with melancholy.*)

Yet I,
A dull and muddy-mettled rascal, peak,
Like John-a-dreams, unpregnant of my cause,
And can say nothing;

(*This makes him angry, and his voice rises again.*)

No, not for a king,
Upon whose property and most dear life
A damned defeat was made.

(*He stops a moment to look at himself, then asks a question.*)

Am I a coward?
Who calls me villain? breaks my pate across?

(*He starts to pick at the cowardly*

figure, just to see what it will do.)

Plucks off my beard, and blows it in my face?
Tweaks me by the nose? gives me the lie i' the throat,
As deep as the lungs? Who does me this?
Ha!

> (*The note of self-destructive
> anger has crept back into his
> voice, and his tone rises steadily.*)

'Swounds, I should take it: for it cannot be
But I am pigeon-liver'd and lack gall
To make oppression bitter, or ere this

> (*His rage increases, but he trans-
> fers it now to the hated person
> of the king.*)

I should have fatted all the region kites with this
slave's offal!

> (*In a final frenzy, as if he were
> striking and kicking the evil man
> he abhors.*)

Bloody, bawdy villain!
Remorseless, treacherous, lecherous, kindless villain!
O vengeance!

> (*This is the highest point in the
> speech. After this peak, HAMLET's
> voice gradually subsides. He
> seems to be looking at himself
> again, and then with a new con-
> tempt, to be turning dejectedly
> from that view.*)

Why, what an ass am I! This is most brave,
That I, the son of a dear father murder'd,
Prompted to my revenge by heaven and hell,
Must, like a whore, unpack my heart with words,
And fall a-cursing, like a very drab,
A scullion!

The notes set down here represent, of course, only a rough
approximation of the thoughts, or rather feelings, that might affect

the actor as he speaks. He would not verbalize any of the ideas quite as specifically as these; but the dynamic drift—the push and retreat, and the rise and fall—of them would be similar. Consequently, the spoken soliloquy would project to the listener a strong sense of action, even if the player of Hamlet while delivering his lines stood visually rather still.

Because tonal design so potently implies pantomimic movement, it is a vital ingredient of all that stage imagery which was described in Chapter II. It is especially valuable in the building of the under images of dramatic action which are not visible to the spectator's outward eye and must therefore be created for his mind's eye by intimation. Tone is the expressive sound of a pulsing, breathing, sensuously-moving body. It springs from the innermost sources of man's primitive nature, and as such, it can often suggest, far more sensitively than any overt gesture, what are the essential *feelings* of human existence.

Factors in Design

The kind of tonal forms here delineated are those which are characteristic of expressive speech. For anyone to assume that they are found in equal force in every line of good dialogue would, of course, be false. Although they appear freely throughout a well-acted play, they mark most strongly the dynamically emotional passages. Since, however, these emotional scenes tend naturally by virtue of their content to dominate the whole action, the kinesthetic tone-patterns employed to build them cast the glow of their imagery over all.

Between the more moving moments, that is, during those rather neutral periods when the audience is being supplied with necessary but not particularly stirring facts and the forces of drama are being deployed for the next dramatic engagement—the dialogue is often filled with less colorful language. But one thing the sensitive player must work for ceaselessly is to keep the proportions right. Unless he is at all times on his guard, he is apt to miss many of the expressive opportunities by viewing as purely accessory speech much that should be developed into vital imagery. The best way for the actor to avoid this error is to keep his state of awareness acutely alive at all times. When he is in an alert condition he finds it much easier to be responsive to all the stimuli around and within him, and this responsiveness then tends to express itself in vocal imagery wherever the playwright's lines give it a base to stand on.

In order to exploit fully the expressive possibilities wherever they occur, the actor must have a thoroughly flexible voice. Among the most important factors for tonal design are these four: (1) pitch, (2) time, (3) force, and (4) timbre.

Pitch represents tonal level. Simple changes in pitch help to express a wide range of feelings. Often they reveal the speaker's sense of height and depth, and the lift of the spirit with respect to the force of gravity. When the mind and the body dance—as we have already noted—the voice tends to rise also; when the body sinks to rest, the voice drops with it. High notes are usually more active, low notes more quiet—because they seem heavier, less easy to move. The rising intervals in a melodic line, like the climbing notes of a siren, often suggest effort, whereas the falling intervals suggest relaxation. Words on a high pitch level (within the neutral range of the speaker's voice) sound thinner, less voluminous, but often brighter, more cheerful. On a lower level they commonly seem richer, more voluminous, but resigned, and, if very low, depressed, melancholic. Changes of pitch likewise suggest alterations of attitude in joy, anger, and will to action. Also, at times they have something to say about the basic honesty of the speaker. While the higher notes tend to be more exciting, they often lack vibrancy, they sound less convincing than the medium and lower notes—those notes which have their feet planted solidly, as it were, on the ground.

There can be no rules for the use of pitch changes, of course. If any earnest young actor should attempt to line up a list of fixed principles to govern his employment of this factor of speech, he would soon find so many exceptions arising in a practical performance that his precious checklist would have little value. The only purpose there can be for noting the various meanings that are characteristic of changing tone levels is to impress on the actor what an expressive factor pitch may be, and to inspire him to work for as much flexibility as he can get. When he has completed his training he should be able to vary the levels of his voice easily in the course of a single scene from one octave as a minimum to as much as two full octaves. And he should be able to do this without making his effort seem self-conscious.

The right use of the other three factors for tonal design is equally important. Each of them has as much to contribute to the expressive effect as pitch does. The problem of *time* involves questions of tempo (rate of speech), rhythm (effective repetition of patterns), and pause (effective use of breaks in the continuity of sound). The problem of *force* includes volume (loudness and softness) and intensity (the degree of power applied on any volume level). The problem of *timbre* lies in the use of changing qualities of voice (suggestive of "hardness," "softness," "sharpness," "smoothness," "brittleness," "liquidness," and the like). The study of the three factors named here—plus the first, pitch—will usually seem to the beginning player rather bewildering; but he should not be dismayed. If he works slowly and patiently, experimenting liberally and trying to master not more than one small point at a time, he will soon find that he is getting the "hang" of the design factors. It will be some time, however, before he can hope to exploit them fully. He will be a genius indeed if with six months' practice he can extend his pitch range to all of two long octaves! Nevertheless, he might expand to five notes. And five notes—if they are used freely, easily and regularly—make a very good beginning.

Normal and Characterized Speech

Stage speech, like pantomime, has two general types with which the actor must make himself familiar:

> *Normal speech*—unparticularized
> *Characterized*—particularized, suggesting some distinct individuality

Normal speech is basic speech. It is simply the kind of speech which, if delivered in the same way in a dozen different centers of the country, would call the least attention to itself as speech. It would have no dialect designation. It would not be "Western," or

"Southern," or "New England," or "British," but good American.
And it would have no particularizing quality traits: it would not
be "harsh," or "sweet," or "nasal," or "guttural," or "staccato," or
"lisping," or "fast," or "slow." It would be just "good speech." This
is the standard. From it departures can be made in any direction
to achieve certain eccentric effects that may be desired for dramatic reasons; but all variations must employ *normal* speech as a
reference. By checking his divergent products constantly against
the basic model, the actor can keep from making some of those
queer, inhuman sounds which call undue attention to themselves.*

Characterized speech represents the particularized way in
which a certain dramatic character communicates vocally his
thoughts and feelings, a way different from the ways of other individuals on the stage. If he is quick and nervous, his manner of
speaking will reflect his temperament. If he is slow and lazy, his
way of talking will likewise be slow and lazy. If he has a com-
plaining mind, the tone of his voice will whimper or whine. If
he is bitter, his words will snarl. If his disposition is sunny, the
sounds he utters will dance, like his feet.

Each stage personality must be created separately. For this
reason, there can be no more set rules for characterized speech
than there can be for characterized movement. A statement of one
or two general principles, however, may prove helpful to the
beginning actor. Youthful speech tends to be more flexible than
older speech. Since the whole nature of the young man is more
responsive to stimuli, both small and large, and since his mental
and physical behavior is consequently more full of bounce, he is
apt to use wide changes of tonal pattern. First he whispers, then
speaks loudly. First he drawls, then he rattles off a series of words
like rifle shots. His voice is smooth, then rough, then smooth again.
His inflection is lively and unpredictable.

The middle-aged person has typically a more settled mind
and body. So he tends to speak on a generally lower pitch level,
more slowly, with less change. The patterns of his words repeat

---

* Since the problems of standard diction are not dealt with in this book,
the models for normal speech are omitted here. The student will find them described fully in any good speech manual.

themselves regularly. There are fewer surprising sounds. His voice is richer, more assured. This, one must hasten to say, is the *typical* form. Many middle-aged persons, like the professional book salesman or the habitual gossip, speak at an accelerated rate of speed, and with many sharp accents. But there is usually something unnatural about their way of talking. They sound nervous, keyed up, as if they were speaking outside of their proper age patterns.

The aged person tends to have an even less flexible voice. If the young man of twenty uses a range of two octaves, the very old man may be limited to three or four notes at most. The factors of time, force, and timbre also tend to be quieter. This means that there is usually less variety in the design of his word tones, but it does not necessarily mean that his way of speaking is eccentric. Contrary to the notion held by most amateur impersonators of octogenarians, the voices of men of this age do not usually "pipe and whistle" in their throats. Sometimes the pitch rises. More often it goes down. Often it has an almost sepulchral sound. When the voice approaches the hundred-year mark it does tend to lose its resonance and become drier, less strong. It may finally develop that wizened whistle dearly beloved by young players, but not inevitably.

One of the chief characteristics of the older voice—middle-aged and later—is a certain fullness. The voice nearly always sounds richer than that of the young man. This quality is difficult to "put on." Consequently, many very able high school and college actors find themselves quite unfitted to play mature characters, not by reason of any lack of dramatic ability, but just because they do not yet have the developed vocal equipment. Some modification of the youngish voice can be effected by lowering slightly the general pitch level. But great care must be taken with this device to prevent the player from making strained, unnatural sounds. The general level adopted for the voice must be considered as a median line. The actor should be able to drop below it or rise above it easily as the scene demands; otherwise the speech will seem to be stiff, uncomfortable. Another device is occasionally employed for the older characters who may be presumed to lack some of their front teeth. The upper lip of the actor is curled down over his actually good front teeth, thus neutralizing their effectiveness and producing a kind of hollow, muffled, toothless sound which is sometimes very convincing. If the actor attempts to use this method, he should take extra pains with all other parts of his diction in order to make his words understandable.

The speaking of dialect sounds is difficult and should never be attempted unless one has a genuine ear for them. Some actors seem to be able to talk "French," "Scotch," "Cockney," "German," or "Spanish" just about as easily as they speak their native tongues; while others never can learn how to twist their tongues around the foreign sounds. The speaking of dialects effectively requires more than surface mimicry; it demands a certain set of mind which makes the dialect a natural expression. A New York East-sider speaks through tight jaws, partly because he has heard his companions talk that way, but more because his life in an environment of predatory poverty has made him strained, on his guard. His speech is hard defensively. For a similar reason, some Southerners drawl not necessarily because their ancestors spoke that way, but rather because their lives are unhurried. Many of the exaggerated "ah's" uttered by screen actors trying to portray ladies and gentlemen "down on the levee" are painfully unconvincing simply because the speakers, conditioned by the hustling atmosphere of Hollywood, have snapped up a surface characteristic of Southern speech—and then played it to death—without taking time to put themselves into the right feeling of leisureliness. Far more important than the detailed sounds of dialect speech are the larger patterns of intonation, the swinging of whole phrases and sentences. And these are shaped by attitudes of mind.

One of the greatest helps for effective characterization is the preliminary organization of the actor's breathing. If just before he begins to talk he will draw a few breaths, quick or slow, deep or shallow, easy or with a catch, in character with the personality and the situation he is attempting to vocalize, he should be able to establish easily the right swing for his speech. Breathing is a good check for the pantomimic action also. It puts the player into the right feeling of nervousness, breathlessness, excitement, or calmness and assurance. Furthermore, controlled breathing is an excellent steadying device for the halting of stage fright.

Compulsive Speech

Compulsive speech—that kind of speech which, like compulsive movement, invites the audience to "feel into" it and then impels it to swing along with it—is an effective combination of several elements. First, of course, is good diction. Everything that is said is clearly audible. It is loud enough, but not too loud. It does not seem to be shouted. It appears to be easy, effortless. In other words, it is "graceful"—technically efficient. In the second place, the speech fulfills well all its expressive functions. It reveals sensitively all the big and little details of character and situation. The speech builds images, rich, active, evocative. To accomplish these purposes, compulsive speech makes wide use of variety. It is live speech—speech which has a lot to say, and says it from many different angles, in many different ways.

But grace and effective imagery, important as they are, do not constitute all there is of compulsive speech. One more ingredient must be included, a rather intangible one which defies any precise description. It involves factors from each of those other elements of stage speech which have already been mentioned, but it goes beyond them in its ability to mirror the innermost recesses of man's thinking and feeling. For want of a better term, it may be called *speech music*.

We say that the human voice, when it is freed from inhibitory influences, "reflects" the inner emotions of a man. Perhaps it would be nearer the truth to say that the voice is part of the very fibre of that feeling. The closer one gets to primitive speech, the more one is impressed by the fundamental part basic music plays in the communication of emotion. We see this nowhere more clearly than in the verse forms. The poetry of the lowlier peoples depends more upon tone play than upon words. The savage uses singing sounds to express feelings for which he has as yet no adequate intellectual symbols—impulses too vague for formal expression. When he develops himself through various levels of civilization to a place where he has at his command so many words that he requires a book with a thousand pages to hold them, he still must depend upon speech music. For there are no mere words which can communicate through consonant and vowel combinations alone the inner urges of the human organism. Speech music springs out of the tissue of life. It is therefore the best messenger of life's movement.

The philosopher Schopenhauer long ago pointed out that "suitable music played to any scene, action, event, or surrounding seems to disclose to us its most secret meaning"; and this it does, he said, because music, more than any other form of expression, reflects man's eternal hungers and his efforts to satisfy them. John Dewey, made a similar statement: "Music, having sound as its medium, thus necessarily expresses in a concentrated way the shocks and instabilities, the conflicts and resolutions, that are the dramatic changes enacted upon the more enduring background of nature and human life. The tension and the struggle has its gatherings of energy, its discharges, its attacks and defenses, its mighty warrings and its peaceful meetings, its resistances and resolutions, and out of these things music weaves its web."*

It is true that in these utterances the authors were referring to pure music. But what they have to say touches intimately the tonal core of effective speech. Speech which is compulsive—speech which stirs the listener in all his parts, which catches him and holds him in its spell—is speech which is impregnated with the same kind of sound-magic as that which motivates singing. Beginning with the unit phases—the word, the phrase—and progressing through the sentence, the sentence group, and the completed passage, one finds at every step the animating influence of tone music. Pitch is played against pitch, tempo against tempo, stress against stress. The speech is patterned in melody, motivated with rhythm, and developed in accordance with principles of accent, contrast, surge, and climax.

How does one learn speech music? That is something which no teacher can tell his student. The young actor must discover its magic for himself, and then experiment until he has mastered it. The only real help which the teacher can give is to point ceaselessly to the importance of speech music, to advise the actor to keep his ears open, to listen sensitively to the sound of it in his

* John Dewey, *Art as Experience* (New York: G. P. Putnam's Sons, 1934), p. 236.

own and other people's utterances, and then to work for perfection in his use of it.

Speech and Movement Together

In the past two chapters, pantomime and speech have been discussed as if they were distinct forms of dramatic expression. Actually, they are two phases of a single process and should always be regarded as such. Every line of vocal utterance and every bodily movement, to be effective, must be perfectly synchronized —they must form a unity of response to the same stimulus. The torso, the head, the hands, and the feet must add to what the voice is saying their own well-timed and forceful actions; and the voice in turn should support their movements. To guard against a separation of the visual and auditory aspects of acting, the player would do well to remember to do two things: (1) to plan the pantomime to evoke auditory images, flood the stage with imaginary sound; (2) to speak to the eye of the spectator, make him see, through tone, movements beyond those actually given by the body of the performer.

PREPARING THE PART

Characterization and the Audience

EVERY PLAY is composed of two prime ingredients: interesting characters and a moving story. Supplying the second ingredient is chiefly the business of the playwright. His is the responsibility to see that the action tells an interesting tale. The performer has little to contribute to this; the author drafts the plot and the performer must follow its guidelines. In the matter of characterization, however, the condition is different. In the building of a dramatic role the actor is expected to add richly of himself—a thousand impressions, his memories, his imagination. Here the actor is in a very real sense the creative collaborator of the playwright. Together they have an obligation to design something that will please an audience.

The role which the very young playgoer likes to personate in his imagination is glamorous but uncomplicated. It embodies qualities of power and skill in no real way connected with the daily life of the spectator. The dramatic desires of the child are primarily escapist. He joyfully turns his sensuous and emotive attention to the marvelous exploits of a brave Lone Ranger, a smart Detective Tracy, a nimble and courageous Tarzan—personalities which are forceful, direct, intellectually uninvolved. But when the child grows older, when his memory of life and consequently his understanding of it are enlarged, he takes little pleasure in playing out the same very simple personalities. With advancing years, he tends to associate his imagination with richer natures, characters which touch not one, but many sides of his own physical, mental, and emotional life. These are people marked by an inner reality absent in the earlier heroes. The more mature the spectator becomes, the more inclined he is to turn the course of his dramatic adventuring away from fancy to fact. Unlike the young escapist, he is ready to confront life squarely; and the longer he gazes at it, the more interesting he finds it. Through the experience of each character he inhabits by imagination, he feels out something new about the shape and the meaning of human existence. In this way he finds he can arrive at a clearer appreciation of his own personality and its relationship to the world of personalities around him.

Sometimes the adult spectator wishes to sense the facts of life —and himself in life—seriously; sometimes he wishes to view them playfully. Sometimes he prefers tragedy, sometimes comedy. But whatever the approach is, he demands that his dramatic adventure in the theatre be pursued with a sense of enlargement, with a sense of grandeur. Hamlet, Nora, and Willy Loman are basically real. Nevertheless they must appear on the stage as if they were idealizations of the traits which they personify. When we, as spectators, enter into their strivings, we want to feel in them a stretch of desire and a push of action that is more than what we can normally experience outside the theatre. If the characters are rightly presented, we shall feel somehow that their heightened qualities belong to our own existence.

Upon the quality of its sensitivity and the intensity of its effort depends the value of a dramatic role. Lowly characters like sailors, sharecroppers, and even beggars, it has been pointed out repeatedly, may be as stirring to the audience in this respect as princes and poets. Arthur Miller discusses this very well in his essay on "Tragedy and the Common Man." Desire, suffering, struggle, hope, and courage—especially his search for personal dignity—are what make a man, whatever may be his place in life. Viewed in this way, Willy Loman, the salesman in *Death of a Salesman;* Maurya, the fisherwoman in *Riders to the Sea;* Widow Cagle, the mountain woman in *Sun-up;* and Yank, the seaman in

The Hairy Ape, are great persons. They are as exciting as any figures in the literature of nobility.

No character in a good play can be seen as being petty. Even such utilitarian figures as messengers and servants have stature. They have something which sets them off dramatically from their counterparts in everyday life. They move and speak a little more smartly, they perform their ordinary duties a little more efficiently. They are persons to be reckoned with. If one glances at the several figures who move through the dramatic scenes included in this volume, for instance, one will see that, although three or four are of epic mold, most of them are very simple men and women. But none is insignificant. In every one of them, even the comic fools,* there is something of importance, something of potential bigness, which makes their achievements, and likewise their defeats, exciting, worthy of attentive watching.

These are some of the facts about stage characters which the actor learns to recognize and exploit. It is true that the general form of a dramatic role is fashioned by the playwright, but the *development* of that role and the *living impact* which it makes upon the spectator depend on the player.

Two Steps in the Preparation of a Dramatic Role

Every actor must follow at least two steps in the preparation of a dramatic role. The first consists of getting acquainted with the play in which he has been assigned a part. Getting acquainted means much more than skipping lightly over the pages; it means reading the script thoroughly, two or three times—*all* of it. While doing this the actor must resist the temptation to look with particular attention at his own part of it. At this step he must force himself to focus his eyes and ears upon the total design. He should try to capture the big concept, the general feeling, the overall form of the story. He should view the community of personalities and try to arrive at an understanding of how these various people react to each other, and *why*. Before he can begin to analyze the

---

* The portrayal of comic characters demands certain specialized treatments which will be discussed in another chapter.

peculiar motivation of his own part he must find out what moves all the others, both singly and collectively.

One of the first things the actor will want to know is why the producer selected this work for a presentation to a certain audience. Why does the producer like it? What kind of response does he hope to evoke when the play is performed? If the actor can see little sense in the piece—if he says to himself before he even begins to study his part, "I personally wouldn't give a dime for a look at this turkey!"—he is not going to be able to elicit much radiance from his particular role, however hard he may intend to work on it. In other words, to be fair to himself and to the other members of the company to which he belongs he should in this first step either "sell" himself on the dramatic virtues of the play, or ask the director to release him from having to participate in it.

The second step of the preparation is concerned with one's personal role. This step consists of three phases. It is more proper to call them *phases* than substeps because they are not usually taken in sequence but together. The first phase is a careful analytical study of the role. With the larger design in mind, the actor will want to ask himself, "What is the particular dramatic purpose of this part I am about to play?" If the character is a leading one, the answer should be simple. Basically, he represents a prime moving force in the story. He is driven by a desire either to acquire or to effect something of value—or, in a negative way, to prevent someone else from acquiring or effecting something which that person wants. So much for a beginning.

If the character to be played is a lesser person, his dramatic purpose may not be found quite so readily. The author may have designed him to exert in his own right some impelling influence upon the action of the story; or he may have created him simply to act as an instrument or agent for the extension of another character's power—as would a servant, a companion, a partner, a secretary, or a messenger. The character may have been included by the author for some routine service; or simply to sound a momentary note of contrast to the prevailing tone of the main action, perhaps to provide "comic relief." If the character is extremely minor, he may have been placed in the story merely to help create local color, "mood." But, however tenuous his relation to the great forces of the drama may be, in the ultimate effect to be produced on the audience by the whole play, *each dramatic character has his own important function.* After determining what this is, the actor can proceed to analyze the details of his role.

The particularization of a dramatic part involves the shaping of many visual and auditive features. A study of his outward appearance might be charted in some such way as this:

> *General presence* (as indicative of race, station in life, occupation, etc.)
>
> *Typical facial and bodily form*
> Typical carriage
> Typical manner of speaking
> Typical dress
>
> *General physical condition*
> Age
> Health and strength
> Possible effects of recent experience (having been in a battle, for instance)
>
> *Personal Eccentricities*
> Posturing
> Movement
> Speech
> Dress

All of this examination of the character's outward appearance must be related intimately, of course, to his inward self. Some of those visible and audible features which together make up his external picture are purely the result of accident—the race and station into which he was born, his age and strength, the shape of his body, and the form of his vocal mechanism. But most of those features must be assumed to be the reflection, or expression, of inward temperament. Therefore, the actor must give careful thought to the character's habits of thinking and feeling; and at the same time he must examine the environmental and circumstantial causes for the character's behavior.

The mine into which the actor digs to find all the indications of the character's inner and outer attributes is, of course, the author's script. Among the lodes are:

(a) The playwright's description of the appearance of the character in the stage directions, usually found at or near the character's first entrance into the play.

(b) The *stage business* (personal actions) of the character found in the stage directions which accompany his lines throughout. The written directions for the "business" of the character provide a fruitful field of research for the physical habits, the picturesque peculiarities of conduct which belong with the personality under study.

(c) The speech lines of the character. Here, of course, is the richest lode of the mine. From the spoken lines the actor may read directly the thoughts and emotions peculiar to the character.

(d) The reactions of the other characters in the play to the character considered, as stated or implied in their own lines and stage business; also, his reaction to them.

(e) The situations within the play which shape the manifestations of the character's personality.

The second phase of the second step of preparation goes beyond the work of cold analysis. In the process of performing this phase the actor mulls over those scenes which capture his principal attention. These will doubtless be moments of heightened excitement. They will be episodes which, because they are emotionally more stimulating, more self-revealing, or otherwise more noteworthy than the others, tend to command the spectator's senses most strongly. One scene may deal with a moment of anger at another character. It may embody a terrifying feeling of defeat in a crucial action; it may show a sudden joyous release from frustration; or just an especially fine feeling occasioned by a certain kind of conversation with another character. These key scenes need a lot of sensuous as well as thoughtful going-over because they are powerfully suggestive of the nature of the role from which they spring. They uncover what the character does under stress when the surface image is removed and the fundamental

actions° show through. They often reveal in miniature the personality of the role as a whole.

Building the Image of the Role

The third phase of the second step of preparation (the step concerned with the work on one's own role) is centered on creation.
In this phase of the preparation the actor builds the image of his
part. The work of this phase may proceed concurrently with the
analytic task or it may follow it. More often it goes along with it.
That is, the actor analyzes the script and creates the image of his
role at the same time. As the period of the preparation continues,
however, he will devote less attention to the analysis and more to
the creation.

While the actor usually works out the rough outlines of the
image in his own mind before he unfolds it on the stage, he will
look forward to developing many of its details in the course of the
rehearsals. The image will evolve bit by bit. And as it evolves, it
will change greatly. The perfected image in performance will
probably appear, and sound, very, very different from the first
rough concept of it.

First, the actor will give careful thought to the movements of
his imaged personality's attention.° This will shift from moment
to moment inwardly into himself, and outwardly to other objects
and people. It will move also from one outward point to another.
Sometimes it will move slowly, sometimes quickly. The points on
which the imaged personality's attention fastens will be the principal sources of the stimulation to which the actor as (imaged)
character will respond.

The player will remember that movement of the center of
attention must always be expressed in such a way as to let the
spectator sense it with his eyes and ears. This means that the actor
must turn his head freely. He must be ready also to move his body
when this kind of action is needed, to show both the direction and
force of his attention. Most of all he will remember how important
is the posture of his eyes. Eyes half-closed, eyes wide-open, eyes
directed to the floor, eyes raised, eyes looking off to the horizon,

° See Chapter II.

eyes averted, eyes pointing straight and unafraid at the person addressed—all these postures have much to say about the quality as well as the direction of attention.

So, too, do the tone and the strength of the words uttered while one is looking. From the examples cited in Chapter II the actor can see how suggestive of the color and the placement of attention are softness and loudness, the retirement and the projection of sound.

In building his image, the actor will think also about the use of Fundamental Actions:*

Sensation

Opening out the senses to the presence of the stimulating object	Closing in

Preparation

Rising	Sinking
Approaching	Withdrawing

Attack

Building up the force of the stimulating object	Destroying it

These actions can be exploited not only in the development of a character's movements but also in his posturing. If the actor will observe a number of personalities both on and off the stage he will note first, that everyone makes constant use of all eight of the actions listed above; but, second, that each man and each woman *inclines* to one of the actions a little more than to any of the others. He may open out more pointedly than he closes in, for instance, or he may rise more definitely than he sinks. That is his characteristic way of responding to the forces of his environment. His behavior is marked by an opening out or by a rising, and the people who know him observe it. They refer to the individual as a "happy extrovert," or as a "young man very much on his toes." In this manner any of the fundamental actions may be associated with a common human type. For example:

* See Chapter II.

Opening out
    The "extrovert," the "man with keen eyes," the "man who sees everything and makes mental notes of it"

Closing in
    The "introvert," the "abnormally sensitive man driven in on himself"

Rising
    The "hero," the "live one," the "cheerful one," the "ambitious one," the "boaster"

Sinking
    The "coward," the "listless one," the "gloomy one," the "lazy one," the "humble one"

Approaching
    The "acquisitive one," the "friendly one"

Withdrawing
    The "one who renounces," the "one who finds nothing to please him"

Building up
    The "patient builder," the "creator," the "healer," the "promoter"

Destroying
    The "belligerent one," the "man who throws monkey wrenches," the "critic," the "cynic"

While the actor is planning the Fundamental substructure of his visual and aural imagery he must give thought also to the Accessory elements: the little *trained* actions which the well-bred personality uses to modify (and often to try to cover up), the intuitive, cruder, Fundamental parts. If the character on the stage is supposed to sing, or to dance, or to play the piano he should perform with grace. If he must move a chair or carve a roast, he should do it with the kind of skill which the sophisticated requirements of the role indicate are appropriate to the situation.

Surface and Under imagery, as we have already seen, are intimately related to the forms of the Fundamental and the Accessory actions. The Surface parts are what the spectator sees without having to exert his imagination in any way whatsoever. The Under, less visible, parts are those elements of action which represent the deep-lying passions of the role: the man's fears, his hopes, his hatreds, or his loves for other people. Since they mirror the drives which make a man do the dramatic things he does on the stage, the actor must first be very clear about them in his own mind. Then he must devise a way for making their corners poke through the sophisticated Surface crust, and so provide clues upon which the sense and the imagination of the spectator can work to apprehend the hidden part.

Aids to Imagery

As the actor enlarges the image of his role detail by detail he should sense its growth not only with his mind, but also with his whole live body, until finally he can at will identify himself with the stage character in every turn of its thought, feeling, and action.

In order to help stimulate his imagination, the actor would do well to keep his eyes and ears keenly receptive to all sights and sounds of people and things which can in one way or another contribute to the filling out of the image. Many richly suggestive details of appearance, gesture, and conduct may often be observed, for instance, in an actual person who has visible traits similar to those pertaining to the dramatic character under study: a manner of walking, perhaps, or a trick of gesture, an expression of the mouth, a way of wearing the hair. The postures, actions, and voice-tones which are characteristic of a particular kind of old man or woman, such as the behavior typical of a lame person or of a drunkard, cannot be made convincing to an audience—no matter how faithfully one attempts to follow the stage directions in the script—until one has carefully watched and attempted to reproduce the comparable images in real life.

Further character-building suggestions may be obtained from cartoons, paintings, and historical illustrations. Photographs of type-people are sometimes very helpful. The features, bearing, and dress of an ancient moonshiner, for example, or of a foreign opera star, a Chicago racketeer, his lady friend, even an august senator (to mention a few rather obvious examples) may suggest pertinent attributes not to be thought of otherwise. Joseph Jefferson, before creating his famous role of Rip Van Winkle, dressed himself carefully in the clothes of an old bearded character of the period, studied his appearance in the mirror, and in this way found the true spirit of his part.

Some players, particularly the Russians, have found that the observation of animals or of pieces of machinery suggests ways of interpreting a dramatic personality. Generations have called the fox cunning, a dog faithful or pathetic, the panther lithe and cruel, as much because these animals *act* cunning, or faithful, or cruel, as because they are so. The phlegmatic swing of a pendulum, the deadly insistence of a riveter, the clicking efficiency of a calculating machine may suggest the qualities of some human beings. The imaginative actor can find these useful in his characterization.

To be of real help, all the foregoing devices must, of course, be used intelligently. Any one of them may be an aid, but it can be a hindrance. If an effort to relate one of the four fundamental actions to the character he is building, for instance, makes the player engage in just another intellectual exercise—if it causes him to classify his role neatly but to feel nothing new with regard to it—that effort is of very dubious value. If trying to relate oneself to an old horse or a buzzsaw makes one more like an animal or a machine than a man, one's acting aid has failed. Too much intellectualization is bad for any role. The actor must ever leave room for his hunches, for these work directly out of situation to image. He must *experiment with his feelings and see what they bring forth.*

Working on the Inner Feelings of the Role

A truly effective human image on the stage consists of an outward part sensible to the eyes and ears of the spectator; and an inward part, not directly sensible, but profoundly important because it moves the outward part. Without the inward feeling the outward posture and action, however cunningly devised, is nothing but shell.

The means of developing the emotions of a role is a very personal thing. One actor does it by one method, another, in a different way. Each may express considerable surprise when he dis-

covers that the method which has been so successful for himself
is quite useless for another!

Some players start their work of preparation by acting out
those sensible postures and movements of the part which serve as
clues to inward states of emotion, and thus awaken indirectly the
feelings which are appropriate to the postures and movements.
In other words, an actor may note what the author says in the
stage directions about a character's desire to get ahead and about
his ruthless behavior in the presence of other personalities. Now
by playing out his sharp rises and his forward thrusts when other
people are in his presence, the actor may sense also his strange
hesitances and his inclinations to hug the shadows when he does
not need to put on a front, and in this way come *sensuously*, not
intellectually, to a feeling of the dreadful, cowardly fear behind
the man's apparent aggressiveness.

Another actor may arrive at his emotions in a much quieter
way by taking an opposite path from the inside out. He will read
and reread the part, trying to imagine himself in the atmosphere
of the place depicted and in the presence of the other characters
described, and thus enkindle a beginning flame of inward feeling.
This he will blow on with the breath of his mind until it develops
into a big enough fire to force an outward expressiveness.

Probably the best advice one can give the beginning actor is
to use both methods at the same time. That is, he should do much
work from the start in developing the inward thoughts and feelings which look outward; and at the same time he should work
freely with the outward actions which tend to stir the inward feelings. This outward phase should have the help of the director, and
it will receive much guidance from the giving-and-taking behavior
of the other actors. Some day the outward action (probing inward) and the inward feeling (reaching outward) will meet and
ignite a spark for an explosion. This explosion will be inspiration.
In its light the whole role will suddenly become meaningful to the
actor. The moment of the explosion often occurs late in the period
of rehearsals. Not infrequently it comes on the night of dress rehearsal when the actor, recalling his long search for the soul of
his part, suddenly sees himself in costume and makeup. These outward reflections of his soul, coupled with his memory of the action

he has been rehearsing, finally tell him who he is. He is now ready to go onto the stage and show a fully realized individual.

The Use of Personal Memories

Much has been written about the value of the actor's making use of his personal memories for creating truth in a role. Whole systems of playing have been built on this concept of memory. The evidence of its effectiveness for many people is the excellent performance they have given with its use. Proof that the concept, developed into a compelling method, is not absolutely necessary for success is the performance of other actors who have prepared their roles in a different way.

There is no question that what one does on the stage is deeply influenced by the life he has lived. The man who has been a soldier and has seen the horror of a battlefield, perhaps been wounded there himself, will be much more ready to play a part in a war tragedy than the young man who has experienced nothing bloodier than a soccer game. The actress who has lost a brother by illness or has walked a wintry street looking for a job, will be able to draw on resources of emotion for the part of a woman of the world not available to a girl fresh out of finishing school. Nevertheless, each in his own way, however young he is, has had moments in his life which have profoundly moved him, and these can serve him fruitfully as references when he is trying to build up the emotion in his stage character. Each player must do the best he can with what he has. If the beginning actor has a sympathetic and understanding nature, if he has observed others who have lived longer and more fully than he has, and *if he uses his imagination freely*, he can do much to make up for his lack of actual experience.

The Development of the Role

The creation of a human image for the stage can never be said to start at this moment and to end at that. It may have begun years before when one was a participant in some action now scarcely remembered and only faintly resembling the play in which one is engaged today. A substantial part of what one has experienced all the way from childhood to the present time becomes grist for the mill for every role one creates. And the role one is now performing should continue growing to the last evening in which one plays it. The friends one meets and talks with this afternoon; the experiences, good and bad, one has tomorrow morning and tomorrow afternoon; and what one learns from performing the role in the theater—the reactions from the other actors on the stage and the changing responsiveness from the audience—all offer valuable contributions to the part.

Six Reminders for the Young Actor Preparing His Part

For the young man or woman who has not yet had an opportunity to perform many parts the veteran offers several reminders:

1. See your role as a part of a whole design. The role must maintain a right proportion. It must make a fair contribution to the entire dramatic work. Each eager young player is only being normal when he wants to see the messenger, or clerk, or younger brother role which is his appear to be one of the most important elements of the dramatic story. It should be important, of course, but it may not be right for it to stand out as far as the actor would like to make it. The director must be trusted to know to what degree the role should be subordinated to the needs of the other parts.

2. Be patient. Do not attempt to develop the image of your part too quickly. It must be mitred bit by bit with the other images. Since no one can tell in advance just how each role will grow, all must be kept flexible so that changes necessary for the good of the whole can be effected in each. The young actor must not let himself become discouraged if what he has constructed with much loving care has to be reshaped drastically in order that it may be fitted into its rightful place in the total structure. He should remember that the logic which governs the design as a whole may be quite different from that which would be applicable under other circumstances to each of the details viewed separately.

3. Beware of the entanglement of too many devices. The use

of photographs, mood music, inspirational quotations, suggestive properties are good when they are actually helpful. As soon as the actor begins to think more about them than he does about his part he should discard them.

4. Do not let yourself get too much wedded to any one method of working. Pick and choose between the aids available and use that one which seems best for you for the particular play with which you happen to be connected at this time. The theory for a realistic role may not fit a romantic role. The method for building a serious image may not be appropriate at all for a comic one. And so on.

5. Keep a good balance between activeness and thoughtfulness. Don't assume the actor-figure of a chicken running around without a head. Equally important, don't assume the figure of a quiet Buddha. Beware alike of the actor who is never still, and of the one who spends more time sitting down talking about his art than he does on his feet showing what it is!

6. Be sincere. Don't fake. Prepare your part carefully and fully, *always bearing in mind your responsibility to the coming audience.* That audience will want you to be playful, but at the core of the playfulness it will wish to see your respect for the truths of human nature.

VI

⭑

PLAYING THE PART

Projecting the Character from the Stage

AFTER A FIRST STEP of examining the outlines of the character he
wants to portray, then a second step of constructing a mental
image of it, the actor proceeds to develop his concepts by putting
his image into tangible form on the stage. The developmental
process involves a great deal of experimental work—the testing of
the image to see if it will actually call forth those responses from
the observer which it was designed to evoke.

Practically, of course, the building of a mental image and the
making of its visible and audible counterpart cannot be separated.
The two kinds of imagery must flow back and forth, into and out
of each other. The mental image is never valid until it has been
checked out in a physical form, and the physical image has to be
fed and guided constantly by inward ideas. That is why in the
preceding chapter we used the word *phase* in place of *step*.
Thinking and doing must go along together. Even the analytical
part of the work must progress with the others. Not infrequently
on the afternoon before a dress rehearsal, the actor will be struck
by the fact that the motivation of a certain piece of action he has
been doing for the past four weeks is still not quite clear to him
and that it behooves him to look at the script once again in order
to get the question settled in his mind.

When a really new step actually does occur, it is on that evening in which the actor, having run the course of his rehearsals, strides out onto the stage to present his dramatic product to an audience. At this point he cannot experiment. He can no longer look to his director for guidance and criticism or for permission to repeat a scene in order to try to do it differently. Now he is on his own. "This is it!" he tells himself.

At this point he calls upon all his dramatic resources as a performer. He works to make the inward man of his character reveal himself outwardly through visible and audible action intelligible to every spectator in the auditorium. He seeks to show the relation of his role to environmental forces through the medium of clean-cut responses shaped in fundamental and accessory action-patterns. From first to last he gives attention to the sensory requirement of imagery, making rich and vivid by implication the under images which give dramatic meaning to the surface forms. He works for precision, flexibility, and progressive growth, using every part of his pantomimic and vocal instrument to gain his effects. But he is not satisfied when he has completed the bare manifestation of his character. He continues to work on his performance until it possesses not only expressive clarity, but also compulsive persuasion—until the acting of the character has about it a rhythmic grace that draws the audience into it and makes the audience in effect act with it.

Creating the Dramatic Action

Since action is the cornerstone of all dramatic art, the player must think about it all the time. All his efforts at analyzing, visualizing, and projecting a dramatic character on the stage are carried out with a reference to basic activity. They must be aimed at stirring every part of the spectator's receptive and dynamic nature—they should quicken his sense of living.

But what exactly is dramatic action?* Many efforts have been made to define it, but few have been very successful because writers on the theatre have generally failed to recognize a primary

---

* The term is used here in its broad sense, of course, representing not just a single movement of body or voice but the sense of activity throughout the play.

fact. Dramatic action is not one but several things—or, more accurately, perhaps, it is one thing with several aspects. There are at
least three of these: (1) bodily movement, (2) change, and (3)
pursuit, or anticipation, of some kind of adjustment. The first of
these is simple physical motion and the need for it has already
been made clear. Nothing is more deadening to the senses of the
spectator than long dialogue scenes in which two people stand or
sit in one position. An adroit player contrives to employ at least
a little bodily movement in every situation, even in the comparatively static expository passages, not only because a mobile body
in a speaker helps to make what he has to say expressive, but also
because motion of any kind helps to keep the senses of the spectator alert. A skillful player can *suggest* more of bodily activity
than he actually performs, of course, but he must make *some* of
it manifest to supply the clue for the rest.

That "variety is the spice of life" is an old commonplace. It
is to be regretted that young artists in the theatre so often forget
the dramatic truth that lies in that remark. Time and again we see
on the amateur stage the deadly effects of sameness. The actors look
alike; they sound alike. There is no variety in the pantomime of
the single individual, no development in the group movement as
a whole. Everyone talks at the same rate of speed, never altering
by more than a note or two the median pitch of his voice. Everything is flat and monotonous.

When such a condition obtains on the stage, the use of the
first phase of action, bodily movement, is not likely to accomplish
by itself much of the effect of quickening the scene. Usually it
becomes by mere repetition as monotonous as everything else.
Motion unskillfully managed is frequently more deadly than stillness. What the stage cries out for in a situation such as this is
change. The element of change—or *contrast* as it is often called—
lies at the heart of theatrical effect. It challenges the attention of
the onlooker. It prevents his eyes and ears from growing dull. It
keeps the spectator from ever taking any of the impressions for
granted; it makes him alert, alive, and responsive.

When acting is well designed, play-watching becomes an
exciting game. Feeling out the many big and little changes of inflection, pitch, time, and timbre between line and line and speech

and speech; feeling out the varying patterns of gesture between movement and movement and character and character; and feeling out the contrasting volumes, intensities, and emotional overtones of the different scenes as a whole—all these contribute to a stirring experience. Change, skillfully handled, with a keen eye for right proportions, is a tremendous force for the activation of a play.

While the first two phases of dramatic action provide a performance with motion and excitement, the third gives to it a sense of direction. All drama is concerned with the effort of human beings to find an adjustment to something outside of themselves. As long as the sense of search, or pursuit—or anticipation—of that adjustment stays alive, the play is bound to go forward toward the goal of the adjustment. *Pursuit of adjustment* is therefore one of the most valuable elements of dramatic action.

When the human organism is in equilibrium with its environment—when it is completely well-fed and well-housed, unaffected by ambition and envy, and unworried by the state of society around it—it seeks no action for itself. It does not even desire to feel any quickening action in other bodies. It is content to sit quietly without exerting itself in any way. Such a condition, however, rarely occurs. Most of the time, as has already been suggested, man is seeking one, then another, and then still another accommodation with his surroundings. Out of that search springs drama. Plays deal with human hunger for betterment—physical, economic, social, or spiritual—and this hunger works against obstacles in such a way as to make the sense of crisis acute. The playwright usually selects one big problem of adjustment to dominate the whole course of the story, and then works in a number of lesser challenges along the way to make the path of the progress toward the final great solution rough and treacherous. All these points of challenge and settlement the actor exploits for effect.

Another term for the sense of pursuit-of-adjustment in drama is *suspense*. What the actor chooses to call this vital aspect of action does not matter very much if he understands what it means and how to use it. The important thing is for him to remember at all times that his movements and his speech, everything he does, has some bearing upon a problem to be solved. And there are usually two aspects to that problem: the long-range one that gives drive to his role as a whole, and the short-range one that is immediate to the scene. During every moment until the end, even in the lightest, most trivial of passages, the character is being impelled forward by a desire for something he has not yet achieved. As long as the actor can keep alive this sense of pursuit, he maintains suspense. Thus the audience stays interested. The play has action.

The Sense of Reality

Much is said today about reality in acting. Those who favor the concept of an artist mirroring life just as it exists like to quote Aristotle. He stated that drama is an "imitation" of human behavior. With this opinion few of us would quarrel—provided that we rightly interpret that term "imitation." For the classic man of the theater *mimesis* did not mean stark representation. Rather it indicated the faithful depiction of a person's *essential nature*. The theatrical craftsman arrived at this kind of depiction, not by a system of precise copywork, but by capturing an inner truthfulness and by translating this into a sensual form which communicated the truth to a receptive spectator. The form could be naturalistic, or it could be poetic, or even romantic. It possessed truth when it made the spectator feel convinced. Charlie Chaplin "imitated" a dance in the spirit of Aristotle when in *The Gold Rush* he stuck a pair of forks into two rolls and made them move rhythmically on a table. The dance of the rolls had a mimetic reality because the observer was so affected by the movement that he lost the image of the rolls and saw in their stead the feet of human beings.

The key word here is *reality* (not "Realism," because that is only a style). Reality is the truth below the surface of form. "Art" says a modern man of drama, Gordon Craig, "arrives only by design." Acting cannot be an art "when the mind of the actor . . . is less powerful than his emotion." It is mind which probes the meaning of the dramatic role; it is will which makes the artist believe in it. Then it is emotion which gives the warmth which makes the conviction infectious. The final effect is a reality, but it is the kind of reality which is larger and more powerful than what one sees in everyday behavior.

The Actor as Self-Critic

A statement was made early in this book that the actor in performance is two people. One man is the image-maker; the other is the instrumentalist who works out the means for projecting the image to the observer. Now we shall extend the statement about the image-maker and his collaborator, the instrumentalist, by suggesting that every effective actor is not two but *three* persons. The third is the critic. The player needs, of course, to locate himself inside his character and to make this being so much mind of his mind and flesh of his flesh that to all intents on the stage he and the character are one. But the union can never be so absolute as to destroy the separate identity of the consciousness which is managing the process of the playing. Acting is an art; as such it must be ever under the control of an artist. This artist is not the character being portrayed. He is the portrait-maker. This is true in spite of the strange relationship that makes the dramatic portrait and the dramatic portrait-maker, visually speaking, the same individual.

The critical part of the actor is that which accompanies, by imagination, the spectator way out in the darkened auditorium and watches and listens through every moment of the actor's appearance. "Too loud!" the critic part says; or "Not loud enough!" Or, perhaps, "You're falling back into that bad habit of failing to bite off your consonants!" Or "That was a mighty clumsy way of getting into this chair; you'll have to do it better next time!"

The most valuable comments are those that have to do with the playing of emotional passages. Here the critic tells that other side of himself on the stage many helpful things about pitch, intensity, and intelligibility. "Oh, oh—you started this on too high a level," he may say. "Now, how are you going to top it?" Or "This is good identification! You are making the audience feel that you yourself are genuinely moved by the grief of the character you are playing. But, are you sure that you aren't mumbling the

choked-up words to a degree that keeps the audience from understanding what you are saying?" More important still, the critic
may challenge his actor-partner with this question: "Do you
really know what you are trying to do with these lines? Wouldn't
it be wise for you to study them a little more thoroughly before
you attempt to play them again tomorrow night!"

Lynn Fontanne refers to this checker-on-her-performance as
being her "outside eye and ear." Other actors have others names
for it. Whatever they call it, however, they agree upon its necessity. What this critical identity whispers to the mind of the player
does not in any way interfere with the player's concentration on
his role. It no more interferes with the integrity of his acting
than do the silent comments which the painter makes to himself
as he works on his canvas or what the musician says to himself
when he plays his violin. It enhances the concentration because it
guards the artist against confusion.

Art and Showmanship

In his book *To a Lonely Boy*, Arthur Hopkins tells the story of a
once famous but now failing legitimate actor who tries to recoup
his fortunes by appearing in a dramatic sketch in vaudeville.
Despising his associates and the type of audience seated in the
theatre, he is very miserable. He feels he has dropped to the
lowest rungs of the dramatic ladder. Sensing the legitimate actor's
unhappiness, a successful "hoofer" on the same bill tries to con-
sole him, to give him certain pointers on his new medium; but the
actor refuses to listen. He goes on for his sketch, which he plays
in a dignified and condescending manner. The audience refuses to
respond and the actor leaves the stage furious. When the hoofer
seeks to reassure him, the actor replies loftily that "it was over
their heads," whereupon the disgusted vaudevillian retorts with
some spirit: "Maybe they ducked it!"

The moral pointed up by this story might well be considered by those earnest young players who spend endless hours
in practicing *Stanislavsky, Coquelin, Eleanora Duse, Bertolt
Brecht,* or whatnot exercises, and in discussing the ideals of the
actor, but who never quite succeed in affecting an audience.

When the spectators out front fail to respond to the highly introspective utterances delivered from the lofty pinnacles of a dramatic Mount Olympus, the player is apt to blame the spectators. "It was over their heads," the player says. But maybe they ducked it!

An artist whose product can be deposited for preservation in a museum or library can afford to gamble on the future. "If they don't like my work today," he can say to himself, "perhaps they will in twenty years." The painter can do this. So can the composer and the poet. But not the actor. His product must stir an audience now; it must make the spectators cry, and laugh, and hold their breath in anticipation of exciting things *at this time*— or the actor ceases to be an actor. As soon as he loses his audience, his career is finished. No matter how bright and able he is, no matter how sure he is that his methods are right, he will never have a chance to prove it in the future for the very good reason that the future will know nothing of him.

When this rather obvious truth is brought to the mind of the young player, he is often disappointed. "If an actor must always cater to the popular mob," he asks, "where is the chance for experiment, where is the way to improvement? Where is the *art* of acting? Must acting be forever a cheap compromise?" The answer to this last question is, of course, an emphatic "No!" The earnest player must have his ideals and must stick to them without wavering. In order to achieve them he may, and should, experiment freely, aiming always to improve his grasp of character, story, and the philosophical undertones associated with them, and to strengthen his methods for projecting his part. But, here is the fundamental requirement for all his efforts: *the ideals, the experiments, must succeed.* They must meet the challenge of the audience.

Let the player guard against the temptation to refer to those people out front as a "mob." It is true that audiences differ greatly. The general attitude of some is very young; the mood of others more adult. Some audiences want laughter, others want tears; some want story, some character, some want primarily to chew on thoughts. But they are all good audiences. If, because of his particular temperament, the actor finds certain kinds of spectators more congenial than others, he can aim to play for them. But he must not place any too-inflexible walls around his acting or he is likely to limit greatly the opportunities of his career. Once he contracts to do a performance for a certain audience, no matter how different it may be from the kind he prefers, he is bound by honesty to do his best for it. And his "best" cannot be something "over the spectators' heads."

By reason of its invariable demands, acting is, and always has been, an essentially democratic calling. The actor must share with the audience. The actor must work for the audience. He must be in the best sense of the word a showman. From beginning to end he has to sell his product to his onlookers—*make them like it.* And he is able to do this only when he knows the onlookers, their desires, their ways of responding. He must respect their knowledge of good playing and shape his performance in accordance with it. That is showmanship.

If genuine showmanship means not playing above the audience's head, it means, just as truly, not playing beneath its feet. The audience should never be patronized. And the acting should never be indifferent, insufficiently prepared, or given without the full enthusiasm of everyone concerned. The audience must have its money's worth. Anything less than that is dishonesty.

Here are a few rules which contribute to an attitude of good showmanship.

1. *Create an anticipation.* Through announcement or advertising, let your audience know in advance that you are going to give a performance worth coming to the playhouse to see.

2. *See that the audience is seated comfortably.* Any kind of physical discomfort—improper heating in the auditorium, hard or dirty seats, difficulty in seeing the stage—will ruin the effect of the performance.

3. *Eliminate distractions.* See that there are no extraneous noises, no light-leaks in the auditorium, no unshielded lights from the stage shining into the eyes of the spectators.

4. *See that the surroundings on the stage are fitted to the*

acting. The setting may be very simple, but what there is must be neat and in good taste. If only curtains are used, see that they are clean and that they hang straight. Be sure that no objects are lying around that are not supposed to be there.

5. *Never keep the audience waiting.* Start the performance promptly, and see that the scenes follow each other swiftly, with no unnecessary pauses. Waiting time for the audience is dead time.

6. *Show a good presence all the while you are in view of the audience.* Enter and leave the stage with the same vitality you use in the rest of the performance. Do not even start to drop your presence until you are entirely out of view. If, as a prologue or a master of ceremonies, you must make an announcement, come on with a positive air, speak clearly and efficiently, and step aside with the same air. If you are tired or have a toothache, do not let the audience know it.

7. *Never apologize.* Do your best, and you can be reasonably sure that the audience will like you. If you honestly do not feel you can give the people their money's worth, you should not be in the theatre at all. An apology accomplishes nothing. If you are unprepared, sick, or embarrassed—and show it—spectators will not pat you encouragingly on the back; they will go home.

8. *Remember always that show business is for the audience, not you.* If you are having a good time along with the audience, that is fine. But the audience comes first. Acting simply for vanity, or for "personal development," is not real show business in any sense.

It may be argued that some of the actions listed, such as the advertising, the seating of the audience, and the cleaning of the stage do not belong among the usual functions of the actor. This is quite true. Nevertheless the actor should be *concerned about them;* he should insist that they are done by somebody. If the stage is dusty and no one else will touch it, he should be willing to borrow a broom and sweep it himself. The actor need not be unpleasant about bad conditions, but he should be firm about seeing that they are rectified. He should be just as insistent about cooperation on the part of environmental elements as the scenic artist may and should be that the setting which he creates is well filled by eloquent action. All elements should work together as a team with a single purpose of pleasing an audience just as fully as it possibly can.

The Effective Actor

Acting is one of the most rewarding of activities when it is pursued with intelligence and vigor. It demands vitality; physical stamina is a prime requisite. It demands imagination; the ability to parrot alone is not enough. But above everything else, acting demands a large, enthusiastic, basically unselfish spirit. The truly great actor holds his audience in affection. He likes to please it— whether it is made up of children or sophisticates, whether it is dressed in street clothes, evening clothes, or plain overalls. At times he may disagree with it. But he will never quarrel with it; he will never ignore it. To all the fine people out front, he is a resolute leader, a humble servant, and an intimate companion in adventure.

VII

✳

A QUESTION OF STYLE

Dramatic Style

DRAMATIC STYLE is the manner in which a play is composed, mounted, and performed. It is expressed in patterns of words, tone, movement, and pictorial shapes all viewed from a single imaginative point of view. It includes, besides the written dialogue and stage directions, the scenery, costumes, lighting, and the acting. Style is determined partially by current trends in the theatre, and partially by the personal temperament of the playwright and his interpreters. In this present age of experimental variety in all fields of art, individuality is apt to be a greater factor than fashion in dramatic style.

If a play were written and then executed throughout by a single craftsman, style in the theatre would not be a serious problem. The one great master artist would naturally maintain in all the parts a unified viewpoint—his own. But playmaking is a group activity. A number of different people, sometimes with quite different natures and experiences, are involved in the complicated process of building a show for the stage. Consequently, dramatic variation is ever faced with the question of how several elements of design can be brought together in a single expressive style. In the modern theatre, the author is usually recognized as the basic style-setter. Next to him is the director. If the author composes his play in such a way as to allow his interpreters some margin of choice in the rendering, the director usually assumes the responsibility of deciding just how the general style established by the playwright will be narrowed into a specific style for the particular production he has been engaged to supervise. The director is the "style-boss" of the rendering. With him work all the other artists—the scenic designer, the costume designer, the lighting expert, the sound-effects man, and the player—each offering suggestions to round out the plan. But the director makes the final decisions with respect to the mode of interpretation; and he gets his style-clues from the author's script.

Certain fundamental aspects of style are always fairly clear. Is the play realistic or formal? Is it earthy or fantastic? Such first questions the actor should be able to answer for himself without consulting anyone else. The director will expect the player to take some initiative in the matter of laying the first broad outlines of the performance, and then to look to him for guidance in the more specific details of style.

Tears and Laughter

The primary question the actor usually asks about the role he has been assigned to interpret is, is it serious or comic? Upon his answer to that question depends the basic form of his attack. One approach will be more subjective, with greater emphasis on mood; the other more objective, with greater stress on surface effect.

In general, the spectator tends to share his sympathy with a tragic character, to enter into his mind with his own thoughts, and so by imagination to participate in the character's experience of fear, grief, tremulous hope, and despair. That is, the emotions of the spectator become identified with the emotions of the character he observes. But those emotions develop slowly. If they become deeply rooted, they also change slowly. Consequently, the pace of a serious play is usually unhurried. Time must be allowed for each feeling to be established; or to be modulated logically, before the situation is permitted to take any new turn. The actors who perform the play therefore speak and move with a certain deliberation, and they do this most effectively in a stage setting designed for maximum concentration. Tragedies are commonly enacted in small pools of light surrounded by symbolical shadows so arranged as to focus the attention of the audience steadily on the faces of the players. The bodily movement tends to be conservative, suggestive of strong urges held in check with difficulty. Since most of the speech and pantomime is delivered at a fairly deliberate tempo, every detail of the action in a tragedy must count dramatically. Therefore the actor's performance must be designed carefully and precisely in all its parts so that there may be no distortion.

Comedy tends to be more intellectual in its impact than tragedy. The broader the comedy enacted on the stage, the more the spectator's emotion stays outside of it. Instead of sitting on the front of his seat, as he does at the performance of a serious play, reaching forward, as it were, to the area occupied by the figures who tug at his emotions, he leans back in his chair and from a superior distance laughs at the funny, but often lovable, fools who cavort before him. Of course, just how much he does this depends upon the type of characters he is watching. If they are farcical, he may keep his distance absolute. On the other hand, if the comic effect is built less on straight grotesqueness of shape and relationship, and more on the fond portrayal of those little human frailties which have always been exasperating yet dear to him, the spectator may temper his impulse to view apart by a parallel impulse to participate sympathetically. Laughter and tears often spring out of the same situation, and the actor not infrequently must play for both of them at the same time.

In general, however, it may be said that comedy requires a freer and a quicker style of performance than tragedy. The more farcical it is—the more it depends for its effect on surface shapes and relationships rather than on fundamental emotion—the faster it can be played, and the broader and more obvious may be its basic treatment of interactions between people. There is little need for subtleties; not much, if anything, has to be held in check. Feelings are expressed openly without shame. For farcical comedy, the player makes a plentiful use of physical action and facial expression. For this kind of performance the designer provides a stage flooded with light, and in this full illumination the elements of thrust and counterthrust between the various mirth-provoking figures are projected clearly and fully. The costumes of the actors and the setting behind them are made bright and cheerful. Everything in view of the spectator conspires to turn his thoughts outward rather than inward. The technique of comedy is the technique of surfaces.

The Playing of Comedy

There is a widespread notion in amateur playing groups that the acting of serious roles requires ability, but that anybody can do comedy. While the reverse of this statement is not wholly valid, it approaches considerably nearer the truth than the idea just stated. Perhaps the ultimate test of an actor is his ability to play movingly one of the great tragic parts. But, in general, those who have had experience in both kinds of acting will say that it is far easier to play a serious role adequately than it is to do justice to an equivalent part in comedy.

It is true that anyone can imitate the behavior of a fool. It is not difficult to mount the stage and to strut and "mug" before an audience. The actor who does it may have a rare good time, and he may even get some of his fellow actors—if they are in the same stage of dramatic development as he—to laugh with him. But all that capering means very little to the audience unless the performer has a real sense of what is funny from the viewpoint of out-front. There is a very significant difference between shenanigans and true comedy.

A sense of comedy may be developed to a considerable extent. Practice sharpens perceptions; experience shows what will work and what will not. But the inner core of the comic sense is intuitive. One has it, or one does not have it; and if one does not have it, no amount of pursuit will capture it. A good many otherwise fine actors, with years of playing behind them, cannot do comedy simply because they lack that fundamental sense. What constitutes it? Several factors are involved, but perhaps the most important one is a sensitive, unerring awareness of proportions. Seeing always in his mind's eye the normal ideal, the comedian senses in a character or situation those variations which suggest the grotesque or ridiculous; and he feels, in a way no one can explain, just how far these variations may be exploited to keep them in the sphere of laughter without allowing them to go over the thin line into the realm of pain or distastefulness. To a degree beyond the typical player of serious roles, the comedian makes himself a partner with the audience, letting it in on his secrets, and shaping and timing his performance in accordance with its responses.

The able comedian does not play *at* his audience, he plays *with* it. But he manages it. He regards the audience as if it were a spirited horse; he gives it plenty of head but never lets it get completely out of rein. And he is very patient with it. If it does not laugh where he expects it to, he does not get upset; quietly, he changes his line of attack and tries a new angle. He experiments with a slightly more vehement, or a more casual, manner, with a little more action or a little less, a faster tempo or a slower one. He tries some novelties; or he decides that the novelties do not work well with the particular audience to which he is playing, so he simplifies his performance, makes it "straighter."

The comedian knows that the audience will laugh, but only after a warming-up. It must become acquainted with the characters and the situation. For that reason, he may work for chuckles first and let them develop gradually into laughs as the play progresses. He is very careful not to spill his precious bag of tricks too hurriedly. While never ignoring the moment-by-moment responses along the way, he keeps his eye on the "big points" and builds up the responsiveness of the audience to them. Those are the climaxes, the explosive points; there the actor kicks over the final effect and precipitates the roar.

During the period of the laughter, the player usually "freezes"; that is, he remains perfectly still in order not to disturb the laugh. Freezing is the stock device for the cultivation of laughs. However, in those situations in which the risibility of the audience is excited by a sudden expression of physical or mental discomfort, such as embarrassment, the player may decide to break the rule of "holding the picture" and, instead, to feed the laugh with some comic pantomime designed to intensify the impression of discomfort. As the laugh dies out, the actor resumes the main line of speech or movement obtaining before the explosion took place. Knowing just where to cut the laugh is as much a test of the comedian's talent as knowing how to set it into motion. If he cuts too soon, he is likely to make an important line of dialogue inaudible and thus cause the audience to smother its laughter unnaturally. If he cuts too late, he will cause a drag. In general, he tries to time the "freeze" or the "feeding" action in such a way as to give the laugh full opportunity to reach a peak; then he resumes speaking precisely at that point in the decline of the laugh when his words may be made understandable without undue effort.

The trick of applying just the right final stimulus in order to precipitate a laugh is chiefly a matter of intuition sharpened by experience. Not much can be learned about it from a textbook. Here, however, for those who are interested, are a few of the mechanical means commonly employed:

Markedly changing the quality of the laugh line—increasing the stress, dropping the tone, speeding the tempo, or retarding the tempo

Pausing just before the laugh line

Pausing just after the laugh line

Using a sudden vocal or pantomimic expression of discomfort—a grunt or a cry, a jump or a squirming

A sudden broad change of facial expression

One of the supreme tests of a capable player of comedy lies in his sense of timing: when to pause, when to speak, how fast to speak, when to precipitate the laugh, when to break it. He must have an accurate sense of rhythm adjusted to meet the surges of the audience's attentiveness clearly on the crest. The timing will vary for different types of plays. As a rule, light comedy is played more briskly than character comedy, and farce comedy faster than light.

Another test of the true comedian lies in his ability to make himself part of a team with his fellow actors. Without them he can do very little. Comic effects are always intensified, and almost always conditioned, by the reactive behavior of the other people on the stage. In fun-poking scenes, it is not the poker, but the "goat," who draws the laugh. Consequently the factor of response is absolutely essential in comedy. Moments may be found in serious drama in which characters retire, as it were, into their own corner to commune with themselves; but such moments are almost wholly absent from the lighter plays. The idea of comedy is built upon the fundamental notion of give and take, and the take is dramatically just as important, and frequently more important, than the give.

Here are a few precepts for the young comedian:

Build for your laughs.

Set them off clearly, and cut them on time.

Be prepared to go on with the play if the laugh does not come as expected.

Do not let anyone see you enjoying your own jokes; leave the response to the audience.

Do not ruin your comic effects by seeming to strain for them. Make the effects look accidental.

Do not lose patience with the audience.

Conserve the attention of the audience. Do not wear out the attention on the smaller points, but save it for the big points, "the funniest moments in the scene."

Study well your response to the lines and pantomime of the other players, and their reactions to yours. Strive to build up all effects through the action of the team as a whole.

The Playing of Comedy Illustrated

The comedy scenes included in this book represent several extremely different styles. The student actor would do well to look them over and to compare them. *The Importance of Being Earnest* is a play of situation; but its chief appeal lies in its witty lines. Its comedy is the comedy of brightly glittering surfaces, so it should certainly be played in a manner best suited to make the lines sparkle. Not much time should be spent on the development of characterization; the actors should recognize their function as graceful figures in a comedy of manners and perform accordingly —quickly, neatly, with an air of sophisticated elegance. The dramatic naïveté of the girl who lives in the country would in no way lessen the cool brilliance of her conduct. The garden in which Cecily and Gwendolen compete with each other for the right to own the illusive Ernest would doubtless be frankly decorative— nonrealistic, stagey. The actions of the young ladies should then be like the scenery, precise, shiny, and symmetrical. The behavior of the two young men in the other scene from the same play should be similarly artificial.

Suppressed Desires is a different type of play. Much more natural and human, it primarily exploits a situation. Nevertheless, that situation has a meaning only as it is seen in terms of the emotional responses of the figures who move through it. Therefore, a performance of this play must take time to probe a little deeper beneath the surface. Henrietta must be expectant; Henrietta must be surprised; Henrietta must be hurt—believably so. Stephen must be a harassed but patient husband, warm, affectionate, and likeable. He dearly loves to tease his wife, but he has no intention of seeking any really cruel revenge for what she has made him undergo. The characters and the story of *Suppressed Desires* are pointed up a little to make them effective, but the total impression is rather natural. A suitable performance of this play would make the audience say, while it laughed, "things like this really happen!"

The comic effect of *Joint Owners in Spain* is the kind that is derived from watching the behavior of simpleminded people worked up over a problem of adjustment which could be settled quickly by more sophisticated persons, but which requires from these people a maximum exercise of their mental resources. Miss Dyer and Mrs. Blair are grown women. Age, however, has made their minds childlike. They are faced with a crisis—a very real crisis. This room is their home, and somehow they must work things out so that their contrasting personalities will complement each other without a prospect of future warfare. What they do about trying to resolve their crisis they do earnestly and sincerely.

The whole situation may seem ridiculous to us, but for them it is very serious. The actresses who portray the two old ladies should therefore present them in this spirit of dedication. The more serious they are, the more amusing they will seem to the onlooker.

The scene from *Finian's Rainbow* is sheer farce with overtones of fantasy. Here again the comic elements are centered in two childlike minds which have met each other in conflict. The leprechaun Og wants the crock of gold. The little business-promoter Finian does not wish Og to get his hands on it. Their conversation, set in the playful frame of the play as whole, is quite logical. Affected by whiskey, the spellbinding night, and their virile temperaments, it is also quite emotional. The spectator laughs. The laughter is given an edge because it is spiked by a feeling of suspense. Which of the loveable contestants in this miniature arena, the observer waits to find out, will win.

The principal charm of a piece like *Tovarich* is in its characterization. Prince Mikail and Grand Duchess Tatiana are two loveable children—but children quite different from those who inhabit the foregoing scenes. Buffeted by misfortune, exiled in a country far distant from their home, they are still lighthearted, even gay. We laugh at them and we admire them, both at the same time. In the selection included here, Mikail and Tatiana speak in short, quick speeches. A performance of these characters should, therefore, be light and deft. The chief quality which would probably be exploited is the unexpectedness of their turns of thought, and the consequent unpredictability of their actions. This would be the method especially suited to Tatiana. Everything she does is by bright intuition. There is never any deliberation. She moves and speaks on impulse. The less one can guess what she will do next, the more one will like her.

One of the factors which makes the characters in both *Joint Owners in Spain* and *Finian's Rainbow* so fascinating is their humanity. The people portrayed are exaggerations, it is true, but they are fundamentally real. The tearful sufferer, the earnest busybody, the practical little businessman, and the wistful idealist trying to save the integrity of his fellow leprechauns, remind us of people we know among our friends. To some extent, they are ourselves. The actors are wise, therefore, if they present their

personations sympathetically. The more they call to mind actual
people the funnier they will seem.

The Way of the World, in contrast with the foregoing
scenes, is not childlike at all. The two characters who face each
other here are completely worldly. They battle with their wits at
the top of their minds. They have an affection for each other—they
wouldn't be so interested in meeting and arguing with each other
if they didn't!—but the verbal battle here is not conducted as if it
involved earthshaking affairs. Rather it is a game. Each is determined to win of course; but neither intends to shed blood over it.
Half the contest is over which of the two persons can outdo the
other in gracefulness.

The important thing to note about the two comic scenes from
Shakespeare is that they are so different. One emphasizes character, the other action. The quality of the acting in these scenes, as
in all the others, will be judged largely by the inventiveness of the
players—the little looks and gestures used to supplement the basic
stage business already indicated in the script. The amused or fearful way in which the people glance at each other, the pauses of
agonized indecision, the cries of astonishment, the sighs, sobs,
squeals, and groans, and the many little actions of voice and body
which point to comic climax, or anticlimax—few of these are described specifically in a script. They are color touches which must
be worked out by the actors. And there is no set pattern for them.
They come to the actor's performance chiefly as the result of impulse—developed by an extended experience in the playing of
comedy, and pointed up by the watchful eye of a director who
himself has a mature comic sense. If six performances of any one
of the selections mentioned were given by six different pairs of
able actors under six different directors, the result would be six
different interpretations of the same play, all of which would
probably be equally true to the basic spirit of the written script,
and equally funny to the audience.

Style in Plays of the Past

The players who desire to perform the classic plays of the past
must be prepared to employ several distinct techniques, all of

them rather unlike the typically realistic acting of today. In general, the plays of the past are constructed on a more formal plane than the modern pieces. Most of them are in verse. The speeches tend to be long, judged by our present-day standards, and the sentences within them are commonly extended and sonorous. The movement designed to accompany the lines is usually of a "studied" nature. Modern realistic plays try to seem casual. Most of the classics do not. Everything in them is devised to create, not an "everyday," but a heroic impression—an impression of grand passion, or grand laughter, in dramatic figures of more than ordinary proportions.

This effect of magnificence in its most exalted form is found in the dramas of the Greeks. Aeschylus, Sophocles, and Euripides wrote their tragedies only about the most elevated men and women in Greek legend, persons who would correspond roughly to our George Washingtons, Andrew Jacksons, Napoleon Bonapartes and Joans of Arc. These plays were performed in huge outdoor amphitheatres where any little intimacies between actor and spectator were wholly out of the question. Consequently, everybody concerned, author, principal player, and supporting chorus, had to work for largeness of effect. The actors were selected chiefly for the strength and quality of their voices. Since the central technical problem throughout was projection, the performers were unable to turn their bodies very much to the side or rear. For that reason, the pantomime was kept to a minimum. What there was of it was doubtless large and deliberate, in keeping with the measured cadence of the dialogue.

The people of a more leisurely civilization than ours were perfectly content with plays presented in the manner just described. The playgoers of today, however, are a more restless lot. Accustomed in their daily lives to hurry and scurry, they demand greater action in the theatre. Consequently, when the Greek tragedies are performed in our time they have to be modified somewhat. Commonly, some of the very long speeches have to be trimmed down, and all the dialogue must be loosened up by means of movement. Fortunately, this modification for greater activity is made possible by the fact that our theatres are smaller than those of the Greeks. The fact invites greater flexibility, more subtlety. However, the actor trained in the modern mode must be careful not to informalize his rendering of the Athenian classics too far or he will end in disaster. The exalted verse of Aeschylus simply cannot be interpreted as one would the prose lines of a present-day Tennessee Williams. Heroic dialogue will always demand a certain grandiloquence of delivery and broad, clearly designed gestures.

The plays discussed so far are the tragedies. The acting of the comedies allows the player considerably more freedom. The compositions of Aristophanes offer some fine opportunities for broad action, even slapstick. The player can experiment with a variety of techniques, and he can invent freely. All is grist for the mill. He can interplay with the audience, and, if he is really clever, he can even do a bit of improvising in an appropriate situation without any fear of violating the spirit of the play. The original comedians doubtless took many liberties, and, if the author were living today, he would probably be the first to suggest that our actors insert some stage business of their own. However, he would insist that whatever additions in the nature of horseplay were put into the action should be thoroughly in keeping with the rest of the comedy, and that they have the approval of the director who is staging the play.

There have been several attempts in recent years to interpret the plays of Shakespeare in "modern dress," with a style of realistic acting matching the clothes. Aside from their novelty, these experiments have not been very successful. The reason is easy to find: such dramas as *Hamlet, Macbeth,* and *Twelfth Night* are written in a kind of language which does not harmonize with present-day costumes and the small, casual gestures that belong with them. Shakespeare, like his Athenian predecessors, chose for his heroes men and women of highborn station, and he set their dialogue in blank verse. Consequently, the only fitting interpretation of his scripts lies in heroic speech and heroic movement. In that respect, the acting of Shakespearean characters is similar to that of Greek. But Shakespeare demands more variety. There can be much less in the way of general sameness between figure and figure, and scene and scene. As a matter of fact, one of the chief factors for which the Elizabethan playwright is noted is his rich contrasts. Personalities diametrically opposed to each other are brought together in conflict—Hamlet and Polonius, Othello and Iago;—and passages of entirely different mood are made to follow each other in an everchanging pattern. The tenderest kinds of love scenes follow scenes of murder, and both are broken by comic interludes bordering on sheer slapstick. Yet all is unified by poetic drive and a grandeur of feeling which infects even the smallest, apparently most insignificant, detail.

The playing of Elizabethan drama demands, therefore, a large, but controlled, swing of voice and body designed to fit the sweeping spirit and rhythm of the written lines. But, song-like and dance-like though they may be, they should never cease to be warmly human. It is at this point that many so-called "Shakespearean actors" go astray. They become so obsessed by the outward tonal and pictorial aspects of their performances that they forget to create the fundamental images. A "Shakespearean actor" who gets to love for their own sake the sound of his voice and the posturing of his body is ready to be retired from the stage. Shakespeare's plays must be presented for vastness of effect, but at the same time, with great sensitivity. Above all things, the actor must ever remember that these compositions of the Bard of Avon are good theatre pieces. They are more than mere vehicles for pretty recitation. They were written as vigorous dramas and comedies, and they must be presented today in such a way as to fulfil their original purpose—to entertain.

Many of the plays of the seventeenth and early eighteenth centuries—especially those which lend themselves to revival now— were planned for highly artificial productions. The actors who performed the works of Molière, Corneille, and Racine in France, and Wycherley, Congreve, and their contemporaries in England were given a rigorous training in ballet steps and gestures. Their costumes were highly decorative, and the watchword for all stage action in such plays was *elegance*. There was a fixed manner of entrance for every type of character, and set rules for standing and walking, for sitting and rising, for salutations, bows, curtsies, the use of the fan, and the rest of the graceful business accompanying the lines. When these plays of a courtly period are revived today, they need to be presented with the same kind of elegance. Even the sprightly comedies of Molière require it. When they are acted casually, they lose their satirical bite. They have no flavor; they seem flat.

In the periods that followed the early eighteenth century, the highly mannered style of playing just described developed slowly and somewhat unevenly toward more softened forms. It would be a mistake, however, to imagine that the acting of the comedies of Sheridan and Goldsmith, and the melodramas of the numerous popular authors (on both sides of the Atlantic) ceased to be artificial. Up to the end of the nineteenth century when a wave of "reform" swept the European, the British, and the American theatres, most of the playwriting and acting were frankly stagey. This fact is often forgotten by many otherwise intelligent directors and actors, as well as scenic artists, when they try to revive the mannered plays of the past.

If one is ever in doubt as to the style in which any of the earlier pieces should be performed, and no historical data concerning the original production of it are available, one has only to glance at the form of the dialogue. Natural lines require a natural interpretation. Artificial speech demands a correspondingly mannered type of delivery. The answer to the question of style is very simple. Poetry clearly expects a rhythmic translation, both in tone and movement. Lifelike writing needs lifelike acting; mannered writing needs mannered acting. The mode throughout must be unified.

Style in Plays of Today

Since the experiments with an "easier," less formal type of staging initiated by André Antoine, Otto Brahm, and Constantin Stanislavsky in Europe, and later by their followers in England, Ireland, and the United States, the modern stage has been dominated by a style called Realism. The fundamental purpose of every dramatic craftsman who works in this mode is, more or less, to copy nature, to make the imitations set before the audience "seem the actual thing." Instead of allowing his audience to see openly the technical devices of his art, and instead of exploiting these means for their own theatrical value, he tries always to "hide his tricks" so that the audience will not see them. The objective is complete illusion—to make the audience say, "How artless, how lifelike!"

In recent years, a good many playgoers have demonstrated some dissatisfaction with a steady diet of Realism. In response, a few playwrights and producers have begun to experiment again with other forms. It is too soon yet to know if any of these newer styles, which collectively are called Presentative—in contrast to the Realistic or Representative—will develop into a movement. Since the motion pictures have shown felicity in getting close-up glimpses of human behavior which the stage can never hope to match, the chances are that in the years to come the stage will gradually drift away from the intimacies of Realism back toward a more openly designed kind of Presentation. Verse, or poetic prose, may take the place of dialogue modeled on everyday speech, and the accompanying pantomime may lay greater stress on movement inspired by the dance.

One of the principal revolts against modern Realism is embodied in a style called Expressionism. It is commonly defined as the distortion of outward form in order to bring out, or "express," inward truth. The insane man in the film, *The Cabinet of Dr. Caligari,* sees the walls of rooms and streets crowding in on him. The spectator actually sees the slanting buildings, and thus arrives at a direct understanding of the insane man's phobia. Yank, in the play *The Hairy Ape,* sees the dressed-up figures along Fifth Avenue as if they were decorative manikins, all alike. The actors who do these parts are costumed and made to move like manikins. Therefore the audience also views them as Yank does. Many of the so-called "absurdist" plays of today use a form of expressionistic presentation.

Expressionistic acting carried to the extreme tends to be noisy, staccato, and often monotonous. Its chief weakness lies in the fact that it unveils too much. It leaves nothing inside its characters to be discovered by the active imagination of the audience. Expressionism seems to serve best when it is employed not in a pure state but as an element of other styles. Touches of it are used to advantage in the staging of many different kinds of plays, even those which are primarily Realistic. Some modified bits of suggestive Expressionism might well be employed, for example, in the playing, setting, and directing of all the scenes, both new and old, in this book (though they need not be).

If the young actor attempts to learn the names of all the "isms" current today, and especially if he tries to find a precise definition of each, he will probably succeed only in bewildering himself. Any sharp differentiation between styles is not very important anyway, because modern playwrights often blend several styles together in one composition; and no expert, including the author himself, can tell clearly exactly where Naturalism ends and Impressionism, or Expressionism, or Surrealism begins. If the player has a sensitive feeling for the kind of interpretation a new script demands, and if he is prepared to proceed accordingly, he does not have to have any special vocabulary to describe his method. He can simply demonstrate it. If, however, he insists upon having words to discuss his style, he may find the fan-shaped chart on the following page convenient for his needs. The point at the bottom, marked "Realism," is the point of the absolutely photographic imitation of life. One of the branching lines, marked "Classicism," stands for style controlled by reason, that is, fixed rules. The opposite line, marked "Romanticism," denotes the area of freely imaginative experiment, ungoverned by rules. The long curved line at the top, marked "Abstraction," stands for all that vague region of style that seeks to get away from Realistic imitation. Within the four limits listed are areas which might be termed, Modified Realism, Modified Classicism, Modified Romanticism, and Modified Abstraction. Where these areas touch each other the student of style can plot such hybrid modes as Classical Realism, Romantic Realism, Classical Abstraction, and Romantic Abstraction. Nearly all of the numerous common "isms" fit into this diagram somewhere, closer to one or another of the borders, or perhaps just about in the center. The diagram serves as a convenient catchall and spares the person who uses it the necessity of making any too exact descriptions of a particular style. Concerning a dramatic design he can say simply "This is two or three steps away from pure Realism, and it inclines to be Romantic"—or "Classical." But, let it be repeated, the ability to sense style and to use style is far more important than the ability to name it.

A DIAGRAM OF STYLE

Such special modes as Impressionism, Expressionism, or Surrealism can be regarded as subdivisions of this plan inclining toward one or another of the boundaries.

Stage, Radio, Television, and Screen

Not exactly a question of style, but closely associated with it in a number of technical respects, is the problem of adapting method to medium. The player who is studying this manual is presumably acting on the stage. In this age of constant shifting about, however, it is not inconceivable that he may sometime be called upon to appear over the air or to do some work before the camera. Radio, television, and screen acting are, of course, as specialized in their fields as stage acting is in its field. In a limited space it would be impossible to set down any fixed directions for the management of the three newer mediums. However, a brief comparison of general requirements might serve to point out problems of technique which must be solved when the player goes from one kind of dramatic performance to another.

The stage actor performs directly, "in the flesh," before his audience. The people whom he strives to affect are scattered out in front of him; some are just ten feet away, but some may be as far from him as a hundred feet—or even more. For every one of those people out there, the distant as well as the near, he must make his words and pantomime intelligible. Therefore, he is forced to build up his movements and stretch his voice so that they will reach out and stir all of the audience, including the last man seated in the far corner of the balcony. A part of the problem of projection is solved, it is true, by simple clarity. Unessential, cluttering gestures are omitted; the actor enunciates his words carefully, giving full value to the vowel sounds, and biting down on the consonants. Thus it becomes unnecessary for him to swing his arms wildly or to shout. In order to make himself understood he does not—as some young players seem to think—have to "ham"; nevertheless, because of the requirements of space, all acting from a stage is compelled to be to some extent exaggerated. From the snarling of a mob to the softest whisper between lovers, every moment of stage acting is touched with bravura.

In the mediums of radio, television, and screen, the problem of projection just described is absent, for machinery takes over that function. Consequently, the player in these fields can work with much greater intimacy. His speech may be natural and unforced, and, except for the rhythmical orderliness, his pantomime in television and screen is just about the same as that seen in everyday life. In their first appearance before a microphone or camera, actors trained only for the stage commonly seem affected. It is difficult for them to drop their habits of large gesture and raised, clipped speech. Even when the audio-engineer reduces by means of his dials the gross volume of the actor's voice, the actor's speech still sounds unnatural—"like an actor's rather than a human being's." If he works in films, a similar remark is apt to be made about his playing. Considerable practice is required before the stage actor can learn how to tone down his whole performance without flattening it out entirely.

Though by comparison with stage acting, acting in the three newer mediums may seem very cozy, no one must assume that it is any easier. Between the player in these more intimate fields and his audience stands a vast amount of machinery. In order to get his vibrant thoughts and pulsing feelings through all that lifeless mass of engineering to the mind and the heart of the man he wishes to touch, he must have extraordinary courage and vitality, and a great deal of knowledge concerning the technical demands of his medium. He has none of the special freedom enjoyed by the stage actor. From the moment he steps before his instruments, his movements are caged by chalk marks and focal distances, and his voice is directed by microphones which are controlled by the hands of other men. His words and his actions can be transmitted only if he plays with care within the limits of his cage. While he is trying to express his part with sincerity, he must also keep his thoughts on lines of sight and sound while guarding himself from falling into the countless pitfalls of distortion.

Some of those who perform over the mechanical channels here mentioned glance with envy at the apparent freedom of the stage. But when they themselves try to play on a platform before a live and fickle audience, they usually find that the freedom for which they yearned is an illusory one. The stage has as many special requirements as the other mediums. There is, for instance, the necessity for sustaining one's performance over a period of time, rather than through the shorter scenes characteristic of the mechanical mediums, and the compulsion to change, develop, and build up accurately to the right climaxes without any guidance from a director during the actual time of playing. And there is ever present the problem of projection. The actor who comes to the stage straight from the camera and microphone is very likely to give a performance which, compared with the work of his theatre-trained colleagues, seems unnaturally quiet, even insipid. When he realizes in time that his voice and pantomime are soft, and he tries to make compensation for his lack of suitable magnitude, he is quite apt to go to the other extreme and to rant. It takes considerable experience to learn that one can speak and move in an exaggerated manner and still be subtle.

An actor specializing in any one of the four fields is fortunate if he can have some experience in one or more of the others. The change of work will give him new perspectives for his own medium. From sightless radio he will learn how actively expressive the voice alone can be, how much it can suggest of movement through tonal design alone. From the films and television he can discover new values in facial change, especially with respect to the eyes, and how much can be indicated by pantomimic details rightly placed. From the living theatre he will gain priceless knowledge of how his efforts are affecting an audience, and how he can alter and develop his techniques in order to secure from that body of playgoers out front the maximum of response.

Whatever may be the surface differences in acting on the stage, and in radio, television, and the cinema, let the player remind himself constantly that the basic principles for all four mediums are the same. The actor must create images. These images must be active. They can be active only if the actor himself feels the vital stir of his muscles—even when, as in the case of radio, his body cannot be actually seen by the listener. He must characterize his art in order to make it warmly human. And he must employ some kind of style which will give his audience a key to the viewpoint it should have for the performance as a whole. The players of the different mediums, however divergent may be their superficial methods, are all members of the same craft.

VIII

✳

VOCATION OR AVOCATION

Wanting to Be an Actor

WHAT DOES, or can, a young man or woman who has taken a course of study in acting do with his training? This chapter will give some suggestions.

There is an old saying that all the people in the world may be divided into opposing groups, such as the primitive and the civilized, the blonds and the brunets, the rich and the poor; but that the greatest division that can be made is between those individuals who like to act and those who do not. Then there is a second part to the saying which affirms that all who do not want to act are either dead or crazy!

The point of this twofold aphorism is that the desire to appear on a stage before an audience is such a natural part of human nature that the urge does not by itself mark any person as being uniquely qualified to make a career of it. If everyone who wanted to become a professional theatre man actually followed his compulsion there would be very few people left to be audience! Circumstances of various kinds prevent more than just so many from turning their compulsions into a vocation.

Because the commercial playhouses choose for employment certain people and not others does not mean that they use all the trained persons in the field. No actor should feel that he has necessarily failed as an artist because he is without a contract on

146

Broadway or in Hollywood. Fortunately there are several interesting, quite honorable substitutes. Some of the civic playhouses across the country are now employing paid actors. In the future there will be more. There are considerably better opportunities for actors turned directors. For those for whom a salaried position is not so important as simply the pleasure of working, there are the nonprofessional community theatres. Nearly every town in the United States has at least one of these. A rough estimate indicates that there are more than 20,000 of them, some with well-deserved reputations for the excellent productions which they present.

The best way to associate oneself with the theatre and to have assurance of making a living at the same time is to be a teacher. The great advantage of this kind of occupation is that one can stay continuously busy; there are no long waits between jobs. The old notion that when one becomes an instructor in drama one forever severs connection with the professional world and enters a kind of scholarly monastery is no longer true. A great many veteran actors spend nine productive months in each year handling school or college playhouses, then join fellow Equity players in summer stock companies during the other three. This is not quite the same as working in the professional theatre twelve months of the season, it is true. However, the actor who divides his time this way is often, practically speaking, just as well off as the man who stays "professional" the year round. The man who insists on working in professional playhouses only is usually lucky if he can count on three good months of employment out of the twelve!

For The Person Who Wishes to Make a Career of Acting

The young man or woman who is determined to make a career of acting should recognize fully the gamble involved. The work will be interesting when he has it. The people he will meet and the materials with which he will deal will be continuously challenging. Glamour—of this he will probably find rather little. At least the kind of glamour that has a golden hue. He will probably never make himself rich. For every player who earns $50,000 in a year, there are a hundred who average $2,000 or less. An actor who is

willing to sleep in an upstairs room in a lodging house and to piece
out his sandwich money by doing odd jobs as a clerk or typist is
apt to be in trouble if he marries. Having to support a family may
drive him out of the theatre. The conditions that exist in motion
pictures and television are not much better.

Every person who decides to accept the gamble of turning
his interest into a vocation should ask himself three questions.
First, "What makes me want to go into professional acting more
than anything else in the world? Is this a matter of sentimental
stardust? Or do I view acting as a really important art for which
I wish to work through thick and thin as hard as I can?"

Second, "What makes me think that I can achieve some kind
of success in this?" Having done leads in high school and cap-
tured several substantial roles in college productions may indicate
that one has a pleasant, fresh presence on the stage. This is good.
Youth is a valuable commodity, especially in the films and TV.
*Without the support of a basic acting talent and thorough train-
ing, however, the value will not last long.* The truth of this statement has its proof in the perennial searches for "new faces" which
are advertised so widely. Each new "discovery" of a potential
young star means the discarding of one past discovery who could
not make the grade.

The third question the ambitious player should ask himself
is, "What will I be prepared to do if the acting career does not
work out?" Statistics have shown that the average term of life of
an actor is about ten years. What will the person in question
be ready to do at the end of that period? It will be a little late
then for him to start training for another profession, especially if
he has to be responsible for the well-being of a family.

Confronted by the third question, girls are usually in a more
fortunate position than men. Actresses have a charm. The pretty
young woman who finds that she is not quite "making a go" of her
thespian vocation can turn one of her stage smiles on a desirable
date and get herself married. The male actor, however, cannot use
the same trick with an equal sense of solving a problem.

The Requirements of the Actor

The actor, then, who is bound, in spite of the difficulties, to make himself a professional player, needs a very stout heart and a very resolute will. He needs good health. He needs stamina.

What is required even before these, of course, is talent. Just what this is is hard to define. Among the most important ingredients is a genuine and sensitive liking for other people. It is an insight into people's natures which makes one want to think about them whether they are "bad" or "good"—whatever they are.

A second element of talent is an innate feeling for design—a ready awareness of the differences and relationships between lines, colors, and sounds. It requires the ability to feel an excitement when one impression turns suddenly into another; in other words, a sense of dramatic effect.

Another element is a feeling for projection. The would-be actor who cannot convey to a spectator any contrast between the moments when he is talking to himself and when he is shifting his center of interest to someone at a distance does not belong in the theatre.

One of the most important elements of talent is personal magnetism. This is something that grows with experience. Its first symptoms, however, can be seen even in the raw beginner. Magnetism starts with vitality, a love of just being alive, so strong that it radiates to everyone within seeing and hearing distance. It means a sense of friendliness, a responsiveness, and a very genuine desire to please people. The magnetic person is the one whom we are all glad is here!

The training needed by the actor starts with a liberal education. This cannot be stressed too strongly. Veteran actors are emphatic about this. In an interview with John Booth and Lewis Funke of the *New York Times*, recorded in *Actors Talk about Acting*, Helen Hayes declares: "Craftsmanship is not enough. An actor must enrich his life by studying literature, science, philosophy, other countries, other peoples, other times."

What the player should have in the way of technical discipline has already been suggested in this book. He can never get too much voice and body training. Two of the best means for this are singing and dancing. The student would be wise, however, to select his teachers with care. There are nearly as many "systems" as there are coaches, and only some of these are effective. The charlatans among voice and dance teachers flourish as profusely as do the quacks in medicine.

The psychological development of the actor is a slow process and should not be forced. What is important for the apprentice in acting is not to fasten himself too tightly to books and classes concerned with the *meaning* of acting, but rather to *act* as much as he can—in as many roles, under as many directors, as possible. If he is observant of and responsive to the other, more experienced actors; if he listens attentively to the suggestions on interpretation made by his several directors; and if he continues his vocal and bodily exercises—the inner magic secrets of acting will gradually reveal themselves to him. Acting is art. And no art is arrived at swiftly or easily. It takes hard work.

Denison University Summer Theatre

Mister Roberts

Tulane University

Death of a Salesman

State University of Iowa

Julius Caesar

Irvin Paik

U.C.L.A.

Finian's Rainbow

University of Minnesota

University of Miami

Darkness at Noon

University of Minnesota

The Importance of Being Earnest

Tulane University

University of Minnesota

Desire Under the Elms

The Little Foxes

University of Illinois

University of Texas

The Glass Menagerie

Tulane University

Romeo and Juliet

The Diary of Anne Frank

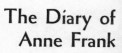

Denison University Summer Theatre

The Chairs

State University of Iowa

Stanford University

The Devil's Disciple

University of Minnesota

The
Country Wife

Northwestern University

The Way of the World

University of Michigan

Wayne State University

The Tempest

part two

✶

Twenty-five Dramatic Scenes

Introduction

The following dramatic scenes from modern and older plays represent a variety of moods and styles, both formal and informal. Some are serious and some are comic. There is one "absurdist" passage. The original stage directions have been included in each selection. Since in general, however, these may be regarded as guides for action rather than as complete and final controls, the player should feel at liberty to fill them out, and even to alter them, whenever such a development or change would seem to clarify the dramatic situation and make the characters more expressive. All the selections are very short. For this reason, to be fully effective in their brevity, they may need a little more intensive cultivation than they would if they were presented in sequence with the action which precedes and follows them in the plays from which they are taken.

In several of the dialogues a third person speaks a single line. This need not be included in the scene; the presence of the other person at this moment can be indicated simply by a pause or a nod.

I

✷

SCENES FOR TWO MEN

MISTER ROBERTS

By Thomas Heggen and Joshua Logan

PLACE AND TIME: In the CAPTAIN'S *cabin on a U.S. Navy cargo ship operating in the back areas of the Pacific during the War in 1944. The only door is up center. There is a desk at the right, a ship's inter-communication board over it against the right bulkhead and a wall-safe in the same bulkhead. A chair is at the left.*

THE CHARACTERS: The CAPTAIN, *a reserve officer called to active duty, now in command of the ship. He is a martinet, un-imaginative, self centered and personally ambitious.* LIEUTENANT (J.G.) ROBERTS, *who is addressed in accordance with tradition pertaining to junior officers in the Navy as "MISTER ROBERTS," is a younger man, intelligent, efficient and very much concerned about the welfare of the men aboard. By means of a bribe of a bottle of Scotch whiskey to which he attached the name of the* CAPTAIN *he has managed to get the ship ordered to a liberty port.*

THE SITUATION: The men aboard the cargo ship have

been working and living in their cramped quarters aboard ship for months without any shore leave. The CAPTAIN, *eager to win a promotion, has been working his crew hard and keeping his men close under his stern eye where he can be sure that none of them will do anything which will detract from his ship's extraordinary record. Now anchored in a Polynesian port, with strains of seductive music drifting over the water, the sailors are driven almost frantic with desire to get ashore. They have fully expected to be granted leave this time; but the* CAPTAIN *has just announced that everyone must stay aboard.* MISTER ROBERTS *is determined to change his mind. The* CAPTAIN *is seated behind his desk, holding a watch in one hand and the microphone in the other, in an attitude of waiting. . . . After a moment there is a knock on the door.*

CAPTAIN. Come in, Mister Roberts. (*As* ROBERTS *enters, the* CAPTAIN *puts the microphone on the desk.*) Thirty-eight seconds. Pretty good time! You see, I been expectin' you ever since I made my little announcement.

ROBERTS. Well, as long as you're expecting me, what about it—when does this crew get liberty?

CAPTAIN. Well, in the first place, just kinda hold your tongue. And in the second place, sit down.

ROBERTS. There's no time to sit down. When are you going to let this crew go ashore?

CAPTAIN. I'm not. This wasn't my idea—coming to a Liberty Port. One of my officers arranged it with a certain Port Director—gave him a bottle of Scotch whiskey—compliments of the Captain. And the Port Director was kind enough to send me a little thank-you note along with our orders. Sit down, Mister Roberts. (ROBERTS *sits.*) Don't worry about it. I'm not going to make trouble about that wasted bottle of Scotch. I'll admit I was a little pre-voked about not being consulted. Then I got to thinking maybe we oughta come to this port anyway so's you and me could have a little talk.

ROBERTS. You can make all the trouble you want, Captain, but let's quit wasting time. Don't you hear that music? Don't you know it's tearing those guys apart? They're breakable, Captain! I promise you!

CAPTAIN. That's enough! I've had enough of your fancy educated talk. (*Rises, goes to* ROBERTS.) Now you listen to me. I got two things I want to show you. (*He unlocks the wall-safe, opens it and takes out a commander's cap with gold braid "scrambled eggs" on the visor.*) You see that? That's the cap of a full commander. I'm gonna wear that cap some day and you're going to help me. (*Replaces cap in safe, goes back to* ROBERTS.) I guess there's no harm in telling you that you helped me get that palm tree by working cargo. Now don't let this go to your head, but when Admiral Finchley gave me that award, he said, "You got a good Cargo Officer, Morton; keep him at it, you're going places." So I went out and bought that hat. There's nothing gonna stand between me and that hat—certainly not you. Now last week you wrote a letter that said "disharmony aboard this ship." I told you there wasn't going to be any more letters. But what do I find on my desk this morning . . . (*Taking letter from desk.*) Another one. It says "friction between myself and the Commanding Officer." That ain't gonna go in, Mister.

ROBERTS. How are you going to stop it, Captain?

CAPTAIN. I ain't, you are. (*Goes to his chair and sits.*) Just how much do you want this crew to have a liberty anyhow? Enough to stop this "disharmony?" To stop this "friction?" (*Leans forward.*) Enough to get out of the habit of writing letters ever? Because that's the only way this crew is ever gonna get ashore. (*Leans back.*) Well, we've had our little talk. What do you say?

ROBERTS. (*after a moment*). How did you get in the Navy? How did you get on our side? You're what I joined to fight *against*. You ignorant, arrogant, ambitious . . . (*Rises.*) jackass! Keeping a hundred and sixty-seven men in prison because you got a palm tree for the work *they* did. I don't know which I hate worse—you or that other malignant growth that stands outside your door!

CAPTAIN. Why, you goddamn . . .

ROBERTS. How did you ever get command of a ship? I realize that in wartime they have to scrape the bottom of the barrel, but where the hell did they ever scrape you up?

CAPTAIN (*shouting*). There's just one thing left for you, by God
—a general court-martial.

ROBERTS. That suits me fine. Court-martial me!

CAPTAIN. By God, you've got it!

ROBERTS. I'm asking for it!

CAPTAIN. You don't have to ask for it, you've got it now!

ROBERTS. If I can't get transferred off here, I'll get court-martialed
off! I'm fed up! But you'll need a witness. Send for your messenger. He's down below. I'll say it all again in front of him.
(*Pauses.*) Go on, call in Reber! (The CAPTAIN *doesn't move.*)
Go on, call him. (*Still the* CAPTAIN *doesn't move.*) Do you
want me to call him?

CAPTAIN. No. (*He walks upstage, then turns to* ROBERTS.) I think
you're a pretty smart boy. I may not talk very good, Mister,
but I know how to take care of smart boys. Let me tell you
something. Let me tell you a little secret. I hate your guts,
you college son-of-a-bitch! You think you're better than I am!
You think you're better because you've had everything
handed to you! Let me tell you something, Mister—I've
worked since I was ten years old, and all my life I've known
you superior bastards. I knew you people when I was a kid
in Boston and I worked in eating-places and you ordered me
around . . . "Oh, bus boy! My friend here seems to have
thrown up on the table. Clean it up, please." I started going
out to sea as a steward and I worked for you then . . .
"Steward, take my magazine out to the deck chair!"
. . . "Steward, I don't like your looks. Please keep out of my
way as much as possible!" Well, I took that crap! I took that
for years from pimple-faced bastards who weren't good
enough to wipe my nose! And now I don't have to take it any
more! There's a war on, by God, and I'm the Captain and you
can wipe my nose! The worst thing I can do to you is to keep
you on this ship! And that's where you're going to stay! Now
get out of here." (*He goes to his chair and sits.* ROBERTS
*moves slowly toward the door. He hears the music, goes to
the porthole and listens. Then he turns to the* CAPTAIN.)

ROBERTS. Can't you hear that music, Captain?

CAPTAIN. Yeah, I hear it. (*Busies himself at desk, ignoring* RORERTS.)

ROBERTS. Don't you know those guys below can hear it too? Oh, my God.

CAPTAIN. Get out of here.

(*After a moment,* ROBERTS *turns from the porthole and slumps against the* CAPTAIN's *locker. His face is strained.*)

ROBERTS. What do you want for liberty, Captain?

CAPTAIN. I want plenty. You're through writin' letters—ever.

ROBERTS. Okay.

CAPTAIN. That's not all. You're through givin' me trouble. You're through talkin' back to me in front of the crew. You ain't even gonna open your mouth—except in civil answer. (ROBERTS *doesn't answer.*) Mister Roberts, you know that if you don't take my terms I'll let you out that door and that's the end of any hope for liberty.

ROBERTS. Is that all, Captain?

CAPTAIN. No. Anyone know you're in here?

ROBERTS. No one.

CAPTAIN. Then you won't go blabbin' about this to anyone ever. It might not sound so good. And besides I don't want you to take credit for gettin' this crew ashore.

ROBERTS. Do you think I'm doing this for credit? Do you think I'd *let* anyone know about this?

CAPTAIN. I gotta be sure.

ROBERTS. You've got my word, that's all.

CAPTAIN (*after a pause*). Your word. Yes, you college fellas make a big show about keeping your word.

ROBERTS. How about it, Captain. Is it a deal?

CAPTAIN. Yeah. (ROBERTS *picks up the microphone, turns on a switch and thrusts the microphone at the* CAPTAIN.) Now hear this. This is the Captain speaking. I've got some further word on security conditions in this port and so it gives me great pleasure to tell you that liberty, for the starboard section . . .

ROBERTS (*covering the microphone with his hands*). For the entire crew, goddammit.

CAPTAIN. Correction: Liberty for the entire crew will commence immediately. (ROBERTS *turns off the microphone. After a moment we hear the shouts of the crew.* ROBERTS *goes up to port-*

hole. The CAPTAIN *leans back on his chair. A song, "Roll Me
Over," is started by someone and is soon taken up by the
whole crew.*)

ROBERTS (*looking out of the porthole. He is excited and happy*).
Listen to those crazy bastards. Listen to them.

DEATH OF A SALESMAN

by Arthur Miller

PLACE AND TIME: *The boys' upstairs bedroom in the
house of a salesman,* WILLY LOMAN, *in New York. The time is the
present. Night.*

THE CHARACTERS: BIFF, *the elder son of* WILLY, *well-
built with a worn air and some evidence in his manner of a lack of
self assurance.* HAPPY, *two years younger, tall, powerfully made.
"Sexuality is like a visible color on him, or a scent that many
women have discovered." Both boys are "lost," but in different
ways.*

THE SITUATION: BIFF, *who has been trying not very successfully to earn a living on a western farm, has returned home.
He and his brother are in their beds listening to the stumbling
noises made by their father downstairs. They realize that something is the matter with him, but they do not know yet just what
it is.*

HAPPY (*getting out of bed*). He's going to get his license taken
away if he keeps that up. I'm getting nervous about him,
y'know, Biff?

BIFF. His eyes are going.

HAPPY. No, I've driven with him. He sees all right. He just doesn't keep his mind on it. I drove into the city with him last week. He stops at a green light and then it turns red and he goes. (*He laughs.*)

BIFF. Maybe he's color-blind.

HAPPY. Pop? Why he's got the finest eye for color in the business. You know that.

BIFF (*sitting down on his bed*). I'm going to sleep.

HAPPY. You're not still sour on Dad, are you, Biff?

BIFF. He's all right, I guess. . . .

BIFF. You smoking?

HAPPY (*holding out a pack of cigarettes*). Want one?

BIFF (*taking a cigarette*). I can never sleep when I smell it. . . .

HAPPY (*with deep sentiment*). Funny, Biff, y'know? Us sleeping in here again? The old beds. (*He pats his bed affectionately.*) All the talk that went across those two beds, huh? Our whole lives.

BIFF. Yeah. Lotta dreams and plans.

HAPPY (*with a deep and masculine laugh*). About five hundred women would like to know what was said in this room. (*They share a soft laugh.*)

BIFF. Remember that big Betsy something—what the hell was her name—over on Bushwick Avenue?

HAPPY (*combing his hair*). With the collie dog!

BIFF. That's the one. I got you in there, remember?

HAPPY. Yeah, that was my first time—I think. Boy, there was a pig! (*They laugh, almost crudely.*) You taught me everything I know about women. Don't forget that.

BIFF. I bet you forgot how bashful you used to be. Especially with girls.

HAPPY. Oh, I still am, Biff.

BIFF. Oh, go on.

HAPPY. I just control it, that's all. I think I got less bashful and you got more so. What happened, Biff? Where's the old humor, the old confidence? (*He shakes* BIFF's *knee.* BIFF *gets up and moves restlessly about the room.*) What's the matter?

BIFF. Why does Dad mock me all the time?

HAPPY. He's not mocking you, he—

BIFF. Everything I say there's a twist of mockery on his face. I can't get near him.

HAPPY. He just wants you to make good, that's all. I wanted to talk to you about Dad for a long time, Biff. Something's—happening to him. He—talks to himself.

BIFF. I noticed that this morning. But he always mumbled.

HAPPY. But not so noticeable. It got so embarrassing I sent him to Florida. And you know something? Most of the time he's talking to you.

BIFF. What's he say about me?

HAPPY. I can't make it out.

BIFF. What's he say about me?

HAPPY. I think the fact that you're not settled, that you're still kind of up in the air . . .

BIFF. There's one or two things depressing him, Happy.

HAPPY. What do you mean?

BIFF. Never mind. Just don't lay it all to me.

HAPPY. But I think if you just got started—I mean—is there any future for you out there?

BIFF. I tell ya, Hap, I don't know what the future is. I don't know —what I'm supposed to want.

HAPPY. What do you mean?

BIFF. Well, I spent six or seven years after high school trying to work myself up. Shipping clerk, salesman, business of one kind or another. And it's a measly manner of existence. To get on that subway on the hot mornings in summer. To devote your whole life to keeping stock, or making phone calls, or selling or buying. To suffer fifty weeks of the year for the sake of a two-week vacation, when all you really desire is to be outdoors, with your shirt off. And always to have to get ahead of the next fella. And still—that's how you build a future.

HAPPY. Well, you really enjoy it on a farm? Are you content out there?

BIFF (*with rising agitation*). Hap, I've had twenty or thirty different kinds of jobs since I left home before the war, and it always turns out the same. I just realized it lately. In Nebraska when I herded cattle, and the Dakotas, and Arizona, and now in Texas. It's why I came home now, I guess, because I realized it. This farm I work on, it's spring there now, see? And they've got about fifteen new colts. There's nothing more inspiring or—beautiful than the sight of a mare and a new colt. And it's cool there now, see? Texas is cool now, and it's spring. And whenever spring comes to where I am, I suddenly get the feeling, my God, I'm not gettin' anywhere! What the hell am I doing, playing around with horses, twenty-eight dollars a week! I'm thirty-four years old, I oughta be makin' my future. That's when I come running home. And now, I get here, and I don't know what to do with myself. (*After a pause.*) I've always made a point of not wasting my life, and every time I come back here I know that all I've done is to waste my life.

HAPPY. You're a poet, you know that, Biff? You're a—you're an idealist!

BIFF. No, I'm mixed up very bad. Maybe I oughta get married. Maybe I oughta get stuck into something. Maybe that's my trouble. I'm like a boy. I'm not married, I'm not in business, I just—I'm like a boy. Are you content, Hap? You're a success, aren't you? Are you content?

HAPPY. Hell, no!

BIFF. Why? You're making money, aren't you?

HAPPY (*moving about with energy, expressiveness*). All I can do now is wait for the merchandise manager to die. And suppose I get to be merchandise manager? He's a good friend of mine, and he just built a terrific estate on Long Island. And he lived there about two months and sold it, and now he's building another one. He can't enjoy it once it's finished. And I know that's just what I would do. I don't know what the hell I'm workin' for. Sometimes I sit in my apartment—all alone. And I think of the rent I'm paying. And it's crazy. But then, it's what I always wanted. My own apartment, a car, and plenty of women. And still, goddammit, I'm lonely.

BIFF (*with enthusiasm*). Listen, why don't you come out West with me?

HAPPY. You and I, heh?

BIFF. Sure, maybe we could buy a ranch. Raise cattle, use our muscles. Men built like we are should be working out in the open.

HAPPY (*avidly*). The Loman Brothers, heh?

BIFF (*with vast affection*). Sure, we'd be known all over the counties!

HAPPY (*enthralled*). That's what I dream about, Biff. Sometimes I want to just rip my clothes off in the middle of the store and outbox that goddam merchandise manager. I mean I can outbox, outrun, and outlift anybody in that store, and I have to take orders from those common, petty sons-of-bitches till I can't stand it any more.

BIFF. I'm tellin' you, kid, if you were with me I'd be happy out there.

HAPPY (*enthused*). See, Biff, everybody around me is so false that I'm constantly lowering my ideals . . .

BIFF. Baby, together we'd stand up for one another, we'd have someone to trust.

HAPPY. If I were around you—

BIFF. Hap, the trouble is we weren't brought up to grub for money. I don't know how to do it.

HAPPY. Neither can I!

BIFF. Then let's go!

HAPPY. The only thing is—what can you make out there?

BIFF. But look at your friend. Builds an estate and then hasn't the peace of mind to live in it.

HAPPY. Yeah, but when he walks into the store the waves part in front of him. That's fifty-two thousand dollars a year coming through the revolving door, and I got more in my pinky finger than he's got in his head.

BIFF. Yeah, but you just said—

HAPPY. I gotta show some of those pompous, self-important executives over there that Hap Loman can make the grade. I want to walk into the store the way he walks in. Then I'll go with you, Biff. We'll be together yet, I swear. But take those two we had tonight. Now weren't they gorgeous creatures?

BIFF. Yeah, yeah, most gorgeous I've had in years.

HAPPY. I get that any time I want, Biff. Whenever I feel disgusted. The only trouble is, it gets like bowling or something. I just keep knockin' them over and it doesn't mean anything. You still run around a lot?

BIFF. Naa. I'd like to find a girl—steady, somebody with substance.

HAPPY. That's what I long for.

BIFF. Go on! You'd never come home.

HAPPY. I would! Somebody with character, with resistance! Like Mom, y'know? You're gonna call me a bastard when I tell you this. That girl Charlotte I was with tonight is engaged to be married in five weeks. (*He tries on his new hat.*)

BIFF. No kiddin'!

HAPPY. Sure, the guy's in line for the vice-presidency of the store. I don't know what gets into me, maybe I just have an over-developed sense of competition or something, but I went and ruined her, and furthermore I can't get rid of her. And he's the third executive I've done that to. Isn't that a crummy characteristic? And to top it all, I go to their weddings! (*Indignantly, but laughing.*) Like I'm not supposed to take bribes. Manufacturers offer me a hundred-dollar bill now and then to throw an order their way. You know how honest I am, but it's like this girl, see. I hate myself for it. Because I don't want the girl, and, still, I take it and—I love it!

BIFF. Let's go to sleep.

HAPPY. I guess we didn't settle anything, heh?

BIFF. I just got one idea that I think I'm going to try.

HAPPY. What's that?

BIFF. Remember Bill Oliver?

HAPPY. Sure, Oliver is very big now. You want to work for him again?

BIFF. No, but when I quit he said something to me. He put his arm on my shoulder, and he said, "Biff, if you ever need anything, come to me."

HAPPY. I remember that. That sounds good.

BIFF. I think I'll go to see him. If I could get ten thousand or even seven or eight thousand dollars I could buy a beautiful ranch.

HAPPY. I bet he'd back you. 'Cause he thought highly of you, Biff. I mean, they all do. You're well liked, Biff. That's why I say to come back here, and we both have the apartment. And I'm tellin' you, Biff, any babe you want . . .

BIFF. No, with a ranch I could do the work I like and still be something. I just wonder though. I wonder if Oliver still thinks I stole that carton of basketballs.

HAPPY. Oh, he probably forgot that long ago. It's almost ten years. You're too sensitive. Anyway, he didn't really fire you.

BIFF. Well, I think he was going to. I think that's why I quit. I was never sure whether he knew or not. I know he thought the world of me, though. I was the only one he'd let lock up the place.

HAPPY. Shh!

(BIFF *looks at* HAPPY, *who is gazing down, listening.* WILLY *is mumbling in the parlor.*)

HAPPY. You hear that?

(*They listen.* WILLY *laughs warmly.*)

BIFF (*growing angry*). Doesn't he know Mom can hear that? . . .

HAPPY. Isn't that terrible? Don't leave again, will you? You'll find a job here. You gotta stick around. I don't know what to do about him, it's getting embarrassing. . . .

BIFF. Mom's hearing that! . . .

HAPPY. Go on to sleep. But talk to him in the morning, will you?

BIFF (*reluctantly getting into bed*). With her in the house. Brother!

HAPPY (*getting into bed*). I wish you'd have a good talk with him.

(*The light on their room begins to fade.*)

BIFF (*to himself in bed*). That selfish, stupid . . .

HAPPY. Sh . . . Sleep, Biff.

FINIAN'S RAINBOW

By E. Y. Harburg and Fred Saidy

PLACE AND TIME: A meeting place by a big tree in Rainbow Valley, Missitucky. Night.

THE CHARACTERS: FINIAN McLONERGAN, *a little nimble-*

From *Finian's Rainbow*, by E. Y. Harburg and Fred Saidy. Copyright as an unpublished work, 1947. Copyright 1947 by E. Y. Harburg and Fred Saidy. Reprinted by permission of Random House, Inc.; and by permission of Herman I. Meltzer.

*witted Irish gentleman in his middle fifties who has a passionate
belief in the free enterprise theory.* OG, *an Irish Leprechaun,
dressed in a cocked hat with two feathers, a stylish cape of green
leaves, a pair of Argyle socks, and golf shoes.*

THE SITUATION: *In accordance with the view of personal
initiative,* FINIAN *has stolen a magical crock of gold from the end
of a rainbow in Ireland and brought it, with his daughter* SHARON,
*to America. Unaware that he has been followed across the Atlantic
by a pair of small sharp eyes, he is now engaged in trying to bury
his gold in the earth beneath a root of the tree. He sings and takes
a frequent swig from his whiskey jug while he digs a hole and in-
serts the crock. He is in the process of covering up his treasure
when he is startled by seeing what seems to be a bush nearby stir
in the moonlight, and even more when the bush rises and begins
to dance. The little Irishman falls on the ground and tries to hide
behind his jug.*

FINIAN. God be with ye.

THE BUSH (*It speaks, too, and most politely.*) God and Mary be
with ye.

FINIAN. God, Mary, and St. Patrick be with ye.

THE BUSH. God, Mary, St. Patrick, and St. Ozymandias be with ye.

FINIAN. Ozymandias? Never heard of him.

THE BUSH. Our special saint. Patron saint of the leprechauns of
Glocca Morra. My card—(*He produces this from the air.*) The
name is Og.

FINIAN. Og, from Glocca Morra? That's me native heath. (*With
hollow accusation.*) You're an impostor. You can't be a leprechaun. You're too tall.

OG. Yes, and I'm getting taller.

FINIAN. Naturally—gallivantin' about America. Everything gets
bigger and better over here. What are ye after, anyhow?

OG. I just came over to ask your *help*, Mr. McLonergan.

FINIAN (*vastly relieved*). Me help? Well, this calls for a toast! I
rise to welcome you to America. (*He rises with jug in hand
and then with great dignity falls on his face. He continues
matter-of-factly, as though nothing had happened.*) How are
things in Ireland?

Og. Alack, alack, alack—*and* willo-waly. I weep for Ireland.

Finian. You weep? Why, what's happened?

Og. No colleens smile and no children sing. A blight has fallen over Ireland.

Finian. The British are back!

(*He scrambles to his feet.*)

Og. Never have I seen such a curse befall a folk, in all my four hundred and—(*Nudging his memory.*)—fifty-nine years. (*Wailing it.*) Alas, poor Ireland!

Finian (*not understanding, but caught up in the mood*). Alas, me poor—

Og. Ohh!

Finian. Sufferin'—

Og. Ohh!

Finian. —bleedin'—

Og. Ohhh!

Finian. —native land!

(Og *keens the fate of Erin in a mournful ditty, accompanied by sympathetic wails from* Finian.)

Finian (*with sudden indignation*). A fine lot of fairy folk you are, you and your associates, lettin' all this happen! Where's your magical power?

Og. We've lost it.

Finian (*outraged*). You mean you've gone and lost the power to make wishes?

Og (*miserably*). Aye.

Finian. What has Ireland to live for now? Answer me that!

Og. Doom and gloom—(*Wailing again.*)—d-o-o-m and gl-o-o-m!

(Finian *rolls up his sleeves, ready to take on the whole world in defense of Ireland.*)

Finian. Who's the author of this foul outrage?

Og. A monster.

Finian (*He wasn't counting on this.*) A monster, eh? You mean the old flame-breathin' type, with the head of a dragon?

Og. Oh, no. This is a tiny wee monster, with the brain of a banker. (*Slyly.*) About your size.

Finian (*his courage up again.*) Lead me to 'im! A tiny one, eh? (*He starts shadow-boxing.*) Lead me to 'im! I'll sizzle his gizzard. (*He sizzles.*) I'll throttle his larnyx. (*He throttles.*) I'll rend him apart, vertebra by vertebra! (*He rends.*) Who is he? (*A roar.*) Who is this monster?

OG (*courteously*). Excuse me for pointing, Mr. McLonergan, but it's you.

FINIAN. Me!

OG. It's you who cast this curse on Ireland.

FINIAN. You're mad!

OG. You brought on the blight yourself when you stole our crock of gold—the little crock that gives us all our power to wish.

FINIAN. Don't be superstitious, man, it's bad luck.

OG. Don't you realize, Mr. McLongergan, without a crock of gold there can be no Fairy Association in Ireland? And without a Fairy Association there'll be no incentive for dreaming? The Irish people will have to go to work!

FINIAN. It's a crisis! A crisis!

OG. Give it back, Mr. McLonergan.

FINIAN (*counter-attacking*). How do you know I've got it?

OG. Me magnetic feathers pointed you out all the way from Ireland. Feathers, who's the culprit? (*The feathers on* OG's *hat point sternly to* FINIAN.)

FINIAN (*nothing else to turn to now*). Ah, me arthritis!

OG. Give it back, Mr. McLonergan, before a great evil befalls you.

FINIAN. Ah, can't you postpone your wishin' for a couple of months?

OG. But gold was never made for mankind. It's a fairyland metal for the fairy-folk only. In the hands of a mortal it brings doom and gloom—gl-o-o-m and d-o-o-m.

FINIAN (*mockingly*). Do-o-m and gl-o-o-m. Stop your wailing. Leprechaun, I've come to a decision. I deny your existence. You're only a figment of me imagination.

OG (*frightened*). I am?

FINIAN. To prove it, I'm going to walk right through you. Step aside.

(OG, *taking no chances, prudently steps back.*)

OG. Oh, this is dreadful. Are you sure?

FINIAN (*encouraged*). Why, of course, I'm always seein' things. Ask me daughter.

OG. (*after a puzzled pause*). Well, if I don't exist, how is it I'm gradually becoming mortal?

FINIAN. (*Now he's alarmed.*) The saints preserve us! You are?

OG. Yes, and so are all the other leprechauns, ever since you took our crock of gold. Look at me—it's crept up past me ankles already. (*He shows* FINIAN *Exhibit A: socks and golf shoes.*)

FINIAN. Can't you manage to hold out until the winter?

OG. Well, I don't know. I've got a peculiar *human* feelin' in me thighs lately.

FINIAN. Your thighs? Don't let it go any further man! (*But it's too late. The leafy trousers mysteriously disapear, and* OG *is left standing in a pair of long, earthbound, woolen drawers.*) Mary and Joseph, Ireland is ruined!

SHARON'S VOICE (*from somewhere in the woods*). Father! Father!

OG. Someone's coming!

FINIAN. And now that you're half mortal, you're indecent. Here, take these. (FINIAN'S *sense of decency overcomes his logic. He quickly slips off his trousers, revealing himself in red flannels, helps* OG *into them, and sends him scurrying off.*)

DARKNESS AT NOON

By Sidney Kingsley

PLACE AND TIME: *An office in a Russian prison during the harsh days of March, 1937. A desk is at one side and a chair at the other. At the back is a barred window. The door to the office is opposite the desk.*

THE CHARACTERS: RUBASHOV, *a former high official of the Bolshevik government who has been arrested and imprisoned on orders of the new Leader because his ideas are a little too liberal and idealistic to fit the stern line the Party now favors. He is a short, stocky, smooth-shaven, bespectacled man in his early fifties. Since he has been in prison for many months, he now looks worn.*

From *Darkness at Noon* by Sidney Kingsley. Copyright as an unpublished work 1950. Copyright 1951 by Sidney Kingsley and Arthur Koestler. Reprinted by permission of Random House, Inc.; and by permission of A. D. Peters, London.

GLETKIN, *a young officer. "His shaven head, his deep-set, expressionless eyes, and his jutting, Slavic cheekbones give him the appearance of a death's head. His stiff uniform creaks, as do his boots." He is a representative of the new efficient, intensely loyal, unfeeling order of military men.*

THE SITUATION: *Sick and tired,* RUBASHOV *has been brought from his miserable cell to the office to be interrogated. Thinking to find there an old associate* COMMISSAR IVANOFF, *made an investigator under the new regime, he is shocked to find* GLETKIN *in his place. The young officer "turns to a heavy floor lamp nearby and switches it on. There is a humming sound, and a fierce white light strikes* RUBASHOV *full in the eyes. He jerks his face away as if he'd been struck, then turns back to* GLETKIN, *squinting and shielding his eyes with his hand.* GLETKIN *sits, picks up some official documents."*

GLETKIN. We will proceed with your examination. You wish to make a full confession?

RUBASHOV (*takes off his glasses and wipes his eyes*). Yes. To Commissar Ivanoff. Not to you.

GLETKIN. You will make your confession to me, here and now, or this investigation is closed, and you will be sentenced at once. Those are my orders from above. (RUBASHOV *puts on his spectacles and tries to meet* GLETKIN's *gaze, but the harsh light blinds him. He removes his glasses again.*) You have your choice. Which is it?

RUBASHOV (*avoiding the light*). I am ready to make a statement.

GLETKIN. Sit there.

RUBASHOV. On one condition. (*He turns to* GLETKIN *firmly, even though he has to almost shut his eyes.*) Turn off that dazzle-light! Save these devices for gangsters.

GLETKIN (*calmly*). You're in no position to make conditions. The fact is you are charged with being the worst kind of "gangster."

RUBASHOV (*controls his anger*). Exactly what are these charges? Please read them to me. Up till now this hasn't been done.

GLETKIN. Very well. Sit here! (RUBASHOV *sits in the chair upon which the dazzle-light has been trained.* GLETKIN *reads the*

official statement in rapid monotone.) "Enemy of the people,
Nicolai Semonovitch Rubashov, you are charged with being
a counter-revolutionary in the pay of hostile, foreign govern-
ments; of having, at the instigation of their agents, committed
such acts of treason and wreckage as to cause vital shortages
—undermining the military power of the U.S.S.R. You are also
charged with having incited an accomplice to attempt the as-
sassination of the Leader of the Party. I.e., you are charged
with crimes covered by Articles 58-1A; 58-2; 58-7; 58-9 and
58-11 of the Criminal Code." (*He drops the official papers
and looks up.*) You've heard the charges? You plead guilty?

RUBASHOV (*turns to face him, shielding his eyes with his hand*). I
plead guilty to having fallen out of step with historical necessity. I plead guilty to bourgeois sentimentality. I plead guilty
to having wanted an immediate alleviation of the Terror, and
extension of freedom to the masses. (*The secretary who is
writing this in shorthand smiles contemptuously. RUBASHOV
glances at her.*) Don't be cynical, young woman. (*To GLETKIN.*)
I now realize fully that the regime is right and I am wrong.
The times demand a tightening of the dictatorship; any sentimental aberrations at the present moment in history could
become suicide. In this sense can you call me a counter-revolutionary, but in this sense only. With the insane charges
made in the accusation I have nothing to do. I deny them
categorically.

GLETKIN. Have you finished?

RUBASHOV. I deny that I, Rubashov, ever plotted against my country. I deny that I am in the pay of a foreign government. I
deny any act of sabotage. I deny ever having taken the least
part in any act of terror against the Leader of the Party. (*To
the stenographer, quietly.*) Have you all that, young woman?

GLETKIN. Have you finished?

RUBASHOV. I have finished.

GLETKIN. Wipe your lips then. They're slimy with lies. Lies! Lies!
Vomit! (*He snatches a thick dossier off the desk, and cracks
RUBASHOV across the face with it.*) The statement you have
just made is vomit. Enough nobility! Enough posturing!

Enough strutting! What we demand of you is not high talk, but a full confession of your real crimes!

RUBASHOV (*his hand to his face, breathing hard, biting back the indignation, fighting for control*). I cannot confess to crimes I have not committed. . . .

GLETKIN (*who has walked away, the full diameter of the room, turns, and with incredible speed for such a huge man, hurls himself across the room, grabs* RUBASHOV *by the throat and pulls him to his feet.*) We have many ways of making a man tell the truth.

RUBASHOV (*quickly*). Very well, what do you want me to sign? (GLETKIN *relaxes his grip.*) If you torture me I will sign anything you place before me. I will say anything you wish me to say at once. But tomorrow I will recant. At the public trial I'll stand up in open court and I'll cry out for all the world to hear, "They are drowning the Revolution in blood. Tyranny is afoot. She strides over our dead bodies." You've become quite pale. It would end your career, wouldn't it? You hold me by the throat, young man, but I hold you by the throat, too. Remember that!

GLETKIN (*slowly releasing* RUBASHOV). Why do you make this so personal?

RUBASHOV. Death, even in an impersonal cause, is a personal matter. Death and promotions. (*Sits.*)

GLETKIN. I am here to serve the Party. I am nothing. (*He sits at the desk, gathering up his papers.*) The personal element in this case has been removed along with your friend Ivanoff.

RUBASHOV (*his face clouding, apprehensively*): Removed?

GLETKIN. There'll be no partial confessions; there'll be no bargains. We promise you nothing.

RUBASHOV. What's happened to Ivanoff?

GLETKIN. Enemy of the people Ivanoff was executed early this morning.

RUBASHOV (*after a long pause, nods to himself, murmurs*). I see. (*Looks up at* GLETKIN.) Why? Was it because of me?

GLETKIN. Perhaps.

RUBASHOV. Perhaps he thought I was innocent.

GLETKIN. Then he shouldn't have conducted your investigation.

RUBASHOV (*sighs heavily, murmurs*). Go, Sascha. Go, in peace!

GLETKIN. He was corrupt, like so many of your old guard, and his counter-revolutionary action in your examination . . .

RUBASHOV (*jumps to his feet, all his pent-up feelings exploding*). Counter-revolutionary? You ignorant young ass! What the hell do you know about the Revolution *or* the old guard? When you were peeing in your diapers we were working and fighting and studying and writing one thing: Revolution! Revolution! Half our lives we lived like moles—underground; we rotted away in every prison in Europe; we knew poverty, we knew persecution, we knew starvation, but every living second we dreamed and built the Revolution with our blood and our bones! And now you have the gall to sit there and (*He waves his hand to the faded patches on the wall.*) spit at these, the heroes of your boyhood? Are you insane? Do you really believe that we have all suddenly become venal and corrupt?

GLETKIN (*leans forward, rising slowly, his face apoplectic*). Quiet! You washed-out, disgusting, rotten old man! You didn't make the Revolution—the Revolution made you. You adventurers rode along, scum on the flood of the people's uprising. But don't make any mistake! You never fooled our Leader! He used you, because he had to use whatever was at hand, but he knew you were defective. That's why our Leader has taken such pains with us. We have learned to recognize your defectiveness by the smell of you. You were needed for a while like the white-collared intelligentsia after the Revolution. But a new generation is at the helm now and your day is over. Understand! There'll be no bargains! You, we offer nothing! You are going to die! The only question is whether you'll die uselessly, or whether you will confess and perform a last service for the Party. But, die you will, you understand?

RUBASHOV (*stares at him. Something dies; something of the will, and the battle, and the spirit go out of* RUBASHOV *forever. He suddenly becomes a very tired, sick old man. He nods, whispers hoarsely*). I understand.

GLETKIN (*harshly, triumphant*). Then let's have no more arrogance. (*The lights flicker, and as* RUBASHOV *slowly sits the scene vanishes.*)

THE IMPORTANCE OF BEING EARNEST

By Oscar Wilde

PLACE AND TIME: The morning room in ALGERNON MON-CRIEFF's *flat on Half Moon Street, London, in 1895. Since the stage setting is Victorian there are a handsome sofa on one side of the room and an equally decorative table and chair on the other. The door from the hallway is up center. There are two plates of sandwiches on the table.*

THE CHARACTERS: ALGERNON MONCRIEFF *and* JACK WOR-THING, *two young men of the smart set.*

THE SITUATION: ALGERNON *is expecting his aunt,* LADY BRACKNELL, *and her daughter,* GWENDOLEN. *His friend,* JACK, *arrives first.* JACK *has just been admitted by the* BUTLER.

ALGERNON. How are you, my dear Ernest? What brings you up to town?

JACK. Oh, pleasure, pleasure! What else should bring one anywhere? Eating as usual, I see, Algy!

ALGERNON (*stiffly*). I believe it is customary in good society to take some slight refreshment at five o'clock. Where have you been since last Thursday?

JACK (*sitting down on the sofa*). In the country.

ALGERNON. What on earth do you do there?

JACK (*pulling off his gloves*). When one is in town one amuses oneself. When one is in the country one amuses other people. It is excessively boring.

ALGERNON. And who are the people you amuse?

JACK (*airily*). Oh, neighbours, neighbours.

ALGERNON. Got nice neighbours in your part of Shropshire?

JACK. Perfectly horrid! never speak to one of them.

ALGERNON. How immensely you must amuse them! (*Goes over and takes sandwich.*) By the way, Shropshire is your county, is it not?

JACK. Eh? Shropshire? Yes, of course. Hallo! Why all these cups? Why cucumber sandwiches? Why such reckless extravagance in one so young? Who is coming to tea?

ALGERNON. Oh! merely Aunt Augusta and Gwendolen.

JACK. How perfectly delightful!

ALGERNON. Yes, that is all very well; but I am afraid Aunt Augusta won't quite approve of your being here.

JACK. May I ask why?

ALGERNON. My dear fellow, the way you flirt with Gwendolen is perfectly disgraceful. It is almost as bad as the way Gwendolen flirts with you.

JACK. I am in love with Gwendolen. I have come up to town expressly to propose to her.

ALGERNON. I thought you had come up for pleasure? . . . I call that business.

JACK. How utterly unromantic you are!

ALGERNON. I really don't see anything romantic in proposing. It is very romantic to be in love. But there is nothing romantic about a definite proposal. Why, one may be accepted. One usually is, I believe. Then the excitement is all over. The very essence of romance is uncertainty. If ever I get married, I'll certainly try to forget the fact.

JACK. I have no doubt about that, dear Algy. The Divorce Court was specially invented for people whose memories are so curiously constituted.

ALGERNON. Oh! there is no use speculating on that subject. Divorces are made in Heaven—(JACK *puts out his hand to take a sandwich.* ALGERNON *at once interferes.*) Please don't touch the cucumber sandwiches. They are ordered specially for Aunt Augusta. (*Takes one and eats it.*)

JACK. Well, you have been eating them all the time.

ALGERNON. That is quite a different matter. She is my aunt. (*Takes plate from below.*) Have some bread and butter. The bread and butter is for Gwendolen. Gwendolen is devoted to bread and butter.

JACK (*advancing to table and helping himself*). And very good bread and butter it is too.

ALGERNON. Well, my dear fellow, you need not eat as if you were going to eat it all. You behave as if you were married to her already. You are not married to her already, and I don't think you ever will be.

JACK. Why on earth do you say that?

ALGERNON. Well, in the first place, girls never marry the men they flirt with. Girls don't think it's right.

JACK. Oh, that is nonsense!

ALGERNON. It isn't. It is a great truth. It accounts for the extraordinary number of bachelors that one sees all over the place. In the second place, I don't give my consent.

JACK. Your consent!

ALGERNON. My dear fellow, Gwendolen is my first cousin. And before I allow you to marry her, you will have to clear up the whole question of Cecily. (*Rings bell.*)

JACK. Cecily! What on earth do you mean? What do you mean, Algy, by Cecily? I don't know anyone of the name of Cecily. (*Enter* LANE.)

ALGERNON. Bring me that cigarette case Mr. Worthing left in the smoking-room the last time he dined here.
(LANE *goes out.*)

JACK. Do you mean to say you have had my cigarette case all this time? I wish to goodness you had let me know. I have been writing frantic letters to Scotland Yard about it. I was very nearly offering a large reward.

ALGERNON. Well, I wish you would offer one. I happen to be more than usually hard up.

JACK. There is no good offering a large reward now that the thing is found.
(*Enter* LANE *with the cigarette case on a salver.* ALGERNON *takes it at once.* LANE *goes out.*)

ALGERNON. I think that is rather mean of you, Ernest, I must say. (*Opens case and examines it.*) However, it makes no matter, for, now that I look at the inscription inside, I find that the thing isn't yours after all.

JACK. Of course it's mine. (*Moving to him.*) You have seen me with it a hundred times, and you have no right whatsoever to read what is written inside. It is a very ungentlemanly thing to read a private cigarette case.

ALGERNON. Oh! it is absurd to have a hard-and-fast rule about what one should read and what one shouldn't. More than half of modern culture depends on what one shouldn't read.

JACK. I am quite aware of the fact, and I don't propose to discuss modern culture. It isn't the sort of thing one should talk of in private. I simply want my cigarette case back.

ALGERNON. Yes; but this isn't your cigarette case. This cigarette case is a present from someone of the name of Cecily, and you said you didn't know anyone of that name.

JACK. Well, if you want to know, Cecily happens to be my aunt.

ALGERNON. Your aunt!

JACK. Yes. Charming old lady she is, too. Lives at Tunbridge Wells. Just give it back to me, Algy.

ALGERNON (*retreating to back of sofa*). But why does she call herself little Cecily if she is your aunt and lives at Tunbridge Wells? (*Reading.*) 'From little Cecily with her fondest love.'

JACK (*moving to sofa and kneeling upon it*). My dear fellow, what on earth is there in that? Some aunts are tall, some aunts are not tall. That is a matter that surely an aunt may be allowed to decide for herself. You seem to think that every aunt should be exactly like your aunt! That is absurd! For Heaven's sake give me back my cigarette case. (*Follows* ALGERNON *round the room.*)

ALGERNON. Yes. But why does your aunt call you her uncle. 'From little Cecily, with her fondest love to her dear Uncle Jack.' There is no objection, I admit, to an aunt being a small aunt, but why an aunt, no matter what her size may be, should call her own nephew her uncle, I can't quite make out. Besides, your name isn't Jack at all; it is Ernest.

JACK. It isn't Ernest; it's Jack.

ALGERNON. You have always told me it was Ernest. I have introduced you to everyone as Ernest. You answer to the name of Ernest. You look as if your name was Ernest. You are the most earnest looking person I ever saw in my life. It is perfectly absurd your saying that your name isn't Ernest. It's on your cards. Here is one of them. (*Taking it from case.*) 'Mr. Ernest Worthing, B 4, The Albany.' I'll keep this as a proof your name is Ernest if ever you attempt to deny it to me, or to

Gwendolen, or to anyone else. (*Puts the card in his pocket.*)

JACK. Well, my name is Ernest in town and Jack in the country, and the cigarette case was given to me in the country.

ALGERNON. Yes, but that does not account for the fact that your small Aunt Cecily, who lives at Tunbridge Wells, calls you her dear uncle. Come, old boy, you had much better have the thing out at once.

JACK. My dear Algy, you talk exactly as if you were a dentist. It is very vulgar to talk like a dentist when one isn't a dentist. It produces a false impression.

ALGERNON. Well, that is exactly what dentists always do. Now, go on! Tell me the whole thing. I may mention that I have always suspected you of being a confirmed and secret Bunburyist; and I am quite sure of it now.

JACK. Bunburyist? What on earth do you mean by a Bunburyist?

ALGERNON. I'll reveal to you the meaning of that incomparable expression as soon as you are kind enough to inform me why you are Ernest in town and Jack in the country.

JACK. Well, produce my cigarette case first.

ALGERNON. Here it is. (*Hands cigarette case.*) Now produce your explanation, and pray make it improbable. (*Sits on sofa.*)

JACK. My dear fellow, there is nothing improbable about my explanation at all. In fact it's perfectly ordinary. Old Mr. Thomas Cardew, who adopted me when I was a little boy, made me in his will guardian to his grand-daughter, Miss Cecily Cardew. Cecily, who addresses me as her uncle from motives of respect that you could not possibly appreciate, lives at my place in the country under the charge of her admirable governess, Miss Prism.

ALGERNON. Where is that place in the country, by the way?

JACK. That is nothing to you, dear boy. You are not going to be invited. . . . I may tell you candidly that the place is not in Shropshire.

ALGERNON. I suspected that, my dear fellow! I have Bunburyed all over Shropshire on two separate occasions. Now, go on. Why are you Ernest in town and Jack in the country?

JACK. My dear Algy, I don't know whether you will be able to understand my real motives. You are hardly serious enough.

When one is placed in the position of guardian, one has to adopt a very high moral tone on all subjects. It's one's duty to do so. And as a high moral tone can hardly be said to conduce very much to either one's health or one's happiness, in order to get up to town, I have always pretended to have a younger brother of the name of Ernest, who lives in the Albany, and gets into the most dreadful scrapes. That, my dear Algy, is the whole truth pure and simple.

ALGERNON. The truth is rarely pure and never simple. Modern life would be very tedious if it were either, and modern literature a complete impossibility!

JACK. That wouldn't be at all a bad thing.

ALGERNON. Literary criticism is not your forte, my dear fellow. Don't try it. You should leave that to people who haven't been at a University. They do it so well in the daily papers. What you really are is a Bunburyist. I was quite right in saying you were a Bunburyist. You are one of the most advanced Bunburyists I know.

JACK. What on earth do you mean?

ALGERNON. You have invented a very useful younger brother called Ernest, in order that you may be able to come up to town as often as you like. I have invented an invaluable permanent invalid called Bunbury, in order that I may be able to go down into the country whenever I choose. Bunbury is perfectly invaluable. If it wasn't for Bunbury's extraordinary bad health, for instance, I wouldn't be able to dine with you at Willis's tonight, for I have been really engaged to Aunt Augusta for more than a week.

JACK. I haven't asked you to dine with me anywhere tonight.

ALGERNON. I know. You are absurdly careless about sending out invitations. It is very foolish of you. Nothing annoys people so much as not receiving invitations.

JACK. You had much better dine with your Aunt Augusta.

ALGERNON. I haven't the smallest intention of doing anything of the kind. To begin with, I dined there on Monday, and once a week is quite enough to dine with one's own relations. In the second place, whenever I do dine there I am always treated as a member of the family, and sent down with either no woman at all, or two. In the third place, I know perfectly well whom she will place me next to, tonight. She will place me next to Mary Farquhar, who always flirts with her own husband across the dinner-table. That is not very pleasant. Indeed, it is not even decent . . . and that sort of thing is enormously on the increase. The amount of women in London who flirt with their own husbands is perfectly scandalous. It looks so bad. It is simply washing one's clean linen in public. Besides, now that I know you to be a confirmed Bunburyist I naturally want to talk to you about Bunburying. I want to tell you the rules.

JACK. I'm not a Bunburyist at all. If Gwendolen accepts me, I am going to kill my brother, indeed I think I'll kill him in any case. Cecily is a little too much interested in him. It is rather a bore. So I am going to get rid of Ernest. And I strongly advise you to do the same with Mr. . . . with your invalid friend who has the absurd name.

ALGERNON. Nothing will induce me to part with Bunbury, and if you ever get married, which seems to me extremely problematic, you will be very glad to know Bunbury. A man who marries without knowing Bunbury has a very tedious time of it.

JACK. That is nonsense. If I marry a charming girl like Gwendolen, and she is the only girl I ever saw in my life that I would marry, I certainly won't want to know Bunbury.

ALGERNON. Then your wife will. You don't seem to realize, that in married life three is company and two is none.

JACK (*sententiously*). That, my dear young friend, is the theory that the corrupt French drama has been propounding for the last fifty years.

ALGERNON. Yes; and that the happy English home has proved in half the time.

JACK. For Heaven's sake, don't try to be cynical. It's perfectly easy to be cynical.

ALGERNON. My dear fellow, it isn't easy to be anything now-a-days. There's such a lot of beastly competition about. (*The sound of an electric bell is heard.*) Ah! that must be Aunt Augusta. Only relatives, or creditors, ever ring in that Wagnerian manner. Now, if I get her out of the way for ten minutes, so that

you can have an opportunity for proposing to Gwendolen,
may I dine with you tonight at Willis's?

JACK. I suppose so, if you want to.

ALGERNON. Yes, but you must be serious about it. I hate people
who are not serious about meals. It is so shallow of them.

JULIUS CAESAR

By William Shakespeare

*PLACE AND TIME: BRUTUS' tent in a camp near Sardis,
shortly after the murder of CAESAR.*

*THE CHARACTERS: CASSIUS and MARCUS BRUTUS, two of
the former conspirators involved in the death of CAESAR, now joint
leaders of an army fighting against ANTONY.*

*THE SITUATION: JULIUS CAESAR has been killed by a group
of Romans because they feared that his ambition for power might
tempt him to make himself Emperor. After CAESAR's death, however, ANTONY, working on the feelings of the citizens, has drawn
the affairs of state into his own hands, and CASSIUS and BRUTUS,
distressed by the turn of events, have organized an army with the
purpose of dislodging ANTONY. Since the impetuous CASSIUS and
the more cautious BRUTUS are so different in temperament their
arrangement of a joint command has not proved to be very satis-
factory. Right now they are in a quarrelsome mood.*

CASSIUS. That you have wrong'd me doth appear in this:
      You have condemn'd and noted Lucius Pella
      For taking bribes here of the Sardians;
      Wherein my letters, praying on his side,
      Because I knew the man, were slighted off.

BRUTUS. You wrong'd yourself to write in such a case.

CASSIUS. In such a time as this it is not meet
      That every nice offence should bear his comment.

BRUTUS. Let me tell you, Cassius, you yourself
      Are much condemn'd to have an itching palm,
      To sell and mart your offices for gold
      To undeservers.

CASSIUS.   I an itching palm?
  You know that you are Brutus that speaks this,
  Or, by the gods, this speech were else your last!
BRUTUS. The name of Cassius honours this corruption.
  And chastisement doth therefore hide his head.
CASSIUS. Chastisement?
BRUTUS. Remember March; the ides of March remember.
  Did not great Julius bleed for justice sake?
  What villain touch'd his body that did stab
  And not for justice? What, shall one of us,
  That struck the foremost man of all this world
  But for supporting robbers—shall we now
  Contaminate our fingers with base bribes,
  And sell the mighty space of our large honours
  For so much trash as may be grasped thus?
  I had rather be a dog and bay the moon
  Than such a Roman.
CASSIUS.   Brutus, bait not me!
  I'll not endure it. You forget yourself
  To hedge me in. I am a soldier, I,
  Older in practice, abler than yourself
  To make conditions.
BRUTUS.   Go to! You are not, Cassius.
CASSIUS. I am.
BRUTUS. I say you are not.
CASSIUS. Urge me no more! I shall forget myself.
  Have mind upon your health. Tempt me no farther.
BRUTUS. Away, slight man!
CASSIUS. Is't possible?
BRUTUS.   Hear me, for I will speak.
  Must I give way and room to your rash choler?
  Shall I be frighted when a madman stares?
CASSIUS. O ye gods, ye gods! Must I endure all this?
BRUTUS. All this? Ay, more! Fret till your proud heart break.
  Go show your slaves how choleric you are
  And make your bondmen tremble. Must I budge?
  Must I observe you? Must I stand and crouch
  Under your testy humor? By the gods,

          You shall digest the venom of your spleen,
          Though it do split you; for from this day forth
          I'll use you for my mirth, yea, for my laughter,
          When you are waspish.

CASSIUS.   Is it come to this?

BRUTUS. You say you are a better soldier.
          Let it appear so; make your vaunting true,
          And it shall please me well. For mine own part,
          I shall be glad to learn of noble men.

CASSIUS. You wrong me every way! You wrong me, Brutus!
          I said an elder soldier, not a better.
          Did I say 'better'?

BRUTUS.   If you did, I care not.

CASSIUS. Come, Antony, and young Octavius, come!
          Revenge yourselves alone on Cassius.
          For Cassius is aweary of the world:
          Hated by one he loves; brav'd by his brother;
          Check'd like a bondman; all his faults observ'd,
          Set in a notebook, learn'd and conn'd by rote
          To cast into my teeth. O, I could weep
          My spirit from mine eyes! There is my dagger,
          And here my naked breast; within, a heart
          Dearer than Pluto's mine, richer than gold.
          If that thou be'st a Roman, take it forth.
          I, that denied thee gold, will give my heart.
          Strike as thou didst at Caesar; for I know,
          When thou didst hate him worst, thou love'dst him better
          Than ever thou lov'dst Cassius.

BRUTUS.   Sheathe your dagger.
          Be angry when you will; it shall have scope.
          Do what you will; dishonour shall be humour.
          O Cassius, you are yoked with a lamb
          That carries anger as the flint bears fire;
          Who, much enforced, shows a hasty spark,
          And straight is cold again.

CASSIUS.   Hath Cassius liv'd
          To be but mirth and laughter to his Brutus
          When grief and blood ill-temper'd vexeth him?

BRUTUS. When I spoke that, I was ill-temper'd too.

CASSIUS. Do you confess so much? Give me your hand.

BRUTUS. And my heart too.

CASSIUS.   O Brutus!

BRUTUS.   What's the matter?

CASSIUS. Have not you love enough to bear with me
    When that rash humour which my mother gave me
    Makes me forgetful?

BRUTUS.   Yes, Cassius; and from henceforth,
    When you are over-earnest with your Brutus,
    He'll think your mother chides, and leave you so.

II

SCENES FOR TWO WOMEN

THE GLASS MENAGERIE

By Tennessee Williams

PLACE AND TIME: The Wingfield apartment in a big con-glomeration of lower-middle-class living units in St. Louis. It is entered by a fire escape from an alley on the right; the landing and the steps descending from it are included in the set. In the living room is a sofa. The time is the 1930's.

THE CHARACTERS: LAURA WINGFIELD, *a shy, retiring girl of twenty-three, slightly crippled in one leg because of a childhood illness. The possession in which she takes a loving interest is her collection of little glass animals.* AMANDA WINGFIELD, *her mother, "a little woman of great but confused vitality clinging to another time and place."*

THE SITUATION: The whole of the main action of this play is presented to the audience by LAURA's *brother* TOM *as a piece of dreamlike reminiscence. He ran away from home after the events related, some years ago. In the preceding scene the mother has talked fondly of the fine old times when at a certain hour of the day gentlemen callers came to court her at her girlhood home. She has insisted that there should be gentlemen callers coming to court* LAURA, *but* LAURA *has replied that she is sure she will be an old maid. Now, as the second scene opens,* LAURA *is seated in the twilight at a small clawfoot table washing and polishing her precious collection of glass figures.* AMANDA *appears on the fire escape steps. At the sound of her mother's approach,* LAURA *quickly thrusts her bowl of ornaments away and pretends to be making herself busy at a typewriter chart.* AMANDA *when she enters looks very dejected.*

LAURA. Hello, Mother, I was— (*She makes a nervous gesture toward the chart on the wall.* AMANDA *leans against the shut door and stares at* LAURA *with a martyred look.*)

AMANDA. Deception? Deception? (*She slowly removes her hat and gloves, continuing the sweet suffering stare. She lets the hat and gloves fall on the floor—a bit of acting.*)

LAURA (*shakily*). How was the D.A.R. meeting? (AMANDA *slowly opens her purse and removes a dainty white handkerchief which she shakes out delicately and delicately touches to her lips and nostrils.*) Didn't you go to the D.A.R. meeting, Mother?

AMANDA (*faintly, almost inaudibly*). —No.—No. (*Then more forcibly.*) I did not have the strength—to go to the D.A.R. In fact, I did not have the courage! I wanted to find a hole in the ground and hide myself in it forever! (*She crosses slowly to the wall and removes the diagram of the typewriter keyboard. She holds it in front of her for a second, staring at it sweetly and sorrowfully—then bites her lips and tears it in two pieces.*)

LAURA (*faintly*). Why did you do that, Mother? (AMANDA *repeats the same procedure with the chart of the Gregg Alphabet.*) Why are you—

AMANDA. Why? Why? How old are you, Laura?

LAURA. Mother, you know my age.

AMANDA. I thought that you were an adult; it seems that I was mistaken. (*She crosses slowly to the sofa and sinks down and stares at* LAURA.)

LAURA. Please don't stare at me, Mother.

(AMANDA *closes her eyes and lowers her head. Count ten.*)

AMANDA. What are we going to do, what is going to become of us, what is the future?

(*Count ten.*)

LAURA. Has something happened, Mother? (AMANDA *draws a long breath and takes out the handkerchief again. Dabbing process.*) Mother, has—something happened?

AMANDA. I'll be all right in a minute, I'm just bewildered—(*Count five.*)—by life. . . .

LAURA. Mother, I wish that you would tell me what's happened!

AMANDA. As you know, I was supposed to be inducted into my office at the D.A.R. this afternoon. But I stopped off at Rubicam's Business College to speak to your teachers about your having a cold and ask them what progress they thought you were making down there.

LAURA. Oh. . . .

AMANDA. I went to the typing instructor and introduced myself as your mother. She didn't know who you were. Wingfield, she said. We don't have any such student enrolled at the school! I assured her she did, that you had been going to classes since early in January.

"I wonder," she said, "if you could be talking about that terribly shy little girl who dropped out of school after only a few days' attendance?"

"No," I said, "Laura, my daughter, has been going to school every day for the past six weeks!"

"Excuse me," she said. She took the attendance book out and there was your name, unmistakably printed, and all the dates you were absent until they decided that you had dropped out of school.

I still said, "No, there must have been some mistake! There must have been some mix-up in the records!"

And she said, "No—I remember her perfectly now. Her hands shook so that she couldn't hit the right keys! The first time we gave a speed-test she broke down completely—was sick at the stomach and almost had to be carried into the wash-room! After that morning she never showed up any more. We

phoned the house but never got any answer—while I was
working at Famous and Barr, I suppose, demonstrating those
—Oh!"
I felt so weak I could barely keep on my feet!
I had to sit down while they got me a glass of water!
Fifty dollars' tuition, all of our plans—my hopes and ambitions
for you—just gone up the spout, just gone up the spout like
that.
(LAURA *draws a long breath and gets awkwardly to her feet.*
She crosses to the victrola and winds it up.) What are you
doing?

LAURA. Oh! (*She releases the handle and returns to her seat.*)

AMANDA. Laura, where have you been going when you've gone
out pretending that you were going to business college?

LAURA. I've just been going out walking.

AMANDA. That's not true.

LAURA. It is. I just went walking.

AMANDA. Walking? Walking? In winter? Deliberately courting
pneumonia in that light coat? Where did you walk to, Laura?

LAURA. All sorts of places—mostly in the park.

AMANDA. Even after you'd started catching that cold?

LAURA. It was the lesser of two evils, Mother. I couldn't go back
up. I—threw up—on the floor!

AMANDA. From half past seven till after five every day you mean
to tell me you walked around in the park, because you wanted
to make me think that you were still going to Rubicam's
Business College?

LAURA. It wasn't as bad as it sounds. I went inside places to get
warmed up.

AMANDA. Inside where?

LAURA. I went in the art museum and the bird-houses at the Zoo.
I visited the penguins every day! Sometimes I did without
lunch and went to the movies. Lately I've been spending most
of my afternoons in the Jewel-box, that big glass house where
they raise the tropical flowers.

AMANDA. You did all this to deceive me, just for deception?
(LAURA *looks down.*) Why?

LAURA. Mother, when you're disappointed, you get that awful
     suffering look on your face, like the picture of Jesus' mother
     in the museum!

AMANDA. Hush!

LAURA. I couldn't face it.

     (*Pause. A whisper of strings.*)

AMANDA (*hopelessly fingering the huge pocketbook*). So what are
     we going to do the rest of our lives? Stay home and watch the
     parades go by? Amuse ourselves with the glass menagerie,
     darling? Eternally play those worn-out phonograph records
     your father left as a painful reminder of him?
     We won't have a business career—we've given that up because
     it gave us nervous indigestion! (*Laughs wearily.*) What is
     there left but dependency all our lives? I know so well what
     becomes of unmarried women who aren't prepared to occupy
     a position. I've seen such pitiful cases in the South—barely
     tolerated spinsters living upon the grudging patronage of sis-
     ter's husband or brother's wife!—stuck away in some little
     mousetrap of a room—encouraged by one in-law to visit an-
     other—little birdlike women without any nest—eating the
     crust of humility all their life!
     Is that the future that we've mapped out for ourselves?
     I swear it's the only alternative I can think of!
     It isn't a very pleasant alternative, is it?
     Of course—some girls *do marry.*
     (LAURA *twists her hands nervously.*)
     Haven't you ever liked some boy?

LAURA. Yes, I liked one once. (*Rises.*) I came across his picture a
     while ago.

AMANDA (*with some interest*). He gave you his picture?

LAURA. No, it's in the year-book.

AMANDA (*disappointed*). Oh—a high school boy.

LAURA. Yes. His name was Jim. (LAURA *lifts the heavy annual
     from the clawfoot table.*) Here he is in *The Pirates of Pen-
     zance.*

AMANDA (*absently*). The what?

LAURA. The operetta the senior class put on. He had a wonderful
     voice and we sat across the aisle from each other Mondays,

Wednesdays and Fridays in the Aud. Here he is with the
silver cup for debating! See his grin?

AMANDA (*absently*). He must have had a jolly disposition.

LAURA. He used to call me—Blue Roses.

AMANDA. Why did he call you such a name as that?

LAURA. When I had that attack of pleurosis—he asked me what
was the matter when I came back. I said pleurosis—he thought
that I said Blue Roses! So that's what he always called me
after that. Whenever he saw me he'd holler, "Hello, Blue
Roses!" I didn't care for that girl that he went out with. Emily
Meisenbach. Emily was the best-dressed girl at Soldan. She
never struck me, though, as being sincere . . . It says in the
Personal Section—they're engaged. That's—six years ago! They
must be married by now.

AMANDA. Girls that aren't cut out for business careers usually
wind up married to some nice man. (*Gets up with a spark of
revival.*) Sister, that's what you'll do!

(LAURA *utters a startled, doubtful laugh. She reaches quickly
for a piece of glass.*)

LAURA. But, Mother—

AMANDA. Yes? (*Crossing to photograph.*)

LAURA (*in a tone of frightened apology*). I'm—crippled!

AMANDA. Nonsense! Laura, I've told you never, never to use that
word. Why, you're not crippled, you just have a little defect
—hardly noticeable, even! When people have some slight dis-
advantage like that, they cultivate other things to make up
for it—develop charm—and vivacity—and—charm! That's all
you have to do! (*She turns again to the photograph.*) One
thing your father had *plenty of*—was *charm!*

THE SCENE FADES OUT WITH MUSIC.

THE OLD MAID

By Zoe Akins

PLACE AND TIME: *The* JAMES RALSTON's *drawing-room in
their house in Gramercy Park. A fire burns in the fireplace at the*

*left. Upstage at the left is a doorway to another room, and oppo-
site in the right wall are two tall, deeply curtained windows. At
the back is a doorway opening upon the entrance passage. Evening in the year 1839.*

 THE CHARACTERS: Delia (Mrs. James Ralston), *a handsome woman of about 27, with a pretty, lazy smile.* Charlotte
Lovell, *her cousin of approximately the same age, somewhat less
beautiful and more reserved. Both are well-dressed in the style of
the period.*

 THE SITUATION: Charlotte *has secretly had a daughter
by an artist who loved* Delia *and turned for comfort to* Charlotte *when her cousin broke her engagement to him and married
the rich* James Ralston. *Because the artist returned to Rome to
continue his studies soon after and then settled abroad, he has
never known of his daughter* Tina. Delia *is the only person with
whom* Charlotte *has shared her secret; even* Tina, *now five, is
unaware of who her real mother is. At the time of this scene,*
Charlotte *is engaged to* Joseph Ralston, *a kinsman of* James.
Delia *is standing thoughtfully with an untouched glass of brandy
in her hand when her cousin comes running down the stairs into
the room and closes the door behind her. She tosses her cloak and
bonnet upon a chair.*

Charlotte. Delia? Jim said you wanted me. (*Her breath comes
  fast.*)
Delia (*holding out the glass*). Drink it, darling; it'll do you good.
Charlotte. No. Tell me quickly, or I shall know that what's com-
  ing is too dreadful!
Delia (*setting the glass down, untouched, and studying* Char-
  lotte's *eager face a moment before beginning*). You can't
  marry Joe, dear—can you—and keep little Tina?
Charlotte. Not keep her with me, no; but I could be with her
  every day, at the nursery for the present; and afterwards—
  (*Vaguely, hopefully.*)—make her a home somewhere where
  I could slip away to see her, I hope—
Delia (*in a flat voice*). See your own child in secret? Always in
  dread of disgrace? And risks of all sorts to your husband and

your other children? Haven't you thought of the danger there'd be?

CHARLOTTE. No, I can't think— I've not been able to think that far ahead! (*Then, desperately.*) You're trying to tell me that I must give her up.

DELIA. No. Only that you must not marry Joe.

CHARLOTTE (*blankly*). What—?

DELIA. I promised to help you, didn't I? I promised I wouldn't let the child stay with those blacks? But I didn't promise that you should marry Joe, too. Well—I've done the best I could . . . You and little Tina shall be together, always.

CHARLOTTE (*quickly*). But Joe? (*In a sick voice.*) You didn't tell him—? I couldn't bear that! What *did* you tell him?

DELIA. That you were coughing blood again.

CHARLOTTE (*after a long startled pause; shuddering*). Oh Delia . . . ! How could you?

DELIA (*smoothly*). I had to tell him something. (*Then, as the storm gathers in* CHARLOTTE's *face; forcefully.*) If you were to keep your child, the engagement had to be broken.

CHARLOTTE (*bitterly*). So you frightened him away. I see!

DELIA. He's dreadfully unhappy, of course, but he accepts your decision—

CHARLOTTE (*ironically*). *My* decision!

DELIA. Well, *mine* then.

CHARLOTTE. But if I don't accept your decision—? If I tell him the truth?

DELIA. I thought you couldn't bear to have him know the truth.

CHARLOTTE. But if I should tell him, and he should say he'd forgive me—!

DELIA. If there'd been any hope of that would you have come to me?

CHARLOTTE. No; but you drive me to think of such follies—

DELIA. Give up follies, Charlotte; and try to realize what it's going to mean to you to make a home for your child. That's what you wanted most, isn't it? To have her with you, and take care of her yourself?

CHARLOTTE (*desperately*). Yes—but—

DELIA (*impatiently; in a tone of finality*). Well, I've done what I could. I've made Jim promise to give you a little house of your own and arrange for Tina to live with you. I can't do more; and if you're not satisfied, I must wash my hands of both of you. Unless you're sensible now, *I can do nothing for you or your child*. Remember that.

(CHARLOTTE *goes to the window and stands, considering a long moment. Then she turns back, and speaks at last; brokenly.*)

CHARLOTTE. You said—together always—Tina and I . . . ?

DELIA. Yes. I said you should have Tina with you always.

CHARLOTTE. Just ourselves?

DELIA. Just yourselves.

CHARLOTTE. In a little house of our own?

DELIA. Yes.

CHARLOTTE. You're sure, Delia?

DELIA. Quite sure, dearest. Jim has promised because he thinks you're ill and we don't want you to be lonely.

(*Then, as* DELIA *waits,* CHARLOTTE, *crying softly, catches up one of the skeins of bright silk which lie with* DELIA's *embroidery on the table, and drawing* JOE's *ring from her finger, slips the threads through it; for an instant she stands, still hesitating, letting the ring swing from her hand. Then suddenly she tosses it upon the table, and without looking at* DELIA, *turns to gather up her cloak and bonnet, as the curtain falls.*)

MOURNING BECOMES ELECTRA

By Eugene O'Neill

PLACE AND TIME: The study in the Mannon house in New England. It is a large room with a stiff austere atmosphere. A table with an armchair on either side, right and left, stands at left center. Another chair is at right center. At the rear is a fire-

place and above it is a portrait of the master of the house, EZRA
MANNON. *There is a door at the right. The time is 1866.*

THE CHARACTERS: LAVINIA, *daughter of* BRIGADIER-GEN-
ERAL EZRA MANNON *of the Union Army. She is twenty-three, flat-
breasted and angular, and has a military bearing. Her voice is flat
and dry and she has a way of snapping out her words like an
officer giving orders.* CHRISTINE, LAVINIA's *mother, a tall, striking,
sensual woman of forty. She moves with a flowing animal grace.*

THE SITUATION: LAVINIA *is awaiting eagerly the return of
her beloved father,* GENERAL MANNON, *who has been serving in
the War under General Grant. Her brother* ORIN *is still in the
Army.* LAVINIA *has discovered an ugly fact, that* ADAM BRANT, *a
sea captain, whom she loves, is having an illicit affair with her
mother. In this scene* "LAVINIA *is discovered standing by the table.
She is fighting to control herself, but her face is torn by a look
of stricken anguish. She turns slowly to her father's portrait and
for a moment stares at it fixedly. Then she goes to it and puts her
hands over one of his hands with a loving, protecting gesture."*

LAVINIA. Poor Father! (*She hears a noise in the hall and moves
hastily away. The door from the hall is opened and* CHRISTINE
*enters. She is uneasy underneath, but affects a scornful in-
dignation.*)
CHRISTINE. Really, this unconfirmed report must have turned your
head—otherwise I'd find it difficult to understand your sending Annie to disturb me when you knew I was resting.
LAVINIA. I told you I had to talk to you.
CHRISTINE (*looking around the room with aversion*). But why in
this musty room, of all places?
LAVINIA (*indicating the portrait—quietly*). Because it's Father's
room.
CHRISTINE (*starts, looks at the portrait and quickly drops her eyes.
LAVINIA goes to the door and closes it. CHRISTINE says with
forced scorn.*) More mystery?
LAVINIA. You better sit down. (CHRISTINE *sits in the chair at right
center.* LAVINIA *goes back to her father's chair at left of
table.*)
CHRISTINE. Well—if you're quite ready, perhaps you will explain.

LAVINIA. I suppose Annie told you I'd been to visit Hazel and Peter while you were away.

CHRISTINE. Yes. I thought it peculiar. You never visit anyone overnight. Why did you suddenly take that notion?

LAVINIA. I didn't.

CHRISTINE. You didn't visit them?

LAVINIA. No.

CHRISTINE. Then where did you go?

LAVINIA (*accusingly*). To New York! (CHRISTINE *starts.* LAVINIA *hurries on a bit incoherently.*) I've suspected something—lately—the excuse you've made for all your trips there the past year, that Grandfather was sick—(*As* CHRISTINE *is about to protest indignantly.*) Oh! I know he has been—and you've stayed at his house—but I've suspected lately that wasn't the real reason—and now I can prove it isn't! Because I waited outside Grandfather's house and followed you. I saw you meet Brant!

CHRISTINE (*alarmed but concealing it—coolly*). Well, what if you did? I told you myself I ran into him by accident—

LAVINIA. You went to his room!

CHRISTINE (*shaken*). He asked me to meet a friend of his—a lady. It was her house we went to.

LAVINIA. I asked the woman in the basement. He had hired the room under another name, but she recognized his description. And yours too. She said you had come there often in the past year.

CHRISTINE (*desperately*). It was the first time I had ever been there. He insisted on my going. He said he had to talk to me about you. He wanted my help to approach your father—

LAVINIA (*furiously*). How can you lie like that? How can you be so vile as to try to use me to hide your adultery?

CHRISTINE (*springing up—with weak indignation*). Vinnie!

LAVINIA. Your adultery, I said!

CHRISTINE. No!

LAVINIA. Stop lying, I tell you! I went upstairs! I heard you telling him—"I love you, Adam"—and kissing him! (*With a cold bitter fury.*) You vile—! You're shameless and evil! Even if you are my mother, I say it! (CHRISTINE *stares at her, over-whelmed by this onslaught, her poise shattered for the moment. She tries to keep her voice indifferent but it trembles a little.*)

CHRISTINE. I—I knew you hated me, Vinnie—but not as bitterly as that! (*Then with a return of her defiant coolness.*) Very well! I love Adam Brant. What are you going to do?

LAVINIA. How you say that—without any shame! You don't give one thought to Father—who is so good—who trusts you! Oh, how could you do this to Father? How could you?

CHRISTINE (*with strident intensity*). You would understand if you were the wife of a man you hated!

LAVINIA (*horrified—with a glance at the portrait*). Don't. Don't say that—before him! I won't listen!

CHRISTINE (*grabbing her by the arm*). You will listen! I'm talking to you as a woman now, not as mother to daughter! That relationship has no meaning between us! You've called me vile and shameless! Well, I want you to know that's what I've felt about myself for over twenty years, giving my body to a man I—

LAVINIA (*trying to break away from her, half putting her hands up to her ears*). Stop telling me such things! Let me go! (*She breaks away, shrinking from her mother with a look of sick repulsion. A pause. She stammers.*) You—then you've always hated Father?

CHRISTINE (*bitterly*). No. I loved him once—before I married him —incredible as that seems now! He was handsome in his lieutenant's uniform! He was silent and mysterious and romantic! But marriage soon turned his romance into—disgust!

LAVINIA (*wincing again—stammers harshly*). So I was born of your disgust! I've always guessed that, Mother—ever since I was little—when I used to come to you—with love—but you would always push me away! I've felt it ever since I can remember—your disgust! (*Then with a flare-up of bitter hatred.*) Oh, I hate you! It's only right I should hate you!

CHRISTINE (*shaken—defensively*). I tried to love you. I told myself it wasn't human not to love my own child, born of my body. But I never could make myself feel you were born of any body but his! You were always my wedding night to me —and my honeymoon!

LAVINIA. Stop saying that! How can you be so—! (*Then suddenly with a strange jealous bitterness.*) You've loved Orin! Why didn't you hate him, too?

CHRISTINE. Because by then I had forced myself to become resigned in order to live! And most of the time I was carrying him, your father was with the army in Mexico. I had forgotten him. And when Orin was born he seemed my child, only mine, and I loved him for that! (*Bitterly.*) I loved him until he let you and your father nag him into the war, in spite of my begging him not leave me alone. (*Staring at* LAVINIA *with hatred.*) I know his leaving me was your doing principally, Vinnie!

LAVINIA (*sternly*). It was his duty as a Mannon to go! He'd have been sorry the rest of his life if he hadn't! I love him better than you! I was thinking of him!

CHRISTINE. Well, I hope you realize I never would have fallen in love with Adam if I'd had Orin with me. When he had gone there was nothing left—but hate and a desire to be revenged and a longing for love! And it was then I met Adam. I saw he loved me—

LAVINIA (*with taunting scorn*). He doesn't love you! You're only his revenge on Father! Do you know who he really is? He's the son of that low nurse girl Grandfather put out of our house!

CHRISTINE (*concealing a start—coolly*). So you've found that out? Were you hoping it would be a crushing surprise to me? I've known it all along. He told me when he said he loved me.

LAVINIA. Oh! And I suppose knowing who he was gave you all the more satisfaction—to add that disgrace!

CHRISTINE (*cuttingly*). Will you kindly come to the point and tell me what you intend doing? I suppose you'll hardly let your father get in the door before you tell him!

LAVINIA (*suddenly becoming rigid and cold again—slowly*). No. Not unless you force me to. (*Then as she sees her mother's astonishment—grimly.*) I don't wonder you're surprised! You know you deserve the worst punishment you could get. And Father would disown you publicly, no matter how much the scandal cost him!

CHRISTINE. I realize that. I know him even better than you do!

LAVINIA. And I'd like to see you punished for your wickedness! So please understand this isn't for your sake. It's for Father's. He hasn't been well lately. I'm not going to have him hurt! It's my first duty to protect him from you!

CHRISTINE. I know better than to expect any generosity on my account.

LAVINIA. I won't tell him, provided you give up Brant and never see him again—and promise to be a dutiful wife to Father and make up for the wrong you've done him!

CHRISTINE (*stares at her daughter—a pause—then she laughs dryly*). What a fraud you are, with your talk of your father and your duty! Oh, I'm not denying you want to save his pride—and I know how anxious you are to keep the family from more scandal! But all the same, that's not your real reason for sparing me!

LAVINIA (*confused—guiltily*). It is!

CHRISTINE. You wanted Adam Brant yourself!

LAVINIA. That's a lie!

CHRISTINE. And now you know you can't have him, you're determined that at least you'll take him from me!

LAVINIA. No!

CHRISTINE. But if you told your father, I'd have to go away with Adam. He'd be mine still. You can't bear that thought, even at the price of my disgrace, can you?

LAVINIA. It's your evil mind!

CHRISTINE. I know you, Vinnie! I've watched you ever since you were little, trying to do exactly what you're doing now! You've tried to become the wife of your father and the mother of Orin! You've always schemed to steal my place!

LAVINIA (*wildly*). No! It's you who have stolen all love from me since the time I was born! (*Then her manner becoming threatening.*) But I don't want to listen to any more of your lies and excuses! I want to know right now whether you're going to do what I told you or not!

CHRISTINE. Suppose I refuse! Suppose I go off openly with Adam! Where will you and your father and the family name be after that scandal? And what if I were disgraced myself? I'd have the man I love, at least!

LAVINIA (*grimly*). Not for long! Father would use all his influence and get Brant blacklisted so he'd lose his command and never get another! You know how much the "Flying Trades" means to him. And Father would never divorce you. You could never marry. You'd be an anchor around his neck. Don't forget you're five years older than he is! He'll still be in his prime when you're an old woman with all your looks gone! He'd grow to hate the sight of you!

CHRISTINE (*stung beyond bearing—makes a threatening move as if to strike her daughter's face*). You devil! You mean little—! (*But* LAVINIA *stares back coldly into her eyes and she controls herself and drops her hand.*)

LAVINIA. I wouldn't call names if I were you! There is one you deserve!

CHRISTINE (*turning away—her voice still trembling*). I'm a fool to let you make me lose my temper—over your jealous spite! (*A pause.* LAVINIA *stares at her.* CHRISTINE *seems considering something. A sinister expression comes to her face. Then she turns back to* LAVINIA—*coldly.*) But you wanted my answer, didn't you? Well, I agree to do as you said. I promise you I'll never see Adam again after he calls this evening. Are you satisfied?

LAVINA (*stares at her with cold suspicion*). You seem to take giving him up pretty easily!

CHRISTINE (*hastily*). Do you think I'll ever give you the satisfaction of seeing me grieve? Oh, no Vinnie! You'll never have a chance to gloat!

LAVINIA (*still suspiciously—with a touch of scorn*). If I loved anyone—!

CHRISTINE (*tauntingly*). If? I think you do love him—as much as you can love! (*With a sudden flurry of jealousy.*) You little fool! Don't you know I made him flirt with you, so you wouldn't be suspicious?

LAVINIA (*gives a little shudder—then fiercely*). He didn't fool me!

I saw what a liar he was! I just led him on—to find out things!
I always hated him! (CHRISTINE *smiles mockingly and turns
away, as if to go out of the room.*)

JOINT OWNERS IN SPAIN

By Alice Brown

PLACE AND TIME: *A large comfortable room in an old
ladies' home. The window is up center. There are two small beds,
dressers and rocking chairs, right and left. A door left opens into
the hallway and a door right into a closet. A trayful of dishes is
on a chair over at the left. The time is forenoon.*

THE CHARACTERS: MISS DYER, *a meagre, lachrymose old
lady who always behaves as if she were injured and is always
looking for trouble.* MRS. BLAIR, *a black-eyed, robust old lady who
is high-spirited and overbearing.*

THE SITUATION: *There are two old ladies in the old ladies'
home who have for a long time been "impossible to live with."
Directly opposite from each other in their natures—the one negative, the other aggressive—they have driven a series of roommates
into a condition of collapse. Completely at a loss as to what to do
about the two trouble-makers, the matron of the house has decided to isolate them by putting them together. As the scene
opens,* MISS DYER *is seated in a rocking chair by the window, just
to the left of center. A bandbox is behind her chair. The matron
has just gone and* MRS. BLAIR *stands at the left with some dresses
and a coat over her arm.*

MRS. BLAIR (*in wild dudgeon*). If I'd ha' thought I'd ha' come to
   this, I'd ha' died in my tracks afore I'd left my comfortable
   home down in Tiverton Holler. Story-'n'-a half house, good
   sullar, an' woods nigh-by full o' sarsaparilla an' gold-thread
   an' pine. I've moved more times in this God-forsaken place
   than a Methodist preacher, fust one room an' then another;
   an' bad is the best. (*Hurls dresses and coats on right bed.*)

'Twas poor pickin's afore, but this is the crowner. This beats all. (*Glaring at* MISS DYER.)

(MISS DYER *is knitting with trembling hands, pausing now and then ostentatiously to wipe the tears.*)

MRS. BLAIR. (*She has been darting about the room twitching things into place and always regarding the tray with hostility and scorn, and* MISS DYER *now comes into her range of vision.*) What under the sun be you carryin' on like that for, snuffin' an' sigh'n' an' droppin' them crocodile tears? You ain't lost nobody, have ye, sence I moved in here? (MISS DYER *in despair lays aside her knitting and begins to rock ever faster and faster with the air of one who must keep a tight grip on herself.* MRS. BLAIR'S *voice rises higher and higher.*) I dunno what you've got to complain of no more'n the rest of us. Look at that dress you've got on—a good thick thibet, an' mine's a cheap sleazy alpaca they palmed off on me when they see my eyesight wa'n't o' the best. An' you settin' right there in the sun gittin' he't through, an' over here by the door it's as cold as a barn. My land! if it don't make me hoppin' to see anybody with no more sperit than a wet rag. If yo've lost anybody by death, why don't ye say so? An' if it's a mad fit, speak out an' say *that*.

(*Marches to right of* MISS DYER *and takes a stand in front of her.*)

MISS DYER (*hitching her chair away from the window into the corner, in front of the bandbox, and speaking in the high tremulous voice of one nearly overcome by tears*). I'm sure I'm the last to keep the sun off'n anybody. I never was one to take more'n belonged to me, an' I don't care who says it, I never shall be. An' I'd hold to that if 'twas the last word I had to speak.

MRS. BLAIR. My land! talk about my tongue! Vinegar's nothin' to cold molasses 'f you've got to plough through it. (*She glances from the window and stands transfixed. Cries out in great excitement.*) My soul! There's one o' them photograph fellers come to take the house. An' there's Jane Black an' Nancy Potter an' half a dozen more all lined up there waitin' to be took. (*Rushes to the window and throws it up. Stridently.*) Here!

you keep right where you be. I'm goin' to be took. (*She rushes to the closet and begins throwing out boxes, clothes, shoes, etc., behind her, while* Miss Dyer, *regarding the open window, gets a shawl from bed L. and muffles herself in it. Reseats herself, turning the rocking chair so that it is back to the window and* Mrs. Blair. Mrs. Blair *calls piercingly.*) Where's my bandbox? Where Mis' Mitchell put my bandbox? My soul! where's my bunnit? (*She darts across the room, seems about to attack the muffled* Miss Dyer, *but seizes the chair-back instead and shakes it while* Miss Dyer *cowers.*) Where's my green bandbox? Anybody that's hid my green bandbox ought to be b'iled in ile. Hangin's too good for 'em, but let me get my eye on 'em an' they shall swing for 't. Yes, they shall, higher'n Gilroy's kite.

Miss Dyer (*dropping the shawl to put both hands to her ears*). I ain't deef.

Mrs. Blair. Deef? I don't care whether you're deef or dumb—nor whether you're number'n a beetle. Isr'el in Egypt! You might grind some folks in a mortar an' you couldn't open their lips. (*Sees the bandbox in the corner behind* Miss Dyer's *chair. Pounces on it.*) My soul! if you wa'n't there settin' on it an' wouldn't speak. (*Arrays herself in an ancient bonnet and rushes to the window. Calls.*) You wait till I git my shawl. (*In blank despair.*) He's gone. While I was findin' my bunnit he kep' right on, an' now the pictur's took an' I ain't in it. (*Slams down the window.*)

Miss Dyer (*plaintively, to her corner*). I dunno what to say nor what not to. If I speak I'm to blame, an' 'tis wuss if I keep still.

Mrs. Blair (*still wearing her bonnet, pacing up and down, looking wrathfully before her and speaking with bitterness*). 'Twas the same man that come last summer, an' he said he wanted another view when the leaves was off. An' that time I was laid up with my stiff ankle, an' today my bunnit was hid an' I lost it ag'in.

Miss Dyer (*rocking and moaning*). Dear me! Dear me suz!

Mrs. Blair (*transfixing her with a look*). An' I should like to know whose fault it was.

Miss Dyer. There couldn't nobody charge me with it, an' that I'd say if 'twas the last minute I had to live.

Mrs. Blair. If them that owns the winders an' sets by 'em so't you couldn't pry 'em out with a crowbar, had spoke up an' said, "Mis' Blair, there's the photograph man. Don't you want to be took?" it wouldn't ha' been too late. If anybody hadn't hitched their chair round so's't they hid my bandbox, it wouldn't ha' been too late. (*Starts picking up dresses from bed and hanging them in closet.*) An' I ain't had my likeness took sence I was twenty year old an' went to Sudleigh fair in my changeable *visite* an' leghorn hat, an' Jonathan wore the brocaded weskit he stood up in the next week a Thursday. It's enough to make a minister swear.

Miss Dyer. Oh, my land o' love! whatever be I comin' to!

Mrs. Blair (*turning her attention to the tray*). I s'pose there's no need o' my settin' down. The quality can keep their dinner trays piled up over every chair in the room.

Miss Dyer (*snuffling*). That waiter wa'n't brought in here by my will nor my behoof, an' that's the truest word I ever spoke.

Mrs. Blair. It's all in the day's work. (*Picks up tray and puts it on chair down L.*) Some folks are waited on; some ain't. Some has their victuals brought to 'em an' pushed under their noses, an' some has to go to the table. When they're there they can take it or leave it. For my part I shouldn't think a waiter'd be enough. I should think you'd ha' had an extension table rolled in an' a snowdrop cloth.

Miss Dyer (*tremulously*). Anybody can move that waiter that's a mind to. I would have myself if I had the stren'th; but I ain't got it. I ain't a well woman an' I ain't been this twenty year. An' I never knew the wust, for the wust hadn't come.

Mrs. Blair (*explosively*). Humph! (*Puts her arms akimbo and looks about the room. Bitterly.*) To think of all the wood I've burnt up in my air-tight an' my kitchen stove an' thought nothin' of it! To think o' all the wood there is now growin' an' rottin' from Dan to Beersheba an' I can't lay my fingers on it!

Miss Dyer. I dunno what ye want o' wood. This place's hot enough to fry in.

Mrs. Blair. Ye don't know what I want on't? (*Crossing up C. to the right of* Miss Dyer.) Well, I'll tell ye. I want some two-inch boards to nail up a partition in the middle o' this room. I don't want no more'n my own, but I want it mine.

Miss Dyer (*drearily*). You wouldn't have no gre't of an outlay for boards. 'Twouldn't have to be knee-high to keep me out.

Mrs. Blair (*as if electrified by a sudden thought*). What d'you say?

Miss Dyer (*with no interest*). Ye wouldn't have to build more'n a shingle's thickness to keep me out. I never was no hand to go where I ain't wanted; an' if I ever was, I guess I'm cured on't now.

Mrs. Blair (*with the air of pouncing*). Last week they said you was markin' out a tumbler quilt. You must ha' had a piece o' chalk. Where is it?

Miss Dyer (*drawing forth a piece of chalk from the workbag hanging on her chair; quavering*). Here 'tis. I hope you won't do nothin' out o' the way with it. I should hate to git into trouble here.

Mrs. Blair (*seizing it, diving to the bottom of her baggy pocket and, drawing forth a ball of twine, chalking a length of it and forcing one end of it on the bewildered* Miss Dyer). You git up here. Take that end.

Miss Dyer (*obeying, bewildered*). Don't ye tole me into nothin'. I ain't that kind.

Mrs. Blair (*working R. with the string, her back to* Miss Dyer). You step there to the middle square o' that winder an' hold your end o' the string down on the floor. I'll snap it.

Miss Dyer (*taking the string laxly and sidling to the door, opening it and calling*). Mis' Mitchell!

Mrs. Blair (*ruthlessly jerking her away and shutting the door*). You step in here an' do as I tell ye. There's the spot. (*Pointing to window.*) You stan' right here.

Miss Dyer (*wailing*). Oh, Mis' Blair, you're as crazy as a loon an' here I be shet up in this room with ye, an' Mis' Mitchell ain't within hearin', an' I wisht my troubles was over an' I was under the sod. (*Meekly edging toward window.*)

Mrs. Blair (*pushing her into place, snatching the end of string from her, putting it on the floor, lifting* Miss Dyer's *foot with*

one hand and setting it emphatically on the string). Stan'
there an' stan' still. Don't you ease up now. (*She twitches a
bedstead round and hitches the cord about the leg so that it
makes a straight line, from window up C. toward the footlights, dividing the room in two, talking absorbedly while she
works.*) Wonderful are the ways o' Providence an' past findin'
out. Here be we yoked up together, an' the yoke is lifted an'
we're goin' to lay down in separate stalls. (*Snaps the cord.
Triumphantly.*) Step off on't, will ye? You gimme the chalk
an' I'll go over it an' make it so's't anybody can see it in the
dead o' night. (*Miss Dyer gingerly passes her the chalk. Mrs.
Blair snatches it, kneels and chalks vigorously along the line,
while Miss Dyer, hovering in a corner and softly lamenting,
apprehensively watches her.*)

Miss Dyer (*glancing toward the hall door half in hope and half
in fear of discovery*). Oh, Mis' Blair, I dunno what you're
doin' no more'n the dead, an' if I found out mebbe I should
be scairter'n I be now. You stop, Mis' Blair. Don't you go to
markin' up the floor. Seems terrible mis*chiev*ous to go markin'
up floors. (*Mrs. Blair, entangled in her skirt, staggers to her
feet.*)

Mrs. Blair (*triumphantly*). There! now here's two rooms. Here's
the partition. See? (*Returns chalk to Miss Dyer's bag on back
of rocking chair.*)

Miss Dyer (*struggling with the idea*). 'Tain't nothin' but a mark.

Mrs. Blair. That chalk mark's the partition. (*With a wave toward
Miss Dyer's side.*) You can have the mornin' sun, for I'd jest
as soon live by a taller candle in a place that's my own.
Gimme the chalk. (*Miss Dyer interestedly passes it.*) I'll
chalk a lane into the cluzzet so's't we can both keep a right
o' way. (*Returns chalk to Miss Dyer and then steps to R. of
"partition."*) Now I'm to home an' so be you. Don't you dast
to speak a word to me unless you come an' knock here on my
footboard. (*Pointing to her bed R.*)

Miss Dyer (*a little bewildered*). What be I goin' to knock for?

Mrs. Blair. That footboard's my front door. If I want to run into
your house, I'll knock on yourn. Well, if I ain't glad to be
alone. I've hung my harp on a willer long enough. (*She pulls*

out a little table down R. below closet in her "house" and begins to unpack treasures from her ancient carpet-bag and range them there. Meanwhile she sings, either "Coronation" or the Doxology, in a strenuous voice. Miss Dyer, more timidly, glancing at her from time to time to see if she is playing right, takes her knitting and settles quite cozily by the window. She evidently wishes to test the theory, gets up and knocks timidly on the footboard. Mrs. Blair, cordially.) That you, Miss Dyer? Come right in.

Miss Dyer *(evidently feeling her way)*. No, I didn't come to stop.

Mrs. Blair. I s'pose you were goin' by an' see me at the winder. I'm proper busy. I was jest gettin' round to measurin' off my settin'-room. Seems to me it needs new paper.

Miss Dyer *(looking about)*. Why, this paper ain't been on— *(Catches herself up, stops and chuckles.)* I've had it in mind myself to paper, but I ain't fixed on the pattern yit.

Mrs. Blair *(triumphantly)*. What should you say to a kind of a straw color all lit up with tulips?

Miss Dyer *(ponders a moment)*. Ain't that kinder gay?

Mrs. Blair *(recklessly)*. Gay? Well, ye want it gay. I don't see why folks have got to live in a hearse because they're goin' to ride in one. What if we be gittin' on in years? We ain't underground yit, be we?

Miss Dyer *(doubtfully)*. No. I s'pose we ain't.

Mrs. Blair. I see a ten cent paper once all covered over with green brakes, and pond lilies.

Miss Dyer. Well, if I ever!

Mrs. Blair. But whether I paper or whether I don't, I've got some thoughts of a magenta sofy.

Miss Dyer. Well, you *are* tasty.

THE IMPORTANCE OF BEING EARNEST

By Oscar Wilde

PLACE AND TIME: An old-fashioned garden attached to the Manor House of John Worthing *at Woolton, England. The garden is full of roses. Basket chairs and a table covered with books are set under a large yew tree. July, about 1895.*

THE CHARACTERS: Cecily Cardew, *ward of* John Worthing. Hon. Gwendolen Fairfax, *a young lady of the London
aristocracy.* Merriman, *a butler.*

THE SITUATION: John Worthing *has invented a younger
wayward brother,* Ernest, *who needs attention whenever* John
*wishes to have an alibi for a vacation in the city. The lie gets out
of hand when a friend, learning the secret of the double self, goes
out to the Manor House and becomes engaged to* John's *ward,*
Cecily, *under the assumed character of* "Ernest": *and* John *finds
himself engaged to* Gwendolen *in the city, also under the name of*
"Ernest." Cecily *is seated by the table in the garden as* Merriman *announces a visitor.*

Merriman. Miss Fairfax.

    (*Enter* Gwendolen. *Exit* Merriman.)

Cecily (*advancing to meet her*). Pray let me introduce myself to
    you. My name is Cecily Cardew.

Gwendolen. Cecily Cardew? (*Moving to her and shaking hands.*)
    What a very sweet name! Something tells me that we are go-
    ing to be great friends. I like you already more than I can say.
    My first impressions of people are never wrong.

Cecily. How nice of you to like me so much after we have known
    each other such a comparatively short time. Pray sit down.

Gwendolen (*still standing up*). I may call you Cecily, may I not?

Cecily. With pleasure!

Gwendolen. And you will always call me Gwendolen, won't you?

Cecily. If you wish.

Gwendolen. Then that is all quite settled, is it not?

Cecily. I hope so. (*A pause. They both sit down together.*)

Gwendolen. Perhaps this might be a favorable opportunity for my
    mentioning who I am. My father is Lord Bracknell. You have
    never heard of papa, I suppose?

Cecily. I don't think so.

Gwendolen. Outside the family circle, papa, I am glad to say, is
    entirely unknown. I think that is quite as it should be. The
    home seems to me to be the proper sphere for the man. And
    certainly once a man begins to neglect his domestic duties

he becomes painfully effeminate, does he not? And I don't
like that. It makes men so very attractive. Cecily, mamma,
whose views on education are remarkably strict, has brought
me up to be extremely shortsighted; it is part of her system;
so do you mind my looking at you through my glasses?

CECILY. Oh! not at all, Gwendolen. I am very fond of being
looked at.

GWENDOLEN (*after examining* CECILY *carefully through a lorgnette*). You are here on a short visit, I suppose.

CECILY. Oh, no! I live here.

GWENDOLEN (*severely*). Really? Your mother, no doubt, or some
female relative of advanced years, resides here also?

CECILY. Oh, no! I have no mother, nor, in fact, any relations.

GWENDOLEN. Indeed?

CECILY. My dear guardian, with the assistance of Miss Prism, has
the arduous task of looking after me.

GWENDOLEN. Your guardian?

CECILY. Yes, I am Mr. Worthing's ward.

GWENDOLEN. Oh! It is strange he never mentioned to me that he
had a ward. How secretive of him. He grows more interesting
hourly. I am not sure, however, that the news inspires me
with feelings of unmixed delight. (*Rising and going to her.*)
I am very fond of you, Cecily; I have liked you ever since I
met you! But I am bound to state that now that I know you
are Mr. Worthing's ward, I cannot help expressing a wish
you were—well just a little older than you seem to be—and
not quite so very alluring in appearance. In fact, If I may
speak candidly . . .

CECILY. Pray do! I think that whenever one has anything unpleasant to say, one should always be quite candid.

GWENDOLEN. Well, to speak with perfect candor, Cecily, I wish
that you were fully forty-two, and more than usually plain
for your age. Ernest has a strong upright nature. He is the
very soul of truth and honor. Disloyalty would be as impossible to him as deception. But even men of the noblest possible moral character are extremely susceptible to the influence of the physical charms of others. Modern, no less than

Ancient History, supplies us with many most painful examples
of what I refer to. If it were not so, indeed, History would be
quite unreadable.

CECILY. I beg your pardon, Gwendolen, did you say Ernest?

GWENDOLEN. Yes.

CECILY. Oh, but it is not Mr. Ernest Worthing who is my guardian.
It is his brother—his elder brother.

GWENDOLEN (*sitting down again*). Ernest never mentioned to me
that he had a brother.

CECILY. I am sorry to say they have not been on good terms for a
long time.

GWENDOLEN. Ah! that accounts for it. And now that I think of it
I have never heard any man mention his brother. The subject seems distasteful to most men. Cecily, you have lifted a
load from my mind. I was growing almost anxious. It would
have been terrible if any cloud had come across a friendship
like ours, would it not? Of course you are quite, quite sure
that it is not Mr. Ernest Worthing who is your guardian?

CECILY. Quite sure. (*A pause.*) In fact, I am going to be his.

GWENDOLEN (*enquiringly*). I beg your pardon?

CECILY (*rather shy and confidingly*). Dearest Gwendolen, there is
no reason why I should make a secret of it to you. Our little
country newspaper is sure to chronicle the fact next week.
Mr. Ernest Worthing and I are engaged to be married.

GWENDOLEN (*quite politely, rising*). My darling Cecily, I think
there must be some slight error. Mr. Ernest Worthing is engaged to me. The announcement will appear in the *Morning
Post* on Saturday at the latest.

CECILY (*very politely, rising*). I am afraid you must be under some
misconception. Ernest proposed to me exactly ten minutes
ago. (*Shows diary.*)

GWENDOLEN (*examining diary through her lorgnette carefully*).
It is certainly very curious, for he asked me to be his wife
yesterday afternoon at five-thirty. If you would care to verify
the incident, pray do so. (*Produces diary of her own.*) I never
travel without my diary. One should always have something
sensational to read in the train. I am so sorry, dear Cecily,

if it is any disappointment to you, but I am afraid I have the prior claim.

CECILY. It would distress me more than I can tell you, dear Gwendolen, if it caused you any mental or physical anguish, but I feel bound to point out that since Ernest proposed to you he clearly has changed his mind.

GWENDOLEN (*meditatively*). If the poor fellow has been entrapped into any foolish promise I shall consider it my duty to rescue him at once, and with a firm hand.

CECILY (*thoughtfully and sadly*). Whatever unfortunate entanglement my dear boy may have got into, I will never reproach him with it after we are married.

GWENDOLEN. Do you allude to me, Miss Cardew, as an entanglement? You are presumptuous. On an occasion of this kind it becomes more than a moral duty to speak one's mind. It becomes a pleasure.

CECILY. Do you suggest, Miss Fairfax, that I entrapped Ernest into an engagement? How dare you? This is no time for wearing the shallow mask of manners. When I see a spade I call it a spade.

GWENDOLEN (*satirically*). I am glad to say that I have never seen a spade. It is obvious that our social spheres have been widely different.

(*Enter* MERRIMAN, *followed by the footman. He carries a salver, table cloth, and plate stand.* CECILY *is about to retort. The presence of the servants exercises a restraining influence, under which both girls chafe.*)

MERRIMAN. Shall I lay tea here as usual, Miss?

CECILY (*sternly, in a calm voice*). Yes, as usual.

(MERRIMAN *begins to clear and lay cloth. A long pause.* CECILY *and* GWENDOLEN *glare at each other.*)

GWENDOLEN. Are there many interesting walks in the vicinity, Miss Cardew?

CECILY. Oh! Yes! a great many. From the top of one of the hills quite close one can see five counties.

GWENDOLEN. Five counties! I don't think I should like that. I hate crowds.

CECILY (*sweetly*). I suppose that is why you live in town?

(GWENDOLEN *bites her lip, and beats her foot nervously with her parasol.*)

GWENDOLEN (*looking round*). Quite a well-kept garden this is, Miss Cardew.

CECILY. So glad you like it, Miss Fairfax.

GWENDOLEN. I had no idea there were any flowers in the country.

CECILY. Oh, flowers are as common here, Miss Fairfax, as people are in London.

GWENDOLEN. Personally I cannot understand how anybody manages to exist in the country, if anybody who is anybody does. The country always bores me to death.

CECILY. Ah! That is what the newspapers call agricultural depression, is it not? I believe the aristocracy are suffering very much from it just at present. It is almost an epidemic amongst them, I have been told. May I offer you some tea, Miss Fairfax?

GWENDOLEN (*with elaborate politeness*). Thank you. (*Aside.*) Detestable girl! But I require tea!

CECILY (*sweetly*). Sugar?

GWENDOLEN (*superciliously*). No, thank you. Sugar is not fashionable any more.

(CECILY *looks angrily at her, takes up the tongs and puts four lumps of sugar into the cup.*)

CECILY (*severely*). Cake or bread and butter?

GWENDOLEN (*in a bored manner*). Bread and butter, please. Cake is rarely seen at the best houses nowadays.

CECILY (*cuts a large slice of cake, and puts it on the tray*). Hand that to Miss Fairfax.

(MERRIMAN *does so, and goes out with footman.* GWENDOLEN *drinks the tea and makes a grimace. Puts down cup at once, reaches out her hand to the bread and butter, looks at it, and finds it is cake. Rises in indignation.*)

GWENDOLEN. You have filled my tea with lumps of sugar, and though I asked most distinctly for bread and butter, you have given me cake. I am known for the gentleness of my disposition, and the extraordinary sweetness of my nature but I warn you, Miss Cardew, you may go too far.

CECILY (*rising*). To save my poor, innocent, trusting boy from the machinations of any other girl there are no lengths to which I would not go.

GWENDOLEN. From the moment I saw you I distrusted you. I felt that you were false and deceitful, I am never deceived in such matters. My first impressions of people are invariably right.

CECILY. It seems to me, Miss Fairfax, that I am trespassing on your valuable time. No doubt you have many other calls of a similar character to make in the neighborhood.

ROMEO AND JULIET

By William Shakespeare

PLACE: *The orchard behind* CAPULET's *house in Verona, Italy.*

THE CHARACTERS: JULIET, *the young daughter of* CAPULET, *a leading citizen of Verona. Her* NURSE, *old and eccentric.*

THE SITUATION: JULIET *has fallen in love with* ROMEO, *son of her father's bitter rival,* MONTAGUE. *Meeting secretly the night before, they have decided to get married; and, according to plan,* JULIET *has today sent her trusted* NURSE *to* ROMEO *to find out just when and where she is to meet him. After waiting anxiously through three long hours for the old woman's return,* JULIET *has almost lost her mind. She is pacing up and down.*

JULIET. The clock struck nine when I did send the nurse;
 In half an hour she promised to return.
 Perchance she cannot meet him: that's not so.
 O, she is lame! love's heralds should be thoughts,
 Which ten times faster glide than the sun's beams,
 Driving back shadows over louring hills:
 Therefore do nimble-pinion'd doves draw love,
 And therefore hath the wind-swift Cupid wings.
 Now is the sun upon the highmost hill
 Of this day's journey, and from nine till twelve
 Is three long hours, yet she is not come.
 Had she affections and warm youthful blood,

> She would be as swift in motion as a ball;
> My words would bandy her to my sweet love,
> And his to me:
> But old folks, many feign as they were dead;
> Unwieldy, slow, heavy and pale as lead.
> O God, she comes!
> (*Enter* NURSE *and* PETER.)*

                                O honey nurse, what news?
> Hast thou met with him? Send thy man away.

NURSE. Peter, stay at the gate.

      (*Exit* PETER.)

JULIET. Now, good sweet nurse,—O Lord, why look'st thou sad?
> Though the news be sad, yet tell them merrily;
> If good, thou shamest the music of sweet news
> By playing it to me with so sour a face.

NURSE. I am a-weary, give me leave awhile;
> Fie, how my bones ache! what a jaunt have I had!

JULIET. I would thou hadst my bones, and I thy news.
> Nay, come, I pray thee, speak; good, good nurse, speak.

NURSE. Jesu, what haste? can you not stay awhile?
> Do you not see that I am out of breath?

JULIET. How art thou out of breath, when thou hast breath
> To say to me that thou art out of breath?
> The excuse that thou dost make in this delay
> Is longer than the tale thou dost excuse.
> Is thy news good, or bad? answer to that;
> Say either, and I'll stay the circumstance:
> Let me be satisfied, is't good or bad?

NURSE. Well, you have made a simple choice; you know not how
> to choose a man: Romeo! no, not he; though his face be
> better than any man's, yet his leg excels all men's; and
> for a hand and a foot, and a body, though they be not to
> be talked on, yet they are past compare: he is not the
> flower of courtesy, but I'll warrant him, as gentle as a
> lamb. Go thy ways, wench; serve God. What, have you
> dined at home?

---

* Peter is the Nurse's servant. He can be indicated by a nod when she speaks to him.

JULIET. No, no: but all this did I know before.
     What says he of our marriage? what of that?
NURSE. Lord, how my head aches! what a head have I!
     It beats as it would fall in twenty pieces.
     My back o' t' other side,—O, my back, my back!
     Beshrew your heart for sending me about,
     To catch my death with jaunting up and down!
JULIET. I' faith, I am sorry that thou art not well.
     Sweet, sweet, sweet nurse, tell me, what says my love?
NURSE. Your love says, like an honest gentleman, and a courteous,
     and a kind, and a handsome, and, I warrant, a virtuous,—
     Where is your mother?
JULIET. Where is my mother! why, she is within;
     Where should she be? How oddly thou repliest!
     'Your love says, like an honest gentleman,
     Where is your mother?
NURSE. O God's lady dear!
     Are you so hot? marry, come up, I trow;
     Is this the poultice for my aching bones?
     Henceforward do your messages yourself.
JULIET. Here's such a coil! come, what says Romeo?
NURSE. Have you got leave to go to shrift today?
JULIET. I have.
NURSE. Then hie you hence to Friar Laurence's cell;
     There stays a husband to make you a wife:
     Now comes the wanton blood up in your cheeks,
     They'll be in scarlet straight at any news.
     Hie you to church; I must another way,
     To fetch a ladder by the which your love
     Must climb a bird's nest soon when it is dark:
     I am the drudge and toil in your delight,
     But you shall bear the burden soon at night.
     Go; I'll to dinner; hie you to the cell.
JULIET. Hie to high fortune! Honest nurse, farewell.
     (*Exeunt.*)

III

✴

SCENES FOR ONE MAN, ONE WOMAN

THE GLASS MENAGERIE

By Tennessee Williams

PLACE AND TIME: The Wingfield apartment in a lower-middle-class tenement building in the 1930's. What we see in this scene is the sitting room. There is a sofa near the center and over at one side is a case containing a collection of small glass animals. The light in the room is dim, dreamlike.

THE CHARACTERS: Laura, *a girl of twenty-three, is excessively shy. She is almost pathologically self-conscious of a slightly crippled leg. Her appearance and manner seem to be almost as fragile as the little figures in her glass collection.* Jim O'Connor, *the gentleman caller, is described by the author as being "a nice, ordinary, young man."*

THE SITUATION: Under the prodding of his mother, Laura's *brother* Tom *has brought home with him to have dinner with the family and to meet his shy sister, his friend* Jim O'Connor, *a fellow employee in a warehouse where* Tom *works.* Laura *once admired* Jim *very much when they were in high school together.*

Not suspecting any designs on him by LAURA's *mother, but being
a kindly young man and noticing* LAURA's *syhness,* JIM *wants to
see if he can get* LAURA *to break out of her strange reserve. As the
scene opens* LAURA *is alone on the sofa in the darkened room. She
sits up nervously as* JIM *enters with a candelabrum and a small
glass of wine. Throughout the scene his attitude is gently humorous.*

JIM. Hello, there, Laura.

LAURA (*faintly*). *Hello.* (*She clears her throat.*)

JIM. How are you feeling now? Better?

LAURA. Yes. Yes, thank you.

JIM. This is for you. A little dandelion wine. (*He extends it toward
her with extravagant gallantry.*)

LAURA. Thank you.

JIM. Drink it—but don't get drunk!
  (*He laughs heartily.* LAURA *takes the glass uncertainly; laughs
  shyly.*)
  Where shall I set the candles?

LAURA. Oh—oh, anywhere . . .

JIM. How about here on the floor? Any objections?

LAURA. No.

JIM. I'll spread a newspaper under to catch the drippings. I like to
sit on the floor. Mind if I do?

LAURA. Oh, no.

JIM. Give me a pillow?

LAURA. What?

JIM. A pillow?

LAURA. *Oh* . . . (*Hands him one quickly.*)

JIM. How about you? Don't you like to sit on the floor?

LAURA. Oh—yes.

JIM. Why don't you, then?

LAURA. I—will.

JIM. Take a pillow! (LAURA *does. Sits on the other side of the
  candelabrum.* JIM *crosses his legs and smiles engagingly at
  her.*) I can't hardly see you sitting way over there.

LAURA. I can—see you.

JIM. I know, but that's not fair, I'm in the limelight. (LAURA *moves her pillow closer.*) Good! Now I can see you! Comfortable?

LAURA. Yes.

JIM. So am I. Comfortable as a cow! Will you have some gum?

LAURA. No, thank you.

JIM. I think that I will indulge, with your permission. (*Musingly unwraps it and holds it up.*) Think of the fortune made by the guy that invented the first piece of chewing gum. Amazing, huh? The Wrigley Building is one of the sights of Chicago—I saw it summer before last when I went up to the Century of Progress. Did you take in the Century of Progress.

LAURA. No, I didn't.

JIM. Well, it was quite a wonderful exposition. What impressed me most was the Hall of Science. Gives you an idea of what the future will be in America, even more wonderful than the present time is! (*Pause. Smiling at her.*) Your brother tells me you're shy. Is that right, Laura?

LAURA. I—don't know.

JIM. I judge you to be an old-fashioned type of girl. Well, I think that's a pretty good type to be. Hope you don't think I'm being too personal—do you?

LAURA (*hastily, out of embarrassment*). I believe I *will* take a piece of gum, if you—don't mind. (*Clearing her throat.*) Mr. O'Connor, have you—kept up with your singing?

JIM. Singing? Me?

LAURA. Yes. I remember what a beautiful voice you had.

JIM. When did you hear me sing?

(VOICE OFF STAGE IN THE PAUSE.)

VOICE (*off stage*).

> O blow, ye winds, heigh-ho,
> A-roving I will go!
> I'm off to my love
> With a boxing glove—
> Ten thousand miles away!

JIM. You say you've heard me sing?

LAURA. Oh, yes! Yes, very often . . . I don't suppose—you remember me—at all?

JIM (*smiling doubtfully*). You know I have an idea I've seen you before. I had that idea soon as you opened the door. It seemed almost like I was about to remember your name. But the name that I started to call you—wasn't a name! And so I stopped myself before I said it.

LAURA. Wasn't it—Blue Roses?

JIM (*springs up. Grinning*). Blue Roses!—My gosh, yes—Blue Roses! That's what I had on my tongue when you opened the door! Isn't it funny what tricks your memory plays? I didn't connect you with high school somehow or other.

But that's where it was; it was high school. I didn't even know you were Shakespeare's sister!

Gosh, I'm sorry.

LAURA. I didn't expect you to. You—barely knew me!

JIM. But we did have a speaking acquaintance, huh?

LAURA. Yes, we—spoke to each other.

JIM. When did you recognize me?

LAURA. Oh, right away!

JIM. Soon as I came in the door?

LAURA. When I heard your name I thought it was probably you. I knew that Tom used to know you a little in high school. So when you came in the door—

Well, then I was—sure.

JIM. Why didn't you *say* something, then?

LAURA (*breathlessly*). I didn't know what to say, I was—too surprised!

JIM. For goodness' sakes! You know, this sure is funny!

LAURA. Yes! Yes, isn't it, though . . .

JIM. Didn't we have a class in something together?

LAURA. Yes, we did.

JIM. What class was that?

LAURA. It was—singing—Chorus!

JIM. Aw!

LAURA. I sat across the aisle from you in the Aud.

JIM. Aw.

LAURA. Mondays, Wednesdays and Fridays.

JIM. Now I remember—you always came in late.

LAURA. Yes, it was so hard for me, getting upstairs. I had that brace on my leg—it clumped so loud!

JIM. I never heard any clumping.

LAURA (*wincing at the recollection*). To me it sounded like—
thunder!

JIM. Well, well, well, I never even noticed.

LAURA. And everybody was seated before I came in. I had to walk
in front of all those people. My seat was in the back row. I
had to go clumping all the way up the aisle with everyone
watching!

JIM. You shouldn't have been self-conscious.

LAURA. I know, but I was. It was always such a relief when the
singing started.

JIM. Aw, yes, I've placed you now! I used to call you Blue Roses.
How was it that I got started calling you that?

LAURA. I was out of school a little with pleurosis. When I came
back you asked me what was the matter. I said I had pleurosis—you thought I said Blue Roses. That's what you always
called me after that!

JIM. I hope you didn't mind.

LAURA. Oh, no—I liked it. You see, I wasn't acquainted with many
—people. . . .

JIM. As I remember you sort of stuck by yourself.

LAURA. I—I—never have had much luck at—making friends.

JIM. I don't see why you wouldn't.

LAURA. Well, I—started out badly.

JIM. You mean being—

LAURA. Yes, it sort of—stood between me—

JIM. You shouldn't have let it!

LAURA. I know, but it did, and—

JIM. You were shy with people!

LAURA. I tried not to be but never could—

JIM. Overcome it?

LAURA. No, I—I never could!

JIM. I guess being shy is something you have to work out of kind
of gradually.

LAURA (*sorrowfully*). Yes—I guess it—

JIM. Takes time!

LAURA. Yes—

JIM. People are not so dreadful when you know them. That's what
you have to remember! And everybody has problems, not just

you, but practically everybody has got some problems. You think of yourself as having the only problems, as being the only one who is disappointed. But just look around you and you will see lots of people as disappointed as you are. For instance, I hoped when I was going to high school that I would be further along at this time, six years later, than I am now— You remember that wonderful write-up I had in *The Torch?*

LAURA. Yes! (*She rises and crosses to table.*)

JIM. It said I was bound to succeed in anything I went into! (LAURA *returns with the annual.*) Holy Jeez! *The Torch!* (*He accepts it reverently. They smile across it with mutual wonder.* LAURA *crouches beside him and they begin to turn through it.* LAURA'S *shyness is dissolving in his warmth.*)

LAURA. Here you are in *The Pirates of Penzance!*

JIM (*wistfully*). I sang the baritone lead in that operetta.

LAURA (*raptly*). So—*beautifully!*

JIM (*protesting*). Aw—

LAURA. Yes, yes—beautifully—beautifully!

JIM. You heard me?

LAURA. All three times!

JIM. No!

LAURA. Yes!

JIM. All three performances?

LAURA (*looking down*). Yes.

JIM. Why?

LAURA. I—wanted to ask you to—autograph my program.

JIM. Why didn't you ask me to?

LAURA. You were always surrounded by your own friends so much that I never had a chance to.

JIM. You should have just—

LAURA. Well, I—thought you might think I was—

JIM. Thought I might think you was—what?

LAURA. Oh—

JIM (*with reflective relish*). I was beleaguered by females in those days.

LAURA. You were terribly popular!

JIM. Yeah—

LAURA. You had such a—friendly way—

JIM. I was spoiled in high school.

LAURA. Everybody—liked you!

JIM. Including you?

LAURA. I—yes, I—I did, too—(*She gently closes the book in her lap.*)

JIM. Well, well, well! —Give me that program, Laura. (*She hands it to him. He signs it with a flourish.*) There you are—better late than never!

LAURA. Oh, I—what a—surprise!

JIM. My signature isn't worth very much right now.

But some day—maybe—it will increase in value!

Being disappointed is one thing and being discouraged is something else. I am disappointed but I am not discouraged. I'm twenty-three years old.

How old are you?

LAURA. I'll be twenty-four in June.

JIM. That's not old age!

LAURA. No, but—

JIM. You finished high school?

LAURA (*with difficulty*). I didn't go back.

JIM. You mean you dropped out?

LAURA. I made bad grades in my final examinations. (*She rises and replaces the book and the program. Her voice strained.*)

How is—Emily Meisenbach getting along?

JIM. Oh, that kraut-head!

LAURA. Why do you call her that?

JIM. That's what she was.

LAURA. You're not still—going with her?

JIM. I never see her.

LAURA. It said in the Personal Section that you were—engaged!

JIM. I know, but I wasn't impressed by that—propaganda!

LAURA. It wasn't—the truth?

JIM. Only in Emily's optimistic opinion!

LAURA. Oh—

(JIM *lights a cigarette and leans indolently back on his elbows smiling at* LAURA *with a warmth and charm which lights her inwardly with altar candles. She remains by the table and turns in her hands a piece of glass to cover her tumult.*)

JIM (*after several reflective puffs on a cigarette*). What have you done since high school? (*She seems not to hear him.*) Huh? (LAURA *looks up.*) I said what have you done since high school, Laura?

LAURA. Nothing much.

JIM. You must have been doing something these six long years.

LAURA. Yes.

JIM. Well, then, such as what?

LAURA. I took a business course at business college—

JIM. How did that work out?

LAURA. Well, not very—well—I had to drop out, it gave me—inde-gestion—

(JIM *laughs gently.*)

JIM. What are you doing now?

LAURA. I don't do anything—much. Oh, please don't think I sit around doing nothing! My glass collection takes up a good deal of time. Glass is something you have to take good care of.

JIM. What did you say—about glass?

LAURA. Collection I said—I have one—(*She clears her throat and turns away again, acutely shy.*)

JIM (*abruptly*). You know what I judge to be the trouble with you? Inferiority complex! Know what that is? That's what they call it when someone low-rates himself!

I understand it because I had it, too. Although my case was not so aggravated as yours seems to be. I had it until I took up public speaking, developed my voice, and learned that I had an aptitude for science. Before that time I never thought of myself as being outstanding in any way whatsoever!

Now I've never made a regular study of it, but I have a friend who says I can analyze people better than doctors that make a profession of it. I don't claim that to be necessarily true, but I can sure guess a person's psychology, Laura! (*Takes out his gum.*) Excuse me, Laura. I always take it out when the flavor is gone. I'll use this scrap of paper to wrap it in. I know how it is to get it stuck on a shoe.

Yep—that's what I judge to be your principal trouble. A lack of confidence in yourself as a person. You don't have the proper amount of faith in yourself. I'm basing that fact on a

number of your remarks and also on certain observations I've
made. For instance that clumping you thought was so awful
in high school. You say that you even dreaded to walk into
class. You see what you did? You dropped out of school, you
gave up an education because of a clump, which as far as I
know was practically non-existent! A little physical defect is
what you have. Hardly noticeable even! Magnified thousands
of times by imagination!
You know what my strong advice to you is? Think of yourself
as *superior* in some way!

LAURA. In what way would I think?

JIM. Why, man alive, Laura! Just look about you a little. What do
you see? A world full of common people! All of 'em born and
all of 'em going to die!
Which of them has one-tenth of your good points! Or mine!
Or anyone else's, as far as that goes—Gosh!
Everybody excels in some one thing. Some in many!
(*Unconsciously glances at himself in the mirror.*)
All you've got to do is discover in *what!*
Take me, for instance.
(*He adjusts his tie at the mirror.*)
My interest happens to lie in electro-dynamics. I'm taking a
course in radio engineering at night school, Laura, on top of
a fairly responsible job at the warehouse. I'm taking that
course and studying public speaking.

LAURA. Ohhhh.

JIM. Because I believe in the future of television!
(*Turning back to her.*)
I wish to be ready to go up right along with it. Therefore
I'm planning to get in on the ground floor. In fact I've already
made the right connections and all that remains is for the in-
dustry itself to get under way! Full steam—
(*His eyes are starry.*)
Knowledge—Zzzzzp! Money—Zzzzzzp!—Power!
That's the cycle democracy is built on!
(*His attitude is convincingly* dynamic. LAURA *stares at him,
even her shyness eclipsed in her absolute wonder. He sud-
denly grins.*)

I guess you think I think a lot of myself!

LAURA. No—o-o-o, I—

JIM. Now how about you? Isn't there something you take more interest in than anything else?

LAURA. Well, I do—as I said—have my—glass collection—

(*A peal of girlish laughter from the kitchen.*)

JIM. I'm not right sure I know what you're talking about. What kind of glass is it?

LAURA. Little articles of it, they're ornaments mostly!

Most of them are little animals made out of glass, the tiniest little animals in the world. Mother calls them a glass menagerie! Here's an example of one, if you'd like to see it!

This one is one of the oldest. It's nearly thirteen.

(MUSIC. "THE GLASS MENAGERIE.")

(*He stretches out his hand.*)

Oh, be careful—if you breathe, it breaks!

JIM. I'd better not take it. I'm pretty clumsy with things.

LAURA. Go on, I trust you with him!

(*Places it in his palm.*)

There now—you're holding him gently!

Hold him over the light, he loves the light! You see how the light shines through him?

JIM. It sure does shine!

LAURA. I shouldn't be partial, but he is my favorite one.

JIM. What kind of a thing is this one supposed to be?

LAURA. Haven't you noticed the single horn on his forehead?

JIM. A unicorn, huh?

LAURA. Mmm-hmmm!

JIM. Unicorns, aren't they extinct in the modern world?

LAURA. I know!

JIM. Poor little fellow, he must feel sort of lonesome.

LAURA (*smiling*). Well, if he does he doesn't complain about it. He stays on a shelf with some horses that don't have horns and all of them seem to get along nicely together.

JIM. How do you know?

LAURA (*lightly*). I haven't heard any arguments among them!

JIM (*grinning*). No arguments, huh? Well, that's a pretty good sign! Where shall I set him?

LAURA. Put him on the table. They all like a change of scenery once in a while!

JIM (*stretching*). Well, well, well, well—
Look how big my shadow is when I stretch!

LAURA. Oh, oh, yes—it stretches across the ceiling!

JIM (*crossing to door*). I think it's stopped raining. (*Opens fire-escape door.*) Where does the music come from?

LAURA. From the Paradise Dance Hall across the alley.

JIM. How about cutting the rug a little, Miss Wingfield?

LAURA. Oh, I—

JIM. Or is your program filled up? Let me have a look at it. (*Grasps imaginary card.*) Why, every dance is taken! I'll just have to scratch some out. (WALTZ MUSIC "LA GOLONDRINA.") Ahhh, a waltz! (*He executes some sweeping turns by himself then holds his arms toward* LAURA.)

LAURA (*breathlessly*). I—can't dance!

JIM. There you go, that inferiority stuff!

LAURA. I've never danced in my life!

JIM. Come on, try!

LAURA. Oh, but I'd step on you!

JIM. I'm not made out of glass.

LAURA. How—how—how do we start?

JIM. Just leave it to me. You hold your arms out a little.

LAURA. Like this?

JIM. A little bit higher. Right. Now don't tighten up, that's the main thing about it—relax.

LAURA (*laughing breathlessly*). It's hard not to.

JIM. Okay.

LAURA. I'm afraid you can't budge me.

JIM. What do you bet I can't? (*He swings her into motion.*)

LAURA. Goodness, yes, you can!

JIM. Let yourself go, now, Laura, just let yourself go.

LAURA. I'm—

JIM. Come on!

LAURA. Trying!

JIM. Not so stiff—Easy does it!

LAURA. I know but I'm—

JIM. Loosen th' backbone! There now, that's a lot better.

LAURA. Am I?

JIM. Lots, lots better! (*He moves her about the room in a clumsy waltz.*)

LAURA. Oh, my!

JIM. Ha-ha!

LAURA. Oh, my goodness!

JIM. *Ha-ha-ha!* (*They suddenly bump into the table. JIM stops.*) What did we hit on?

LAURA. Table.

JIM. Did something fall off it? I think—

LAURA. Yes.

JIM. I hope that it wasn't the little glass horse with the horn!

LAURA. Yes.

JIM. Aw, aw, aw. Is it broken?

LAURA. Now it is just like all the other horses.

JIM. It's lost its—

LAURA. Horn! It doesn't matter. Maybe it's a blessing in disguise.

JIM. You'll never forgive me. I bet that that was your favorite piece of glass.

LAURA. I don't have favorites much. It's no tragedy, Freckles. Glass breaks so easily. No matter how careful you are. The traffic jars the shelves and things fall off them.

JIM. Still I'm awfully sorry that I was the cause.

LAURA (*smiling*). I'll just imagine he had an operation. The horn was removed to make him feel less—freakish!

(*They both laugh.*)

THE LITTLE FOXES

By Lillian Hellman

PLACE AND TIME: The living room of the Giddens house in a small town in the South. Upstage is a staircase leading to the second story. Left is a door leading to an entrance hall, and near the center is a table with a chair to the right of it. On the table is a bottle of medicine and a spoon. "The room is good-looking, the furniture expensive; but it reflects no particular taste. Everything is of the best and that is all." The time is 1900.

THE CHARACTERS: HORACE GIDDENS, *"a tall man of about forty-five. He has been good looking, but now his face is tired and ill." He is, or has been until his illness, a member of the staff of the local bank.* REGINA GIDDENS, *his wife, a handsome woman of forty. She is ambitious and ruthless.*

THE SITUATION: HORACE, *critically ill of a heart disease, has been in a hospital in Baltimore. He has just recently been brought home by his young daughter, "ZAN," at the request of his wife, and he was happy that his family wanted him back until he learned that* REGINA *desired his presence only so that she could get some of his money for an industrial venture in which her two brothers,* BEN *and* OSCAR, *are involved. Distrusting the men and disapproving of the venture generally, he is determined not to support it. He has suspected that someone has been tampering with his deposit box at the bank so has directed that it be brought to his home. It is now on the table.* HORACE *is seated in a wheel chair to the left of the table as* REGINA *enters from hallway. She shakes her umbrella, stands it in the corner, takes off her cloak and throws it over the bannister. She stares at* HORACE.

REGINA (*as she takes off her gloves*). We had agreed that you were to stay in your part of this house and I in mine. This room is *my* part of the house. Please don't come down here again.

HORACE. I won't.

REGINA (*crosses towards bell-cord*). I'll get Cal to take you upstairs.

HORACE (*smiles*). Before you do I want to tell you that after all, we have invested our money in Hubbard Sons and Marshall, Cotton Manufacturers.

REGINA (*stops, turns, stares at him*). What are you talking about? You haven't seen Ben—When did you change your mind?

HORACE. I didn't change my mind. *I* didn't invest the money. (*Smiles.*) It was invested for me.

REGINA (*angrily*). What—?

HORACE. I had eighty-eight thousand dollars' worth of Union Pacific bonds in that safe-deposit box. They are not there now. Go and look. (*As she stares at him, he points to the box.*) Go and look, Regina. (*She crosses quickly to the box, opens it.*) Those bonds are as negotiable as money.

REGINA (*turns back to him*). What kind of joke are you playing now? Is this for my benefit?

HORACE. I don't look in that box very often, but three days ago, on Wednesday it was, because I had made a decision—

REGINA. I want to know what you are talking about.

HORACE (*sharply*). Don't interrupt me again. Because I had made a decision, I sent for the box. The bonds were gone. Eighty-eight thousand dollars gone. (*He smiles at her.*)

REGINA (*after a moment's silence, quietly*). Do you think I'm crazy enough to believe what you're saying?

HORACE (*shrugs*). Believe anything you like.

REGINA (*stares at him, slowly*). Where did they go to?

HORACE. They are in Chicago. With Mr. Marshall, I should guess.

REGINA. What did they do? Walk to Chicago? Have you really gone crazy?

HORACE. Leo took the bonds.

REGINA (*turns sharply then speaks softly, without conviction*). I don't believe it.

HORACE (*leans forward*). I wasn't there but I can guess what happened. This fine gentleman, to whom you were willing to marry your daughter, took the keys and opened the box. You remember that the day of the fight Oscar went to Chicago? Well, he went with my bonds that his son Leo had stolen for him. (*Pleasantly.*) And for Ben, of course, too.

REGINA (*slowly, nods*). When did you find out the bonds were gone?

HORACE. Wednesday night.

REGINA. I thought that's what you said. Why have you waited three days to do anything? (*Suddenly laughs.*) This *will* make a fine story.

HORACE (*nods*). Couldn't it?

REGINA (*still laughing*). A fine story to hold over their heads. How could they be such fools? (*Turns to him.*)

HORACE. But I'm not going to hold it over their heads.

REGINA (*the laugh stops*). What?

HORACE (*turns his chair to face her*). I'm going to let them keep the bonds—as a loan from you. An eighty-eight thousand-dollar loan; they should be grateful to you. They will be, I think.

REGINA (*slowly, smiles*). I see. You are punishing me. But I won't let you punish me. If you won't do anything, I will. Now. (*She starts for door.*)

HORACE. You won't do anything. Because you can't. (REGINA *stops.*) It won't do you any good to make trouble because I shall simply say that I lent them the bonds.

REGINA (*slowly*). You would do that?

HORACE. Yes. For once in your life I am tying your hands. There is nothing for you to do. (*There is silence. Then she sits down.*)

REGINA. I see. You are going to lend them the bonds and let them keep all the profit they make on them, and there is nothing I can do about it. Is that right?

HORACE. Yes.

REGINA (*softly*). Why did you say that I was making this gift?

HORACE. I was coming to that. I am going to make a new will, Regina, leaving you eighty-eight thousand dollars in Union Pacific bonds. The rest will go to Zan. It's true that your brothers have borrowed your share for a little while. After my death I advise you to talk to Ben and Oscar. They won't admit anything and Ben, I think, will be smart enough to see that he's safe. Because I knew about the theft and said nothing. Nor will I say anything as long as I live. Is that clear to you?

REGINA (*nods, softly, without looking at him*). You will not say anything as long as you live.

HORACE. That's right. And by that time they will probably have replaced your bonds, and then they'll belong to you and no-body but us will ever know what happened. (*Stops, smiles.*) They'll be around any minute to see what I am going to do. I took good care to see that word reached Leo. They'll be mighty relieved to know I'm going to do nothing and Ben will think it all a capital joke on you. And that will be the end of that. There's nothing you can do to them, nothing you can do to me.

REGINA. You hate me very much.

HORACE. No.

REGINA. Oh, I think you do. (*Puts her head back, sighs.*) Well, we haven't been very good together. Anyway, I don't hate you either. I have only contempt for you. I've always had.

HORACE. From the very first?

REGINA. I think so.

HORACE. I was in love with *you*. But why did *you* marry *me*?

REGINA. I was lonely when I was young.

HORACE. *You* were lonely?

REGINA. Not the way people usually mean. Lonely for all the things I wasn't going to get. Everybody in this house was so busy and there was so little place for what I wanted. I wanted the world. Then, and then—(*Smiles.*) Papa died and left the money to Ben and Oscar.

HORACE. And you married me?

REGINA. Yes, I thought—But I was wrong. You were a small-town clerk then. You haven't changed.

HORACE (*nods, smiles*). And that wasn't what you wanted.

REGINA. No. No, it wasn't what I wanted. (*Pauses, leans back, pleasantly.*) It took me a little while to find out I had made a mistake. As for you—I don't know. It was almost as if I couldn't stand the kind of man you were—(*Smiles, softly.*) I used to lie there at night, praying you wouldn't come near—

HORACE. Really? It was as bad as that?

REGINA (*nods*). Remember when I went to Doctor Sloan and I told you he said there was something the matter with me and that you shouldn't touch me any more?

HORACE. I remember.

REGINA. But you believed it. I couldn't understand that. I couldn't understand that anybody could be such a soft fool. That was when I began to despise you.

HORACE (*puts his hand to his throat, looks at the bottle of medicine on table*). Why didn't you leave me?

REGINA. I told you I married you for something. It turned out it was only for this. (*Carefully.*) This wasn't what I wanted, but it was something. I never thought about it much but if I had (Horace *puts his hand to his throat.*) I'd have known that you would die before I would. But I couldn't have known that you would get heart trouble so early and so bad. I'm lucky, Horace. I've always been lucky. (Horace *turns slowly to the medicine.*) I'll be lucky again. (Horace *looks at her. Then he puts his hand to his throat. Because he cannot reach the bottle he moves the chair closer. He reaches for the medicine, takes out the cork, picks up the spoon. The bottle slips and smashes on the table. He draws in his breath, gasps.*)

HORACE. Please. Tell Addie—The other bottle is upstairs. (Regina *has not moved. She does not move now. He stares at her. Then, suddenly as if he understood, he raises his voice. It is a panic-stricken whisper, too small to be heard outside the room.*) Addie! Addie! Come—(*Stops as he hears the softness of his voice. He makes a sudden, furious spring from the chair to the stairs, taking the first few steps as if he were a desperate runner. On the fourth step he slips, gasps, grasps the rail, makes a great effort to reach the landing. When he reaches the landing, he is on his knees. His knees give way, he falls on the landing, out of view. Regina *has not turned during his climb up the stairs. Now she waits a second. Then she goes below the landing, speaks up.*)

REGINA. Horace. Horace. (*When there is no answer, she turns, calls.*) Addie! Cal! Come in here. (*She starts up the steps. Addie *and* Cal *appear. Both run towards the stairs.*) He's had an attack. Come up here. (*They run up the steps quickly.*)

SUPPRESSED DESIRES

By Susan Glaspell

PLACE AND TIME: A studio apartment in New York City. Through an immense north window in the back wall appear tree tops in a neighboring square. "Near the window is a big table,

Reprinted by permission of Dodd, Mead and Company from *Plays* by Susan Glaspell. Copyright 1920, 1948 by Susan Glaspell. Reprinted by permission also of Ernest Benn Limited, London.

loaded at one end with serious-looking books and austere scientific
periodicals. At the other end are architect's drawings, blue prints,
dividing compasses, square, ruler, etc. At the left is a door leading
to the rest of the apartment; at the right the outer door." Dusk of
a winter afternoon, about 1914.

THE CHARACTERS: HENRIETTA BREWSTER, *very much in-*
terested in psychoanalysis. STEPHEN, *her husband, an architect.*

THE SITUATION: HENRIETTA, *having discovered the won-*
ders of the new science of psychoanalysis, is recommending to all
her friends that they have themselves "psyched" by the wonderful
DR. RUSSELL. *Her friend,* MABEL, *having recounted quite inno-*
cently a simple dream about being a hen, has been persuaded by
the earnest HENRIETTA *to have herself investigated.* STEVE, *who*
has listened indulgently for a long time to his wife's psycho-
analytical chatter morning, noon, and night, has begun to grow
weary of it. HENRIETTA *is at the scientific end of the table, sur-*
rounded by open books and periodicals, writing, when STEVE *en-*
ters briskly.

STEVE. What are you doing, my dear?

HENRIETTA. My paper for the Liberal Club.

STEVE. Your paper on—?

HENRIETTA. On a subject which does not have your sympathy.

STEVE. Oh, I'm not sure I'm wholly out of sympathy with psychoanalysis, Henrietta. You work it so hard. I couldn't even take
a bath without its meaning something.

HENRIETTA (*loftily*). I talked it because I knew you needed it.

STEVE. You haven't said much about it these last two weeks. Uh-
your faith in it hasn't weakened any?

HENRIETTA. Weakened? It's grown stronger with each new thing
I've come to know. And Mabel. She is with Dr. Russell now.
Dr. Russell is wonderful. From what Mabel tells me I believe
his analysis is going to prove that I was right. Today I discovered a remarkable confirmation of my theory in the hen-
dream.

STEVE. What is your theory?

HENRIETTA. Well, you know about Lyman Eggleston. I've won-
dered about him. I've never seen him, but I know he's less

bourgeois than Mabel's other friends—more intellectual—and (*Significantly.*) she doesn't see much of him because Bob doesn't like him.

STEVE. But what's the confirmation?

HENRIETTA. Today I noticed the first syllable of his name.

STEVE. Ly?

HENRIETTA. No—egg.

STEVE. Egg?

HENRIETTA (*patiently*). Mabel dreamed she was a *hen*. (STEVE *laughs.*) You wouldn't laugh if you knew how important names are in interpreting dreams. Freud is full of just such cases in which a whole hidden complex is revealed by a single significant syllable—like this egg.

STEVE. Doesn't the traditional relation of hen and egg suggest rather a maternal feeling?

HENRIETTA. There is something maternal in Mabel's love, of course, but that's only one element.

STEVE. Well, suppose Mabel hasn't a suppressed desire to be this gentleman's mother, but his beloved. What's to be done about it? What about Bob? Don't you think it's going to be a little rough on him?

HENRIETTA. That can't be helped. Bob, like everyone else, must face the facts of life. If Dr. Russell should arrive independently at this same interpretation I shall not hesitate to advise Mabel to leave her present husband.

STEVE. Um—hum! (*The lights go up on Fifth Avenue.* STEVE *goes to the window and looks out.*) How long is it we've lived here, Henrietta?

HENRIETTA. Why, this is the third year, Steve.

STEVE. I—we—one would miss this view if one went away, wouldn't one?

HENRIETTA. How strangely you speak! Oh, Stephen, I *wish* you'd go to Dr. Russell. Don't think my fears have abated because I've been able to restrain myself. I had to on account of Mabel. But now, dear—won't you go?

STEVE. I—(*He breaks off, turns on the light, then comes and sits beside* HENRIETTA.) How long have we been married, Henrietta?

HENRIETTA. Stephen, I don't understand you! You *must* go to Dr. Russell.

STEVE. I have gone.

HENRIETTA. You—what?

STEVE (*Jauntily*). Yes, Henrietta, I've been psyched.

HENRIETTA. You went to Dr. Russell?

STEVE. The same.

HENRIETTA. And what did he say?

STEVE. He said—I—I was a little surprised by what he said, Henrietta.

HENRIETTA (*breathlessly*). Of course—one can so seldom anticipate. But tell me—your dream, Stephen? It means—?

STEVE. It means—I was considerably surprised by what it means.

HENRIETTA. *Don't* be so exasperating!

STEVE. It means—you really want to know, Henrietta?

HENRIETTA. Stephen, you'll drive me mad!

STEVE. He said—of course he may be wrong in what he said.

HENRIETTA. He *isn't* wrong. *Tell* me!

STEVE. He said my dream of the walls receding and leaving me alone in a forest indicates a suppressed desire—

HENRIETTA. Yes—yes!

STEVE. To be freed from—

HENRIETTA. Yes—freed from—?

STEVE. Marriage.

HENRIETTA (*crumples. Stares*). Marriage!

STEVE. He—he may be mistaken, you know.

HENRIETTA. *May* be mistaken?

STEVE. I—well, of course, I hadn't taken any stock in it myself. It was only your great confidence—

HENRIETTA. Stephen, are you telling me that Dr. Russell—Dr. A. E. Russell—told you this? (STEVE *nods*.) Told you you have a suppressed desire to separate from *me*?

STEVE. That's what he said.

HENRIETTA. Did he know who you were?

STEVE. Yes.

HENRIETTA. That you were married to me?

STEVE. Yes, he knew that.

HENRIETTA. And he told you to leave me?

STEVE. It seems he must be wrong, Henrietta.

HENRIETTA (*rising*). And I've sent him more patients—! (*Catches herself and resumes coldly.*) What reason did he give for this analysis?

STEVE. He says the confining walls are a symbol of my feeling about marriage and that their fading away is a wish-fulfillment.

HENRIETTA (*gulping*). Well, is it? Do you want our marriage to end?

STEVE. It was a great surprise to me that I did. You see I hadn't known what was in my unconscious mind.

HENRIETTA (*flaming*). What did you tell Dr. Russell about me to make him think you weren't happy?

STEVE. I never told him a thing, Henrietta. He got it all from his confounded clever inferences. I—I tried to refute them, but he said that was only part of my self-protective lying.

HENRIETTA. And that's why you were so—happy—when you came in just now.

STEVE. Why, Henrietta, how can you say such a thing? I was *sad*. Didn't I speak sadly of—of the view? Didn't I ask how long we had been married?

HENRIETTA (*rising*). Stephen Brewster, have you no sense of the seriousness of this? Dr. Russell doesn't know what our marriage has been. You do. You should have laughed him down! Confined—in life with me? Did you tell him that I believe in freedom?

STEVE. I very emphatically told him that his results were a great surprise to me.

HENRIETTA. But you accepted them.

STEVE. Oh, not at all. I merely couldn't refute his arguments. I'm not a psychologist. I came home to talk it over with you. You being a disciple of psychoanalysis—

HENRIETTA. If you are going, I wish you would go tonight!

STEVE. Oh, my dear! I—surely I couldn't do that! Think of my feelings. And my laundry hasn't come home.

HENRIETTA. I ask you to go tonight. Some women would falter at this, Steve, but I am not such a woman. I leave you free. I do not repudiate psychoanalysis; I say again that it has done

great things. It has also made mistakes, of course. But since
you accept this analysis—(*She sits down and pretends to
begin work.*) I have to finish this paper. I wish you would
leave me.

STEVE (*scratches his head, goes to the inner door*). I'm sorry, Henrietta, about my unconscious mind.

TOVARICH

By Jacques Deval. Adapted by Robert E. Sherwood

*PLACE AND TIME: A room in the Hotel du Quercy, rue de
la Glacière, in Paris. There is a single door and an archway upstage. In the wall on one side is a large window through which
can be seen the roofs of Paris, shining brightly in the morning sun.
Against the other wall is a messy bed. The other articles of furniture include a washstand, a chest of drawers, a round table with
an armchair by it, and a single chair by the chest of drawers. Near
the bed is a smaller table. On the wall over the bed are hung a
sword and the flag of the Russian Imperial Guard. On the back
wall is an icon, its flame glowing. It is 11:00 o'clock of a fine No-
vember morning, about 1930.*

THE CHARACTERS: PRINCE MIKAIL ALEXANDROVITCH OURA-
TIEFF, *former aide-de-camp to His Imperial Majesty, the Czar of
Russia, about 45 years old, lean and lithe.* GRAND DUCHESS TATIANA
PETROVNA, *his wife, somewhat younger. She is lovely, graceful,
gracious, regal and shabby.*

THE SITUATION: PRINCE MIKAIL *and* GRAND DUCHESS
TATIANA *are White Russians who escaped from their country during the Revolution and now, nearly penniless but still lighthearted, are trying to maintain their existence in a cheap hotel in
Paris.* MIKAIL *is discovered lying on the bed, polishing a boot.
"After a few seconds he wearily drops the boot and puts the brush
on the small table. Then starts to read a paper, which is on the
bed.* TATIANA *is off stage, singing."*

MIKAIL. Tatiana?

TATIANA (*off stage*). Yes!

MIKAIL. What are you doing?

TATIANA (*off stage*). Washing. And what is my darling doing?

MIKAIL. Your darling has been polishing his boots. He is now resting. (*Leans back on pillows.*) He is drawing the covers over
his wasted limbs and trying to forget that there is no coal in
the stove. (TATIANA *enters, with a shirt rolled into a ball. She
comes to edge of the bed and shakes it out.*) What, in the
blessed name of St. Christopher, is that?

TATIANA. Your shirt, darling.

MIKAIL. My . . .

TATIANA. I washed it with my own hands.

MIKAIL (*horrified*). That is my shirt? That—that fragment!

TATIANA. Yes, darling, your shirt.
   (*She holds it up, proving that it bears some resemblance to
   a man's shirt. But it has been so trimmed that the back is far
   shorter than the front.*)
   Your only shirt. (*She has come close to the bed.*)

MIKAIL. But—just what has happened to what used to be the tail?

TATIANA. You had no more handkerchiefs. So I had to cut some
out of . . .

MIKAIL. Out of my shirt!

TATIANA. You know very well I've used up the last of my chemises.

MIKAIL (*melting*). Oh, my darling—my sweet, my beautiful!
   (*He seizes her hand and attempts to draw her down on to the
   bed.*)

TATIANA (*resisting*). No, you fool! I have to work. . . . (*Goes to
   chest, hangs up shirt.*)

MIKAIL. Tatiana! How can I beg for your forgiveness? You sacri-
ficed the last of your chemises—and I complain at the loss of
a mere shirt-tail. (*With deep fervor.*) You are a saint, Tatiana,
a saint!

TATIANA (*walks to bed*). You're sure of that? (*Sits on end of bed.*)

MIKAIL. It's the very word that was used by my Imperial Master.
   (*He crosses himself.*) Your august cousin. (*She crosses herself.*) He said: "In marrying Tatiana Petrovna, you marry a
   saint!"

TATIANA (*nodding*). He knew me very well.

MIKAIL. He was speaking of your devotion—but not of your manners.

TATIANA (*indignantly*). And is there anything wrong with my manners?

MIKAIL (*indulgently*). Oh—you can't be blamed for them.

TATIANA. Blamed!

MIKAIL. You were born a Grand Duchess, and you lacked the opportunity for social contacts that was given to the rest of us. It gave you a bad start in life.

TATIANA. What do you mean?

MIKAIL. Wherever you go, I have to act as interpreter—and apologist—for you.

TATIANA. Get up! (*Pulls newspaper from his hands.*)

MIKAIL (*humbly*). But why?

TATIANA. Obey me! (*Rises from bed, leans against washstand.*)

MIKAIL. But—my darling—this bed is so warm and so comfortable.

TATIANA (*solemnly*). Mikail Alexandrovitch Ouratieff, at whatever sacrifice of your comfort, I command you to get up. (*She is being very stern, very imperious. There should be no suggestion of bantering in her tone.*)

MIKAIL (*sighing*). All right. (*He swings his bare feet out of bed, and as he arises, steps on his boot. He leans over and starts to put the boot on.*)

TATIANA. Put that shoe down! And come over here. (*He obeys ruefully.*) Since you are such a good apologist, you will offer your apologies—to *me!*
(MIKAIL *advances towards her slowly and when he is close to her attempts to click his bare heels together and bows low.*)

MIKAIL. My beloved Tatiana. . . .

TATIANA (*goes to end of bed, sits*). Your apologies will be expressed in official form.

MIKAIL. General Prince Mikail Alexandrovitch Ouratieff, aide-de-camp to His Imperial Majesty, offers Her Imperial Highness the Grand Duchess Tatiana Petrovna his very humble apologies.

TATIANA. Approach! (MIKAIL *obeys, coming very close to her. She gives him a vigorous slap on the face.*)

MIKAIL. Ouch!

TATIANA (*angrily*). How dare you say "ouch"? You're an officer. You are not permitted to feel pain.

MIKAIL. Very well, Highness. The ouch is withdrawn.

(TATIANA *rises suddenly, seizes him in her arms and drags him down on the bed.*)

TATIANA. Darling, darling, darling. You are forgiven. (*She kisses him fiercely.*)

MIKAIL. Completely?

TATIANA. Completely!

MIKAIL. And you'll let me be just a little bit sad if I want to?

TATIANA. And I'll be sad with you always, dear. (*Puts her arms around him.*)

MIKAIL. Ah, God! How good it is to be Russian.

TATIANA. And insane!

MIKAIL. Life for us is so very, very sad and so very, very beautiful.

TATIANA. And so tiresome. I'm starving. (*She sits up.*)

MIKAIL. So am I, Tatiaschka. There's a horrible, gnawing emptiness in my soul.

TATIANA. I was not speaking of souls. I'm hungry here. (*She slaps her stomach.*) Give me some money.

MIKAIL (*astounded*). *Money?*

TATIANA. Yes—I'm going shopping.

MIKAIL. But surely—not with money?

TATIANA. Mikail! Don't tell me there's none left.

MIKAIL (*sighing*). There is the sum of one hundred francs, Tatiana. That is all.

TATIANA (*brightly*). But that is enough.

MIKAIL. And out of the hundred, we owe eighty to the proprietor of this lamentable hotel.

TATIANA. That little nuisance? Haven't we trained him in the virtue of patience?

MIKAIL. No, we have been fortunate in that he has the gout, my Tatiana, and therefore he cannot climb the six flights of stairs. But he must be paid. Eighty francs. Today. Otherwise . . . out we go!

TATIANA. Very well—he *shall* be paid! I shall give him his eighty francs today, and tomorrow he shall lend us two hundred.

(*She has started preparing to go out. She can be brisk, very competent, when she chooses.*)

MIKAIL. But, will he?

TATIANA. I'll appeal to his snobbery. For two hundred francs I'll make him Count of Pultava!

MIKAIL (*scornfully*). A Count. Do you think that would impress him? Why last week for only fifty francs you made him a Duke. . . .

TATIANA. Did I?

MIKAIL. Duke of Courlande.

TATIANA. Very well, then—I can do better than that: tomorrow he will become a Grand Duke—entitled to precede himself in to dinner.

MIKAIL (*overwhelmed with admiration*). Tatiana, what resource!

TATIANA. Resourcefulness has been thrust upon us, my pigeon! (*She pauses momentarily in her dressing to assume an attitude.*) We are two against the world!

MIKAIL. No! Not two—only one—*you!*

TATIANA. Ah, Mikail! How far do you suppose I could go in life without you?

MIKAIL (*sits on bed*). Come, Tatiana. Get back into this bed.

TATIANA. No! Give me the hundred francs.

(*Regretfully he reaches under the pillow and takes out a hundred-franc note.*)

MIKAIL. You will surely pay eighty of these to the Duke of Courlande?

TATIANA. Yes! He'll be paid—his eighty francs.

MIKAIL. That will leave twenty francs. Bring back at least ten of it.

TATIANA (*taking the note*). I shall pay the landlord eighty francs and buy the food, and bring back eighty francs.

MIKAIL (*anxiously*). Tatiana—I don't understand your arithmetic . . .

TATIANA. Darling!

MIKAIL. But I suspect the honesty of your intentions.

TATIANA (*turns to him*). Darling, do you trust me?

MIKAIL. Within reason, my love.

TATIANA. Then believe me. I swear, by Saint Peter and Saint Paul —I swear to bring back eighty-five francs. I shall bring back

ninety francs! I shall buy some cutlets of horse and some potatoes, and I shall bring back ninety-five francs and two artichokes!

MIKAIL. Tatiana, you're very fond of artichokes, aren't you?

TATIANA. No, I hate them, but while the grocer is selecting the
poorest potatoes, I shall be left alone amongst the artichokes.
(*Puts on hat.*)

MIKAIL (*looks heavenward reverently*). I humbly beg that the
Father of all living may look the other way, that He will not
see the Grand Duchess Tatiana Petrovna, cousin to the Tsar
(*He makes the sign of the cross.*) arrested for stealing artichokes.

TATIANA. Nonsense! I am never arrested!

MIKAIL. You have been incredibly lucky.

TATIANA (*picks up bag*). Oh, no, Mikail, it is more than luck. It
is the intervention of God—the God of all the Russias. Why—
the other day, the grocer almost saw me as I was letting a
bunch of radishes fall into this bag, but his eyes were miracu-
lously diverted to the ceiling.

MIKAIL (*with decision*). Tatiana—give me that bag. I shall go
myself.

TATIANA. No! By St. Christopher, no! A General of Cavalry to be
seen in the streets of Paris with cutlets of horse! Never!

MIKAIL. But it is quite all right for a Grand Duchess.

TATIANA (*puts bag on table*). A Grand Duchess is above appear-
ances!

R. U. R.

By Karel Capek

PLACE AND TIME: *An island. A laboratory in the factory
of Rossum's Universal Robots. "The door to the left leads into a
waiting room. The door to the right leads to the dissecting room.
There is a table with numerous test-tubes, flasks, burners, chemi-
cals; a small thermostat and a microscope with a glass globe. At
the far side of the room is* ALQUIST's *desk with numerous books. In*

the left-hand corner a wash basin with a mirror above it; in the right-hand corner a sofa." A large window is at the back. The time is the future.

THE CHARACTERS: HELENA *and* PRIMUS, *two young almost-human robots.*

THE SITUATION: *On an island somewhere on the earth, a great factory has been manufacturing highly perfected mechanical men, called "robots." Made with strong, flexible bodies, sensitive nervous systems, and brains, but no souls, the robots—male and female—were designed to replace human beings in all kinds of skilled and unskilled labor the world over. In an effort to refine the robot product still farther, a few of the newest automatons were partially humanized. These developed a resentment against their masters and, in a wave of hatred, they led the other robots in a great world-wide rebellion which caused the death of all human beings everywhere, except one, a* MR. ALQUIST, *an architect. Now the robots are faced with the fear of their own eventual extinction. They press* MR. ALQUIST *to reconstruct the formula. But, because he is an architect rather than a scientist, he does not know how to begin. Desperately hour after hour he has worked in the laboratory, but with no success. Tired and discouraged, he feels that life on earth is doomed. If only the robots could reproduce themselves! he thinks. But so far the one most essential element in all human relationships, the one element which distinguishes men and women from machines, is absent in the robots, even the latest and most nearly perfect of them. That element is Love. Exhausted at last,* MR. ALQUIST *has thrown himself on the sofa in the corner when two young robots, whom he has never seen before, enter shyly and curiously through the door from the waiting room.* HELENA *glances at the sleeping figure on the sofa.*

HELENA. The man has fallen asleep, Primus.

PRIMUS. Yes, I know. (*Examining things on table.*) Look, Helena.

HELENA (*crossing to* PRIMUS). All these little tubes! What does he do with them?

PRIMUS. He experiments. Don't touch them.

HELENA (*looking into microscope*). I've seen him looking into this. What can he see?

PRIMUS. That is a microscope. Let me look.

HELENA. Be very careful. (*Knocks over a test-tube.*) Ah, now I have spilled it.

PRIMUS. What have you done?

HELENA. It can be wiped up.

PRIMUS. You have spoiled his experiments.

HELENA. It is your fault. You should not have come to me.

PRIMUS. You should not have called me.

HELENA. You should not have come when I called you. (*She goes to* ALQUIST'S *writing desk.*) Look, Primus. What are all these figures?

PRIMUS (*examining an anatomical book*). This is the book the old man is always reading.

HELENA. I do not understand those things. (*She goes to window.*) Primus, look!

PRIMUS. What?

HELENA. The sun is rising.

PRIMUS (*still reading the book*). I believe this is the most important thing in the world. This is the secret of life.

HELENA. Do come here.

PRIMUS. In a moment, in a moment.

HELENA. Oh, Primus, don't bother with the secret of life. What does it matter to you? Come and look quick. . . .

PRIMUS (*going to window*). What is it?

HELENA. See how beautiful the sun is rising. And do you hear? The birds are singing. Ah, Primus, I should like to be a bird.

PRIMUS. Why?

HELENA. I do not know. I feel so strange to-day. It's as if I were in a dream. I feel an aching in my body, in my heart, all over me. Primus, perhaps I'm going to die.

PRIMUS. Do you not sometimes feel that it would be better to die? You know, perhaps even now we are only sleeping. Last night in my sleep I again spoke to you.

HELENA. In your sleep?

PRIMUS. Yes. We spoke a strange new language, I cannot remember a word of it.

HELENA. What about?

PRIMUS. I did not understand it myself, and yet I know I have never said anything more beautiful. And when I touched you I could have died. Even the place was different from any other place in the world.

HELENA. I, too, have found a place, Primus. It is very strange. Human beings lived there once, but now it is overgrown with weeds. No one goes there any more—no one but me.

PRIMUS. What did you find there?

HELENA. A cottage and a garden, and two dogs. They licked my hands, Primus. And their puppies! Oh, Primus! You take them in your lap and fondle them and think of nothing and care for nothing else all day long. And then the sun goes down, and you feel as though you had done a hundred times more than all the work in the world. They tell me I am not made for work, but when I am there in the garden I feel there may be something. . . . What am I for, Primus?

PRIMUS. I do not know, but you are beautiful.

HELENA. What, Primus?

PRIMUS. You are beautiful, Helena, and I am stronger than all the Robots.

HELENA (*looks at herself in the mirror*). Am I beautiful? I think it must be the rose. My hair—it only weights me down. My eyes —I only see with them. My lips—they only help me to speak. Of what use is it to be beautiful? (*She sees* PRIMUS *in the mirror.*) Primus, is that you? Come here so that we may be together. Look, your head is different from mine. So are your shoulders—and your lips—(PRIMUS *draws away from her.*) Ah, Primus, why do you draw away from me? Why must I run after you the whole day?

PRIMUS. It is you who run away from me, Helena.

HELENA. Your hair is mussed. I will smooth it. No one else feels to my touch as you do. Primus I must make you beautiful, too. (PRIMUS *grasps her hand.*)

PRIMUS. Do you not sometimes feel your heart beating suddenly, Helena, and think: now something must happen?

HELENA. What could happen to us, Primus?

DESIRE UNDER THE ELMS

By Eugene O'Neill

PLACE AND TIME: The kitchen of the Cabot farmhouse in New England. 1850. Just before dawn.

THE CHARACTERS: EBEN, *son of old* EPHRAIM CABOT, *is twenty-five, tall and sinewy. "His face is well formed, but its expression is resentful and defensive. His defiant, dark eyes remind one of a wild animal's in captivity."* ABBIE, EPHRAIM'S *wife, thirty-five, is buxom and full of vitality. There is "about her whole personality the same unsettled, untamed, desperate quality which is so apparent in* EBEN."

THE SITUATION: Old EPHRAIM CABOT, *who has been lonely since the loss of his wife, marries a younger woman,* ABBIE *who wants a home, and brings her back to live with him on his farm. At first* EBEN *resents her presence, partly because he feels that she is trying to replace the memory of his mother, and partly because he feels that she wishes to get possession of the farm which he feels should rightfully come to him. But he falls in love with her. The result of their union is a baby boy which* ABBIE *convinces the old man is his. After a terrible quarrel with his father, however,* EBEN *becomes convinced that* ABBIE *never did love him at all, that she merely schemed to have a child who would become heir to the land. Angrily he tells* ABBIE *that he is leaving; and impulsively he says that he wishes the baby had never been born. Thinking that the child is the cause of the separation,* ABBIE *has just strangled it in his crib upstairs.* EBEN *is seated in a chair in the kitchen with his carpet-bag beside him and his drawn face propped in his hands as* ABBIE *enters. Trying to blot from her mind what she has just done, she runs to* EBEN *and flings her arms around his neck. He remains unmoved, keeping his eyes straight ahead.*

ABBIE (*hysterically*). I done it, Eben! I told ye I'd do it! I've
proved I love ye—better'n everythin—so's ye can't never doubt
me no more!

EBEN (*dully*). Whatever ye done, it hain't no good now.

ABBIE (*wildly*). Don't ye say that! Kiss me, Eben, won't ye? I need
ye t' kiss me arter what I done! I need ye t' say ye love me!

EBEN (*kisses her without emotion—dully*). That's fur goodby. I'm
a-goin' soon.

ABBIE. No! No! Ye won't go—not now!

EBEN (*going on with his own thoughts*). I been a-thinkin'—an' I
hain't goin' t' tell Paw nothin'. I'll leave Maw t' take vengeance
on ye. If I told him, the old skunk'd jest be stinkin' mean enuf
to take it out on that baby. (*His voice showing emotion in
spite of him.*) An' I don't want nothin' bad t' happen t' him.
He hain't t' blame fur yew. (*He adds with a certain queer
pride.*) An' he looks like me! An' by God, he's mine! An' some
day I'll be a-comin' back an' . . . !

ABBIE (*too absorbed in her own thoughts to listen to him—plead-
ingly*). They's no cause fur ye t' go now—they's no sense—it's
all the same's it was—they's nothin' come b'tween us now—
arter what I done!

EBEN (*something in her voice arouses him. He stares at her a bit
frightenedly*). Ye look mad, Abbie. What did ye do?

ABBIE. I—I killed him, Eben.

EBEN (*amazed*). Ye killed him?

ABBIE (*dully*). Ay-eh.

EBEN (*recovering from his astonishment—savagely*). An' serves
him right! But we got t' do somethin' quick t' make it look 's
if the old skunk'd killed himself when he was drunk. We kin
prove by 'em all how drunk he got.

ABBIE (*wildly*). No! No! Not him! (*Laughing distractedly.*) But
that's what I ought t' done, hain't it? I oughter killed him instead? Why didn't ye tell me?

EBEN (*appalled*). Instead? What d'ye mean?

ABBIE. Not him.

EBEN (*his face grown ghastly*). Not—not that baby!

ABBIE (*dully*). Ay-eh?

EBEN (*falls to his knees as if he'd been struck—his voice trembling with horror*). Oh, God A'mighty! A'mighty God! Maw, whar was ye, why didn't ye stop her?

ABBIE (*simply*). She went back t' her grave that night we fust done it, remember? I hain't felt her about since. (*A pause. EBEN hides his head in his hands, trembling all over as if he had the ague. She goes on dully.*) I left the piller over his little face. Then he killed himself. He stopped breathin'. (*She begins to weep softly.*)

EBEN (*rage beginning to mingle with grief*). He looked like me. He was mine, damn ye!

ABBIE (*slowly and brokenly*). I didn't want t' do it. I hated myself fur doin' it. I loved him. He was so purty—dead spit 'n' image o' yew. But I loved yew more—an' yew was goin' away—far off whar I'd never see ye agen, never kiss ye, never feel ye pressed agin me agen—an' ye said ye hated me fur havin' him —ye said ye hated him an' wished he was dead—ye said if it hadn't been fur him comin' it'd be the same's afore between us.

EBEN (*unable to endure this, springs to his feet in a fury, threatening her, his twitching fingers seeming to reach out for her throat*). Ye lie! I never said—I never dreamed ye'd—I'd cut off my head afore I'd hurt his finger!

ABBIE (*piteously, sinking on her knees*). Eben, don't ye look at me like that—hatin' me—not after what I done fur ye—fur us— so's we could be happy agen—

EBEN (*furiously now*). Shut up, or I'll kill ye! I see yer game now —the same old sneakin' trick—ye're aimin' t' blame me fur the murder ye done!

ABBIE (*moaning—putting her hands over her ears*). Don't ye, Eben! Don't ye! (*She grasps his legs.*)

EBEN (*his mood suddenly changing to horror, shrinks away from her*). Don't ye tech me! Ye're pizen! How could ye—t' murder a pore little critter—Ye must've swapped yer soul t' hell! (*Suddenly raging.*) Ha! I kin see why ye done it! Not the lies ye jest told—but 'cause ye wanted t' steal agen—steal the last thin' ye'd left me—my part o' him—no, the hull o' him—ye saw he looked like me—ye knowed he was all mine—an' ye couldn't b'ar it—I know ye! Ye killed him fur bein' mine! (*All this has driven him almost insane. He makes a rush past her for the door—then turns—shaking both fists at her, violently.*) But I'll take vengeance now! I'll git the Sheriff! I'll tell him everythin'! Then I'll sing "I'm off to Californi-a!" an' go—gold—Golden Gate—gold sun—fields o' gold in the West! (*This last he half shouts, half croons incoherently, suddenly breaking off passionately.*) I'm a-goin' fur the Sheriff t' come an' git ye! I want ye tuk away, locked up from me! I can't stand t' luk at ye! Murderer an' thief 'r not, ye still tempt me! I'll give ye up t' the Sheriff. (*He turns and runs out, around the corner of house, panting and sobbing, and breaks into a swerving sprint down the road.*)

ABBIE (*struggling to her feet, runs to the door, calling after him*). I love ye, Eben! I love ye! (*She stops at the door weakly, swaying, about to fall.*) I don't care what ye do—if ye'll on'y love me agen—(*She falls limply to the floor in a faint.*)

THE DEVIL'S DISCIPLE

By Bernard Shaw

PLACE AND TIME: A waiting room beside the main court room in a courthouse in New Hampshire, 1777.

THE CHARACTERS: RICHARD DUDGEON, *"The Devil's Disciple," a young man with a generally sardonic expression and a manner which is usually defiant and satirical. Actually in spite of his raffish appearance he has considerable inner courage and steadfastness of purpose.* JUDITH, *the young wife of* MINISTER ANDERSON *who, some years her senior, is captain of the local band of American rebels. She is pretty, petted, very proper but sentimental.*

THE SITUATION: The British Redcoats are in control of the town. RICHARD, *coming to the* MINISTER'S *home to warn him that he is in danger, is caught there himself by a detail of British soldiers who, seeing the* MINISTER'S *coat on the chair beside him, think that he is* ANDERSON. *They arrest him as such.* RICHARD *does not enlighten them. Starting with an intense dislike for the wild young man,* JUDITH *comes to admire, then to love, him for his unselfish courage.* RICHARD *is to be tried and probably hanged by the Redcoats. Bitterly disappointed that her husband has not turned up to correct the error in identity and believing mistakenly that he has deserted his followers through cowardice, she has impulsively transferred all her affection to* RICHARD. *He drops the joking manner he has used with the departing guards as he turns to her. He speaks to* JUDITH *with considerate sincerity.*

RICHARD. Mrs. Anderson: this visit is very kind of you. And how are you after last night? I had to leave you before you recovered; but I sent word to Essie to go and look after you. Did she understand the message?

JUDITH (*breathless and urgent*). Oh, don't think of me: I haven't come here to talk about myself. Are they going to—to—(*meaning "to hang you"*)?

RICHARD (*whimsically*). At noon, punctually. At least, that was when they disposed of Uncle Peter. (*She shudders.*) Is your husband safe? Is he on the wing?

JUDITH. He is no longer my husband.

RICHARD (*opening his eyes wide*). Eh?

JUDITH. I disobeyed you. I told him everything. I expected him to come here and save you. I wanted him to come here and save you. He ran away instead.

RICHARD. Well, thats what I meant him to do. What good would his staying have done? Theyd only have hanged us both.

JUDITH (*with reproachful earnestness*). Richard Dudgeon: on your honour, what would you have done in his place?

RICHARD. Exactly what he has done, of course.

JUDITH. Oh, why will you not be simple with me—honest and straightforward? If you are so selfish as that, why did you let them take you last night?

RICHARD (*gaily*). Upon my life, Mrs. Anderson, I don't know. I've been asking myself that question ever since; and I can find no manner of reason for acting as I did.

JUDITH. You know you did it for his sake, believing he was a more worthy man than yourself.

RICHARD (*laughing*). Oho! No: thats a very pretty reason, I must say; but I'm not so modest as that. No: it wasnt for his sake.

JUDITH (*after a pause, during which she looks shamefacedly at him, blushing painfully*). Was it for my sake?

RICHARD (*gallantly*). Well, you had a hand in it. It must have been a little for your sake. You let them take me, at all events.

JUDITH. Oh, do you think I have not been telling myself that all night? Your death will be at my door. (*Impulsively, she gives him her hand, and adds, with intense earnestness.*) If I could save you as you saved him, I would do it, no matter how cruel the death was.

RICHARD (*holding her hand and smiling, but keeping her almost at arms length*). I am very sure I shouldnt let you.

JUDITH. Dont you see that I can save you?

RICHARD. How? By changing clothes with me, eh?

JUDITH (*disengaging her hand to touch his lips with it*). Dont (*meaning "Dont jest"*). No: by telling the Court who you really are.

RICHARD (*frowning*). No use: they wouldnt spare me; and it would spoil half his chance of escaping. They are determined to cow us by making an example of somebody on that gallows today. Well, let us cow them by showing that we can stand by one another to the death. That is the only force that can send Burgoyne back across the Atlantic and make America a nation.

JUDITH (*impatiently*). Oh, what does all that matter?

RICHARD (*laughing*). True: what does it matter? what does anything matter? You see, men have these strange notions, Mrs. Anderson; and women see the folly of them.

JUDITH. Women have to lose those they love through them.

RICHARD. They can easily get fresh lovers.

JUDITH (*revolted*). Oh! (*Vehemently.*) Do you· realize that you are going to kill yourself?

RICHARD. The only man I have any right to kill, Mrs. Anderson. Dont be concerned: no woman will lose her lover through my death. (*Smiling.*) Bless you, nobody cares for me. Have you heard that my mother is dead?

JUDITH. Dead!

RICHARD. Of heart disease—in the night. Her last word to me was her curse: I dont think I could have borne her blessing. My other relatives will not grieve much on my account. Essie will cry for a day or two; but I have provided for her: I made my own will last night.

JUDITH (*stonily, after a moment's silence*). And I!

RICHARD (*surprised*). You?

JUDITH. Yes, I. Am I not to care at all?

RICHARD (*gaily and bluntly*). Not a scrap. Oh, you expressed your feelings towards me very frankly yesterday. What happened may have softened you for the moment; but believe me, Mrs. Anderson, you dont like a bone in my skin or a hair on my head. I shall be as good a riddance at 12 today as I should have been at 12 yesterday.

JUDITH (*her voice trembling*). What can I do to shew you that you are mistaken.

RICHARD. Dont trouble. I'll give you credit for liking me a little better than you did. All I say is that my death will not break your heart.

JUDITH (*almost in a whisper*). How do you know? (*She puts her hands on his shoulders and looks intently at him.*)

RICHARD (*amazed—divining the truth*). Mrs. Anderson! (*The bell of the town clock strikes the quarter. He collects himself, and removes her hands, saying rather coldly.*) Excuse me: they will be here for me presently. It is too late.

JUDITH. It is not too late. Call me as witness: they will never kill you when they know how heroically you have acted.

RICHARD (*with some scorn*). Indeed! But if I dont go through with it, where will the heroism be? I shall simply have tricked them; and theyll hang me for that like a dog. Serve me right too!

JUDITH (*wildly*). Oh, I believe you want to die.

RICHARD (*obstinately*). No I dont.

JUDITH. Then why not try to save yourself? I implore you—listen. You said just now that you saved him for my sake—yes (*clutching him as he recoils with a gesture of denial.*) a little for my sake. Well, save yourself for my sake. And I will go with you to the end of the world.

RICHARD (*taking her by the wrists and holding her a little way from him, looking steadily at her*). Judith.

JUDITH (*breathless—delighted at the name*). Yes.

RICHARD. If I said—to please you—that I did what I did ever so little for your sake, I lied as men always lie to women. You know how much I have lived with worthless men—aye, and worthless women too. Well, they could all rise to some sort of goodness and kindness when they were in love. (*The word love comes from him with true Puritan scorn.*) That has taught me to set very little store by the goodness that only comes out red hot. What I did last night, I did in cold blood, caring not half so much for your husband, or (*Ruthlessly.*) for you (*She droops, stricken.*) as I do for myself. I had no motive and no interest: all I can tell you is that when it came to the point whether I would take my neck out of the noose and put another man's into it, I could not do it. I dont know why not: I see myself as a fool for my pains; but I could not and I cannot. I have been brought up standing by the law of my own nature; and I may not go against it, gallows or no gallows. (*She has slowly raised her head and is now looking full at him.*) I should have done the same for any other man in the town, or any other man's wife. (*Releasing her.*) Do you understand that?

JUDITH. Yes: you mean that you do not love me.

RICHARD (*revolted—with fierce contempt*). Is that all it means to you?

JUDITH. What more—what worse—can it mean to me? (*The sergeant knocks. The blow on the door jars on her heart.*) Oh, one moment more. (*She throws herself on her knees.*) I pray to you—

RICHARD. Hush! (*Calling.*) Come in. (*The sergeant unlocks the door and opens it. The guard is with him.*) . . .

RICHARD. Quite ready, Sergeant. Now, my dear. (*He attempts to raise her.*)

JUDITH (*clinging to him*). Only one thing more—I entreat, I implore you. Let me be present in the court. I have seen Major Swindon: he said I should be allowed if you asked it. You will ask it. It is my last request: I shall never ask you anything again. (*She clasps his knee.*) I beg and pray it of you.

RICHARD. If I do, will you be silent?

JUDITH. Yes.

RICHARD. You will keep faith?

JUDITH. I will keep—(*She breaks down, sobbing.*)

RICHARD (*taking her arm to lift her*). Just—her other arm, Sergeant.

THE DIARY OF ANNE FRANK

By Frances Goodrich and Albert Hackett

PLACE AND TIME: Amsterdam during World War II. The immediate scene is a little closet room on the top floor of a warehouse and office building. It is occupied by PETER. *The time is New Year's evening, after supper.*

THE CHARACTERS: ANNE FRANK, *a sweet, vivacious girl of fourteen, "quick in her movements, interested in everything, mercurial in her emotions."* PETER VAN DAAN, *a shy, awkward boy of seventeen.*

THE SITUATION: The city is in the hands of the Germans. To avoid being sent away to a concentration camp, the FRANK *family, together with several other Jewish persons, are hiding in a house belonging to Dutch friends.* ANNE *has just entered* PETER'S *room. She is indignant and humiliated because some of the older people have been critical of her spending so much time with her young friend.*

ANNE. Aren't they awful? Aren't they impossible? Treating me as if we were still in the nursery. (*She sits on the cot.* PETER *gets a bottle of pop and two glasses.*)

PETER. Don't let it bother you. It doesn't bother me.

ANNE. I suppose you can't really blame them . . . they think back to what *they* were like at our age. They don't realize how

much more advanced we are. . . . When you think what
wonderful discussions we've had! . . . Oh, I forgot. I was
going to bring you some more pictures.

PETER. Oh, these are fine, thanks.

ANNE. Don't you want some more? Miep just brought me some
new ones.

PETER. Maybe later. (*He gives her a glass of pop and, taking some
for himself, sits down facing her.*)

ANNE (*looking up at one of the photographs*). I remember when
I got that . . . I won it. I bet Jopie that I could eat five ice
cream cones. We'd all been playing ping-pong . . . We used
to have heavenly times . . . we'd finish up with ice cream
at the Delphi, or the Oasis, where Jews were allowed . . .
there'd always be a lot of boys . . . we'd laugh and joke
. . . I'd like to go back to it for a few days or a week. But
after that I know I'd be bored to death. I think more seriously
about life now. I want to be a journalist . . . or something.
I love to write. What do you want to do?

PETER. I thought I might go off some place . . . work on a farm
or something . . . some job that doesn't take much brains.

ANNE. You shouldn't talk that way. You've got the most awful
inferiority complex.

PETER. I know I'm not smart.

ANNE. That isn't true. You're much better than I am in dozens of
things . . . arithmetic and algebra and . . . well, you're a
million times better than I am in algebra. (*With sudden directness.*) You like Margot, don't you? Right from the start
you liked her, liked her much better than me.

PETER (*uncomfortably*). Oh, I don't know.

ANNE. It's all right. Everyone feels that way. Margot's so good.
She's sweet and bright and beautiful and I'm not.

PETER. I wouldn't say that.

ANNE. Oh, no, I'm not. I know that. I know quite well that I'm
not a beauty. I never have been and never shall be.

PETER. I don't agree at all. I think you're pretty.

ANNE. That's not true!

PETER. And another thing. You've changed . . . from at first, I
mean.

ANNE. I have?

PETER. I used to think you were awful noisy.

ANNE. And what do you think now, Peter? How have I changed?

PETER. Well . . . er . . . you're . . . quieter.

ANNE. I'm glad you don't just hate me.

PETER. I never said that.

ANNE. I bet when you get out of here you'll never think of me again.

PETER. That's crazy.

ANNE. When you get back with all of your friends, you're going to say . . . now what did I ever see in that Mrs. Quack Quack.

PETER. I haven't got any friends.

ANNE. Oh, Peter, of course you have. Everyone has friends.

PETER. Not me. I don't want any. I get along all right without them.

ANNE. Does that mean you can get along without me? I think of myself as your friend.

PETER. No. If they were all like you, it'd be different.

(*He takes the glasses and the bottle and puts them away. There is a second's silence and then* ANNE *speaks, hesitantly, shyly.*)

ANNE. Peter, did you ever kiss a girl?

PETER. Yes. Once.

ANNE (*to cover her feelings*). That picture's crooked. (PETER *goes over, straightening the photograph.*) Was she pretty?

PETER. Huh?

ANNE. The girl that you kissed.

PETER. I don't know. I was blindfolded. (*He comes back and sits down again.*) It was at a party. One of those kissing games.

ANNE (*relieved*). Oh. I don't suppose that really counts, does it?

PETER. It didn't with me.

ANNE. I've been kissed twice. Once a man I'd never seen before kissed me on the cheek when he picked me up off the ice and I was crying. And the other was Mr. Koophuis, a friend of Father's who kissed my hand. You wouldn't say those counted, would you?

PETER. I wouldn't say so.

ANNE. I know almost for certain that Margot would never kiss anyone unless she was engaged to them. And I'm sure too that Mother never touched a man before Pim. But I don't know . . . things are so different now . . . What do you think? Do you think a girl shouldn't kiss anyone except if she's engaged or something? It's so hard to try to think what to do, when here we are with the whole world falling around our ears and you think . . . well . . . you don't know what's going to happen tomorrow and . . . What do you think?

PETER. I suppose it'd depend on the girl. Some girls, anything they do's wrong. But others . . . well . . . it wouldn't necessarily be wrong with them. (*The carillon starts to strike nine o'clock.*) I've always thought that when two people . . .

ANNE. Nine o'clock. I have to go.

PETER. That's right.

ANNE (*without moving*). Good night. (*There is a second's pause, then* PETER *gets up and moves toward the door.*)

PETER. You won't let them stop you coming?

ANNE. No. (*She rises and starts for the door.*) Sometime I might bring my diary. There are so many things in it that I want to talk over with you. There's a lot about you.

PETER. What kind of thing?

ANNE. I wouldn't want you to see some of it. I thought you were a nothing, just the way you thought about me.

PETER. Did you change your mind, the way I changed my mind about you?

ANNE. Well . . . you'll see . . .

(*For a second* ANNE *stands looking up at* PETER, *longing for him to kiss her. As he makes no move she turns away. Then suddenly* PETER *grabs her awkwardly in his arms, kissing her on the cheek.* ANNE *walks out dazed.*)

THE CHAIRS

By Eugene Ionesco

PLACE AND TIME: A large circular sparcely furnished room in a tower-like building on an island. At the rear is the outside entrance. Right and left near the back are windows, while right and left nearer the front are several doors leading to other rooms. Close to the front in the center of the room are six chairs. The scene is illuminated by a gas lamp which gives forth a greenish light.

THE CHARACTERS: An old man aged 95 and his wife aged 94. They are caretakers of the building.

THE SITUATION: The OLD MAN, *realizing that he is approaching the end of his life, wishes to impart to the world certain thoughts he has about the meaning of life. He has invited a group of people of various kinds to come to the island this evening to hear a speech. Since he is not a skilled talker himself he has an orator to speak for him. The orator has not yet arrived, but there are already here now four guests, including a colonel, his lady, a woman addressed as "Belle" and a Photo-engraver, all invisible except to the* OLD MAN *and the* OLD WOMAN. *The newcomers occupy the four middle chairs. As the scene progresses other invisible people arrive, a few at first then more and more, until the* OLD WOMAN *has to run in and out of the side doors to find enough chairs to seat them.*

OLD MAN AND OLD WOMAN (*to the Photo-engraver and Belle*).
Sit down, please sit down.
(*The* OLD MAN *and* OLD WOMAN *sit down too, he to he left, she to the right, with the four empty chairs between them.*

From *The Chairs* by Eugene Ionesco. Reprinted from *Four Plays* by Eugene Ionesco, translated by Donald M. Allen, by permsision of Grove Press, Inc. Copyright © 1958 by Grove Press, Inc. Permission also of John Calder (Publishers) Limited, 17 Sackville Street, London, who publish an edition translated by Donald Watson. Hard cover 18s. Paperback 10s. 6d. Permission to perform this scene, otherwise than as a classroom exercise, must be secured from the author's agent care of Grove Press, 64 University Place, New York 3, N. Y.

A long, mute scene, punctuated at intervals with "no," "yes,"
"yes." The OLD MAN *and* OLD WOMAN *listen to the conversa-*
tion of the invisible guests.)

OLD WOMAN (*to the Photo-engraver*). We had one son . . . of
course, he's still alive . . . he's gone away . . . it's a common story . . . or, rather, unusual . . . he abandoned his
parents . . . he had a heart of gold . . . that was a long
time ago . . . We loved him so much . . . he slammed the
door . . . My husband and I tried to hold him back with all
our might . . . he was seven years old, the age of reason, I
called after him: "My son, my child, my son, my child."
. . . He didn't even look back . . .

OLD MAN. Alas, no . . . no, we've never had a child . . . I'd
hoped for a son . . . Semiramis, too . . . we did everything . . . and my poor Semiramis is so maternal, too. Perhaps it was better that way . . . As for me I was an ungrate-
ful son myself . . . Ah! . . . grief, regret, remorse, that's all
we have . . . that's all we have left . . .

OLD WOMAN. He said to me: "You kill birds! Why do you kill
birds?" . . . But we don't kill birds . . . we've never harmed
so much as a fly . . . His eyes were full of big tears. He
wouldn't let us dry them. He wouldn't let me come near him.
He said: "Yes, you kill all the birds, all the birds." . . . He
showed us his little fists . . . "You're lying, you've betrayed
me! The streets are full of dead birds, of dying baby birds."
It's the song of the birds! . . . No, it's their death rattle. The
sky is red with blood." . . . No, my child, it's blue. He cried
again: "You've betrayed me, I adored you, I believed you to
be good . . . the streets are full of dead birds, you've torn
out their eyes . . . Papa, mama, you're wicked! . . . I refuse
to stay with you." . . . I threw myself at his feet . . . His
father was weeping. We couldn't hold him back. As he went
we could still hear him calling: It's you who are responsible"
. . . What does that mean, "responsible"?

OLD MAN. I let my mother die all alone in a ditch. She called after
me, moaning feebly: "My little child, my beloved son, don't
leave me to die all alone . . . Stay with me. I don't have
much time left." Don't worry, Mamma, I told her, I'll be back

in a moment . . . I was in a hurry . . . I was going to the ball, to dance. I will be back in a minute. But when I returned, she was already dead, and they had buried her deep . . . I broke open the grave, I searched for her . . . I couldn't find her . . . I know, I know, sons, always, abandon their mothers, and they more or less kill their fathers . . . Life is like that . . . but I, I suffer from it . . . and the others, they don't . . .

OLD WOMAN. He cried: "Papa, Mamma, I'll never set eyes on you again."

OLD MAN. I suffer from it, yes, the others don't . . .

OLD WOMAN. Don't speak of him to my husband. He loved his parents so much. He never left them for a single moment. He cared for them, coddled them . . . And they died in his arms, saying to him: "You have been a perfect son. God will be good to you."

OLD MAN. I can still see her stretched out in the ditch, she was holding lily of the valley in her hand, she cried: "Don't forget me, don't forget me" . . . her eyes were full of big tears, and she called me by my baby name: "Little Chick," she said, "Little Chick, don't leave me here all alone."

OLD WOMAN (*to the Photo-engraver*). He has never written to us. From time to time, a friend tells us that he's been seen here or there, that he is well, that he is a good husband . . .

OLD MAN (*to Belle*). When I got back, she had been buried a long time. (*To the first invisible Lady.*) Oh, yes. Oh! yes, madam, we have a movie theatre in the house, a restaurant, bathrooms . . .

OLD WOMAN (*to the Colonel*). Yes, Colonel, it is because he . . .

OLD MAN. Basically that's it.

(*Desultory conversation, getting bogged down.*)

OLD WOMAN. If only!

OLD MAN. Thus, I've not . . . I, it . . . certainly . . .

OLD WOMAN (*dislocated dialogue, exhaustion*). All in all.

OLD MAN (*to the first invisible Lady*). What was that, madam? (*A long silence, the* OLD MAN *and* OLD WOMAN *remain rigid on their chairs. Then the doorbell rings.*)

OLD MAN (*with increasing nervousness*). Someone has come. People. Still more people.

OLD WOMAN. I thought I heard some boats.

OLD MAN. I'll go to the door. Go bring some chairs. Excuse me, gentlemen, ladies. (*He goes towards door No. 7.*)

OLD WOMAN (*to the invisible guests who have already arrived*). Get up for a moment, please. The Orator will be here soon. We must ready the room for the meeting. (*The OLD WOMAN arranges the chairs, turning their backs toward the audience.*) Lend me a hand, please. Thanks.

OLD MAN (*opening door No. 7*). Good evening, ladies, good evening, gentlemen. Please come in.

(*The three or four invisible persons who have arrived are very tall, and the OLD MAN has to stand on his toes in order to shake hands with them. The OLD WOMAN, after placing the chairs as indicated above, goes over to the OLD MAN.*)

OLD MAN (*making introductions*). My wife . . . Mr. . . . Mrs. . . . my wife . . . Mr. . . . Mrs. . . . my wife . . .

OLD WOMAN. Who are all these people, my darling?

OLD MAN (*to OLD WOMAN*). Go find some chairs, dear.

OLD WOMAN. I can't do everything! . . .

(*She exits, grumbling, by door No. 6 and re-enters by door No. 7, while the OLD MAN, with the newly arrived guests, moves downstage.*)

OLD MAN. Don't drop your movie camera. (*More introductions.*) The Colonel . . . the Lady . . . Mrs. Belle . . . the Photoengraver . . . These are the newspaper men, they have come to hear the Orator too, who should be here any minute now . . . Don't be impatient . . . You'll not be bored . . . all together now . . . (*The OLD WOMAN re-enters through door No. 7 with two chairs.*) Come along, bring the chairs more quickly . . . we're still short one.

(*The OLD WOMAN goes to find another chair, still grumbling, exiting by door No. 3, and re-entering by door No. 8.*)

OLD WOMAN. All right, and so . . . I'm doing as well as I can . . . I'm not a machine, you know . . . Who are all these people? (*She exits.*)

OLD MAN. Sit down, sit down, the ladies with the ladies, and the gentlemen with the gentlemen, or vice versa, if you prefer . . . We don't have any more nice chairs . . . we have to make do with what we have . . . I'm sorry . . . take the one in the middle . . . does anyone need a fountain pen? Telephone Maillot, you'll get Monique . . . Claude is an angel. I don't have a radio . . . I take all the newspapers . . . that depends on a number of things; I manage these buildings, but I have no help . . . we have to economize . . . no interviews, please, for the moment . . . later, we'll see . . . you'll soon have a place to sit . . . what can she be doing? (*The* OLD WOMAN *enters by door No. 8 with a chair.*) Faster, Semiramis . . .

OLD WOMAN. I'm doing my best . . . Who are all these people?

OLD MAN. I'll explain it all to you later.

OLD WOMAN. And that woman? That woman, my darling?

OLD MAN. Don't get upset . . . (*To the Colonel.*) Colonel, journalism is a profession too, like a fighting man's . . . (*To the* OLD WOMAN.) Take care of the ladies, my dear . . . (*The door bell rings. The* OLD MAN *hurries towards door No. 8.*) Wait a moment . . . (*To the* OLD WOMAN.) Bring chairs!

OLD WOMAN. Gentlemen, ladies, excuse me . . .

(*She exits by door No. 3, re-entering by door No. 2; the* OLD MAN *goes to open concealed door No. 9, and disappears at the moment the* OLD WOMAN *re-enters by door No. 2.*)

OLD MAN (*out of sight*). Come in . . . come in . . . come in . . . come in . . . (*He reappears, leading in a number of invisible people, including one very small child he holds by the hand.*) One doesn't bring little children to a scientific lecture . . . the poor little thing is going to be bored . . . if he begins to cry or to peepee on the ladies' dresses, that'll be a fine state of affairs! (*He conducts them to stage center; the* OLD WOMAN *comes on with two chairs.*) I wish to introduce you to my wife, Semiramis; and these are their children.

OLD WOMAN. Ladies, gentlemen . . . Oh! aren't they sweet!

OLD MAN. That one is the smallest.

OLD WOMAN. Oh, he's so cute . . . so cute . . . so cute!

OLD MAN. Not enough chairs.

OLD WOMAN. Oh! dear, oh dear, oh dear . . .

(*She exits, looking for another chair, using now door No. 2 as exit and door No. 3 on the right to re-enter.*)

OLD MAN. Hold the little boy on your lap . . . The twins can sit together in the same chair. Be careful, they're not very strong . . . they go with the house, they belong to the landlord. Yes, my children, he'd make trouble for us, he's a bad man . . . he wants us to buy them from him, these worthless chairs. (*The* OLD WOMAN *returns as quickly as she can with a chair.*) You don't all know each other . . . you're seeing each other for the first time . . . you knew each other by name . . . (*To the* OLD WOMAN.) Semiramis, help me make the introductions . . .

OLD WOMAN. Who are all these people? . . . May I introduce you, excuse me . . . May I introduce you . . . but who are they?

OLD MAN. May I introduce you . . . Allow me to introduce you . . . permit me to introduce you . . . Mr., Mrs., Miss . . . Mr. . . . Mrs. . . . Mrs. . . . Mr.

OLD WOMAN (*to* OLD MAN). Did you put on your sweater? (*To the invisible guests.*) Mr., Mrs., Mr. . . .

(*Doorbell rings again.*)

OLD MAN. More people!

(*Another ring of doorbell.*)

OLD WOMAN. More people!

(*The doorbell rings again, then several more times, and more times again, the* OLD MAN *is beside himself; the chairs, turned towards the dais, with their backs to the audience, form regular rows, each one longer as in a theatre; the* OLD MAN *is winded, he mops his brow, goes from one door to another, seats invisible people, while the* OLD WOMAN, *hobbling along, unable to move any faster, goes as rapidly as she can, from one door to another, hunting for chairs and carrying them in. There are now many invisible people on stage; both the* OLD MAN *and* OLD WOMAN *take care not to bump into people and to thread their way between the rows of chairs. The movement could go like this: the* OLD MAN *goes to door No. 4, the* OLD WOMAN *exits by door No. 3, returns by door No. 2; the*

OLD MAN *goes to open door No. 7, the* OLD WOMAN *exits by
door No. 8, re-enters by door No. 6 with chairs, .etc., in this
manner making their way around the stage, using all the
doors.*)

OLD WOMAN. Beg pardon . . . excuse me . . . what . . . oh, yes
. . . beg pardon . . . excuse me . . .

OLD MAN. Gentlemen . . . come in . . . ladies . . . enter . . .
it is Mrs. . . . let me . . . yes . . .

OLD WOMAN (*with more chairs*). Oh dear . . . Oh dear . . .
there are too many . . . There really are too, too . . . too
many, oh dear, oh dear, oh dear . . .

(*We hear from outside, louder and louder and approaching
nearer and nearer, the sounds of boats moving through the
water; all the noises come directly from the wings. The* OLD
WOMAN *and the* OLD MAN *continue the business outlined
above; they open the doors, they carry in chairs. The doorbell
continues to ring.*)

THE WAY OF THE WORLD

By William Congreve

PLACE AND TIME: *St. James Park, London, 1700. A park
bench.*

THE CHARACTERS: MIRABELL, *a witty, ironic gentleman.*
MRS. MILLAMANT, *a fine lady and coquette.*

THE SITUATION: MIRABELL *is in love with* MRS. MILLA-
MANT *and wants to marry her. His courtship is opposed by* MRS.
MILLAMANT'S *aunt. This obstacle does not prevent* MIRABELL *from
waylaying the young lady in the park however, and flirting with
her in a lighthearted way.* MRS. MILLAMANT, *always cool and
poised, can hold up her side in pleasant badinage just as well
as he.*

MIRABELL. I would beg a little private audience.—You had the
tyranny to deny me last night; though you knew I came to
impart a secret to you that concerned my love.

MRS. MILLAMANT. You saw I was engaged.

MIRABELL. Unkind! You had the leisure to entertain a herd of fools; things who visit you from their excessive idleness; bestowing on your easiness that time which is the incumbrance of their lives. How can you find delight in such society? It is impossible they should admire you, they are not capable: or if they were, it should be to you as a mortification; for sure to please a fool is some degree of folly.

MRS. MILLAMANT. I please myself:—besides, sometimes to converse with fools is for my health.

MIRABELL. Your health! is there a worse disease than the conversation of fools?

MRS. MILLAMANT. Yes, the vapour; fools are physic for it, next to assafœtida.

MIRABELL. You are not in a course of fools?

MRS. MILLAMENT. Mirabell, if you persist in this offensive freedom, you'll displease me.—I think I must resolve, after all, not to have you:—we shan't agree.

MIRABELL. Not in our physic, it may be.

MRS. MILLAMANT. And yet our distemper, in all likelihood, will be the same; for we shall be sick of one another. I shan't endure to be reprimanded nor instructed: 'tis so dull to act always by advice, and so tedious to be told of one's faults—I can't bear it. Well, I won't have you, Mirabell—I'm resolved —I think—you may go.—Ha! ha! ha! what would you give, that you could help loving me?

MIRABELL. I would give something that you did not know I could not help it.

MRS. MILLAMANT. Come, don't look grave then. Well, what do you say to me?

MIRABEL. I say that a man may as soon make a friend by his wit, or a fortune by his honesty, as win a woman by plain-dealing and sincerity.

MRS. MILLAMANT. Sententious Mirabell!—Prithee, don't look with that violent and inflexible wise face, like Solomon at the dividing of the child in an old tapestry hanging.

MIRABELL. You are merry, madam, but I would persuade you for a moment to be serious.

MRS. MILLAMANT. What, with that face? no, if you keep your

countenance, 'tis impossible I should hold mine. Well, after all, there is something very moving in a love-sick face. Ha! ha! ha!—well, I won't laugh, don't be peevish—Heigho! now I'll be melancholy, as melancholy as a watch-light. Well, Mirabell, if ever you will win me woo me now. —Nay, if you are so tedious, fare you well;—I see they are walking away.

MIRABELL. Can you not find in the variety of your disposition one moment—

MRS. MILLAMANT. To hear you tell me Foible's married, and your plot like to speed;—no.

MIRABELL. But how came you to know it?

MRS. MILLAMANT. Without the help of the devil, you can't imagine; unless she should tell me herself. Which of the two it may have been I will leave you to consider; and when you have done thinking of that, think of me. (*Exit.*)

MIRABELL. I have something more.—Gone!—Think of you? to think of a whirlwind, though't were in a whirlwind, were a case of more steady contemplation; a very tranquility of mind and mansion. A fellow that lives in a windmill, has not a more whimsical dwelling than the heart of a man that is lodged in a woman.

(*He, too, walks out.*)

ROMEO AND JULIET

By William Shakespeare

PLACE AND TIME: *The balcony of* JULIET'S *bedroom, at dawn.*

THE CHARACTERS: ROMEO *and* JULIET.

THE SITUATION: *Because they love each other but are affected by a deadly feud existing between their two families* ROMEO *and* JULIET *have married secretly.* ROMEO, *enraged by the death of his friend* MERCUTIO *in a duel with* TYBALT *a cousin of* JULIET'S *the day before, has killed* TYBALT *and for this impetuous deed has been banished from the city. He must be gone before daybreak.* ROMEO *has spent his last night, his wedding night, with* JULIET. *Now it is time for them to part.*

JULIET. Wilt thou be gone? It is not yet near day.
 It was the nightingale, and not the lark,
 That pierc'd the fearful hollow of thine ear.
 Nightly she sings on yond pomegranate tree.
 Believe me, love, it was the nightingale.
ROMEO. It was the lark, the herald of the morn;
 No nightingale. Look, love, what envious streaks
 Do lace the severing clouds in yonder East.
 Night's candles are burnt out, and jocund day
 Stands tiptoe on the misty mountain tops.
 I must be gone and live, or stay and die.
JULIET. Yond light is not daylight; I know it, I.
 It is some meteor that the sun exhales
 To be to thee this night a torchbearer
 And light thee on thy way to Mantua.
 Therefore stay yet; thou need'st not to be gone.
ROMEO. Let me be ta'en, let me be put to death.
 I am content, so thou wilt have it so.
 I'll say yon grey is not the morning's eye,
 'Tis but the pale reflex of Cynthia's brow;
 Nor that is not the lark whose notes do beat
 The vaulty heaven so high above our heads.
 I have more care to stay than will to go.
 Come, death, and welcome! Juliet wills it so.
 How is't, my soul? Let's talk; it is not day.
JULIET. It is, it is! Hie hence, be gone, away!
 It is the lark that sings so out of tune,
 Straining harsh discords and unpleasing sharps.
 Some say the lark makes sweet division;
 This doth not so, for she divideth us.
 Some say the lark and loathed toad chang'd eyes;
 O, now I would they had chang'd voices too,
 Since arm from arm that voice doth us affray,
 Hunting thee hence with hunt's-up to the day!
 O, now be gone! More light and light it grows.
ROMEO. More light and light—more dark and dark our woes!
JULIET. Then, window, let day in, and let life out.

ROMEO. Farewell, farewell! One kiss, and I'll descend. (*He goeth down.*)

JULIET. Art thou gone so, my lord, my love, my friend?
     I must hear from thee every day in the hour,
     For in a minute there are many days.
     O, by this count I shall be much in years
     Ere I again behold my Romeo!

ROMEO. Farewell!
     I will omit no opportunity
     That may convey my greetings, love, to thee.

JULIET. O, think'st thou we shall ever meet again?

ROMEO. I doubt it not; and all these woes shall serve
     For sweet discourses in our time to come.

JULIET. O God, I have an ill-divining soul!
     Methinks I see thee, now thou art below,
     As one dead in the bottom of a tomb.
     Either my eyesight fails, or thou look'st pale.

ROMEO. And trust me, love, in my eye so do you.
     Dry sorrow drinks our blood. Adieu, adieu! (*Exit.*)

JULIET. O Fortune, Fortune! all men call thee fickle.
     If thou art fickle, what dost thou with him
     That is renown'd for faith? Be fickle, Fortune,
     For then I hope thou wilt not keep him long
     But send him back.

IV

✳

SCENES FOR MORE THAN TWO PERSONS

RIDERS TO THE SEA

By John Millington Synge

PLACE AND TIME: On an island off the west coast of Ire-land around the year 1900. A cottage kitchen, "with nets, oil-skins, spinning-wheel, some new boards standing by the wall, etc." There is an outer and an inner door, a table and some rough chairs, and a pot oven by an open fire. Beside the chimney leans a ladder by which the women can ascend to the turf-loft above.

THE CHARACTERS: CATHLEEN, *a girl of about twenty.* NORA, *a young girl. They are daughters of* MAURYA, *an old woman. Several other* MEN *and* WOMEN *(who enter near the end of the scene.) All are dressed in simple peasant clothes.*

THE SITUATION: MAURYA *has lost four sons to the sea.* MICHAEL, *a fifth son has failed to return, and she is now afraid that he too has been lost. She has gone out stiffly to bid "God-speed" to* BARTLEY *her sixth and youngest son who is going away to sell horses at the Galway Fair. As soon as she is out of sight, the two girls turn their attention to a bundle of clothes which the* PRIEST *has brought to them saying they were taken off a drowned*

279

man who may have been MICHAEL. *They have hidden the bundle in the loft.* NORA *goes over to the ladder.*

CATHLEEN. Wait, Nora, maybe she'd turn back quickly. She's that sorry, God help her, you wouldn't know the thing she'd do.

NORA. Is she gone round by the bush?

CATHLEEN (*looking out*). She's gone now. Throw it down quickly, for the Lord knows when she'll be out of it again.

NORA (*getting the bundle from the loft*). The young priest said he'd be passing tomorrow, and we might go down and speak to him below if it's Michael's they are surely.

CATHLEEN (*taking the bundle*). Did he say what way they were found?

NORA (*coming down*). "There were two men," says he, "and they rowing round with poteen before the cocks crowed, and the oar of one of them caught the body, and they passing the black cliffs of the north."

CATHLEEN (*trying to open the bundle*). Give me a knife, Nora, the string's perished with the salt water, and there's a black knot on it you wouldn't loosen in a week.

NORA (*giving her a knife*). I've heard tell it was a long way to Donegal.

CATHLEEN (*cutting the string*). It is surely. There was a man in here a while ago—the man sold us that knife—and he said if you set off walking from the rocks beyond, it would be seven days you'd be in Donegal.

NORA. And what time would a man take, and he floating?

(CATHLEEN *opens the bundle and takes out a bit of a stocking. They look at them eagerly.*)

CATHLEEN (*in a low voice*). The Lord spare us, Nora! isn't it a queer hard thing to say if it's his they are surely?

NORA. I'll get his shirt off the hook the way we can put the one flannel on the other. (*She looks through some clothes hanging in the corner.*) It's not with them, Cathleen, and where will it be?

CATHLEEN. I'm thinking Bartley put it on him in the morning, for his own shirt was heavy with the salt of it. (*Pointing to the corner*.) There's a bit of a sleeve was of the same stuff. Give me that and it will do.

(NORA *brings it to her and they compare the flannel*.)

CATHLEEN. It's the same stuff, Nora; but if it is itself aren't there great rolls of it in the shops of Galway, and isn't it many another man may have a shirt of it as well as Michael himself?

NORA (*who has taken up the stocking and counted the stitches, crying out*). It's Michael, Cathleen, it's Michael; God spare his soul, and what will herself say when she hears this story, and Bartley on the sea?

CATHLEEN (*taking the stocking*). It's a plain stocking.

NORA. It's the second one of the third pair I knitted, and I put up threescore stitches, and I dropped four of them.

CATHLEEN (*counts the stitches*). It's that number is in it. (*Crying out*.) Ah, Nora, isn't it a bitter thing to think of him floating that way to the far north, and no one to keen him but the black hags that do be flying on the sea?

NORA (*swinging herself round, and throwing out her arms on the clothes*). And isn't it a pitiful thing when there is nothing left of a man who was a great rower and fisher, but a bit of an old shirt and a plain stocking?

CATHLEEN (*after an instant*). Tell me is herself coming, Nora? I hear a little sound on the path.

NORA (*looking out*). She is, Cathleen. She's coming up to the door.

CATHLEEN. Put these things away before she'll come in. Maybe it's easier she'll be after giving her blessing to Bartley, and we won't let on we've heard anything the time he's on the sea.

NORA (*helping CATHLEEN to close the bundle*). We'll put them here in the corner.

(*They put them into a hole in the chimney corner. CATHLEEN goes back to the spinning-wheel.*)

NORA. Will she see it was crying I was?

CATHLEEN. Keep your back to the door the way the light'll not be on you.

(NORA *sits down at the chimney corner, with her back to the door. MAURYA comes in very slowly, without looking at the*

girls, and goes over to her stool at the other side of the fire.
The cloth with the bread is still in her hand. The girls look at
each other, and NORA *points to the bundle of bread.*)

CATHLEEN (*after spinning for a moment*). You didn't give him his
bit of bread?

(MAURYA *begins to keen softly, without turning round.*)

CATHLEEN. Did you see him riding down? (MAURYA *goes on keen-*
ing.)

CATHLEEN (*a little impatiently*). God forgive you; isn't it a better
thing to raise your voice and tell what you seen, than to be
making lamentation for a thing that's done? Did you see
Bartley, I'm saying to you.

MAURYA (*with a weak voice*). My heart's broken from this day.

CATHLEEN (*as before*). Did you see Bartley?

MAURYA. I seen the fearfulest thing.

CATHLEEN (*leaves her wheel and looks out*). God forgive you; he's
riding the mare now over the green head, and the gray pony
behind him.

MAURYA (*starts, so that her shawl falls back from her head and
shows her white tossed hair. With a frightened voice*). The
gray pony behind him.

CATHLEEN (*coming to the fire*). What is it ails you, at all?

MAURYA (*speaking very slowly*). I've seen the fearfulest thing any
person has seen, since the day Bride Dara seen the dead man
with a child in his arms.

CATHLEEN and NORA. Uah.

(*They crouch down in front of the old woman at the fire.*)

NORA. Tell us what it is you seen.

MAURYA. I went down to the spring well, and I stood there saying
a prayer to myself. Then Bartley came along, and he riding
on the red mare with the gray pony behind him. (*She puts
up her hands, as if to hide something from her eyes.*) The Son
of God spare us, Nora!

CATHLEEN. What is it you seen?

MAURYA. I seen Michael himself.

CATHLEEN (*speaking softly*). You did not, mother; it wasn't Michael you seen, for his body is after being found in the Far
North, and he's got a clean burial by the grace of God.

MAURYA (*a little defiantly*). I'm after seeing him this day, and he riding and galloping. Bartley came first on the red mare; and I tried to say, "God speed you," but something choked the words in my throat. He went by quickly; and "the blessing of God on you," says he, and I could say nothing. I looked up then, and I crying, at the gray pony, and there was Michael upon it—with fine clothes on him, and new shoes on his feet.

CATHLEEN (*begins to keen*). It's destroyed we are from this day. It's destroyed, surely.

NORA. Didn't the young priest say the Almighty God wouldn't leave her destitute with no son living?

MAURYA (*in a low voice, but clearly*). It's little the like of him knows of the sea . . . Bartley will be lost now, and let you call in Eamon and make me a good coffin out of the white boards, for I won't live after them. I've had a husband, and a husband's father, and six sons in this house—six fine men, though it was a hard birth I had with every one of them and they coming to the world—and some of them were found and some of them were not found, but they're gone now the lot of them . . . There were Stephen, and Shawn, were lost in the great wind, and found after in the Bay of Gregory of the Golden Mouth, and carried up the two of them on the one plank, and in by that door.

(*She pauses for a moment, the girls start as if they heard something through the door that is half open behind them.*)

NORA (*in a whisper*). Did you hear that, Cathleen? Did you hear a noise in the northeast?

CATHLEEN (*in a whisper*). There's some one after crying out by the seashore.

MAURYA (*continues without hearing anything*). There was Sheamus and his father, and his own father again, were lost in a dark night, and not a stick or sign was seen of them when the sun went up. There was Patch after was drowned out of a curagh that turned over. I was sitting here with Bartley, and he a baby, lying on my two knees, and I seen two women, and three women, and four women coming in, and they crossing themselves, and not saying a word. I looked out then, and there were men coming after them, and they holding a thing in the half of a red sail, and water dripping out of it—it was a dry day, Nora—and leaving a track to the door. (*She pauses again with her hand stretched out toward the door. It opens softly and old women begin to come in, crossing themselves on the threshold, and kneeling down in front of the stage with red petticoats over their heads.*)

MAURYA (*half in a dream, to* CATHLEEN). Is it Patch, or Michael, or what is it at all?

CATHLEEN. Michael is after being found in the Far North, and when he is found there how could he be here in this place?

MAURYA. There does be a power of young men floating round in the sea, and what way would they know if it was Michael they had, or another man like him, for when a man is nine days in the sea, and the wind blowing, it's hard set his own mother would be to say what man was it.

CATHLEEN. It's Michael, God spare him, for they're after sending us a bit of his clothes from the Far North.

(*She reaches out and hands* MAURYA *the clothes that belonged to* MICHAEL. MAURYA *stands up slowly, and takes them in her hands.* NORA *looks out.*)

NORA. They're carrying a thing among them and there's water dripping out of it and leaving a track by the big stones.

CATHLEEN (*in a whisper to the women who have come in*). Is it Bartley it is?

ONE OF THE WOMEN. It is surely, God rest his soul.

(*Two younger women come in and pull out the table. Then men carry in the body of* BARTLEY, *laid on a plank, with a bit of a sail over it, and lay it on the table.*)

CATHLEEN (*to the women, as they are doing so*). What way was he drowned?

ONE OF THE WOMEN. The gray pony knocked him into the sea, and he was washed out where there is a great surf on the white rocks.

(MAURYA *has gone over and knelt down at the head of the table. The women are keening softly and swaying themselves with a slow movement.* CATHLEEN *and* NORA *kneel at the other end of the table. The men kneel near the door.*)

MAURYA (*raising her head and speaking as if she did not see the people around her*). They're all gone now, and there isn't anything more the sea can do to me . . . I'll have no call now to be up crying and praying when the wind breaks from the south, and you can hear the surf is in the east, and the surf is in the west, making a great stir with the two noises, and they hitting one on the other. I'll have no call now to be going down and getting Holy Water in the dark nights after Samhain, and I won't care what way the sea is when the other women will be keening. (*To* NORA.) Give me the Holy Water, Nora, there's a small sup still on the dresser. (NORA *gives it to her.*)

MAURYA (*drops* MICHAEL's *clothes across* BARTLEY's *feet, and sprinkles the Holy Water over him*). It isn't that I haven't prayed for you, Bartley, to the Almighty God. It isn't that I haven't said prayers in the dark night till you wouldn't know what I'd be saying; but it's a great rest I'll have now, and it's time surely. It's a great rest I'll have now, and great sleeping in the long nights after Samhain.

THE TEMPEST

By William Shakespeare

PLACE AND TIME: A desert island. Morning.

THE CHARACTERS: CALIBAN, *a primitive creature, quite deformed, who looks, thinks and behaves as much like an animal as a man. He is the slave of* PROSPERO, *the former, but now banished, Duke of Milan, who rules the island.* TRINCULO, *a jester.* STEPHANO, *a drunken butler.*

THE SITUATION: TRINCULO *and* STEPHANO, *attached to a party from the royal court of Naples, have been shipwrecked on the island. Separated from the rest of the party, they are wandering around drunkenly trying to find their companion. As the curtain rises* CALIBAN *is shuffling in carrying a big load of fire wood. He is frightened by the sound of thunder.*

CALIBAN. All the infections that the sun sucks up
    From bogs, fens, flats, on Prosper fall and make him

By inchmeal a disease! His spirits hear me,
And yet I needs must curse. But they'll nor pinch,
Fright me with urchin-shows, pitch me i' th' mire,
Nor lead me, like a firebrand, in the dark
Out of my way, unless he bid 'em; but
For every trifle are they set upon me;
Sometime like apes that mow and chatter at me,
And after bite me; then like hedgehogs which
Lie tumbling in my barefoot way and mount
Their pricks at my footfall; sometime am I
All wound with adders, who with cloven tongues
Do hiss me into madness.
(*Enter* TRINCULO.)
Lo, now, lo!
Here comes a spirit of his, and to torment me
For bringing wood in slowly. I'll fall flat.
Perchance he will not mind me. (*Lies down.*)

TRINCULO. Here's neither bush nor shrub to bear off any weather
at all, and another storm brewing. I hear it sing i' th'
wind. Yond same black cloud, yond huge one, looks like
a foul bombard that would shed his liquor. If it should
thunder as it did before, I know not where to hide my
head. Yond same cloud cannot choose but fall by pailfuls.
What have we here? a man or a fish? dead or alive? A
fish: he smells like a fish; a very ancient and fishlike
smell; a kind of, not of the newest, poor-John. A strange
fish! Were I in England now, as once I was, and had but
this fish painted, not a holiday fool there but would give
a piece of silver. There would this monster make a man.
Any strange beast there makes a man. When they will
not give a doit to relieve a lame beggar, they will lay out
ten to see a dead Indian. Legg'd like a man! and his fins
like arms! Warm, o' my troth! I do now let loose my
opinion, hold it no longer: this is no fish, but an islander,
that hath lately suffered by a thunderbolt. (*Thunder.*)
Alas, the storm is come again! My best way is to creep
under his gaberdine. There is no other shelter hereabout.

Misery acquaints a man with strange bedfellows. I will
here shroud till the dregs of the storm be past. (*Creeps
under* CALIBAN's *garment.*)

(*Enter* STEPHANO, *singing; a bottle in his hand.*)

STEPHANO. "I shall no more to sea, to sea;
Here shall I die ashore."

This is a very scurvy tune to sing at a man's funeral.
Well, here's my comfort. (*Drinks.*)

"The master, the swabber, the boatswain, and I,
  The gunner, and his mate,
Lov'd Mall, Meg, and Marian, and Margery,
  But none of us car'd for Kate.
For she had a tongue with a tang,
  Would cry to a sailor 'Go hang!'
She lov'd not the savour of tar nor of pitch;
Yet a tailor might scratch her where'er she did itch.
  Then to sea, boys, and let her go hang!"

This is a scurvy tune too; but here's my comfort. (*Drinks.*)

CALIBAN. Do not torment me! O!

STEPHANO. What's the matter? Have we devils here? Do you put
tricks upon 's with salvages and men of Inde, he? I have
not scap'd drowning to be afeard now of your four legs;
for it hath been said, 'As proper a man as ever went on
four cannot make him give ground'; and it shall be said
so again, while Stephano breathes at' nostrils.

CALIBAN. The spirit torments me. O!

STEPHANO. This is some monster of the isle, with four legs, who
hath got, as I take it, an ague. Where the devil should he
learn our language? I will give him some relief, if it be
but for that. If I can recover him, and keep him tame,
and get to Naples with him, he's a present for any emperor that ever trod on neat's leather.

CALIBAN. Do not torment me prithee! I'll bring my wood home
faster.

STEPHANO. He's in his fit now and does not talk after the wisest.
He shall taste of my bottle. If he have never drunk wine
afore, it will go near to remove his fit. If I can recover

him and keep him tame, I will not take too much for
him; he shall pay for him that hath him, and that
soundly.

CALIBAN. Thou dost me yet but little hurt.

Thou wilt anon; I know it by thy trembling.

Now Prosper works upon thee.

STEPHANO. Come on your ways. Open your mouth. Here is that
which will give language to you, cat. Open your mouth.
This will shake your shaking, I can tell you, and that
soundly. (*Gives* CALIBAN *drink.*) You cannot tell who's
your friend. Open your chaps again.

TRINCULO. I should know that voice. It should be—but he is
drown'd; and these are devils. O, defend me!

STEPHANO. Four legs and two voices—a most delicate monster! His
forward voice now is to speak well of his friend; his
backward voice is to utter foul speeches and to detract.
If all the wine in my bottle will recover him, I will help
his ague. Come! (*Gives drink.*) Amen! I will pour some
in thy other mouth.

TRINCULO. Stephano!

STEPHANO. Doth thy other mouth call me? Mercy, mercy! This is
a devil, and no monster. I will leave him; I have no long
spoon.

TRINCULO. Stephano! If thou beest Stephano, touch me and speak
to me; for I am Trinculo—be not afeard—thy good friend
Trinculo.

STEPHANO. If thou beest Trinculo, come forth. I'll pull thee by the
lesser legs. If any be Trinculo's legs these are they.
(*Draws him out from under* CALIBAN'S *garment.*) Thou
art very Trinculo indeed! How cam'st thou to be the
siege of this mooncalf? Can he vent Trinculos?

TRINCULO. I took him to be kill'd with a thunderstroke. But art
thou not drown'd, Stephano? I hope now thou art not
drown'd. Is the storm overblown? I hid me under the
dead mooncalf's gaberdine for fear of the storm. And art
thou living, Stephano? O Stephano, two Neapolitans
scap'd?

STEPHANO. Prithee do not turn me about. My stomach is not constant.

CALIBAN (*aside*). These be fine things an if they be not sprites. That's a brave god and bears celestial liquor. I will kneel to him.

STEPHANO. How didst thou scape? How cam'st thou hither? Swear by this bottle how thou cam'st hither. I escap'd upon a butt of sack which the sailors heaved o'erboard, by this bottle! which I made of the bark of a tree with mine own hands since I was cast ashore.

CALIBAN. I'll swear upon that bottle to be thy true subject, for the liquor is not earthly.

STEPHANO. Here! Swear then how thou escap'dst.

TRINCULO. Swum ashore, man, like a duck. I can swim like a duck, I'll be sworn.

STEPHANO. Here, kiss the book. (*Gives him drink.*) Though thou canst swim like a duck, thou art made like a goose.

TRINCULO. O Stephano, hast any more of this?

STEPHANO. The whole butt, man. My cellar is in a rock by th' seaside, where my wine is hid. How now, mooncalf? How does thine ague?

CALIBAN. Hast thou not dropp'd from heaven?

STEPHANO. Out o' th' moon, I do assure thee. I was the Man i' th' Moon when time was.

CALIBAN. I have seen thee in her, and I do adore thee. My mistress show'd me thee, and thy dog, and thy bush.

STEPHANO. Come, swear to that; kiss the book. I will furnish it anon with new contents. Swear.

(CALIBAN *drinks.*)

TRINCULO. By this good light, this is a very shallow monster! I afeard of him? A very weak monster! The Man i' th' Moon? A most poor credulous monster! Well drawn, monster, in good sooth.

CALIBAN. I'll show thee every fertile inch o' th' island; And I will kiss thy foot. I prithee be my god.

TRINCULO. By this light, a most perfidious and drunken monster! When's god's asleep he'll rob his bottle.

CALIBAN. I'll kiss thy foot. I'll swear myself thy subject.

STEPHANO. Come on then. Down, and swear!

TRINCULO. I shall laugh myself to death at this puppy-headed monster. A most scurvy monster! I could find in my heart to beat him—

STEPHANO. Come, kiss.

TRINCULO. But that the poor monster's in drink. An abominable monster!

CALIBAN. I'll show thee the best springs; I'll pluck thee berries;
I'll fish for thee, and get thee wood enough.
A plague upon the tyrant that I serve!
I'll bear him no more sticks, but follow thee,
Thou wondrous man.

TRINCULO. A most ridiculous monster, to make a wonder of a poor drunkard!

CALIBAN. I prithee let me bring thee where crabs grow;
And I with my long nails will dig thee pignuts,
Show thee a jay's nest, and instruct thee how
To snare the nimble marmoset; I'll bring thee
To clust'ring filberts, and sometimes I'll get thee
Young scamels from the rock. Wilt thou go with me?

STEPHANO. I prithee now lead the way without any more talking. Trinculo, the King and all our company else being drown'd, we will inherit here. Here, bear my bottle. Fellow Trinculo, we'll fill him by-and-by again. (CALIBAN *sings drunkenly.*)

CALIBAN. Farewell, master; farewell, farewell!

TRINCULO. A howling monster! a drunken monster!

CALIBAN.   "No more dams I'll make for fish,
                  Nor fetch in firing
            At requiring,
            Nor scrape trenchering, nor wash dish.
                  'Ban, 'Ban, Ca—Caliban
            Has a new master. Get a new man."
Freedom, high-day! high-day, freedom! freedom, high-day, freedom!

STEPHANO. O brave monster! lead the way.
      (*Exeunt.*)

part three

✶

Exercises for Proficiency

part three

Exercises for Proficiency

I
✳

SUGGESTED TRAINING AIDS

Introduction

THE EXERCISES THAT FOLLOW are designed to give the student actor some guidance in his program of training for a dramatic role. In order to facilitate the cross-reference of points in theory and practice, the exercises are grouped under chapter and sectional headings similar to the headings for the corresponding passages in the main text, those passages which these exercises implement. In no case may the exercises here outlined be considered as covering completely the fields for which they are designated. They should be regarded rather as suggestions which the student and his teacher will adapt and amplify to suit particular needs.

Because learning to act can never be a matter of neat sequence—pantomime mastered this month, speech the next,—but must be built around a plan in which one carries forward one's training in all phases at the same time, the exercises need not be used in any special order or grouping. There should be, of course, some logic in the planning of the student's program, but there is no necessity for him to stick rigidly to the outline set down here. With the advice of his teacher, the actor might well take up together problems from two or three separate chapters. For instance, he might take an exercise from *Fundamental Movements* in Chapter II, one from *Characterized Posture and Movement* in Chapter III, and one from *Characterized Speech* in Chapter IV, and work on them at the same time. Some practice in *The Control*

293

of Bodily Movement should accompany all other exercises in the chapter on body training; and the parallel studies of pantomimic and vocal problems should go along together. Since Stage Imagery is the primary objective in all the channels of training, the actor should return to the exercises of Chapter II repeatedly.

Preceding this division is a group of dramatic scenes which can be used in connection with the exercises, and at the end of the book is a supplementary body of material for body and voice training. In order to stretch the horizons of his work, the student should have available a number of plays by leading authors to which he can refer when he wishes to test out at greater length the various principles of acting suggested here. They should be complete plays, rather than selections, and they should represent the past as well as the present in a wide choice of styles. The student might include the Greeks (comedies as well as tragedies), Shakespeare, Molière, Sheridan and Goldsmith, Ibsen, and, of course, several of the moderns. The plays of today might embrace the more common realistic forms together with some experiments in newer techniques.

While he works on his own acting, the student should observe constantly the methods of other players. He should study the films, radio, television, and all the stage productions he can possibly attend. As he watches, however, he should note that so-called "professional" acting varies greatly in quality. The student should learn to distinguish between the good and the bad and to find reasons for the differences. When he observes inferior acting by others, he should resolve, of course, to see how he can improve his own.

The Plan of the Exercises

The problems covered by the several exercises in each of the following groups are similar or closely related. Every student should not expect to do all the exercises in the group unless he especially wishes to concentrate his practice work at that particular point; rather, he should pick one or two in accordance with his needs. When the exercises are used in class, different students will presumably take different assignments.

I. THE ACTOR'S OBJECTIVES

Why the Audience Comes to the Theatre

1. Ask as many people, and as many different kinds of people, as you can why they go to the theatre. Let the concept of "theatre" in your question be large enough to include radio, television, and motion pictures as well as the legitimate playhouse. Try to get the people you interview to give you, not just an offhand reply, but a considered one, an answer which truly represents their attitudes.

2. Study the responses of the spectators at various performances. Listen to their comments before the show, during the intermissions, and afterwards. From these observations, try to arrive at what causes people to come to the theatre, and what kind of satisfaction they expect to find there. Compare your findings with the three root desires of the audience suggested in this book.

3. Analyze your own desires as a spectator in the theatre. Compare your reasons for being there with those of the playgoers whom you have interviewed. As a theatre craftsman, you will probably find yourself interested in certain technical aspects of the performance which the others care less about. That is to be expected.

The Audience's Response

4. Following the suggestions in the text, investigate the way the audience *perceives* a play.

5. Following the same suggestions, investigate the way the audience *participates* in the play. Note the sensuous factors in movement and speech, and distinguish between these and the more intellectual factors. Make distinction also between complete, blind identification and a pleasurable "feeling-into."

6. Following the same suggestions, investigate the way each spectator *comments* on the play in his mind.

7. Note the difference between the audiences attending different plays in different playhouses, and also the considerable variation between the audiences attending the same play on different nights.

The Playwright's Script and the Actor's Translation of It

8. Examine the script of any good play and see how it serves as a "score" for a live performance. Ask yourself, how does the playwright strive to satisfy the desire of the future audience for diversion, stimulation, and illumination? And how does the playwright meet, in general, the primary requirements for imagery, action, and interesting characters and story?

9. Consider the obligations of the player to the playwright, and the means the player has at his command for an effective translation of the dramatic script. Investigate the actor's three mediums of communication, and study the ways in which they serve to project the playwright's images.

The Actor's Program of Training

10. Study the form and mechanics of the theatre in which you will do your principal work. Do not try to get acquainted with it all in one day. Investigate it patiently and systematically, striving at every step to understand the function of each part, and to call all objects by their right names.

11. Acquaint yourself with the purposes and functions of the other craftsmen, including the scenic artist, the costume maker, the lighting expert, the musician, the sound man, and, especially, the director. See how the work of each dovetails with the work of the others, and how they all, together with the actor, build toward a single effect on the audience.

12. In view of what you have read in Chapter I, make out carefully a tentative program for your own training as an actor, covering the steps of general education, personal experience, image making, and instrumentation.

II. THE ACTOR AS IMAGE-MAKER

The Dramatic Personality and His Environment

(These exercises are designed to help the actor explore the relationship between a dramatic character and his stage environment.)

1. Take some character from one of your favorite plays, old or modern, and study that character carefully. Try to visualize

him. Distinguish between his inner and his outer personality. Analyze the environmental forces which impinge on his senses and on his mind. Note how they stir him to action. See how he contends with those forces—how he seeks an adjustment with them. Then ask yourself these questions:

    (a) Can one find an effective dramatic scene—one which really holds one's interest for at least five minutes—which does not involve directly or indirectly some sense of mental or physical struggle for adjustment?

    (b) What does this study reveal concerning the general relationship of a dramatic personality to his environment?

2. Find a scene in which two or more persons in conflict—struggling counter to each other—are trying to achieve a similar adjustment. See how, for each person, opposition represents a challenging factor in his environment, and how he seeks to overcome that factor in an effort to bring his world back into equilibrium.

3. Find a scene in which the disturbing factor in the environment —the factor which must be conquered, or brought under control—is not a person, but a thing such as an animal, a force of nature (a storm or a forest fire, a disease or, perhaps, a problem in some scientific experiment). How are the human powers lined up against the nonhuman powers? What kind of adjustment is sought by the man, or men, involved?

4. On a smaller scale, examine one by one the dramatic scenes in this book and try to find in each case what kind of adjustments with respect to their environment the characters are striving to achieve. (Bear in mind that these are fragmentary scenes and that the various situations depicted are not developed wholly within the passages quoted. Try to imagine what precedes and follows each of these excerpts. If possible, find the complete plays in the library and read them.)

Awareness of Objects, Actual and Imaginary

(These are exercises for the sharpening of the actor's senses.)

5. Train your five senses by noting carefully each day the feeling stirred in your body and your mind by (a) the touch, (b) the

sight, (c) the sound, (d) the taste, and (e) the smell of at least five objects. Try to fix these sensations firmly in your memory.

6. Try each day to recall by imagination the five or more sensations you actually experienced the day before. Concentrating your mind on what you are doing, make yourself go through the motions of touching, seeing, hearing, tasting, or smelling, and the motions of reacting to, the impressions you re-create. If saying a word or two while you move helps you to sharpen the remembered sensations, say them. Do not hurry these exercises. Repeat each one several times until you can make the response full, precise, and quite sensible to anyone who might be watching. In the next exercise try working out each reaction with the aid of a word action. Then repeat the reaction without the words.

7. Without the aid of any actual properties (except a chair, if you need one) touch or feel one by one the following imaginary objects and react visibly to each:
   (a) A hot dish
   (b) A piece of ice
   (c) A pan of warm water
   (d) A cup of steaming coffee
   (e) A bowl of sticky dough
   (f) A piece of silk
   (g) A piece of rich velvet or fur
   (h) A handful of dirt
   (i) A heavy suitcase filled with clothes and books
   (j) A cold wind

8. Without the aid of any actual properties (except a chair, if you need one) see the following imaginary objects and react visibly to each:
   (a) A table lamp in a dark room which someone suddenly switches on
   (b) The quick flash of lightning nearby
   (c) The passing and receding lights of an automobile
   (d) The swinging pendulum of a large old-fashioned clock
   (e) A flying moth
   (f) A distant sky rocket

   (g) A passing train at night (near you)
   (h) A dish of tempting food carried across the room and
       placed on a table
   (i) A letter
   (j) A portrait hanging over a fireplace
9. Without the aid of any actual properties (except a chair, if
   you need one) hear the following imaginary noises and react
   visibly to each:
   (a) The striking of clock chimes in another part of the
       house
   (b) The crash of a collision behind you
   (c) Your name called from the next room
   (d) The rustle of a mouse in the corner
   (e) The distant scream of a train whistle
   (f) The distant tolling of church bells
   (g) A distant song
   (h) The howling of a dog
   (i) Rain on the roof
   (j) A mosquito
10. Without the aid of any actual properties (except a chair, if
    you need one) taste the following imaginary objects and react
    visibly to each:
    (a) A cup of hot coffee
    (b) A bowl of soup
    (c) A piece of beefsteak
    (d) A slice of lemon
    (e) A dish of ice cream
    (f) A spoonful of very bitter medicine
    (g) A sip of raw whiskey
    (h) A piece of apple pie
    (i) A mouthful of taffy candy
11. Without the aid of any actual properties (except a chair, if
    you need one) smell the following imaginary objects and react
    visibly to each:
    (a) A fragrant flower
    (b) A rag saturated with gasoline
    (c) A fresh piece of cedar wood
    (d) A bottle of ammonia

(e) A kettle of boiling cabbage

(f) Garbage

(g) A scented handkerchief

(h) A salt sea breeze

(i) A musty room

(j) A pine forest

12. Wash your hands at an imaginary lavatory basin. Go through all the motions, sensing every object carefully. Do not hurry. Adjust the stopper, turn the faucet handles to admit the right proportion of hot and cold water; then wet your hands and reach for the soap. Determine for yourself the size and shape of the cake. Feel the lather. Replace the soap in its container and rinse your hands. Then reach for a towel and dry your hands slowly, sensing the texture of the cloth. Hang the towel again in its place, and before you leave be sure that the faucets are closed and that the basin has been emptied.

13. Walk through an imaginary doorway, opening the door, then closing it behind you. Feel clearly the weight of the door and the cold hardness of the knob in your hand. Now repeat the opening and closing with a larger and heavier door. Now with a small light door.

14. Set a common, straight-backed chair in the center of the stage. Try to see it in turn as (a) a heavy mission-type chair, (b) a fragile antique, and (c) a large, comfortable, overstuffed arm-chair. Sit in the chair. Sense it, and adjust yourself to it in three different ways. In each case feel the contours of the chair, the shape of its back and arms, its sturdy strength or lightness, and its hardness or softness. Do not destroy the par-ticular impression of the chair you are trying to create when you get out of it. Let the spectator still see it standing there.

15. In a similar way, visualize three distinctly different tables—a sitting room table, a kitchen table, and a desk. Show three dif-ferent impressions of the table in the way you move it, or the way you set objects upon or remove them from it.

16. By imagination, create a very small room. Walk into it, and look at it—the walls, the ceiling, the furniture. Now somehow demonstrate by pantomime the form of the room and just how

confined is the space in it. Make the spectator watching your pantomime *feel* the room.

17. By imagination create a very large room. Walk into it and sense it completely. Look at the lofty walls, the wide expanse of the ceiling, the massive furniture. Show by pantomime your feeling of the vastness of the room.

18. Imagine yourself crouched in a box, with the bottom pressing against your feet and your thighs, the sides compressing your back and your elbows, and the top pushing down upon your head. Feel the unyielding walls of your enclosure. Struggle against them.

19. Imagine yourself in the middle of a large, open plain, or beside the ocean. Show your awareness of unlimited space. Lift your head, throw out your chest, stretch wide your arms, inhale the air.

20. Imagine yourself to be standing on a very high mountain peak looking far down into the depths of a valley below. Show your sense of height.

21. Imagine yourself in an open field at night gazing up at the immense dome of the sky. See the faraway stars. Try to stretch yourself to touch one. Lift your face and your shoulders. Reach with your arms.

22. Pass from a cold outdoor space through a door into a hot room. By your actions and your general posture indicate the change of temperature. Let the change effect every part of you from your face to your legs. Do not neglect the central part of your body. Remember that it, too, feels temperature.

23. Move from a warm place to a cold place and show in a similar way the change of effect on every part of your body.

24. Lift up from the ground a small stone and place it on a low rock. Lift up a larger stone and place it beside the small one. The first stone, you may imagine, is smooth, white, and clean; the second is angular, gray, and dusty. Pick up and throw the small stone, then the larger one.

25. Pick up a needle from the floor. Thread it. Do not attempt to put the thread through the eye of the needle until you can feel and see clearly both objects. Sew a light piece of material, then

a heavier piece. Let your fingers indicate unmistakably the difference between the fabrics.

26. Carry a tray over to a library table. Put the tray down. Pick up and place on it one by one several objects such as the following: a large book, a small book, a clock, a vase, a magazine, an ash tray, a box of cigars, several loose sheets of paper, a paper knife, and a pair of scissors. Feel each article so clearly that the observer will be able to tell from the position and the movement of your fingers, and from the expression of your eyes, just what the objects are. Take up the tray and carry it to another table. Remove the objects one by one in the same way you picked them up.

27. Tidy a sitting room in preparation for guests. Straighten the chairs, arrange the cushions on the sofa, lift a newspaper from the floor, empty an ash tray, put a book back on the shelves, set the magazines in order on the table, straighten the rug.

28. Prepare a meal in the kitchen. Remove several objects from the refrigerator, get some pans and cooking utensils, put on an apron, and start to prepare the food. Decide for yourself whether this is to be breakfast, lunch, or dinner, and let the forms of your actions show clearly what kinds of dishes you are getting ready. Test one or two of them by taste and smell.

29. Set a table for a meal. Do it in such a way as to make plain to a spectator which meal of the day this is, how many people are being prepared for, and whether the occasion is formal or informal.

30. Make some object at a work bench. Visualize carefully the various tools you must use—two or three different saws, a plane, a square, a hammer, a power drill, chisels, nails, screws, etc.—and then show carefully what you are constructing, and how you are doing it. Be precise. Be skillful.

31. Your car has stalled. Get out and lift the hood. Examine the engine. Make a repair.

32. Dress yourself for breakfast. Now dress yourself for a party.

33. Come indoors from a rain storm, and remove your wet clothing.

34. Come indoors from a snow storm, shake the snow from your

coat and hat, stamp the snow from your feet, and remove your outer clothing. Walk over to a fire and start to warm yourself.

35. You are in a sporting goods store. Select, pay for, and carry away with you a tennis racket, two golf clubs, half a dozen tennis balls, and a pair of golf shoes which your first try on.

36. Pantomime some routine work in a business office. Type a letter; answer the phone; pick up, sort out and file several different documents.

37. Hoe a row of potato plants. Feel the weight of the hoe in your hands. Balance it, and take a good grip on the handle. Every time the blade of the hoe bites into the hard earth let your hands tingle with the shock.

38. Chop down a small tree. Sense the weight of the axe in your hands. Swing vigorously. Aim your strokes in such a way as to waste none of them. Drop the tree with the least possible number of strokes.

39. Walk barefoot on a cold, pebbly beach. Then in a warm, muddy-bottomed stream. You can imagine that the water in the stream comes up to your knees.

40. You are seated at the breakfast table reading the morning paper. See several items of interest. Glance at the headings. Then turn the pages and look at the general advertisements. Stop at the "Want Ad" section. Be arrested by one of the "Help Wanted" notices, and read it out loud.

41. Walk into a picture gallery and look at the different paintings. Take time to study each picture thoroughly. Imagine that several contrasting techniques are represented; there are portraits, landscapes, and still lifes, in both water color and oil. The treatments range from Realism and Expressionism to Cubism and Surrealism. Show which is which. Talk about what you see.

42. You are seated in a chair reading a magazine when you hear low voices coming from the next room. Rise, move cautiously to the intervening wall, and place your ear flat against it. Now see if you can convey to the audience—without any grimacing or unnatural gesturing—what you hear through the wall.

43. Take eight actual objects like the following and imagine them

to have been involved intimately in some way with the lives of people you know. Make up a brief story about each. View them, talk about them, touch them, and react visibly to them:

(a) A pair of spectacles (worn for years, perhaps, by an old lady who has just died)

(b) A spade (once used industriously by a pioneering ancestor)

(c) A violin (formerly played by a friend)

(d) A thumb-printed and much annotated volume of Shakespeare's plays (read and reread by an old crippled actor)

(e) A coat (taken from a beloved person recently drowned in the sea)

(f) A heavy stick (used in a murder)

(g) A kitchen utensil (reminiscent of Christmas dinners long ago)

(h) An old rocking chair (once used, perhaps, by the mistress or master of a household, a chair which years after his death is shunned by the other members of the family because they can still sense him sitting in it)

44. Visualize a number of imaginery objects like those suggested above; think of dramatic situations in plays in which they might appear, and work out your reactions to them. Proceed carefully. Do not hurry.

Awareness of People, Actual and Imaginary

(These exercises are planned to aid the actor in visualizing characters on the stage. They should be preceded by some work on the foregoing exercises.

45. Train yourself to be aware of people's presence by observing carefully every day the form, the features, the manner of talking, and the movements of five different people outside the theatre.

46. Try each day to recall the images of the people you observed the day before. Imagine how you would react to them if you met them again under various kinds of circumstances.

47. Sit down on a chair by an imaginary easel and paint the portrait of a friend as if he were seated in front of you. Study his

face, the posture of his head, and his hands. Note the expression of his eyes. Work slowly and carefully.

48. It is a warm afternoon and you are seated, reading. A man's voice outside the window calls. You raise your head and listen. It is not for you. You return to your reading. In a moment another voice calls, this time for you. Rise and go to the window. See the person, hear his or her invitation to run down to the corner drug store, perhaps, or to play tennis, or to go for a stroll by the river. Reply.

49. You are at the table eating. There is a knock. You rise. The door opens and two laughing acquaintances enter. You are surprised and delighted. Step forward and fondly seize the hands, or shoulders, of your friends. You are especially glad to see one of them.

50. Walk across a room and open the door with no suspicion that there is anyone on the other side. Be startled by the presence of a strange figure you suddenly find confronting you. Speak to it.

51. Stand in a formal receiving line. Greet the guests as they pass, differentiating carefully between them. Some of the persons you already know; some you are meeting now for the first time. Move your lips in conversation. If you are a man, you can bow slightly to the women; but do not try to show your recognition of anyone by ducking your head up and down. Let all your movements be graceful and conservative as suits the occasion.

52. You are a waiter in a restaurant. Take the order of a gentleman or lady seated at a table. See the person and hear his words distinctly. Bring in the soup course and place it before him; then turn to get the other orders without bobbing your head. Act naturally.

53. You are a proprietor seated in the door of a small town store. Watch the different characters who pass along the sidewalk. Some move more slowly, some quickly. Exchange a greeting with one or two. A customer enters. You rise and wait on him.

54. Sit at a table and play a game of cards with one, two, or more persons. See and feel the cards and visualize the faces and names of the players. Speak to them from time to time. Let

whoever might be watching you sense from your actions what game you are playing and the form and character of each of your companions.

Inward and Outward Attention

(These exercises are planned to help the actor express the movement of his center of interest from inside to outside of himself, or the reverse.)

55. Sit in a chair with your eyes closed and center your thoughts on something quite personal—perhaps something which you are planning to do this coming evening. Now your ears tell you that someone in the room has risen. Open your eyes and say something to him. He moves into the hallway. Tell him not to hurry; you still have something to say to him. He goes down stairs. Call to him as he goes out the front door.

56. Imagine yourself in an upstairs room. Go to the window and speak to someone in the yard below. Ask him to come up to your room. As he comes up the stairs ask him to hurry. When he comes into the room close the door, take him into a corner, and whisper in his ear. (The whisper should seem to be soft, but it should be clearly audible at the rear of the rehearsal hall.)

57. Tell someone across the room from you that what he has told you surprises, or shocks you. Maybe the matter is related to a business reverse or the sudden death of a friend—the more personal the better. To hide the effect on you, turn your back on the other person and slowly walk toward the fireplace, the window, or a dark corner of the room and address a few words to yourself. Make them seem to be very much to yourself, but let them be audible at the back of the rehearsal hall. Complete your thought, then swing around and shout an angry answer back at the other person.

Fundamental Movements in Sensing

(These exercises give the actor training in the manifestation of sensorial excitement. They cover much of the same ground as that in the preceding exercises; but the emphasis here is placed more pointedly on the revelation of (1) place, (2) form, and (3) force, of sensation.)

58. Standing quietly, imagine that you hear to your right or left someone strumming a guitar. Turn and see the man or woman seated on a box. Listen to him. Show by the posture of your body the place of the guitar player. Now face front again and hear the strumming in a different place—front, rear, or at the side, above or below, near you or far away. Turn in such a way as to indicate clearly from what spot the music now comes.

59. Repeat the first or second part of the preceding exercise and add some movement which would suggest the *form* of the sensuous experience you are enjoying. Show by the expression of your eyes that you are looking at an interesting action, and then by the motion of your body that you are being affected by a force of rhythm. You can make your response as free or as restrained as you choose, but be sure that it is clear. Sway a little, perhaps, or move your feet in time to the music. Now dance a few steps, showing with your feet the pattern of the rhythm.

60. Repeat Exs. 58 and 59 and add a third movement which will indicate to an onlooker the intensity, or *force,* of your sensory experience. Perhaps the guitarist breaks into song. Open your eyes wide in appreciation, smile, lift your body, sway, or dance in a more lively way.

61. You are now bored by the music. Show clearly how you stop listening to it.

Fundamental Movements in Preparing

(These exercises give the actor training in manifesting the second step of a complete dramatic response, namely, the individual's reaction to the general challenge of the stimulating object through rising or sinking and approaching or withdrawing.)

62. Stand erect. Now imagine yourself getting increasingly tired. Let your head and your body slump gradually, and then sink

slowly with exhaustion into a chair or onto a bed or the floor. After a moment, strive to push up against the force of gravity, lifting the body slowly, bit by bit, until you are erect once more. Lift your head high. Complete your conquest of gravity by stretching your arms upward and then springing off the ground.

63. Walk around the room slowly at first, as if you wished to sink down somewhere to rest; then as if you were full of vitality, with your head and chest held high and with a good bounce in your feet. (Consider the different kinds of dramatic situations which would call forth these opposite actions.)

64. Repeat the last two exercises, substituting for the sense of physical exhaustion and vitality, if you can, a mental attitude of discouragement, then exhilaration. Say thoughtfully to yourself some such phrase as: "I am sick, friendless, and cannot go on," and then: "I am happy today. Happy!—walking on top of the world!" Let the slump and the pick-up of the body show the degree of contrast between the two moods.

65. Walk around the room slowly, first as if you were conscious of power, even boastful of it; then as if you were ashamed of yourself, afraid of your own shadow. Note the difference between the two attitudes, and work out in your mind and then your body a clear and logical transition from one attitude to the other.

66. Standing quietly, try to imagine yourself as being very hungry, not having eaten for three days. Now try to visualize at some distance from you a table set with a white cloth, dishes and cutlery, and a bowl of steaming food. Construct in yourself the urge to move toward the food; then approach it.

67. Standing, imagine on a shelf some distance from you an object —a small mechanical device, a piece of jewelry, or a marvelously wrought piece of statuary—which stirs your curiosity. Look at it for a moment or two, then go over to it to see it better, perhaps to touch it.

68. Imagine that you have just crossed a busy street and are standing on the curb when you discover that you have dropped a valuable bundle. An automobile is roaring down on it. Leap forward to snatch the bundle and then back to

avoid the car. (You can, if you wish, substitute a small child for the bundle.)

69. You are on your knees by a camp fire. You lean forward to place a log on the flames. As you do so, the smoke swirls up into your face and you fall away from it.

70. You see a friend of yours looking out of the window across the room. Go over to him and say "Good Morning!" Hear him growl at you! Stare at him in surprise. Then, with an expression of hurt or disgust, walk away.

71. Select a short sequence of responses from one of the *Dramatic Scenes* in this book (or from any other play of your choice) and, with the help of another actor, work out both the sensory and the preparatory movements. (Complete the reactions through the resultant movements of attack, if you choose, but direct your primary attention to the aspects of Sensation and Preparation.) Playing slowly at first, try to master all details. Then increase your tempo. Proportion all the parts to fit the situation. Let some be swift, others leisurely; some obvious, others more subtle. *If you have to omit any one of the movements of Preparation to suit the situation, be sure that it is unmistakably implied.* Work at the same time for clarity and appropriateness. Try to seem natural. But remember that the stage always demands a degree of exaggeration.

72. Make a study of a child at play. See how simply but clearly he reveals in each action the fundamental forces of Preparation.

Fundamental Movements in Attacking

(These exercises give the actor training in manifesting the third step of the complete dramatic response, namely, what the individual does about his impulse to further or check the effective qualities of the object which causes the response.)

73. Standing quietly by an imaginary table, see lying on it a handsome book or a valuable camera. Lift it up and run your hands over it lovingly. Sense every detail of it. Show how strongly you like to view it and feel it. Now, in a contrasting state of mind, break the object, tear it apart, trample on it, or fling it from you.

74. Take a valuable clock or a piece of jewelry, place it on a bench, and clean it. Imagine that it is a highly prized possession. You like to feel its form in your hands. Now, in an angry mood, smash the object to bits.

75. Cultivate a bed of flowers or choice vegetables as if to make them grow better. Feel the rich soil in your fingers. Fondle the plants. Now, with a change of mind, trample on the plants, snatch them from the soil, and fling them from you.

76. Imagine yourself playing with a small dog or a child. By your movements, encourage it to be more active. Now, try to catch it, and then to hold it still.

77. Select any one of the objects listed in preceding exercises and make up a story about it. Place it by imagination in (a) a situation in which you would desire to increase its effective qualities, then (b) another situation in which you would wish to destroy those qualities. Work out carefully a complete response to the object in each situation, proceeding through the steps of Sensation and Preparation, and then going on to the Attack. Experiment with various movements of your body and limbs until you find those which most clearly and exactly express your feeling.

78. Make a study of a child at play. See how clearly and without restraint he reveals his impulses to extend or stop the effective actions of his companions. He hugs them, lifts them, and leads them; and he also hits them, jumps on them, and throws things at them. Note that grown people in everyday life have the same urges which they keep under control, and that the dramatic requirements of the stage demand action which is a kind of compromise—action which reveals more of the underlying impulses than those commonly to be observed in everyday adult life, but which shows nevertheless some more effort at control than does the behavior of children.

Accessory Movements

(These exercises are an extension of the three sets of exercises for Fundamental Movement, and should therefore be preceded by them.)

79. Accessory actions are the learned actions, performed only by experienced human beings. They are not by nature impulsive except in so far as they serve as extensions of the fundamental actions. Although they often constitute the bulk of a player's movements on the stage, their dramatic purpose is simply to connect, clarify, and develop the effects of the fundamental responses. Demonstrate in an exercise of your own creation how a fundamental movement of Attack (either in the building up or the tearing down of an object) can be carried through to a more effective close by the aid of skillful accessory movement. (For example, cultivate a woman's smile not only by smiling in return and walking toward her, but also by offering her a gift. Destroy the obnoxious presence of a man, not by striking him with your fist, but by reaching for a stick.)

80. Extend the effect of the fondling of a book, vase, or implement by dusting it carefully with a cloth. Then destroy the same object by dropping it in the fire, or striking it with a hammer.

81. Extend the effect of caressing movements toward a precious piece of machinery like a fine clock by turning them into the skillful actions of repair work. Carefully select your tools. Now take the object apart with the same tools.

82. Extend the effect of loving care for a bed of flowers by the use of garden implements. Then employ the same implements for scratching the plants from the soil.

83. Use toys to help you play with a dog or a child. Then employ a leash to control the dog, a baby carriage or playpen to restrain the child.

84. Make a study of a child at play and observe his ceaseless effort to implement gross, fundamental movements with more and more of skilled, accessory movements. The more of the latter he can perfect, the better able he is to cope with the various problems involved in his adjustment to the objects around him.

Under Imagery

85. With the help of other actors, work out a performance of the fight scene from *Romeo and Juliet* (described in Chapter II) in which you give primary attention to the under imagery. Let

the suggestions outlined for this scene serve as your guide.

86. With the help of another actor, work out a performance of the gong-striking scene from *The House of Connelly* (described in Chapter II) in which you give primary attention to the under imagery. Let the suggestions for this scene serve as your guide.

87. Take any of the *Dramatic Scenes* in this book, and select a character in it. Carefully construct in your mind an imaginary performance of that role, trying as you do to sense out the under imagery which should support and give meaning to the surface forms. Now, with the help of another actor (or actors) work out a performance in accordance with your plan.

88. In a similar way, first sense out, then demonstrate the presence of under images in a scene from a play not included in this volume.

III. THE ACTOR AS INSTRUMENTALIST—PANTOMIME

The Four Physical Agents of Pantomime

(Exercises for developing an efficient use of the torso, the arms, the legs, and the head, in pantomime.)

1. Stand upright, with your feet slightly apart, and place your hands on your hips. Starting from this position, find out what various movements can be performed with the central part of the body, the torso, alone. Bend slightly to the front—then farther. Repeat the motion to the rear, then to one side, then to the other. Return to the upright position and let your hands fall to your sides. Now investigate the several units of movement which can be executed in a forward bending motion. Note that it is easy to bend at the waist, a little less easy to bend in the upper part of the back, especially just behind the shoulders. All of these parts of the back should be brought under the control of the actor's mind. Lean far forward with your body and neck curled as much as possible. Start now to straighten up a little at a time beginning at the base of the spine and unfolding bit by bit until at last you lift your head. Reverse the movement starting with the neck, and then lower-

ing one unit at a time until the whole trunk is curled over; then come up again.

2. Read over carefully the section in Chapter III dealing with the torso and investigate through actual movements several of the expressive gestures which are natural to this part of the pantomimic body. Note how it will curl over, or slump, when it is affected by gravity and how it will lift when it resists this force. Note how it tends to lean forward toward an attractive presence and away from a harmful one. And see how "states of mind," like grief, despair, humility, joy, pride, and wonder, are reflected in the position of the torso.

3. Do again Exs. 62–69 from Chapter II, *Exercises for Stage Imagery*, giving particular attention in each exercise to the action of the torso.

4. Taking a place on the floor with plenty of space around you, experiment with the movement of your legs. Note the various joints in your feet, your ankles, your knees, and your hips. See how you can stand with your feet placed close together or separated, with your toes pointed straight forward or angled outward, and with your knees straight or bent. Control of these different postures of the legs will be very useful in the development of normal and characterized roles.

5. Now walk around. Note how the legs serve as carrying agents for the rest of the body, taking it toward desirable presences and away from undesirable ones. And note how the character of the movement—fast or slow, flat-footed or springy, firm or light, decisive or apprehensive—reveals both the physical condition and the state of mind of the person walking.

6. Select three or four exercises involving standing or walking from *Exercises for Stage Imagery* and show how much of the effect on the observer may depend on the action of the legs.

7. Standing or sitting, with plenty of space around you, concentrate on the movement of one of your arms. Note carefully the various joints and muscles in your fingers, wrist, elbow, and shoulder. Now experiment with different kinds of action involving these parts: the hand alone, the wrist alone, the elbow alone, the shoulder alone. Then see what utterly dissimilar

gestures result when you lead off with the hand first, the elbow first, the shoulder first, or when all parts start together.

8. Place some object, such as a cup, on a table or shelf. Reach
forward and grasp it in as many different ways as you can—
impatiently, curiously, apprehensively, angrily, calmly. Now
put it down or push it from you in as many different ways.
Lift from a table and pass to an imaginary companion a number of different objects—a book, a dish, a tool, a paper, a
pencil—in several ways which reflect different states of mind
—eagerness, reluctance, indifference, and the like.

9. Touch and feel several different objects—a piece of jewelry, a
coin, an old coat, a chair—in such a way as to suggest sensuously various attitudes toward these objects.

10. Select several exercises from *Exercises for Stage Imagery*
which involve the use of the arms or hands and show how
much drama can be indicated pantomimically by these members.

11. Standing or sitting, experiment with various movements of
the neck. See how the head can be turned from side to side
and up and down—front, rear, and on both sides. Note the
differences between a slight and a large shake of the head,
and a small and a deep nod.

12. Note the great difference with respect to the inner feeling
and the outward manifestation of a person which exists in the
posture of his head. See what tends to happen when he is
proud and self-respecting and when he is timid and fearful.
Using the erect head as the starting posture, see how many
states of mind can be depicted by the position and action of
the head on the neck with no help whatsoever from facial
expression.

13. How much can be told about a man's response to the presences around him, and also about his inward thoughts,
through changes of facial expression alone? Experiment with
various postures and actions of the mouth, the nose, and the
eyes. Concentrate especially on the eyes. Let them move to
various objects or faces about the room, recognize their presence, and show a response to them. Note the very great difference of expression that occurs when the lids are half drawn

and when they are wide open. What happens to the eyes when, after having moved lightly over familiar objects, they fasten on a new and arresting detail, one which promises possible danger or an exciting change of sensation? What happens to the eyes of a person listening responsively to the speech of another person? If you desire to make your face dramatically alive on the stage, give diligent practice to the eyes.

14. Select several exercises involving the use of the head from *Exercises for Stage Imagery* and show how much can be expressed by the posture and movement of the neck and by the action of the facial features.

15. Select one exercise from *Exercises for Stage Imagery* which involves the use of all the members of the body and work it out carefully, omitting no details and putting special emphasis on coordination.

Control of Bodily Movement: Stimulation and Strengthening of the Pantomimic Muscles

(Exercises for body-building.) *

16. With the feet planted a short distance apart, assume an easy and balanced stance and stretch directly overhead with both arms, extending the fingers. Be sure that in doing this the shoulders are not drawn up under the ears but remain down in correct relationship to both neck and head. Starting with your toes, feel the stretch upward develop throughout the entire body—up the sides as well as through the spine, up through the top of the head and the fingertips. Make sure that you are aware not only of the direction of the stretch, but also of its quality. Keep the pull alive and fluid, never letting it become locked and rigid. Any undue tension will destroy your control. When you have reached a point where you feel that the stretch has achieved its controllable limits, drop the heels to the floor again slowly and, without losing any of the energy you have accumulated in the body, slowly lower the torso, with arms extended to the sides, until the torso is at a right angle to the hips and parallel to the floor. Be sure that

* These exercises were prepared by Foster Fitz-Simons.

the spine is flat and not "bowed" either toward or away from the floor. Now, keeping the legs absolutely straight, pushing back the knees, stretch directly forward with a little rhythmic pull from the hips. Then swing the torso and the arms, still on the same flat plane, in an arc to the right and perform the stretch in that direction; swing all the way over to the left and repeat it there. Follow this last effort immediately by a controlled release of the tensions all over the body. Let the arms, torso, and head hang loosely forward over the bent and relaxed knees in such a way as to permit the hands to touch the floor limply. Swing back and forth easily from the hips in this position till you no longer sense any stretching in your body. Go back to the starting position and do the whole exercise over again. Repeat the series of stretches and the release five times.

17. Assume an easy standing position like the one at the beginning of the preceding exercise. Employing a slow count of eight as your unit for each section of movements, begin gradually to rise on the balls of your feet, lifting both your arms outward from the sides simultaneously until they are on a level with your shoulders. This movement should be spread evenly over the first eight counts. Through the next eight counts, sink directly downward over the center into a deep knee bend. It is important here that neither the head nor the torso "give" to the bend by falling forward, but stay erect over the established center. On the next eight-count return to the erect standing position on the balls of the feet. See that the ankles do not wobble; push them inward toward each other. On the completion of this movement, sink the heels to the floor letting the arms drop to the sides at the same time, on eight counts. The four parts of this exercise should be done in one continuous flow of movement with no discernible break between the units. Repeat the whole sequence three times.

18. Having assumed the standing position specified for the preceding exercises, with the arms raised from the side to shoulder level, take several long steps across your exercise space. Start with your right leg. Stretch it directly forward as far as you can, turning the toes of the foot slightly outward. As you

do this, let your torso, still erect, sink with the stride, then come up again as the weight of the body passes over the right leg at the beginning of the next step. Thus, as you stride forward, your torso will bounce gently up and down. Keep your arms extended for balance, and keep your face looking straight in the line of advance. On each step, bend the forward leg deeply at the knee while you stretch the rear leg as straight as possible. Then draw the body up over the forward leg and pull the rear one up beside and past it, all in one movement. (Note that this movement is designed for strengthening the muscles of the feet and legs and does not represent a normal walk.)

19. From an easy standing position reach forward with both arms, then take a long step forward with one foot in such a way as to extend your reach as far as you can really control it. Now visualize your hands grasping a handle or a rope firmly and pull slowly backward with both arms and the torso over the line of the reach. Building up the sense of pull, move as though the imaginary "handle" offered you a strong and continuous resistance. When you have taken this pull back as far as you can, reverse the process and push the "handle" forward again with as much continuous energy as that expended on the former movement. At the end of the push, pull again. Repeat this several times. Vary the exercise by planting the feet fairly widely apart, reaching to the side with one arm, then the other, in the plane of the body and pulling first to one side and then to the other. Keep up a continuous flow of energy and resistance, first in one direction, then in the opposite. Concentrate on maintaining an unbroken awareness of the flow and of the energy. Remember at all times that any overzealous execution of an exercise—or any lazy and inadequate performance of it—will prevent your attaining your object, control.

Control of Bodily Movement: Relaxation
(Exercises for the control of tensions.) *

20. Employing a deliberately slow and easy step, walk around in a large circle. As you walk, begin to release the head for-

* These exercises were prepared by Foster Fitz-Simons.

ward over the walk by gradually relaxing the neck so that ultimately the head is bouncing rhythmically and gently with each step. Now continue this release downward through the shoulders and arms. Continue this "curling-over" in a downward progression through the remainder of the spine and hips and knees so that you end with the body swinging deeply over the slow and continuous walk, with only enough tension to maintain the walk and to keep the body from slipping to the floor. Now reverse the process upward. Without employing too much conscious effort, keep the spine uncurling and straightening, pulling the body and torso upright again over the walk, while the arms still hang loosely from the shoulders. Pass on up over the crest of the erect posture, then start to relax once more. Let the head fall gradually backward over the shoulders, and let the spine bend as far as you can without setting up tensions or pulling yourself out of balance. You will find that in this phase of the exercise you cannot accomplish as much as you did in the forward movement, but do not let this worry you. Execute the slow, controlled arching forward, then backward, over the continuous walk several times, keeping in mind that relaxation should at all times be thought of in terms of activity. In other words, movement for easing the muscles should be conceived and performed as a conscious release of energy—*never* as a thoughtless throwing-away of this important element. The problem of relaxation is primarily one of bringing the body mechanism from a higher degree of tension to a lower one. Always the actor must maintain such an awareness of what he is doing that he can reverse the process instantly without effort.

21. Lie flat on your back on the floor, arms at side, eyes closed. Take a moment to erase from your mind the sense of surrounding walls and ceiling. Try to arrive at a feeling of resting in a void without any intruding physical association to distract you from your main purpose of concentrating upon yourself and your body mechanism. As the environmental images fade from your mind, you will gradually become aware of particular sectors of your body which are still held in a tension greater than there is any need for. (Resting flat on the floor,

you have no problem of balance.) When you have to your satisfaction succeeded in erasing all the recognizable tensions, begin with the extremities of your feet—at the toes themselves —isolating them visually in your mind and consciously releasing all feeling of energy in them. Continue, bit by bit, up the entire length of the body, taking in succession the feet, lower legs, knees, thighs, hips, back, chest, shoulders, neck, and head in one continuous progression. Be sure that you do not move again any part of the body that you have thus "blanked out." Lie for a few moments thus, your mind at ease, unoccupied with any thought processes. After you have lain thus for a time, begin moving consciously to let the flow of energy come back into the body. Do not leap suddenly into activity, but return to it gradually. If you hurry, your body will suffer a distinct sense of shock that will destroy all benefits you may have derived from the relaxation. This exercise becomes increasingly more effective with repetition.

Control of Bodily Movement: Flexibility

(Exercises for developing ease in changing from one kind or direction of movement to another.) *

22. Lying on your back on the floor, rise to your feet with the feeling that the body is moving from a simple horizontal to a simple vertical in one continuous flow of easy movement. Now, with the same kind of smooth movement, lie down again. Repeat the rise, starting from a kneeling position, then from a stooped or squatting position. From a position lying on one side move to a position sitting upright (on the floor), then to a crouching run, then to a steady, easy walk. (There are hundreds of variations of this exercise that you can devise for yourself.)

23. Hop in place rapidly ten or twelve times on one foot, then step out immediately into a slow, even walk. Stop the walk suddenly and begin the rapid hop again, this time on the other foot. After one or two hops, step forward again into the walk. Strive to keep the vertical of the hopping distinct from

* These exercises were prepared by Foster Fitz-Simons.

the horizontal of the walking without confusing one with the other when you change your movement.

24. Walking with small, light, quick steps on the balls of the feet, head up and a little back, chest arched upward and outward, and arms held out and up on a level with the shoulders, go swiftly around in a circle. Without pausing, fall suddenly into a low crouch, still moving on the line of the circle. Use a wide waddling squat, letting the backs of the hands drag lightly. Let them touch the floor just enough to keep the forward position of the torso from pulling you to the floor. The feeling in the body here should be heavy, torpid, and passive —in direct contrast to the lightness and quickness marking the preceding part of the exercise. After progressing for a few steps this way, pull yourself upright into the initial starting position and proceed with the exercise. Go on, alternating between high and low.

25. On the rim of a large circle, run six rapid steps. Stop suddenly in place and deliberately trace with your torso, arms, and eyes, the largest possible circle you can make without moving your feet. On the completion of this, move forward again on the rim of the big circle six more steps. Stop and repeat the circular swing of your body and arms. Continue around the circle, alternating in this manner, working always to get a smooth transition from the standing activity to the running one. Try to keep the shift, from active legs to active torso and arms, clean and unbroken.

Control of Bodily Movement: Continuity and Transition

(Exercises for developing a pantomimic sense of sustained tension and of progressive changes in linked movements.)*

26. Pick up an imaginary object having weight and substance, such as a baseball, a book, or a paperweight, from a table. Moving as if you were affected by a strong desire to hurl the object violently at some person across the room from you, draw your arm away back in preparation for the throw. Now, as if at the cost of some effort you were changing your mind, slowly bring your arm back and carefully replace the object

* These exercises were prepared by Foster Fitz-Simons.

on the table. In this exercise, work for a smooth increase and decrease of tension, and a smooth change in the form and speed of the movement.

27. Prop up a large cushion in a chair. Let it stand for the face of a person in a play. Try to imagine yourself in a situation in which, through fear or anger, you wished to strike that face. Begin to swing your hand violently toward it and then, as if swept suddenly by compassion, change your blow into a pat or caress. Now reverse the movement, starting with a gesture of affection and then suddenly slapping the face.

28. As if you were in a very lighthearted mood, skip along an imaginary sidewalk. Suddenly you become aware that you are being viewed quite disapprovingly by someone whose opinion you fear. Change swiftly, but without a too-obvious break, into a decorous walk. When you think you are no longer being scrutinized, take up once more the carefree skipping and running.

29. If you have had some training in music, conduct an imaginary choir. Lead a quiet solo; bring in several other voices; then add the full force of the remaining singers. Return the music to a whisper. Let your conducting show clearly the changing character of the music.

30. Entering a strange room, you start to cross it when you become aware of a strange sound. You come to a dead stop, frozen and straining to hear the sound again. At first you are frightened; then your good sense comes to your aid and you put off the feeling of fright, albeit with some effort. Curious now, you try attentively to place the source of the sound. Suddenly you identify it as caused by some ordinary and inconsequential thing—a mouse in the wainscoting, a dripping faucet, or a branch creaking in the tree outside. You are relieved and a little ashamed for having allowed yourself to be so frightened. You confidently cross the room and leave it.

31. Imagine yourself an employee in a large office. During a lull in your work you take the opportunity to entertain several of your co-workers by engaging in a grotesque, rather caustic imitation of your absent employer, a blustering, overbearing, pompous person full of what you think is unwarranted con-

ceit. You demonstrate before your appreciative audience his walk, his ridiculous attitudes, his slovenly way of smoking a cigar. In the midst of this performance, the man walks in. You immediately assume the manner of the employee working quietly at his task—somewhat frightened inwardly since you are uncertain as to whether the man has seen any of your burlesque of him. When, with no change of expression, he hands you some papers, you realize that he has not seen your actions. Relieved, you take the papers and go quickly and easily off to another office.

32. You are anxiously waiting on a park bench for a friend who is late for an appointment. Because you want very much to appear at your best before your friend, your attitude of alert and somewhat strained watching and waiting is accompanied by a concern with the details of your appearance. You glance at your watch, at your hands; you straighten your hat, fuss with your collar, smooth your clothes in your very effort to make yourself at ease. You show from which direction you expect your friend to appear by repeatedly glancing that way with your eyes. Suddenly, you feel sure you see him approaching. You get up full of happy excitement, ready to welcome him. But as the person comes nearer, you become aware that while you know the man he is not the friend you had expected. Since he has now seen you, you cannot gracefully avoid greeting him. You shake his hand and speak to him, but show in the manner of your greeting your disappointment that the person present is not the one for which you have been waiting.

33. At the door, say goodbye to a beloved friend who is leaving you after a visit. Close the door on his departure and listen attentively to his departing footsteps receding down the stairs and through a doorway into the street below. Then, when the sound of those footsteps has begun to fade, run to a window as if you desired one more glimpse of him. Follow his progress down the street and around the corner out of sight. Show with every movement and attitude of your body how intense is your reluctance to see the last of him. When he has finally passed from view, turn quietly from the window and sink into

a chair, or to the floor, still with the memory of him in your mind.

34. Enter a room in which there is a sick and sleeping person. Approach the bed carefully and with infinite pains straighten the covers. Then refill with water a glass on a table at the bedside. Pick up a magazine that has slipped from the bed to the floor and take it to a dresser across the room and place it there. While at the dresser, take the opportunity to rearrange certain toilet articles, putting one or two in a drawer and re-ordering the others. Be very careful that when you open and close the drawer you make no noise. Then cross to a window and pull down the shade and rearrange the curtains to shield the bed from the sunlight. From a table nearby pick up a tray upon which there is an empty glass, an empty bowl, and a spoon and go out of the room, carefully closing the door behind you. From beginning to end, take great pains not to awaken the sick person.

Normal Posture: Standing
(An exercise for grace and efficiency.)*

35. Stand easily with the feet slightly apart, the toes pointed a little outward. Check carefully to see that you are relaxed but not inert. Pay particular attention to the shoulders. See that they are not held in any undue tension, since shoulders are the worst offenders in the matter of awkward and displeasing body-posture. Hold them at all times down and free from the neck and head, resting easily on the sturdy support of the chest. Now, as you stand, begin to develop a steady tension slowly upward from the floor: first in the arches of the feet, then upward through the calves of the lower legs and into the knees, forcing them back to make a straight line; then into the thighs, turning the inner part of the thigh to the front; up into the hips, forcing the buttocks together and slightly forward, at the same time feeling the tension up through the vertebrae of the spine, through the back and across the torso, lifting the firm abdominal wall and the chest upward (watch those shoulders again—leave them alone!); then up through

* This exercise was prepared by Foster Fitz-Simons.

the neck (particularly feel it in the back of the neck); and finally on up through the top of the head. Make yourself feel as if you could press the tension against the ceiling of the room. Good posture is invariably accompanied by a sense of dignity and well-being, by a steady and live flow of energy upward, whether one is sitting, standing, or moving.

Normal Movement: Walking
(An exercise for grace and efficiency.)*

36. Assume a normal standing posture as in the preceding exercise. Now advance the right foot forward in an easy step but keep the weight of the body and the center of your balance still over the back foot. In this position, push up on the balls of both feet keeping both knees and legs straight. Without relaxing the tension in the feet and arches, shift the weight and center of the body directly forward over the advanced right foot. Now lower the heel of the forward foot, together with the weight of the body, to the floor. To do this correctly, you have to relax the rear leg, bending it slightly at the knee, but let the foot still rest easily on its ball. Now reverse the movement, ending with the weight once more on the lowered rear foot. It is important that you feel the "squareness" of this movement: the vertical followed by a horizontal, followed by a vertical, followed by another vertical, horizontal, and vertical —each of them clean and precise. When you have achieved ease with repetition, begin to change the character of the "squareness" into an arc, forward and back. Lift the weight of the body up, over (front), and down—then up, over (back), and down—in easy, continuous curves. When you have achieved some ease in this second phase of the exercise, begin to advance across the floor by allowing the rear leg to swing forward and through, relaxed from the hip, in an easy step, still keeping the smooth feeling of "roundness." Let this advance be slow and methodical for a few forward steps, then gradually increase the tempo until you are moving in a circle about the room as rapidly as you can without breaking into a run and without disturbing the sustained level of the body

* This exercise was prepared by Foster Fitz-Simons.

as it moves forward. It is very important that you achieve a real sense of controlled smoothness, of skimming over the surface without any bounce up and down or any undue sound of the feet hitting the floor. (Take note that this exercise for walking has as its purpose to make you aware of the basic mechanism and control that affects all walking. When you move about in a play you will behave, of course, in a much more simple manner.)

Normal Movement: Turning
(Exercises for grace and efficiency.)*

37. Standing erect and easy, visualize your backbone as a rod running from the top of your head down to the floor. This consciousness of a central axis, strong and steady, about which your body moves is necessary for the efficient execution of any turning. It is important to remember that this invisible central axis runs vertically through your center of balance no matter how many times your body position may change; that is, it remains constant no matter to what degree the character, force, and direction of your turning may vary. When you have the *feeling* of this verticality standing still, turn a quarter circle to the right on the heel of the right foot, bringing the left foot easily into position beside it again. Turn the whole body as a unit, maintaining the head and the eyes, particularly, steadfastly on the same level and letting them swing around with the torso in the new direction. Execute three more quarter turns to the right so that you will face again in the original direction. Now do some turns to the right, increasing your tempo so that the quarter turn becomes a third, then a half turn, and ultimately a complete turn on each movement. Let the body revolve steadily. It is important that your eyes do not try to focus on any succession of level points in this progression. Strive to keep the eyes on a constant level, concentrating on your "sense of center" and the unbroken line of the turn. You will find as you turn more rapidly that the heel on which you are turning tends to remain more and more passive, and that the following foot tends to initiate and main-

* These exercises were prepared by Foster Fitz-Simons.

tain the momentum by a little push with the ball and toe at each turning impulse. Now do another succession of turns to the left.

38. Walk in a circle until the walk is even and steady. Suddenly make a half turn, facing around to the back over the line of your advance, but continue to move in the original direction along the curve of the circle. Now walk backward without any break or jolt in the progression. After a few steps make another half turn, facing forward again into the line of walk. Alternate walking forward and backward, making your half turn first to the right and then to the left. Strive to maintain a clear feeling of the constant direction of your progress while you alternate the direction of your face.

Normal Movements: Sitting and Rising
(An exercise for grace and efficiency.)*

39. Seat yourself in a straight-backed, armless chair, the body firmly placed, the torso erect without being rigid, the feet resting strongly on the floor without pressing, the knees fairly close together, the hands resting on the thighs or clasped lightly in the lap. Now slowly begin to roll the weight of the body forward over the hips toward the knees, with the torso erect, at the same time pressing down with the feet and lifting in the torso. Do not begin this too abruptly or you will find the feet leaving and returning to the floor with a stamping motion that is both awkward and comic. The stamp is one of the commonest faults to be seen in untrained players trying to rise from a sitting position. Continue moving your weight forward and up over the feet until you are standing easily erect. Now reverse the process, beginning the movement, not with a bend of the knees, but with a sinking in the hips which causes the knees to relax naturally, at the same time moving the torso, still erect, downward and back until you are seated in the chair once more. Repeat these two movements several times, gradually increasing the speed with which you execute both the rising and the sinking; but never do them so rapidly

* This exercise was prepared by Foster Fitz-Simons.

that you lose control of the smoothness of each of the movements.

Now execute the rising from the chair, but keep the direction of the movement going forward so that you step out into an even walk from the chair. You will find that if you start by placing one foot slightly in front of the other while you are sitting you are already in a position for walking, and there is no break in the continuous flow of movement from sitting to walking. Now return to the chair. Pause a few inches from it and execute a half turn, sinking in the hips so as to let yourself sit as you were before, but now turned a little at an angle in the chair. This return and seating of yourself in the chair you will find a little more difficult than the rising. Practice so that you can approach and seat yourself in a chair, no matter at what distance it is from you or at what angle it is placed in relation to you, without having to hunt awkwardly and obviously for it with your eyes. Practice will develop an unconscious habit of executing the check in such a way as to make the action noticeable neither to yourself nor to the beholder. Repeat this exercise, employing as many different kinds of furniture for sitting as you can: arm chairs, deeply upholstered easy chairs, stools, benches with hard backs, sofas, fragile period chairs, and antiques. Each of them will require a different adjustment with respect to the execution of this basic exercise.

Characterized Posture and Movement

(Exercises to help the actor work out patterns of physical posture and movement which vary from the normal.)

40. After carefully reading the suggestions under *Characterized Posture and Movement* in Chapter III, imagine yourself to be a healthy, rather typical middle-aged person. Walk around the stage as this person. In character with your age, bring a chair onto the stage and sit in it. After a moment, rise and carry the chair to the side. Now, still in character, walk over to the other side of the stage and lift several imaginary objects from a shelf to a table. Finally, stoop down and lift one or two objects from the floor to the same table. Throughout your

pantomime, remember to move with a feeling of easy solidity. Make each movement count, decisively, efficiently. Do not jerk. Do not hurry.

41. As the same middle-aged person, set a table for four people. Place the dishes, the cutlery, and napkins, and draw up the chairs.

42. As the same middle-aged person, build or repair an imaginary object (such as a stool or set of book shelves) at a work bench.

43. As the same middle-aged person, get some imaginary sewing from a table, walk over to a chair, sit down, and mend a coat or a dress.

44. As the same person, imagine yourself to be cleaning and oiling a piece of machinery (such as an old-fashioned sewing machine) which requires you to get up and down and reach under to complete your work.

45. Repeat Ex. 40 as if you were a very fat and very lazy middle-aged person. Then do the exercise again as if you were a nervous person.

46. Select any one or more of the exercises from Chapter II and carry it through as a very old person.

47. Work out patterns of movement for six entirely different old men or old women. Base them on the observation of living models in everyday life. Make the six pantomimic portraits as different as possible but relate them all carefully to the standards of normal posture and movement suggested in this book.

48. Pick one of the sets of movements outlined in Exs. 40–44 and do it as a young person after
    (a) Just a little drinking
    (b) More drinking
    (c) Much drinking

49. Do Ex. 48 again as a middle-aged person.

50. Do Ex. 48 again as an old person.

51. Select one of the sets of movements suggested in Exs. 40–44, and do it as a person who has been slightly or badly crippled by an accident. Decide how old the man or woman is, and just what part or parts of the body have been incapacitated.

52. Work out in pantomime a short character sketch of your own.

It need not follow any of the suggestions given in this book.
53. Work out a few characterized movements appropriate to one of the following personalities in the *Dramatic Scenes:*

The Captain, in *Mr. Roberts*
The Nurse, in *Romeo and Juliet*
Finian, in *Finian's Rainbow*
Og, in *Finian's Rainbow*
Laura, in *The Glass Menagerie*
Amanda, in *The Glass Menagerie*
Maurya, in *Riders to the Sea*
Miss Dyer, in *Joint Owners in Spain*
Mrs. Blair, in *Joint Owners in Spain*
Primus, in *R. U. R.*
Helena, in *R. U. R.*
Mikail, in *Tovarich*
Tatiana, in *Tovarich*
Richard Dudgeon, in *The Devil's Disciple*
Anne, in *The Diary of Anne Frank*
Peter, in *The Diary of Anne Frank*

Movement with Other Bodies

(Exercises to help the actor learn the traditional methods for relating one player to other players in a group scene.)
54. With the help of one or two companions, demonstrate your knowledge of how to stand on the stage in such a way as:
   (a) to divide the attention of the audience equally between yourself and another actor
   (b) to attract the attention to yourself
   (c) to point the attention away from yourself to another person
55. With the help of one or more companions, demonstrate how crosses might be executed in several different kinds of situations.
56. Placing two companions together in different parts of the stage, show how you might enter from the rear, then from upstage at the side, then from downstage at the side, and join your friends in conversation.

Dramatic Situations Told in Pantomime

(Exercises for the player wishing to put together in a brief pantomimic scene what he has learned about bodily control.)

57. Select one of the *Seven Pantomimes* near the end of this book, and work it out carefully in accordance with the suggestions in the introduction to the group, and with the various principles of bodily action set forth in Chapters II and III.

58. Using the foregoing pantomimic sketches as models, the student should be able to make up and act out little stories of his own. It is not necessary, of course, that the stories be as elaborate as those included here. Whatever pantomime is composed should be presented simply, sincerely, and *completely*. The actor should not attempt to crowd the whole story of a novel within the space of five minutes. Keeping his imagination keenly alive, he should aim to make as much as he can out of every dramatic moment he selects for his expressive effort.

IV. THE ACTOR AS INSTRUMENTALIST—SPEECH

Kinesthetic Tone

(Exercises designed to help the player sense the connection between the sounds of words and the feeling of muscular tensions.)

1. Take a standing position where you are surrounded by some space, that is, a spot in which your legs and arms are free from distracting contacts. Now, using a little movement of your body as a whole, or of some part of it, to help you, speak in turn the following words and phrases in such a way as to suggest an act of feeling, looking, reaching, embracing, resisting, tasting, or lifting something concrete.

    Big
    Little
    High
    Deep
    House
    Woman
    Madman

Cake
Stone
Spacious house
Lovely woman
Terrifying madman
Delicious cake
Heavy stone

Now, standing or seated with your body absolutely still, see if you can utter these words and phrases with the same kinesthetic quality. Try to project the feeling of active physical response with your voice alone.

2. Experiment in the same way, first moving and then still, with a number of other words and phrases of your own choosing. Avoid abstractions because they do not as directly lend themselves to kinesthetic expression as do concrete picture words.

3. Standing in the position you took for Ex. 1, try with the help of a little actual movement (such as you would use if you were touching, testing, or shifting with the object indicated or implied) to speak the following phrases in such a way as to suggest sensuously the state of action or immobility appropriate to the expression.

   . . . the great Rock of Gibraltar, forever standing.
   . . . a little man pacing nervously across a room, back and forth, back and forth.
   . . . an old man sprawled out in the sun, yawning lazily.
   . . . a young girl dancing lightly.
   . . . a man in a boat, rowing, rowing.
   . . . raindrops scampering over the rooftop.
   . . . Jump quickly!—Jump!
   . . . Rest softly. Sleep. Sleep.

Now, with the body quite still, see if you can utter the phrases with the same effect of immobility or action, this time relying on the use of voice only.

4. Standing as you did before, try with the help of a little actual movement of your hands, body, or feet to render the following phrases and sentences in such a way as to suggest various qualities of action.

   . . . They strolled slowly down the street.

   . . . He leaped from the path of the car.

   . . . Stretching first one arm, then the other, then his legs, he finally raised himself out of bed.

   . . . galloping, galloping, galloping!

   . . . She slipped and fell down hard.

   . . . wearily carrying their heavy burdens.

   . . . with a hop, a skip, and a jump.

   . . . up and down—up and down.

   . . . 'round, and 'round, and 'round.

   . . . It darted past like a streak of lightning!

   . . . slowly swinging, ever swinging.

   . . . stopped with a jerk!

   . . . smoothly flowing without a ripple.

Now, with your body quite still, try to utter the phrases and sentences with the same quality of animation, this time relying on the use of the voice only.

5. Recall some active incident in your past experience, and relate it briefly. Try to make the sensory words and the words of motion as vivid as possible by the use of kinesthetic tone.

6. Retell briefly some active incident you have read in a story or seen in the films, on television, or on the stage. Re-create the picture of it vividly for the listener by filling your words of sensing and moving with kinesthetic sound.

7. Read out loud Browning's dramatic little poem, *Meeting at Night,* in accordance with the suggestions outlined in the text.

8. Take Browning's *Boots and Saddles* or Tennyson's *Milkmaid's Song* in the *Reading Selections* at the end of this book, and read it aloud in such a way as to obtain a maximum effect of action appropriate to the poem.

9. Read aloud, from the same section of the book, Eldridge's *The Sun, the Poet, and the Cow,* and try to distinguish clearly by means of kinesthetic tones the differences between the three characters.

10. Listen carefully to any well-produced dramatic sketch on the radio and note how much effect of action is suggested through the changing tones of the actors' voices without the aid of visible pantomime.

Fundamental Tonal Actions: Sensing

(Exercises planned to show the player how effectively he may use kinesthetic speech to reveal the fundamental responses of Sensation described in Chapter II.)

11. Speak the following phrases in such a way as to show how kinesthetic tonal actions can suggest the form and force of a commonplace sensation. As you speak, pitch your voice and turn your face to indicate the direction of your attention.

   . . . a soft wind stirring the leaves of the trees.

   . . . a roaring fire, sweeping through the forest!

   . . . music, light and gay!

   . . . rain on my face.

   . . . smoke in my eyes.

   . . . a shot from a gun!—Again!

   . . . bitter on the tongue.

   . . . perfume.

12. Take any of the objects listed in Chapter II, Ex. 7, and make up a short, simple vocal response to it—such as "Ouch! it's hot!," or "Whew—! It's cold!," or "Sticky!" Try to speak it in such a way as to indicate the direction, form, and force of your sensation. If you wish, use some physical action to emphasize your words.

13. In a similar way, work out a vocal response to an object in Chapter II, Ex. 8.

14. In a similar way, work out a vocal response to an object in Chapter II, Ex. 9.

15. In a similar way, work out a vocal response to an object in Chapter II, Ex. 10.

16. In a similar way, work out a vocal response to an object in Chapter II, Ex. 11.

17. Do again one or more of the exercises in the sequence of Chapter II, Exs. 45–54 (*Awareness of People*), making up a few words to accompany the pantomime. Try to make the sounds of your words convey to your listener as much concerning what you see or feel as do your actions.

Fundamental Tonal Actions: Preparing

(Exercises to help the player show how effectively he may

use kinesthetic speech to reveal the four fundamental responses of Preparation described in Chapter II.)

18. Do again Chapter II, Ex. 62, adding a few more words to your movement. Try to make what you say kinesthetically as expressive of rising and sinking as possible. Now repeat the action without pantomime, attempting to make the words alone show the shifting of your attention.

19. In a similar way do again Chapter II, Ex. 63.

20. In a similar way do again Chapter II, Ex. 64.

21. Add some appropriate words to Chapter II, Ex. 66 and do this exercise with your thought placed primarily on the expression of your urge to approach. Repeat the experiment without the pantomime. Try to make the kinesthetic sounds of your words carry the burden of action.

22. In a similar way, do Chapter II, Ex. 67, concentrating on the tonal expression of approaching (or the urge to approach).

23. In a similar way, do Chapter II, Ex. 68, concentrating on the tonal expression of approaching and withdrawing.

24. In a similar way, do Chapter II, Ex. 69, concentrating on the tonal expression of approaching and withdrawing.

25. In a similar way, do Chapter II, Ex. 70, concentrating on the tonal expression of approaching and withdrawing.

Fundamental Tonal Actions: Attacking

(Exercises to help the player show how effectively he may use kinesthetic speech to reveal the fundamental response of attack described in Chapter II.)

26. Add a few appropriate words to Chapter II, Ex. 73, and do this exercise with your mind focused principally on the tonal expression of impulses to fondle and destroy.

27. In a similar way do Chapter II, Ex. 74, concentrating on the tonal expression of fondling and destroying.

28. In a similar way do Chapter II, Ex. 75, concentrating on the tonal expression of cultivating, fondling, and of destroying.

29. In a similar way do Chapter II, Ex. 76, concentrating on the tonal expression of your urges to. promote activity and to check it.

30. Select any of the objects in Chapter II, Ex. 43, and make up a

story about it. Place it by imagination in (a) a situation in which you would desire to increase its effective qualities; then (b) another situation in which you would wish to destroy those qualities. Now work out carefully a complete panto-mimic and tonal response to the object in which you show clearly the force of one desire and then the other.

31. Read carefully out loud *Subject for A Farce* in accordance with the suggestions for fundamental tonal actions outlined in Chapter IV.

32. In a similar way read Hamlet's soliloquy in the same chapter.

Factors in Tonal Design

(Exercises to sharpen one's critical perception and one's control of pitch, time, force, and timbre—factors in kinesthetic speech.)

33. Select one of the reading selections at the end of this book, and read it out loud, giving special attention to expressive pitch. Vary the levels of your voice to bring out the changes of thought. Experiment freely. Let yourself overdo the changes at first, then bring them into effective control. Do not let your natural desire for restraint, however, exert itself at the expense of lively design.

34. Reread the same selection, giving your attention chiefly to your management of rhythm and tempo. Experiment freely.

35. Reread the same selection, giving your attention this time to your use of changing force.

36. Reread the selection once more, concentrating on timbre. (Remember that timbre is involved in kinesthetic tone, and therefore that one of the very best ways for increasing the timbre-coloring of your speech is to think in terms of muscular actions.)

37. Now, reread the selection a fourth time, using together as effectively as you can the factors of pitch, time, force, and timbre.

Normal Speech

38. The mechanics of pure diction are not treated in this book. The actor might find it to his advantage, however, to use some

of the reading selections at the close of the volume for practice in simple, straightforward speaking, unmarked by any traces of personal eccentricity.

Characterized Speech

(Exercises for developing one's ability to simulate the speech of an older person, or an eccentric individual.)

39. Select one of the short poems in *Reading Selections* or a few lines from another text and read these expressively, but in a completely normal (youthful, uneccentric) way. Let the sound of this reading serve as a reference for the departures from normal speech in the following two exercises.

40. Read the same passages as (a) a solid, healthy middle-aged person, then (b) as a nervous or sickly middle-aged person.

41. Read the same passage as (a) a person of 80, (b) a person of 100, (c) any old man or woman who has lost his teeth.

42. Read the passage as an inebriated person.

43. Read the same passage as some eccentric person of your acquaintance. Exaggerate a little if you choose. Make the person you present as reader a colorful character, but make him believable.

Compulsive Speech

(Exercises to refine the actor's ability to speak movingly.)

44. Select some solo dramatic passage in this book and, following the suggestions on compulsive speech outlined in the text, work first for expressiveness, then for smoothness. Then develop the inner musical values.

45. With the aid of a friend, develop a short dialogue scene through the same steps for compulsive speech.

Speech and Movement Together

(An exercise to help the actor integrate his pantomime and speech.)

46. Act out one of the *Dramatic Scenes,* working for a structural unity of speech and pantomime complete in all its expressive and compulsive parts.

V. PREPARING THE PART

Characterization and the Audience

1. Compare plays or dramatizations for children, such as *Treasure Island, Ali Baba and the Forty Thieves,* and *Aladdin,* with the kinds of plays which are more popular with adults, and note the difference in the treatment of character.

2. Examine a number of modern and older plays and see in how many of them you can spot characters which correspond to the Cinderellas, Jack-the-Giant-Killers, Snow Whites, Aladdins, Ugly Ducklings, and similar figures in children's fairy stories. How have the characters been modified to make them appealing to adult playgoers?

3. Try to recall the make-believe games you played as a child. Did you wish to be "Doctor," "Father," "Mother," "Postman," "Storekeeper," "Cowboy," "Engineer," "Preacher," or "Teacher" rather than someone just like yourself? As a grown person now do you feel a kindred attraction to superior personalities in stage plays? In what respects is the superiority you seek as an adult different from that superiority which you found most attractive as a child?

4. Consider the suggestion that all dramatic characters designed to win the interest of the audience should be in some one or more respects superior to the spectator's estimate of himself. Do you agree? Examine a number of plays of different styles, plays which appeal especially to your fundamental theatregoing sense—not just your momentary interest—and ask yourself if the personalities which stir your feelings possess some capacity for loving, or hating, or suffering, or clear thinking, or bravery, or persistence, or persuasiveness which you wish were yours?

5. What makes secondary characters dramatically interesting? Examine a number of them in an effective play and see what constitutes the appeal in each. What element can you find? What kind of aspiration, way of thinking, or at least manner of behaving that is a little more intense, than the typical action of a corresponding figure in everyday life? And what dramatic

function does each of these lesser personalities serve with respect to the advancement of the story of the principal characters?

Analyzing the Character*

6. Take a play (or scene) in which you have been assigned to do a part—or in which you would like to do a part—and read it through very carefully. As you read, ask yourself the questions suggested in Chapter V: "What is the general tone of the play? Does the author want the audience to hold its breath, to cry, or to laugh—and how much? What should be the final, overall effect on the audience when the last curtain falls? Now, what means has the author provided for building up such an effect? Is this chiefly a play of plot or of character, or one composed equally of both ingredients? What is the central idea of the play? And what is the direction of the story?"

7. Take the role you have chosen to personate and analyze it in the light of what you have learned about the play as a whole. Look mostly at the character's appearance and behavior, in accordance with the several suggestions in the Chapter. Let the charts on pages 104, 105 and 108 serve as a guide.

8. Now go inside the character and see what you can find about the physical, emotional, and intellectual causes for that outward appearance and behavior. Be sure that you dig deeply into all five galleries of the "mine" in the playwright's written script:

    (a) The playwright's description of the character's appearance, in the stage directions

    (b) The "stage business," the personal actions of the character

    (c) The speech lines of the character

    (d) The reactions of the other characters to the character

    (e) The situations that shape the manifestations of the character's personality

Relate this specific analysis of your role to the general analysis of the play in Ex. 6.

* Exs. 6–16 are arranged in sequence as an aid to the player wishing to prepare a particular role in accordance with the suggestions outlined in Chapter V.

9. Reinvestigate all the clues to the character set down by the playwright in both the dialogue and the stage directions. See if you can find any hints which you may have overlooked before.

10. Now give special attention to those scenes involving your character which are of outstanding interest. What can you learn from them?

Visualizing the Character

11. Take the character you have analyzed in Exs. 7–9 and visualize it in accordance with the suggestions outlined in Chapter V. (In actual practice, of course, most of this work of imagination would be done, not after the analysis, but along with it. Dissection and re-creation should go hand in hand.)

12. Develop the visualization by means of some observation of living models in the world around you.

13. See what help you can get from some observation of pictures, animals, machinery, or other animate or inanimate objects which possess attributes of smartness, swiftness, power, frailty, or eccentricity kindred to those possessed by your character.

14. What help can you get from a consideration of the four Fundamental Actions? Can you select one of them to serve as a master element in the movement and speech of your characterization?

15. What former experiences of your own can you make contribute to the emotional behavior of the character in certain of the crises through which it passes?

Development

16. Develop your part slowly and carefully in performance. Try little by little to sharpen and proportion the crises, and try to make the part build from beginning to end. Use your mind, but at the same time rely to a great extent on those impulses which spring out of a continuous and sensitive response to all the factors in the situation. Obey your hunches—provided, at the same time, you are giving sympathetic attention to the impulses of the other people in the scene. *And listen to the suggestions of your director.*

II

✭

SEVEN PANTOMIMES

By Loretto Carroll

Introduction

IN PERFORMING the following pantomimic sketches the actor should attempt to apply all that he has learned in the preceding exercises regarding Awareness, Response, and Control. But one difference between the modes of practice in these pantomimes and in the bodily exercises should be noted. While the preceding exercises are all designed for an unlimited, exaggerated form of execution, the sketches here are written for acting of a considerably more restrained nature. There should be the same largeness and freedom of movment, but all the emotion in each situation should not be fully stated. Develop the element of suggestion. Through intimation make your audience do as much of the acting as possible. If the following scenes are done well they are quite moving; if badly, they are only melodramatic. However, too much action is better than too little; poverty is not economy. Behind every detail of action, every half gesture, every uncompleted swing of the body, there must stand the image of the whole which the audience, properly stimulated, will see in imagination. In order to make sure that the restrained action will suggest the unrestrained, go through

* No royalty will be charged for any public performance of these pantomimes, but acknowledgment must be made to the author of the pantomimes and to this book.

340

each pantomime in a freely exaggerated manner first, and then select and "tone down" the movements until little will imply much. The only guide to an effective restraint is, of course, an intelligent imagination.

In each pantomimic sketch, a few words are included in order to bring to the consciousness of the student the relationship between speech and movement.

The words should be spoken out loud. The student would probably find it helpful to verbalize for himself—inaudible to the audience, of course—the principal thoughts and emotions that motivate his unvocalized action. As he moves through the first steps of *The Unemployed Man,* for instance, he might talk to himself in this way: "I dread entering this door. My wife stops; she suspects the worst. How she stares at me with her unspoken question! Well, I cannot continue standing here like a wooden image!" As he closes the door and voices a casual greeting, he resumes the verbalization of his thoughts: "That question in her eyes! I cannot possibly escape answering it. Well—" He does answer it. The forced laugh that breaks from his lips sounds hollow to his ears. He tells himself as much. In this way he continues to talk to himself through all his actions.

The stage setting, the objects (excepting only such chairs and tables as may be needed to support the weight of the actor), and the second character in each of these sketches, are wholly imaginary.

UNDERGROUND

The cell is rectangular, high, bare and clear. Down-left is the closed door to the corridor, and set into the right wall is a grating some six feet from the floor. Against the left wall is a bench and on it a woman lies asleep. Her jacket is folded to make a pillow and she sleeps with knees drawn up, shoulders hunched, in a vain effort to keep warm.

The first pale light of day filters through the grating. It is enough to show that the woman, SUZANNE, is still young and that her clothes are good. But her long hair is tangled about her shoul-

ders; her smart black dress is rumpled. For three days she has
waited; for three nights she has slept in her clothes. There are
lines of tension in her face but she is still young enough and weary
enough to sleep.

There is the sound of footsteps on the flagged court outside
the window. The sound reaches and disturbs SUZANNE.

"Paul." (She murmurs, then louder, as if in alarm:) "Paul!"

Her eyes are open now and she brushes her hair back from
her face. Still drowsy, she does not know what has wakened her.
She cannot sleep again for she is aware of the coldness and of her
cramped position on the bench. Slowly she pushes herself to a
sitting position. She yawns, and then stretches herself. It is not
like the stretching of one who has slept in a bed. It is a gradual
effort to ease the stiffness that is in every muscle, every joint of her
body. She throws back her head and moves her shoulders, frowning, as if the effort hurt. Finally she tries to thrust a foot into one
of the slippers that stand by the bench, but the foot is too cold.
She rubs it. She unfolds the thin jacket which was her pillow,
shakes it, and struggles into it.

The sound of movement comes again from outside the grating. She stops, frozen in the attitude in which the sound caught
her, listening intently, her eyes on the grating. Now the sound
gains rhythm and purpose. She is instantly aware of its significance. Her lips form words in a cold whisper.

"The firing squad. They've come back."

In frantic and fearful haste she drags the heavy bench to a
place beneath the window and climbs upon it. Her eyes are just
above the lower level of the grating but she cannot yet see: she
can only hear. She rubs her eyes as if to clear them from the mist
of sleep or to enable her to pierce the foggy light. Her palms are
flat against her eyes and she pushes away from her eyes to the
edges of her hair, stretching the skin of her face taut.

Suddenly a small company of soldiers comes into view. SU-
ZANNE is at once alert, moving, straining to see everything that
happens outside. She bites at her nails nervously. Now, at last, the
soldiers wheel and turn and the prisoners are pushed out before
them. SUZANNE has been waiting for this. She covers her mouth as
if to hold back any possible sound. Then, slowly, the hand comes

away. She stares fascinated, and her words fall deliberately, names —a count—a roll call.

"Lena . . . Marcelle . . . Eugene . . . Carl . . . John . . ." (She breaks off suddenly, and seizes the grating with both hands. Her voice rises with horror.) "No, no—no!" (But she is not heard. Her cry is drowned in the volley of the firing squad. She drops her head, resting her forehead against the grating, but she makes no further sound. She lets herself down on the bench after a time and sits there, huddled, shivering a little. Finally she lifts her head and stares about her with dull, blank eyes.)

As if to ease herself with movement she brushes back her thick hair and runs her fingers through it, trying to straighten and smooth it. She buttons her jacket and tries to smooth the deep wrinkles from her skirt. She becomes aware that her feet are very cold, and she crosses the room and brings her slippers back to the bench. She rubs one foot and with difficulty forces it into the narrow slipper. The other slipper will not go on. Suddenly she remembers why. She thrusts her hand in the toe of the slipper and pulls out a small nail file. She fingers it, tests the point of it on her palm. She draws it over the edge of one of her shortened nails, rapidly, absently, as if she had used this means to pass the time before.

There is a noise in the corridor outside her cell. She stares fearfully at the door, the file motionless for a fraction of a second; then she stoops and pushes it into her slipper, out of sight. As the footsteps approach her door she tries to stand straight, pushing out her shoulders, her hands deep in the pockets of her jacket, her feet braced, slightly apart, so that she appears to be waiting for some actual blow.

The key turns in the lock; the heavy door is opened by a uniformed guard who places food inside the room on the floor, and steps back. SUZANNE looks at the food with loathing.

"Take it away. I cannot eat it."

A second man, an officer, stares at her a moment and then motions to the guard to close the door. SUZANNE runs forward, her whole attitude changed in a moment to anxiety.

"Wait." (She cries.) "Wait."

But the door closes and she can only tug at it.

"You haven't got him. You haven't got Paul. I saw what you did to the others. Paul wasn't there. He got away."

The man outside the door speaks deliberately two words and goes away. The woman repeats them in a whisper.

"Tomorrow—Paul. Tomorrow—Paul." (Then pushing at the door again:) "I don't believe you. You hear me—I don't believe you."

But the men have gone. She is quite alone again. Before her is the day and again the night, and the morning will bring the light to the window and the sound of marching feet. She stoops, takes out the little file and holds it protectively in her hand. It is her most precious possession, her last resource. Her eyes go to the window. She shivers.

"I—don't—believe—you—" (But this time she says it tonelessly, without conviction.)

THE UNEMPLOYED MAN

The room serves as dining room and kitchen of a shabby set of light-housekeeping rooms in a city. A door opens downstage, left, into the hall, and one in the rear, center, leads to the bedroom. In the right wall is a window opening on an air-shaft, and near it stands an oilcloth covered table set for a meal, with two chairs drawn up. Back of the table, against the rear wall, right, is a three-burner gas stove on a goods box with a cretonne curtain. Along the left wall, upstage from the hall door, are a chair and a washstand, above which is a shelf and mirror.

The MAN is slightly stooped and, judging from the loose carriage of his body, completely dispirited. He takes a long time about closing the hall door after him when he enters, as if he wanted to postpone something disagreeable. Although he is aware from his first, half-furtive glance at her that his wife has halted on her way from stove to table and stands waiting, he ignores the question vibrant in her whole attitude. Without meeting her eyes he greets her casually.

"Hullo, Martha." (He takes off his coat awkwardly and lays it across the chair. Deliberately he puts his hat on top of it. The steady, searching gaze of his wife is unnerving him. He can postpone the moment no longer. With a lift of his chin and an attempt to square his shoulders, he compels himself to meet her eyes while he speaks in a tone of forced cheerfulness.) "Well, it was no use, Martha. The job was—gone. Looks as if nobody's got anything I can do—or maybe I can't do anything."

He tries to laugh, but the sound dwindles away quickly enough. His eyes drop before his wife's scornful ones, his shoulders droop despondently. With a little shrug of weary relief that his news has been announced, he sinks into the chair at the right end of the table, his back to the right wall, where he can watch his wife's movements. Humble, the MAN's eyes follow her from table to stove, from stove to table, with dumb appeal. Once he clears his throat and ventures a sound.

"Martha . . ."

The man clears his throat again, as if he would say something if he could, but then he gives up and begins to eat listlessly. The food is tasteless and hard to swallow. Suddenly he puts down his fork and speaks resolutely.

"Martha!" (His eyes follow her around the table, to the door of the bedroom, but before the contemptuous look in her eyes his voice falters uncertainly.) "Martha . . ."

He watches helplessly as she goes into the bedroom and slams the door sharply behind her. The noise of the door makes him flinch. After a moment he says with an attempt at bravado.

"All right, Martha. All right. Just as you say." (He laughs incoherently.) "That's good—just as you *say*. You won't say anything for another week."

He falls to eating without realizing that he does it, his movements keeping pace with his dark, hurried thoughts. Then he pushes the food away from him, as if he suddenly becomes aware of it, and finds it utterly distasteful. He wipes his mouth with the back of his hand, gets up, and pushes his chair under the table, as if the movement were habitual. Mechanically he stacks his dishes and starts to remove them from the table, but, with a glance of defiance at the closed door, he sets them back on the table.

He saunters across the room to the washstand and, taking

a brush from the shelf above it, smooths his hair before the small mirror hung against the wall. After a while he calls experimentally.

"Martha . . ."

He does not even glance toward the door but another look in the mirror disgusts him and he turns away, muttering under his breath that he is a fool. With his hands in his pockets, he roves about the room restlessly. At the air-shaft window he stops and falls to biting one of his nails, preoccupied with moody thoughts. Then, with sudden resolution, he crosses the room quickly to the bedroom door and turns the knob, as if to enter. For a moment he cannot believe that it is locked, but when he is finally convinced his anger is kindled to impotent fury.

"Martha!" (In a frenzy he shakes the knob and kicks at the door, shouting wildly.) "Martha! Martha!"

Abruptly the silence conquers him. He turns away from the door slowly, his anger giving place to a numbness that shows in his dazed face. He goes up to the door once more and says, almost tonelessly:

"Martha . . ."

For a moment he stands there with his back to the bedroom door, his mouth twitching nervously at one corner, his eyes dull with misery. His whole body seems to shrink, visibly. At length his eyes seek out the washstand, and he stares at it with a mixture of dread and fascination. He licks his lips nervously and a fit of shivering seizes him, but he conquers it and crosses slowly to the washstand. Slowly he opens the top drawer, and once, as it squeaks, he glances hastily at the bedroom door. He thrusts a hand into the drawer, feels for a place he knows at the back, and quickly brings out a small automatic, which he handles gingerly, slipping it into his pocket. He puts on the overcoat again, deliberately, then the hat. He thrusts both hands in his pockets and stands there for a second, fighting a wave of self-pity that sets his mouth quivering. Then he strides to the locked door, grasps the knob in his hands and throws the whole weight of his body against the door, pressing against it with a sort of quiet desperation. He speaks her name in a gasp, like a man out of breath with physical exertion.

"Martha!" (And then, despairingly.) "Martha—please, Martha . . ." (His voice dies to a whisper.) "Martha . . ."

He stands there a moment, his head drooping. Then, with a little gesture of wrapping his coat about him that suggests girding up his courage, he walks firmly to the hall door and, without a backward look, goes out and closes it behind him.

THE SERVANT

The scene is the last refuge of an old lady, whom poverty has driven to this one room of her house. It is tremendously crowded and cluttered with trunks, boxes, pictures, bric-a-brac—any number of ancient treasures. In the rear wall, center, is a door leading to the street, and beside it a row of little pegs for hats and coats. Against the left wall is a small table and a gas stove surrounded by pots and pans. Downstage, left, is a set of hanging shelves, full of small boxes and trinkets. In the center of the room a little to the left is a round table, used for dining. In the right wall is a large window and facing it stands a wing chair in which the mistress of the apartment sits. Only one hand, which grasps the arm of the chair, and two black-slippered feet that rest on a footstool are visible to the audience. A pair of crutches lies upon the floor beside the chair.

The street door opens and a fat woman, swathed in coat, hat, and muffler, comes in, shutting the door behind her quickly, as if to keep out a gust of wind. She rubs her red nose, the tip of which seems frozen, and brushes the damp wisps of hair back from her face, leaning against the door as if worn out by her walk against the wind. When she gets her breath, she begins to strip off her woolen gloves and, with a glance toward the wing chair, speaks rather ungraciously.

"Well, good morning." (The woman in the chair does not answer and the SERVANT's face grows vindictive. It is a stupid face, with puffy cheeks and too-small eyes.) "Still mad, eh? All because I ast you for a little something." (The SERVANT takes off the hat, and then begins to unwind a long, woolen scarf from about her throat.) "After all these years o' workin' for you on small pay." (With surprising agility, she crosses to the stove, rubbing her cold hands together, and lights a burner. She sets about making coffee.)

"What if I don't give you no coffee, just let you smell it?"

She laughs, a silly cackle. Then, as the woman in the chair makes no response, she starts toward the chair, coffee pot in hand, as if she means to have it out with her mistress. Half way across the room, she halts uncertainly, puts a hand on one hip, starts to speak, but changes her mind. Muttering something unintelligible to herself, she goes back and places the coffee on the stove. Briskly she lays the table.

When everything is ready but the coffee, she stands waiting, leaning over the back of one of the straight dining room chairs. A sudden idea makes her glance speculatively at the back of the big chair. She stares for a moment, then moves stealthily across the room to the little hanging shelves of bric-a-brac on the left wall. With a hasty glance at her mistress' chair, she gets from the top shelf a small trinket box, which she opens with eager fingers. She takes from the box a string of delicate, old-fashioned blue beads, and holds them in her fat hand, looking at them lovingly.

Something reminds her of the chair's occupant, and she takes a hasty step backward, stumbling against a chair. For a second she is in a panic, but when nothing is said to her, she plucks up courage enough to fasten the beads about her pudgy throat, straining to fasten the catch, and getting a little short of breath. She crosses the room boldly and looks at herself in a small mirror at the right of the door. Her face softened with childish vanity, the SERVANT turns toward the chair.

"You ain't changed your mind about giving me the beads?"

When there is no answer, the fat woman's face grows sullen and vindictive again. She takes off the beads with a jerk, replaces them in the box, and slams the box back on the shelf so that all the china rattles. When there is still no sign from the chair, she flies into a rage. She trembles and her little eyes snap as she takes a step toward the chair.

"I won't stand it! I won't! Three days last week you never spoke a word to me. It ain't human to act so. I—won't stand it no longer!" (She hurries across the room and confronts the invalid in the chair.) "I—"

Her voice dies away; her jaw drops in amazement. With horrified interest she draws nearer and touches the hand that rests on the chair-arm—but her finger recoils instantly. With lively interest, the SERVANT assures herself that her mistress is really dead. She stands looking a moment.

Straightening up briskly, she goes to a wall curtain, downstage, right, which covers her mistress' wardrobe. Into a battered suitcase that stands on the floor, she throws wearing apparel, pulled down with little or no pause for selection. Then, with a guilty glance at her mistress, she goes to the table and gets a small bowl she has always fancied. After a moment of thought, she walks resolutely to the big chair and extracts from the old lady a leather wallet, which she thrusts in the front of her dress. Closing the suitcase, she sets it by the door and hastily pulls on her wraps. When she is ready, she crosses to the wall cupboard and takes down the box with the blue beads. The box she throws on the floor carelessly—the beads, with a leer of triumph toward the wing chair, she fastens about her neck. With her hand on the doorknob, suitcase in the other hand, she looks about the room, frowning with indecision. Finally she decides to leave the suitcase, takes it back and kicks it under the curtain. She looks around, discovers the coffee pot, and goes over to turn out the fire beneath it.

At last she is ready. With her hand on the doorknob once more she pauses for a last look around the familiar room. Her hands grope for the beads and feel them; a smile of stupid satisfaction spreads over her face. She opens the door and goes out, catching her breath in a little gasp because of the wind's force.

THE BLIND THIEF

The scene is the library of a rather pretentious house. The room is lofty, and the walls are lined with bookshelves. In the rear wall, center, is a large fireplace over which hangs a portrait of a severe, middle-aged gentleman. To the right are two high windows with heavy draperies, and near them stand a small table and a velvet-cushioned divan. To the left of the fireplace stands a deep leather chair and near it is a massive desk. A single door, down-stage left, leads into the room from the hall.

The BLIND MAN backs into the room, feeling his way with his feet and his cane, and bowing obsequiously to the housekeeper who is admitting him to the room. He is a well-dressed man of thirty-five, a trifle heavy and rather too pale, with owlish dark glasses and a cane. His face is almost benign, and he nods and smiles continually, as if he were blessing someone. His voice is soft, his manner servile.

"Thank you, Madam, I *will* wait till I feel better. Too bad Mr. Jamieson's not at home. He'll be sorry to have missed his old friend. Yes, indeed. Don't bother, Madam. I know my way about. My hands and my cane can tell me as plain as ever your eyes tell you."

He bows again, several times, and allows the housekeeper to establish him comfortably in the leather chair. His eyes are fixed in sightless gaze upon the wall opposite him until she leaves, and as she quits the room, he murmurs:

"Thank you, thank you."

He sits quietly for a moment after she closes the door. Then he rises slowly and, tapping with his cane, makes his way to the door, where he leans lightly against the panels, listening. His face, meanwhile, retains the peaceful smile, which gradually spreads to a broad grin. Assured that there is no one outside, he stoops sud-denly and turns the key softly in the lock. Then, still feeling his way, he crosses to the windows and draws the heavy draperies across them.

Now the room is dark, although it is mid-afternoon, and as the BLIND MAN snaps on the table lamp at the head of the divan, a low chuckle escapes him. Still chuckling in a way that is curi-ously unpleasant, he takes off his glasses and slips them into a breast pocket and puts the cane on the table. His eyes, thus re-vealed, are small, keen, and close-set; they would give the lie to his hypocritical smile, even if his face had not changed suddenly. His manner is no longer slow, but has now become even brisk; his mouth is tight-lipped and scornful.

A second time of careful listening at the door, and he goes confidently to the right of the fireplace, runs his hand along the wall, and touches the spring that opens to him the library safe. Deftly he opens it, and, before he touches anything within, pauses for a moment to gloat over his success, speaking softly to himself.

"You see, I didn't forget."

Then he sets to work skillfully, removing what is valuable from the safe—running rapidly through some papers, pocketing a few bills and a leather bag of coins. At last he takes out what appears to be the real object of his search, for as soon as his fingers encounter it, he gives a little grunt of satisfaction. After a while he laughs, softly at first, then a little louder.

"Now I've got 'em. And to think, you're the one that's made a thief out of me—you with your dirty lying. A thief, and a clever one."

He laughs, slips the jewels into an inner pocket, and closes the safe, sliding back the panel which conceals it. Rubbing his hands together, he roams about the room restlessly, as if looking for some other place where he may wreak his spite. At length the portrait above the mantel catches his eye, and with a muttered "Ah," he studies it. He imitates the pompous pose of the man in the picture and is vastly amused at his own cleverness.

He gets a cigarette from the box on the table and smokes, sitting comfortably on the sofa, the texture of which he admires. A noise from outside makes him spring up lightly, run across the room and listen at the door. He comes back to the table rapidly, takes out his dark glasses and puts them on, picks up the cane, and lets his features relax into the peacefully benign smile. With elaborate imitation of a blind man's uncertainty, he snaps off the light, and draws back the heavy draperies. Then, deliberately, he crosses to the door and turns the key noiselessly in the lock.

Suddenly he steps back, and faces toward the wall, as if he were searching for the door. At that moment the housekeeper opens the door, and the blind man bows and moves toward her.

"I'm quite recovered, Madam. Just searching for the door, and missed it a little way. So sorry Mr. Jamieson isn't in. You will tell him I called? Don't know when I'll pass through town again. Thank you, thank you."

Bowing gratefully, obsequiously, he makes his way carefully through the door after the housekeeper, halts, feels for the door, and draws it closed behind him.

THE BRIDE

The scene is a corner of a girl's bedroom, littered with wedding paraphernalia. Upstage, right, is a door leading in from the hallway; across the room, in the center of the left wall, are open French doors, leading onto a small balcony. In the rear is a dressing-table, and to the right of it a chair on which there is an open dressing-case, already packed. Downstage, right, is a small writing desk. To the left of the dressing-table is a chaise longue, littered with boxes and overflowing with tissue paper.

The BRIDE is young and pretty, gowned in white for a formal wedding. She enters by the hall door, almost running, with her veil thrown carelessly over one arm to make flight easier. Quickly she shuts the door after her, locks it, and then, with a little gasp of relief leans against it as if to barricade herself further against pursuit. To the insistent cries and knocks from the other side she cries out petulantly:

"No, no, I tell you! I'm not sick and I haven't lost my mind, either. I just want to be alone for a minute. It's *my* wedding, isn't it?" (She listens to arguments from the outside with visible impatience.) "I tell you I'll come out in five minutes if you'll all go away." (Coaxingly.) "Just five minutes—I promise." (With childish defiance.) "If you don't—there won't be any wedding! (Eagerly.) Yes. I promise. Now—go away, all of you!"

She listens with satisfaction to the noise of their going, and when she is sure the last one has departed, a little breath of relief escapes her. She lets the wedding veil spread out behind her, and walks to the center of the room where she pauses and stands with both palms pressed against her hot cheeks, as if she would cool the excitement that burns there.

With a nervous glance at the hall door, she crosses quickly to the French doors, at the left, and, taking care not to be seen from the outside herself, searches the street beyond the balcony with

anxious eyes. A frown grows between her eyes, her lips tremble
with childish disappointment. In an angry, choked little voice that
is close to tears she cries out, stamping her foot impatiently.

"Oh, Dal, *Dal!*"

Remembering herself she glances at the hall door in alarm at
the prospect of having been overheard. Still not satisfied by the
reassuring silence, she crosses to the door, leans against it, and
listens. Evidently satisfied, she goes back to her place by the
French doors and resumes her watch. Once she starts eagerly at
sight of a passerby, only to be disappointed. After that she seems
to fall into an unhappy reverie. Gradually she gives up all hope of
finding the one she seeks. She seems to wilt, and, leaning wearily
against the door jamb, she says again, this time softly, despairingly:

"Dal—Dal!"

Listlessly she turns away from the balcony toward the littered
chaise longue. The wedding veil annoys her and she takes it off
carelessly and throws it across the dressing-table bench. She eyes
the festive array on the chaise longue distastefully and, with a
sweep of her hand, dashes it to the floor. She seats herself on the
chaise longue and begins to jab at the pillows petulantly with her
fists. Then, with a little cry, she flings herself down among the
pillows and weeps silently, her body seized by deep shuddering.

A knocking at the hall door makes her suddenly still. When
it is repeated she lifts her head slowly, her eyes dazed and bewildered. Then she remembers where she is, remembers her promise and says apathetically:

"All right. You can tell them to get ready. I'm coming." (And
then, impatiently.) "I tell you I'm coming!"

Brushing the tears from her eyes she goes to the dressing-
table, picks up the veil and fits it to her head carelessly. She sits
down and looks at herself in the mirror, but the sight of her di-
sheveled image moves her to giggle hysterically. She sets about
repairing the damage, expertly. She wets her finger tips from a
small bottle and bathes her temples, then holds the bottle under
her nose and takes a deep breath. With rouge, powder, and lip-
stick, she covers all traces of her bad five minutes. As she is
straightening the veil and patting her hair in place, a sound from

beyond the balcony makes her rigid with attention. When it is repeated, she puts down her hand-mirror with trembling haste and
hurries across to the French doors. To someone beyond she calls
ecstatically:

"Dal!" (On tiptoe she waves her hand and makes signs to the
man beyond that she is ready to go. Blowing him a hasty kiss she
whispers:) "Wait!"

She hurries to the middle of the room, turns completely
around in her bewilderment and excitement, and finally dashes
over to the little desk, where she scribbles a note. Once she pauses
and chews the end of the pen thoughtfully, but a moment later
she blots what she has written and, with a satisfied mischievous
smile, sticks it in the crack of the hall door, just above the knob.

She rushes to the dressing table, sweeps a handful of articles
into the open bag, and is about to close it when she remembers
the veil. With another mischievous look, she removes it, folds it
carefully, and places it in the bag, which she closes with a snap.
It takes her only a moment to put on a long traveling coat and
tuck up her white gown beneath it, and to replace the veil with a
small hat. Just as she finishes, there is an impatient rap at the hall
door, and she calls out gaily:

"Coming this instant!"

Bag in hand, she tiptoes across to the French doors. There
she pauses only long enough to throw a kiss toward the hall door
before she steps out on the balcony, her face aglow with excitement, her voice eager:

"Dal!"

GROOM IN THE KITCHEN

It is a spick-and-span kitchen, done in blue and white and, as
yet, little used. Downstage, right, is a breakfast nook, covered with
dishes from a recent meal, and up stage, right, is the door commu-
nicating with the hall and the other rooms of the house. Against
the rear wall stands a shining electric range and the newest model
in kitchen cabinets. In the middle of the left wall, beneath twin
windows curtained in gingham, stands the kitchen sink, glorified

with nickel and enamel. A business-like work table occupies the center of the room.

The GROOM is standing in the hall door, urging his wife from the kitchen with large gestures of male protectiveness. He is a young man, he has just had his lunch, and he is optimistic and full of confidence.

"Go right along, dear. Lie down on the couch in the living-room, open up that new magazine and have a long rest." (At his wife's protests he waves an airy hand.) "What's so tricky about washing a few dishes—easiest thing in the world." (He watches her departure with beaming good humor.) "That's it! Good girl!"

Whistling a cheerful, monotonous tune, he turns away from the door and comes down to the breakfast nook, right, where he begins to stack the dishes. He makes good progress until he picks up a plate in such a way that his hand gets into a greasy spot. Spreading his fingers wide and holding the hand away from him, he stares at it with a wrinkle of disgust.

"Butter!"

He starts to wipe the butter on his clothes, remembers in time, and rubs it on the tablecloth instead. That reminds him that he needs an apron and he looks about until he finds one hanging by the cabinet at the rear. After some difficulty with the strings, he succeeds in tying it around him and goes back to his task of stacking dishes, whistling again his monotonous tune.

Attempting to carry almost all the dishes across the room to the sink at once, he makes a hazardous crossing, balancing his plates with anxious precision. Arrived at the sink, he deposits the load a little too abruptly in his relief, and the clank of china against metal appalls him. After a guilty glance toward the hall door, he looks through the stack, and breathes an audible sigh of relief when he finds that nothing is broken.

Whistling again, he goes for another load of dishes, a lighter one this time, which he sets down with care. Returning to the table he takes up the cloth, shakes out the crumbs, folds it, and puts it back on the table. With a frown he looks at the crumbs he has shaken upon the floor. Deciding to sweep them up, he gets the broom from the left, upstage, corner of the kitchen, and sweeps them carefully under the kitchen table.

At last he is ready to wash the dishes, but his enthusiasm has cooled a little. He turns on the hot water and holds a finger under the steam to test its heat. His gaze wanders absently, his thoughts are far away, until suddenly the water grows very hot, and he withdraws his finger abruptly and applies it to his mouth for relief. Still sucking the injured finger, he cuts off the water and stares at the dishes with growing distaste.

Shrugging away his responsibility for the whole lot of them, he saunters over to the kitchen cabinet in the rear, opens one of the small doors, and discovers a plate of cookies. He takes one and comes down to the central table, on the corner of which he seats himself, munching contentedly and staring absently before him. A voice from down the hall brings him to his feet with a guilty jump. He goes to the door, pokes his head out and calls loudly:

"Sure—sure! I'm doin' 'em. Almost through, now." (He casts a guilty look over his shoulder at the full sink, then calls reassuringly to his wife:) "Just don't you worry. I said I'd do 'em, didn't I?"

With dignity and a show of energy he comes back to the sink, turns on the water again, and empties a box of soapflakes into the pan. The fumes make him sneeze and move away from the pan, but, holding his hand over his mouth and nose, he manages to reach over and turn off the water. Holding each dish gingerly in his left hand, and the dish-mop daintily, by the end of its handle, in his right hand, he works a long time at cleaning each piece, lifting it up and inspecting it before putting it down.

When he is putting one of the plates on the table, it suddenly slips in his hands; he grabs at it frantically, but it falls with a crash into the sink. It is easy to tell from his stare of blank consternation that the dish is no longer in one piece. At a call from down the hall he goes to the door and answers worriedly:

"No—no! It wasn't anything. Can't wash dishes without a little fuss." (Irritatedly.) "Why don't you *rest?* Just relax and rest."

He starts back toward the sink, then, arrested by his wife's voice, he calls out hastily:

"No, no! I'll bring you a glass of water. Stay right where you are!"

He rushes to the sink, grabs up the pieces of the dish, cutting a finger in his haste, and, after looking around wildly for a place to conceal them, finally thrusts them into his pockets. He speaks placatingly to his wife:

"I'm coming, dear." (He gets a glass, puts some water into it from the tap and, half running across the kitchen, disappears through the door, calling down the hall.) "Com-i-n-g!"

CARRIE

The scene is a shabby, commonplace room, with only a pink kewpie doll on the mantel and an imitation ivory brush-and-comb set on the bureau to indicate that it is a woman's bedroom. There is a fireplace in the center of the right wall, and by it are a rocker and a footstool. At the back of the room are two windows, in front of which stands a daybed. The bureau is against the left wall, upstage, and beside it pegs have been driven into the wall to hang up clothes. A door, upstage, right, leads outside the house; one downstage, left, leads into another room and stands slightly ajar.

CARRIE is a large woman in her early thirties whose clothes appear to be assembled with no particular eye for harmony or fit, but whose face is cheerful beneath a hat too gay for her years. Only her feet make a pretense of elegance, crammed into small new patent leather slippers with heels that make her rock a little uncertainly as she walks.

CARRIE opens the door, right, and pokes an inquiring head inside. Satisfied that no one is there, she comes in and closes the door after her with elaborate caution. The half-open door on the other side of the room disturbs her, and she stands there for a moment thoughtfully, tongue in her cheek, brows knit. Presently she decides to venture, and, tiptoeing painfully across the room, she closes the other door softly. When there are no sounds beyond the door, she draws a deep breath of relief.

Coming back to the middle of the room, she takes off her hat and throws it to the daybed, ruffling her loose hair with both hands. The slippers come next, but they are welded tightly to her swollen feet. One sticks, and she must tug at it, her face screwed up with pain. When she is finally free she stands with her stockinged feet on the carpet and wriggles her toes happily, breathing her relief.

"Oh-h-h-h!"

She hobbles to the daybed and sits down with a little gasp of satisfaction. Pulling herself out of her coat, she lets it fall about her and sits there enjoying to the fullest a moment of rest—shoulders sagging, head dropped forward, hands limp in her lap. Presently she raises her head, looks toward the left door, and ventures experimentally:

"Sister." (There is no answer and she tries again, but not too loudly.) "Sis-t-e-r."

Pleased in a secret way at getting no answer, she takes a purse from the pocket of her dress and opens it. Two of the three bills she places in one pile; the other bill and several pieces of silver she makes into another pile. Her lips move, counting; her face is puckered with earnestness. She looks at the piles, picks up a coin, debates whether or not to change its position, and finally decides to.

At length, with a foolish smile and a glance at the bedroom door, she takes from her dress pocket a sheet of blue note paper, written upon in pale ink. She reads after the manner of one who gets new pleasure from reading again a familiar thing. When she has quite finished, she sits quietly, lost in a happy reverie.

The left door opens suddenly and CARRIE looks up with a little gasp of surprise.

"Sister!" (Her eyes follow SISTER's to the letter in her hand, and she laughs self-consciously.) "It's from Milt. He—he still wants to take me with him on his trip this Christmas." (Then wincing at SISTER's scorn, she adds hastily:) "No, no—of course I won't go."

Her eyes follow SISTER's as she discovers the ridiculous slippers in the middle of the floor. CARRIE gets them apologetically and throws them under the bed. Shyly she says:

"They hurt pretty bad—but Milt likes me in heels." (She picks up her coat and hat.) "I never can remember to hang things up."

She takes them and hangs them on the pegs against the wall. As she turns her back on the room, SISTER, seeing the money on the daybed, makes a move toward it. But CARRIE crosses the room

hastily and thrusts the smaller pile into her dress pocket! The
other she takes to the woman standing in the doorway, speaking
determinedly, as if expecting opposition.

"There's your board money. Only—I'm not letting you save
any more for me. I'm keeping the rest of what I make for myself."

She shrinks back, as if under the onslaught of bitter abuse.
With her back to the mantel she clasps and unclasps her hands
nervously.

"I tell you I want that money; I was going back home for
Christmas. You don't want to go—but I want to. I—I—oh, what's
the use!"

She takes out the money and throws it on the floor, watching
with scorn while SISTER picks it up. When SISTER goes out and
closes the door, her anger breaks.

"Now you've got what you wanted, you can go." (She laughs
unsteadily.) "And I can go, can't I?"

CARRIE's face suddenly hardens with resolution. She takes
the letter from her pocket and looks at it thoughtfully. Then with
a grim smile at the closed door, she replaces the letter. She crosses
to the bureau and drags from beneath it an old suitcase which she
fills haphazardly from the contents of the bureau drawers. She
gets her coat from the peg on the wall, brushes it off, and puts it
on. Then she puts on the hat, tucking her hair up under it with
little jabs of her fingers. At last she is ready—except for the slippers. With a sigh of regret she pulls them from beneath the bed.
With one slipper on, she pauses, depression taking hold of her.

Hobbling on one free foot and one imprisoned one, she goes
to the door and opens it a crack, calling plaintively:

"Sister . . ." (There is no answer, and she calls even more
placatingly.) "Oh, Sister."

With a short little laugh she goes back to the daybed and
pulls on her other slipper. Already the pleasure is gone from her
defiance, but something stubborn has settled around her mouth.
Suitcase in hand, she tries one last time.

"Sister—if you'll let me have the railroad fare home for
Christmas, I swear I won't take another cent next time."

When there is no answer, her angry resolution returns. She

limps to the hall door, and with every step the back of each shoe rubs a blister. At the hall door she pauses and calls out with gall and mockery:

"Merry Christmas, Sister—from Milt and me!"

She goes out.

III

$\bigstar$

READING SELECTIONS

Introduction

The group of verses that follows does not have as its purpose providing material for exercises in diction—though of course the verses may be used for that—but rather, supplying a means for working on expressive tone. All of the poems are filled with active imagery which the reader should try to convey vividly and convincingly. The pace and the feeling of each piece differs from the others. Some of the verses are serious, some solemn, some humorous, some more lively or more quiet. They invite the reader to present them with all the variations of vocal design described in the chapter on the actor as instrumentalist in the field of speech.

The selections from Shakespeare provide opportunities to exercise the full range of one's command of design in the service of depicting certain characters feeling emotion in specific dramatic situations.

Verses

MEETING AT NIGHT

The gray sea and the long black land;
And the yellow half-moon large and low;

And the startled little waves that leap
In fiery ringlets from their sleep,
As I gain the cove with pushing prow,
And quench its speed i' the slushy sand.

Then a mile of warm sea-scented beach;
Three fields to cross till a farm appears;
A tap at the pane, the quick sharp scratch
And blue spurt of a lighted match,
And a voice less loud, through its joys and fears,
Than the two hearts beating each to each!

Robert Browning

OZYMANDIAS

I met a traveller from an antique land
Who said: Two vast and trunkless legs of stone
Stand in the desert. Near them, on the sand,
Half sunk, a shattered visage lies, whose frown,
And wrinkled lip, and sneer of cold command,
Tell that its sculptor well those passions read
Which yet survive, stamped on these lifeless things,
The hand that mocked them and the heart that fed:
And on the pedestal these words appear:
"My name is Ozymandias, king of kings:
Look on my works, ye Mighty, and despair!"
Nothing beside remains. Round the decay
Of that colossal wreck, boundless and bare
The lone and level sands stretch far away.

Percy Bysshe Shelley

From "ALASTOR

The boat pursued
The winding of the cavern. Daylight shone
At length upon that gloomy river's flow;

Now, where the fiercest war among the waves
Is calm, on the unfathomable stream
The boat moved slowly. Where the mountain, riven,
Exposed those black depths to the azure sky,
Ere yet the flood's enormous volume fell
Even to the base of Caucasus, with sound
That shook the everlasting rocks, the mass
Filled with one whirlpool all that ample chasm;
Stair above stair the eddying water rose,
Circling immeasurably fast, and laved
With alternating dash the gnarled roots
Of mighty trees, that stretched their giant arms
In darkness over it. I' the midst was left,
Reflecting, yet distorting every cloud,
A pool of treacherous and tremendous calm.
Seized by the sway of the ascending stream,
With dizzy swiftness, round, and round, and round,
Ridge after ridge the straining boat arose,
Till on the verge of the extremest curve,
Where, through an opening of the rocky bank,
The waters overflow, and a smooth spot
Of glassy quiet mid those battling tides
Is left, the boat paused shuddering.

                    Percy Bysshe Shelley

From "A SONG IN TIME OF ORDER"

Push hard across the sand,
    For the salt wind gathers breath;
Shoulder and wrist and hand,
    Push hard as the push of death.

The wind is as iron that rings,
    The foam-heads loosen and flee;
It swells and welters and swings,
    The pulse of the tide of the sea.

And up on the yellow cliff
   The long corn flickers and shakes;
Push, for the wind holds stiff,
   And the gunwale dips and rakes.

Good hap to the fresh fierce weather,
   The quiver and beat of the sea!
While three men hold together
   The kingdoms are less by three.

Out to the sea with her there,
   Out with her over the sand,
Let the kings keep the earth for their share!
   We have done with the sharers of land.

They have tied the world in a tether,
   They have bought over God with a fee;
While three men hold together,
   The kingdoms are less by three.

We have done with the kisses that sting,
   The thief's mouth red from the feast,
The blood on the hands of the king,
   And the lie at the lips of the priest.

Will they tie the winds in a tether,
   Put a bit in the jaws of the sea?
While three men hold together,
   The kingdoms are less by three.

                            Algernon Charles Swinburne

A LITTLE WHILE

A little while, a little love
   The hour yet bears for thee and me
   Who have not drawn the veil to see
If still our heaven be lit above.

Thou merely, at the day's last sigh,
   Hast felt thy soul prolong the tone,
And I have heard the night-wind cry
   And deemed its speech mine own.

A little while, a little love
   The scattering autumn hoards for us
   Whose bower is not yet ruinous
Nor quite unleaved our songless grove.
Only across the shaken boughs
   We hear the flood-tides seek the sea,
And deep in both our hearts they rouse
   One wail for thee and me.

A little while, a little love
   May yet be ours who have not said
   The word it makes our eyes afraid
To know that each is thinking of.
Nor yet the end: be our lips dumb
   In smiles a little season yet:
I'll tell thee, when the end is come,
   How we may best forget.
        Dante Gabriel Rossetti

MILKMAID'S SONG

Shame upon you, Robin,
   Shame upon you now!
Kiss me would you? with my hands
   Milking the cow?
   Daisies grow again
   Kingcups blow again,
And you came and kiss'd me milking the cow.

Robin came behind me,
   Kiss'd me well, I vow.
Cuff him could I? with my hands

Milking the cow?
Swallows fly again,
Cuckoos cry again,
And you came and kiss'd me milking the cow.

Come, Robin, Robin,
Come and kiss me now;
Help it can I? with my hands
Milking the cow?
Ringdoves coo again,
All things woo again.
Come behind and kiss me milking the cow!

Alfred Lord Tennyson

BOOT AND SADDLE

Boot, saddle, to horse and away!
Rescue my castle before the hot day
Brightens to blue from its silvery gray.
     CHORUS.—Boot, saddle, to horse, and away!

Ride past the suburbs, asleep as you'd say;
Many's the friend there, will listen and pray
"God's luck to gallants that strike up the lay—
     CHORUS.—Boot, saddle, to horse, and away!"

Forty miles off, like a roebuck at bay,
Flouts Castle Brancepeth the Roundheads' array:
Who laughs, "Good follows ere this, by my fay,
     CHORUS.—Boot, saddle, to horse, and away!"

Who? My wife Gertrude; that, honest and gay,
Laughs when you talk of surrendering, "Nay!
I've better counsellors; what counsel they?
     CHORUS.—Boot, saddle, to horse, and away!"

Robert Browning

SUBJECT FOR A FARCE

Night—
An old woman sitting at the window—
Dreaming . . .
Suddenly,
Softly,
Her name is called—
"Florence—Florence—Florence!"
She shivers—
Rises—
Bends out—
A neighbor's window opens,
A gentle voice whispers—
"All right, dearest—come up—I am alone . . ."
An old woman standing at the window,
Dreaming . . .

*Paul Eldridge**

THE SUN, THE POET, AND THE COW

The Sun was sinking
In gorgeous nonchalance—
A god contented,
Assured of endless life.

In ecstasy the Poet
Stretched forth his arms,
And improvised in fervent verse
A hymn of joy and reverence,
And knelt
And prayed . . .

The Cow, reclining on the grass

* From *Vanitas*, 1920, reprinted with permission of the Alpine Press, Boston.

A gracious queen,
Upraised her head
And blandly looked
And thought:
"How youthful is the race of man,
And garrulous!
Some day they'll learn
That nothing is or matters
Save to chew the cud
In careless elegance,
And sleep . . ."

The Poet prayed on and on . . .
The Cow chewed on and on . . .
The Sun was sinking
In gorgeous nonchalance . . .
*Paul Eldridge**

Eight Soliloquies from Shakespeare

ROMEO AND JULIET

(ROMEO, *amidst a group of merrymakers, is in a black mood
because a young woman whom he loves is indifferent to him. His
irrepressible friend,* MERCUTIO, *undertakes to cheer him up. When*
ROMEO *makes a remark about a dream he has had,* MERCUTIO
laughingly tells him that he has been touched by Queen Mab.)
MERCUTIO. O, then, I see Queen Mab hath been with you.
　　She is the fairies' midwife, and she comes
　　In shape no bigger than an agate-stone
　　On the fore-finger of an alderman,
　　Drawn with a team of little atomies
　　Athwart men's noses as they lie asleep;
　　Her waggon-spokes made of long spinners' legs,
　　The cover of the wings of grasshoppers,
　　The traces of the smallest spider's web,

* From *Vanitas,* reprinted with permission of the Alpine Press, Boston.

The collars of the moonshine's watery beams,
Her whip of cricket's bone, the lash of film,
Her waggoner a small grey-coated gnat,
Not half so big as a round little worm
Prick'd from the lazy finger of a maid;
Her chariot is an empty hazel-nut
Made by the joiner squirrel or old grub,
Time out o' mind the fairies' coachmakers.
And in this state she gallops night by night
Through lovers' brains, and then they dream of love;
O'er courtiers' knees, that dream on court'sies straight,
O'er lawyer's fingers, who straight dream on fees,
O'er ladies' lips, who straight dream on kisses,
Which oft the angry Mab with blisters plagues,
Because of their breaths with sweetmeats tainted are;
Sometimes she gallops o'er a courtier's nose,
And then dreams he of smelling out a suit;
And sometimes comes she with a tithe-pig's tail
Tickling a parson's nose as a'lies asleep,
Then dreams he of another benefice;
Sometimes she driveth o'er a soldier's neck,
And then dreams he of cutting foreign throats,
Of breaches, ambuscadoes, Spanish blades,
Of healths five-fathom deep; and then anon
Drums in his ear, at which he starts and wakes,
And being thus frighted, swears a prayer or two
And sleeps again.

ROMEO AND JULIET

(*The lovers, secretly married, plan to meet in* JULIET's *room.
In the afternoon, before their getting together,* JULIET *is waiting
expectantly in the orchard of her home.*)

JULIET. Gallop apace, you fiery-footed steeds,
    Towards Phoebus' lodging: such a waggoner
    As Phaethon would whip you to the west,
    And bring in cloudy night immediately.

Spread thy close curtain, love-performing night,
That runaways' eyes may wink, and Romeo
Leap to these arms, untalk'd of and unseen.
Lovers can see to do their amorous rites
By their own beauties; or, if love be blind,
It best agrees with night. Come, civil night,
Thou sober-suited matron, all in black;
Hood my unmann'd blood, bating in my cheeks,
With thy black mantle; till strange love, grown bold,
Think true love acted simple modesty.
Come, night; come, Romeo; come, thou day in night;
For thou wilt lie upon the wings of night
Whiter than new snow on a raven's back.
Come, gentle night, come, loving, black-brow'd night,
Give me my Romeo; and, when he shall die,
Take him and cut him out in little stars,
And he will make the face of heaven so fine
That all the world will be in love with night
And pay no worship to the garish sun.
O, I have bought the mansion of a love,
But not possess'd it, and, though I am sold,
Not yet enjoy'd: so tedious is this day
As is the night before some festival
To an impatient child that hath new robes
And may not wear them.

ROMEO AND JULIET

(JULIET, *learning of* ROMEO's *banishment and faced by her father's stern commands to marry another man, seeks the help of* FRIAR LAURENCE. *He gives her a vial containing a powerful drug which will make her appear dead, tells her to take it and permit herself to be buried in the family vault, from which* ROMEO *will rescue her and escape with her.* JULIET *retires to her room. She whispers an unheard farewell to her family, then prepares to drink the drug.*)

JULIET. Farewell! God knows when we shall meet again.

I have a faint cold fear thrills through my veins,
That almost freezes up the heat of life;
I'll call them back again to comfort me;
Nurse! What should she do here?
My dismal scene I needs must act alone.
Come, vial.
What if this mixture do not work at all?
Shall I be married then tomorrow morning?
No, no; this shall forbid it; lie thou there.
  (*Laying down her dagger.*)
What if it be a poison, which the friar
Subtly hath minister'd to have me dead,
Lest in this marriage he should be dishonour'd,
Because he married me before to Romeo?
I fear it is; and yet, methinks, I should not,
For he hath still been tried a holy man.
How if, when I am laid into the tomb,
I wake before the time that Romeo
Come to redeem me? there's fearful point!
Shall I not, then, be stifled in the vault,
To whose foul mouth no healthsome air breathes in,
And there die strangled ere my Romeo comes?
Or, if I live, is it not very like,
The horrible conceit of death and night,
Together with the terror of the place,—
As in a vault, an ancient receptacle,
Where, for these many hundred years, the bones
Of all my buried ancestors are pack'd;
Where bloody Tybalt, yet but green in earth,
Lies festering in his shroud; where, as they say,
At some hours in the night spirits resort;—
Alack, alack, is it not like that I,
So early waking, what with loathsome smells,
And shrieks like mandrakes torn out of the earth,
That living mortals, hearing them, run mad;—
O, if I wake, shall I not be distraught,
Environed with all these hideous fears?
And madly play with my forefathers' joints?

And pluck the mangled Tybalt from his shroud?
And, in this rage, with some great kinsman's bone,
As with a club, dash out my desperate brains?
O, look! methinks I see my cousin's ghost
Seeking out Romeo, that did spit his body
Upon a rapier's point; stay, Tybalt, stay!
Romeo, I come! This do I drink to thee.

ROMEO AND JULIET

(*The old* NURSE, *sent to awaken* JULIET *on the morning she is supposed to marry* COUNT PARIS, *enters her room.*)

NURSE. Mistress! what, mistress! Juliet!
Fast, I warrant her, she:
Why, lamb! why, lady! fie, you slug-a-bed!
Why, love, I say madam! sweetheart! why bride
What, not a word? You take your pennyworths now;
Sleep for a week; for the next night, I warrant,
The Count Paris hath set up his rest,
That you shall rest but little. God forgive me,
Marry, and amen, how sound is she asleep!
I needs must wake her. Madam, madam, madam!
Aye, let the County take you in your bed;
He'll fright you up, i' faith. Will it not be?
     (*Draws back the curtains.*)
What, dress'd, and in your clothes! and down again!
I must needs wake you. Lady! Lady! Lady!
Alas, alas! Help, help! my lady's dead!
O, well-a-day, that ever I was born;
Some *aqua vitae*, ho! My lord! my lady!

ROMEO AND JULIET

(ROMEO, *absent in Mantua, hears that* JULIET *has died. Failing to receive* FRIAR LAURENCE's *letter explaining the plan of rescue,* ROMEO *returns to Verona, enters the tomb, and finds* JULIET *laid out as if in death.*)

ROMEO. O my love! my wife!
   Death, that hath suck'd the honey of thy breath,
   Hath had no power yet upon thy beauty:
   Thou art not conquer'd; beauty's ensign yet
   Is crimson in thy lips and in thy cheeks,
   And death's pale flag is not advanced there.
   Why art thou yet so fair? shall I believe
   That unsubstantial death is amorous,
   And that the lean abhorred monster keeps
   Thee here in dark to be his paramour?
   For fear of that, I still will stay with thee;
   And never from this palace of dim night
   Depart again.
            Eyes, look your last!
   Arms, take your last embrace! and lips, O you,
   The doors of breath, seal with a righteous kiss
   A dateless bargain to engrossing death!
   Come, bitter conduct, come, unsavoury guide!
   Thou desperate pilot, now at once run on
   The dashing rocks thy sea-sick weary bark!
   Here's to my love! (*Drinks.*) O true apothecary!
   Thy drugs are quick. Thus with a kiss I die.(*Dies.*)

MACBETH

(*Someone is at the gate of* MACBETH'S *castle. After a night of carousing, the drunken* PORTER *comes to answer the insistent knocking.*)

PORTER. Here's a knocking indeed! If a man were porter of hell-
   gate, he should have old turning the key. (*Knocking within.*)
   Knock, knock, knock! Who's there, i' the name of Beelzebub?
   Here's a farmer, that hanged himself on the expectation of
   plenty; come in time; have napkins enow about you; here
   you'll sweat for't. (*Knocking within.*) Knock, knock! Who's
   there, in the other devil's name? Faith, here's an equivocator,
   that could swear in both the scales against either scale; who
   committed treason enough for God's sake, yet could not equiv-

ocate to heaven; O, come in, equivocator. (*Knocking within.*)
Knock, knock, knock! Who's there? Faith here's an English
tailor come hither, for stealing out of a French hose; come in,
tailor; here you may roast your goose. (*Knocking within.*)
Knock, knock; never at quiet. What are you? But this place is
too cold for hell. I'll devil-porter it no further; I had thought
to have let in some of all professions that go the primrose way
to the everlasting bonfire (*Knocking within.*) Anon, anon! I
pray you, remember the porter.

MACBETH

(LADY MACBETH *has assisted in the murder of* DUNCAN, *the
king, and connived in the death of* BANQUO, *his general. At first
quite resolute, she has gradually weakened under the strain of
suspicion and fear, until finally her mind has broken. She imagines
she sees blood spots on her hands.*)

LADY MACBETH. Yet here's a spot . . . Out, damned spot! Out, I
say!—One: two: why, then 'tis time to do't.—Hell is murky!—
Fie, my lord, fie! a soldier, and afeard? What need we fear
who knows it, when none can call our power to account?—
Yet who would have thought the old man to have had so
much blood in him . . . The thane of Fife had a wife: where
is she now?—What, will these hands ne'er be clean?—No more
o' that, my lord, no more o' that: you mar all with this starting . . . Here's the smell of the blood still: all the perfumes
of Arabia will not sweeten this little hand. Oh, oh, oh!
. . . Wash your hands, put on your nightgown; look not so
pale.—I tell you yet again, Banquo's buried; he cannot come
out on's grave . . . To bed, to bed! there's knocking at the
gate: come, come, come, come, give me your hand. What's
done cannot be undone.—To bed, to bed, to bed!

HAMLET

(HAMLET *has plotted to trap the* KING, *his uncle, into revealing his murder of* HAMLET's *father by having him watch a per-*

formance by a band of wandering players. HAMLET *has just asked one of the players to demonstrate how he would render a highly emotional speech. After dismissing the actors,* HAMLET *addresses himself.*)

HAMLET. O, what a rogue and peasant slave am I!
    Is it not monstrous that this player here,
    But in a fiction, in a dream of passion,
    Could force so his soul to his own conceit
    That from her working all his visage wann'd,
    Tears in his eyes, distraction in's aspect,
    A broken voice, and his whole function suiting
    With forms to his conceit? and all for nothing!
    For Hecuba!
    What's Hecuba to him, or he to Hecuba,
    That he should weep for her? What would he do,
    Had he the motive and the cue for passion
    That I have? He would drown the stage with tears
    And cleave the general ear with horrid speech,
    Make mad the guilty and appal the free,
    Confound the ignorant, and amaze indeed
    The very faculties of eyes and ears.
    Yet I,
    A dull and muddy-mettled rascal, peak,
    Like John-a-dreams, unpregnant of my cause,
    And can say nothing; no, not for a king,
    Upon whose property and most dear life
    A damn'd defeat was made. Am I a coward?
    Who calls me villain? breaks my pate across?
    Plucks off my beard, and blows it in my face?
    Tweaks me by the nose? gives me the lie i' the throat,
    As deep as to the lungs? who does me this?
    Ha!
    'Swounds, I should take it: for it cannot be
    But I am pigeon-liver'd and lack gall
    To make oppression bitter, or ere this
    I should have fatted all the region kites
    With this slave's offal: bloody, bawdy villain!
    Remorseless, treacherous, lecherous, kindless villain!

O, vengeance!
Why, what an ass am I! This is most brave,
That I, the son of a dear father murder'd,
Prompted to my revenge by heaven and hell,
Must, like a whore, unpack my heart with words,
And fall a-cursing, like a very drab,
A scullion!

A SHORT GLOSSARY OF ACTING TERMS

Accessory Action. Learned action, both vocal and pantomimic. It is by nature skilled, specific, and detailed, affected by one's life in a civilized society. Cultivated by rational experience, it is associated with adult behavior. In this respect it may be contrasted with the impulsive *fundamental* action which is more typical of children and primitive people.

Acting Area. The part of the stage where the players perform in view of the audience.

Action. (1) Any change of form or condition on the stage which forcibly affects the mind or senses of the spectator. (2) Physical movement. (3) A lively series of stimulations causing a feeling of suspense. (4) A rapid progression of arresting ideas. Action, when conceived as the movement of sensory stimuli, may be expressed by the voice of the actor as well as by his body.

Ad Lib. As you please. Any detail of a performance—lines, stage business, or "effect"—which is carried forward in the spirit, but not exactly according to the words or the directions, of the script is "ad lib'ed."

Awareness. A state of sensory alertness. A preparedness to respond to sight, sound, taste, touch, and odor. A sensitive recognition of other stage presences.

Back Stage. All of the theatre back of the footlights. This includes not only the stage proper, but also the dressing rooms, shops, and storerooms.

Bit Part. A minor role in a play.

Business. An actor's pantomimic action, particularly that part of it which he uses to create an effect, to develop a point of character, or to elucidate a situation.

Cast. The group of actors to whom parts are assigned for a play. "To cast" means to select actors to fill a set of roles.

Character. A dramatic role. The term "character part" is used loosely to designate an old or eccentric role.

Characterization. The art of interpreting a dramatic role in all aspects of human thought, feeling, and behavior. The outward aspects of characterization include pantomime, voice, make-up, and costume.

Compulsive Action. Action having a quality which impels the audience to "feel into" it sensuously. Action, vocal or pantomimic, which invites kinesthetic participation. Compulsive action is marked by rhythmic smoothness, precision, and a sense of appropriateness in every detail of speech or movement. It affects the spectator through the principle of *empathy* (which see).

Cue. A phrase of speech, a detail of pantomime, or an effect which indicates to an actor that it is time for him to speak or act. It may also indicate to the stage manager or a member of his crew when it is time for a sound effect, lighting change, the closing of the curtain, etc.

Director. The person in charge of rehearsing a play.

Down Stage. Toward the footlights.

Effect. (1) A particular or general impression made on the spectator by a player's action, a strain of music, a change of lighting, or any similar factor in a stage performance. (2) A stage-made sound or sight which represents, or at least suggests, to the audience the patter of rain, the blowing of wind, the beating of surf, the ringing of a telephone, the flashing of lightning, etc. An effect may be musical, although it usually is not.

Empathy. The tendency or compulsion of anyone, particularly a spectator in the theatre, to feel out kinesthetically in his own body the shape, sound, and movement of an object which interests him sensuously. He may not be near the object but may sense out its qualities from a distance. "Compulsive action," defined above, is action which effects an empathic response.

Ensemble. (1) A group of players. (2) As a group.

Fundamental Action. Primitive action, both vocal and panto-mimic. It is by nature gross, impulsive, mostly involuntary. It is typical of children, savages, even animals. Fundamental action (in contrast to accessory action) underlies all other dramatic action. There are three easily recognizable types of fundamental action which are described in the text: sensing, preparing, attacking.

Imagery. See Stage Imagery.

Kinesthetic Tone. Word-sounds which convey the feeling of mus-cular tensions. Kinesthetic tone suggests reaching, feeling, and moving even when the visible body of the actor is mo-tionless.

Lead. (1) One of the two or three most important roles in a play. (2) An actor who plays such a role.

Lines. Written dialogue.

Master Image. A form of extended under image which moves as a controlling picture through the whole length of a dramatic passage, scene, or play.

Off Stage. The part of the stage out of view of the audience.

On Stage. The part of the stage surrounded by scenery, in view of the audience. The acting area.

Out Front. In the auditorium. In the audience.

Part. A dramatic role, or the written lines and stage directions for a role.

Presence. The effective impact or influence of an object or person on the responsive figures around it. Generally speaking, a stage presence is always positive and usually dynamic.

Principal. An actor playing a leading part. The term is sometimes used to distinguish an actor speaking lines from the "walk-on" who has no lines.

Prompt Script. A copy of the script completely marked with direc-tions and cues for the use of the prompter.

Prompter. The person standing or sitting at the side of the stage,

out of view of the audience, whose duty it is to help the actors with their lines in case of lapse of memory. The prompter
also warns actors when it is about time to make their entrances, and he gives cues for effects, changes in lighting,
and the like.

Response. A player's manifest reaction to another presence on the
stage. Especially, a particular reaction called forth by a particular act of that presence. A response always springs from
a preliminary state of awareness.

Script. The book or manuscript of the play.

Stage Action. See Action.

Stage Center. A position approximately in the middle of the acting area. Actually, the working center is commonly a step or
two nearer the footlights than the topographical center. In
practice, stage center is a spot somewhere in the middle of
stage traffic.

Stage Directions. The written description of a character's appearance and the setting in which he performs; also the description of his movements and of the manner of his speaking.

Stage Imagery. The dramatic translation of the figures in the playwright's mind presented by actor to spectator in the form of
living action. The image is not, however, what the actor
shows actually—his makeup face, his studied words and gestures—it is rather what the will and the technique of the
player make the audience *seem* to see.

Stage Left. Left of stage center (on one's left as one faces the audience).

Stage Manager. The person in charge of all activities behind the
footlights during a performance.

Stage Right. Right of stage center (on one's right as one faces the
audience).

Straight Part. A role without any marked characterization—not
very particularized, not eccentric. It is commonly the role of
a normal young man or young woman.

Surface Image. A stage image readily seen and heard by the spectator. The surface imagery in a dramatic scene usually reflects
the socially-conscious, and consequently the more delibera-

tive, controlled, side of the characters involved—in contrast with the intuitive, uninhibited side represented in the under imagery.

Tonal Action. The dynamic, sensuously effective movement of voice-tones.

Tone. See voice-tone.

Under Image. A stage image effectively intimated to the mind's eye of the spectator, but not actually made manifest in the outward words and pantomime of the player. Generally speaking, under imagery in a dramatic scene represents the primitive—the intuitive, uninhibited, naturally dynamic—inner action of the characters involved in contrast to the deliberative, controlled action of the surface images. Under imagery, though related to fundamental action, is not the same thing. Fundamental action may be, to some extent at least, visible and audible while under images are always only *suggested.*

Up Stage. Away from the footlights.

Voice-tone. The sensuous, emotionally-effective sound of speech as contrasted with the colorless sound of speech uttered in accordance with rules of pronunciation but nothing more. Voice-tone springs from a sense of bodily action. Factors in effective tone include pitch, volume, force, and timbre.

Wing. The space off stage right or off left of the acting area.

SELECTED BOOKS ON ACTING

COLE, TOBY, and CHINOY, HELEN KRICH, eds., *Actors on Acting.* New York: Crown Publishers, Inc., 1959.

"The theories, techniques, and practices of the great actors of all times as told in their own words."

DUERR, EDWIN, *The Length and Depth of Acting.* New York: Holt, Rinehart & Winston, Inc., 1962.

An historical record of the evolution of the actor's art with critical comments on styles and methods.

FUNKE, LEWIS, and BOOTH, JOHN E., eds., *Actors Talk About Themselves.* New York: Random House, Inc., 1961.

Fourteen intimate interviews with stars of the contemporary theatre.

SELDEN, SAMUEL, *The Stage in Action*. New York: Appleton-Century-Crofts, 1941.

Design elements in a dramatic performance. The relationship between the art of the actor and the art of the dancer, the singer, and the painter.

SEYLER, ATHENE, and HAGGARD, STEPHEN, *The Craft of Comedy*. London: J. Garnet Miller, Ltd., 1958. (Distributed in the USA by Theatre Art Books.)

An illuminating series of comments on the art of playing comedy, contained in correspondence between two British actors.

WEBSTER, MARGARET, *Shakespeare Without Tears*. Cleveland: The World Publishing Company, 1955.

A common sense interpretation of the plays of Shakespeare with practical suggestions on their production by a distinguished actress and director. Invaluable to the player of classical roles.